THE SUBVERSION OF POLITICS

European Autonomous Social Movements
and the Decolonization of Everyday Life

GEORGY KATSIAFICAS

The Subversion of Politics
European Autonomous Social Movements
and the Decolonization of Everyday Life

Copyright © Georgy Katsiaficas 1997, 2006

First published in 1997 by Humanities Press International
This updated edition published in 2006 by AK Press

ISBN 1 904859 53 4
ISBN13 9781904859536

Library of Congress Control Number 2006920973

AK Press
674-A 23rd St
Oakland CA
94612 USA
www.akpress.org

AK Press
PO Box 12766
Edinburgh, Scotland
EH8 9YE
www.akuk.com

Printed in Canada by union labor
Cover design by Josh Warren-White
Interior design by jankyHellface

for Ron Brazao and
Ingrid Schmidt-Harzbach

CONTENTS

Introduction to the AK Press edition (2006)   *iii*
Introduction to the Korean edition (2000)   *x*
Preface to the first edition (1997)   *xiii*
Acknowledgements   *xxi*
Chronology   *xxii*
Abbreviations   *xxiv*
List of Illustrations   *xxv*
Federal Republic of Germany (map)   *xxvi*

From 1968 to Autonomy   **1**
The European Context   3
The Meaning of Autonomy   6
The Autonomen: An Invisible Movement   9
Media and Marginality   13

Italian Autonomia   **17**
Worker Roots Of Autonomy   18
The Women's Movement   27
Student And Youth Roots Of Autonomy   36
1977: A Year Of Crisis   43
Repression And Resistance   51

Sources of Autonomous Politics in Germany   **59**
The Autonomous Women's Movement   67
The Antinuclear Movement   80
Müslis And *Mollis*: From The New Left To The Punk Left   88
The Elections In Berlin   97
The Structure Of Spontaneity   100

European Autonomous Movements   **107**
Amsterdam   111
Copenhagen   117
Hafenstrasse: International Symbol   124
The Guerrillas And The Movement   128
The Red Zoras   132
May Day 1988: A Personal Note   135

Photos   **139**

The Autonomen in Unified Germany   153

Neo-Nazis And The State   155
Autonomy And Antifascism   165
The Battle For Mainzerstrasse   168
The Contradictions Of Autonomy   174
The German Problem   180

The (Anti)Politics of Autonomy   187

Autonomy And The Greens   196
Autonomy And The Left   209
In Defense of the Dialectic   217
From the Fetishization of Production to the Production of Fetish   220
The Centrality of Patriarchy   222
Neo-Leninist Rectitude   224
Strategic Concerns   226
Toward A Rationality Of The Heart   228

The Theory of Autonomy   235

Late Capitalism's Postmodern Features   238
Colonization Of Everyday Life   244
New Social Movements And The Politics Of Identity   248
From The Invisibility Of The Private To Its Rationalization:
    A Reasonable Project?   255
The Atomized Individual And The Constraint Of Autonomy   257
The Autonomy Of Theory?   259
Decolonization And Democracy   263

Notes   *269*
Index   *297*

INTRODUCTION TO THE AK PRESS EDITION (2006)

The Autonomen are dead—autonomous social movements are everywhere emerging. Neither side of this contradictory formulation is completely accurate, yet taken together, they are not completely false.

Often marginalized and almost always transient, autonomous movements are increasingly influential—toppling dictatorships, changing the course of civil society, and altering global institutions' priorities. The visibility of the Seattle protests in 1999 made the US appear to be at the center of such changes. Yet tragically, people here remain largely aloof. Significant anti-corporate antecedents were profoundly present prior to Seattle and long after it—but seldom in the belly of the beast.

Latin America is today undergoing its most profound wave of movements since the early 1970s. Vast popular mobilizations are at the center of these developments. The accumulation of decades of struggle against corporate globalization means today that progressives and radicals are being elected across the continent. Transnational capital is unwelcome, not only at the ballot boxes but often in the streets as well. In the space of a few short years, regimes friendly to the US have largely disappeared. People power movements have caused the resignations of governments in Peru, Argentina, Bolivia and Ecuador, and electoral victories have been won in Brazil, Uruguay, Bolivia and Venezuela. Nowhere else in the world are the local and the global so intimately understood in their connections.

Beginning in the 1980s in East Asia, a series of revolts accomplished a shift in regional political power. The Gwangju Uprising in 1980 ushered in this new era; soon thereafter, country after country exploded: in the Philippines (1986), South Korea (1987), Nepal (1989) and Indonesia (1997), dictatorships were overthrown; in China (1989), Burma (1990) and Thailand (1992), thousands of people were massacred as the established order reigned supreme—at least for now.

From these brief remarks, readers might sense that I believe we are heading toward a situation in which global transformation is possible. Indications of the system's inability to govern wisely are evident in the indecent response to Hurricane Katrina. Proof of its irrational character is abundantly clear in the starvation and disease at the margins of the corporate economy, and the permanence of war as a feature of our political landscape. As Bono, Bob Geldorf and others with good hearts come to realize that the corporate system needs war and starvation at its periphery in order for profits to rise, they may join the rest of us who already understand the need for global system transformation. In the meantime, we cannot wait for them.

The vital need for system change is painfully evident today to millions of us, and we have learned how People Power revolutions are possible. As the impetus for new global institutions increases (buoyed by such gatherings as the World Social Forum and confrontations with summits of global elites), ways to move forward beyond marching and voting need to be found. Europe's Autonomen are one example from which we can learn. Their incipient forms of dual power, especially in their communes and collective institutions make apparent the capacity of human beings to govern themselves. In Argentina today, self-managed factories, hotels and offices provide further indications of the capacity of ordinary people to act with wisdom and justice.

While Europe's autonomous movements provide concrete historical examples of the form of anti-systemic movements, their "conscious spontaneity" was developed when the movement was a small minority of the population. Never in Italy or Germany did autonomous movements even approach having the support of a majority of the society. In Italy, the Fordist organization of the economy in the 1970s (i.e. its reliance on assembly lines and large factories) meant that the movement's impact was greater among the working class than in Germany, where the economy's post-industrial forms accorded the movement less of a "class" character. In Chapter 7 of this book, I note that German firms globally expanded and incorporated astonishing gains in productivity, profoundly altering the process of production.

The surge of movement actions described in this book has decidedly subsided. While the usual Mayday festivities continue in Berlin and elsewhere, no longer do hundreds—or even dozens—of squats provide the movement with continuity, with a space for deepening activists' ability to resist the contamination of our everyday lives by competition, domination and hierarchy. Even if the Autonomen from the 1980s are no longer in the forefront, their movement showed that the collective wisdom of thousands of people is superior to the decision-making apparatus of the German political class, whose blind rush into behemoth political control-centers continues in new forms. To be sure, while the movement has long passed its high point, its ability to rekindle interest and commitment among new generations of activists is impressive. Scattered building occupations occur; squatted bars and collective centers remain open; and a university strike for more than a year led to a new Berlin Open University. Significantly, the activist scene includes many youth under twenty-five.

Among industrialized countries, it was in Germany that massive protests against the institutions of global capital first appeared, as did the Black Bloc, a product of their movement, which has since become internationally relevant. Autonome tactics have diffused and their experiences remain a practical contribution to the question of organization of the avant-garde. Yet are the representative assemblies and collectives of the Autonomen sufficiently powerful organizational forms for today? Clearly the answer is no.

The form of organization gleaned from their experiences is charted in Chapter 6 of this book in the form of concentric circles with an activist core surrounded by its "scene" and sympathizers. Today it might make sense to understand the global movement's situation as dozens—perhaps even hundreds—of such circles of varying size and intensity overlapping in their impact and influences. No doubt one of the main energy points of the past decade has been the Zapatistas. In 1999, they used the internet to call for demonstrations against neoliberalism, and activists in several cities responded. Besides the Zapatistas, Gwangju increasingly plays an international role. An even earlier call for coordinated actions came in 1972, when the Vietnamese revolution meticulously prepared an internationally synchronized offensive. After convening a Paris conference to coordinate the action calendars of anti-war movements in over eighty countries, the Vietnamese launched a military offensive in April 1972, during which they declared the existence of the Provisional Revolutionary Government.

Confrontations with the principal summits of global corporate domination (the IMF, G8, World Bank and WTO) also help to create a global dynamic that spreads throughout the world like a wave in a stadium. When people confront elite summits, they create an intuitive dynamic of solidarity and struggle. The experiences gleaned in such moments are often life-formative—as are friendships and identities formed during them. Perhaps most importantly, these actions accumulate energy that may crystallize an "eros effect," a sudden intuitive awakening of massive opposition to the powers-that-be. Instances of revolt profoundly resonate among us, spurring action within formerly quiet areas and crossing national borders. Most apparent in the globally interconnected uprisings of 1968, instances of the eros effect continue to animate political change. Neither armed insurrection nor general strikes, the massive contestation of public space, spilling across regions and erupting with unforeseen intensity, the refusal of people to simply return to business as usual until changes are made, is a new tactic in the arsenal of popular movements. A global eros effect—a people power revolution compelling systemic change in the structures of the world system—could be a vehicle for the coming liberation of the species from inherited structures and outmoded forms of social organization which today mean misery for so many human beings. To rely on the awakening of a global eros effect alone to transform the world system would be shortsighted. Yet to deny its efficacy as a vehicle for social transformation would be to ignore the dynamics of the past forty years of media culture.

If the world system can be transformed, it must be from within its core areas—as the history of revolution and counterrevolution in the 20th century bitterly reminds us. Since the Autonomen arose within an economically advanced region, their collective form has great relevance for emergent movements. While their communes and direct democracy are of value in themselves, there is no metaphysical solution to the dilemma of liberatory organization. Rather, effective organizations arise within popular movements in specific situations: SDS on both German and the US campuses, like SNCC in the South and the Black Panther Party in the ghettos, arose under different conditions in the 1960s; and Autonomen forms in Germany were created under conditions of urban marginalization and militant opposition.

Popular movements have an intelligence that is matched by few theorists. In my understanding, the empirical history of popular movements reveals an inner logic of unfolding reasonability, comparable to the logic of mind uncovered by 18th century German philosophy. This logical progression can be concretely observed in the actions of thousands—sometimes millions—of people in definite historical moments. Comparing the development of movements from 1789 to 1848, 1905, 1917 and 1968, the multitude's contestation of ever-expanding concerns of power in everyday life becomes apparent, and popular struggles become increasingly self-organized and autonomously intelligent. In May 1968 in France, ten million striking students and workers enacted norms of international solidarity, overthrowing the dominating presence of French patriotism; simultaneously they replaced institutional hierarchy with self-management. In May 1970 in the US, more than four million students and faculty went on strike against Nixon's invasion of Cambodia and murderous attacks on the Black Panther Party: American chauvinism and racism were negated by international solidarity; in place of competition and hierarchy, cooperation and egalitarianism became people's values; instead of individual advancement and accumulation of wealth being individuals' primary concerns, social justice and alleviation of inequality were the center of action.

People's capacity to create autonomous organizations has dramatically altered the dialectical relationship of spontaneity and consciousness. In 1871, the Paris Commune arose as the existing National Guard seized control of Paris; while in Gwangju in 1980, people spontaneously created a Citizens' Army that drove the South Korean military out of the city and held it for nearly a week. Popular movements intuit new tactics and appropriate new tools: in China in 1989, the fax machine; in Thailand in 1992, cell phones; and the Zapatistas more recently, the internet. This intelligence and intuition of popular movements, the basis of people power and the eros effect, is one of humanity's great resources.

As popular intuition and intelligence have deepened, millions of people around the world today have the capability to rule more wisely and with better results than ensconced elites. Millions of us in nearly every country focus our energies on transforming the character of the global economic system, because we recognize it as the root cause of permanent war, systemic starvation and misery, and catastrophe for the earth.

The multitude's rationality, our wisdom produced from the inner logic of centuries of movements, far surpasses that of elites today who control political power and economic wealth. Would anyone argue with the notion that the peace movement is far more intelligent than Bush, Cheney and Co.? Would anyone propose that the South Korean military dictators were wiser than the people of Gwangju—who risked life and limb to bring about democracy? How much longer will we allow the corporate elite's greed, rather than human need, to direct the use of the vast wealth our species has produced over generations of labor? Can we find an alternative, redirect the use of banks and insurance company assets for human need, downsize corporate behemoths and dismantle military might?

In the disintegration of the Soviet Union, we find an optimistic model, especially for the future of the USA. While the destruction of power is an absolutely vital question today, those who would write off any attempt by liberatory movements to wield power prepare us for disappointment and failure. In a situation where global capital's power is already being contested, regional organs of dual power arise and even national governments oppose transnational capital's domination.

When it was first published in 1997, this book appeared to have a bleak future because of the near simultaneous bankruptcy of Humanities Press. Although it was co-winner of the Michael Harrington Award in political science in 1998, the book was scarcely available. After repeated inquires from interested readers, I finally put it as a free download on my website (www.eroseffect.com). AK Press's decision to republish this book at the same time as a new Korean translation is being prepared, and Turkish, Greek, Spanish and Russian editions are also at work, is one indication among many that we are moving toward a new upsurge of active confrontations with the powers-that-be.

In preparing for this new publication, I considered rewriting the book. Although I have changed some minor details and updated the critique of Antonio Negri, the text is essentially unchanged. I felt it better to leave it intact, since the writing itself was part of the Autonome Zeitgeist at the end of the 20th century.

The Subversion of Politics is the second volume in a trilogy that seeks to uncover the hidden logic and reasonability of social movements in contemporary urbanized societies. My first volume portrayed the global imagination of movements in 1968. Rather than writing a national history of any one of the insurgencies that emerged in nearly every country, I wrote a global history of these movements, emphasizing their synchronic ties to each other. I situated these movements' imagination in the actions of millions of people during moments of profound upheaval in France and the US. Among other things, I found that movements in Czechoslovakia, Poland and Yugoslavia were closely related to these insurgencies in the "free world," and I developed the concept of the "eros effect" to better comprehend the fundamental connectedness of social movements to each other.

This book focuses on autonomous movements in Central Europe from 1968 to 1996. As in my study of 1968, I reveal hidden dimensions of these movements and tie them to theoretical concerns not generally understood in relationship to social movements. The range of my analysis of theory and practice indicates that autonomous movements at their best pose a species awareness that transcends ethnic exclusivity, patriarchal power and class divisions. In Germany, they critically posed the failure of even some of the most progressive Germans to go beyond their German identity; they took the feminist universal to a higher level, interweaving it with class oppression on a global scale; and they similarly subsumed the workerist imperative of Italian Autonomia without its hierarchical connotations. While guerrillas and parliamentarians are inherently elitist groupings, autonomous social movements insist on a global egalitarianism. At their best, their vision and actions embody a new species-universality, the source today of activism aimed at transforming the world system in the anti-corporate globalization movement.

The final volume in my study, *Unknown Uprisings: South Korean Social Movements Since World War 2*, will deal with the successive waves of social movements which won democracy, greater individual liberties and trade union rights in South Korea. Focusing on the Gwangju Uprising, I trace the eros effect in the beloved community of this unique city in 1980 and follow its impact to the Great June Struggle of 1987, when nineteen consecutive days of demonstrations overthrew the military dictatorship. South Korean workers then became the main force animating Korea, winning trade union rights after decades of struggle. Recently Korean farmers have been in the lead of anti-corporate struggles in Cancun and Hong Kong. I also discuss East Asian movements in the 1980s and 1990s, when an unfolding logic of popular contestations of power affected country after country.

The world has never been changing more rapidly—and never been more brutally savage. The time for our species to seize control of its destiny is rapidly approaching. Let us hope we are worthy of the task before us.

Cambridge, Massachusetts
January 15, 2006

INTRODUCTION TO THE KOREAN EDITION (2000)

People will ask: How can Katsiaficas tolerate holding up European social movements as a model for those in Korea when Eurocentrism is rampant in the attitude and actions of so many people? In two words, the answer is, I don't. The movements I describe and analyze here are specific to the political and cultural conditions that formed certain European countries' action-possibilities in a specific period of time. The conditions in these countries have already changed—as have their movements. Nowhere do they exist today as I have portrayed them in this book.

It will be said: Katsiaficas brings owls to Athena (or as the British would express it, coals to Newcastle). Korean social movements are so lively and have accomplished so much, how can he even think of attempting to teach Korean activists about autonomous movements? Autonomous Korean movements already have won democracy—more of an accomplishment than any European movement discussed here. Emergent Korean workers movements have won legalized autonomous trade unions and continue massively to struggle for a decent standard of living and economic justice. Feminist movements increasingly challenge patriarchal domination and question long-held social conventions. The history of the Korean student movement is as glorious as anywhere. And that is just the beginning. Autonomous uprisings as in Kwangju astonish the world.

Compared to Korean movements, the European Autonomen are small and marginalized. While Italian workers movements momentarily challenged the social order in the 1970s, they were thoroughly repressed when they resisted, marginally integrated if they would play by the rules of corporate hegemony. Although Dutch squatters were able for a short period of time to control much of Amsterdam, they were soon defeated, and similar German, Danish and Swiss movements never were able to move beyond the margins of the political order.

All this would be rightfully said.

At the same time, the script for the future trajectory of Korean movements has yet to be written. No doubt the blood and sacrifices of too many people will be the price of future struggles and gains. If this book's contribution to the future of Korea is to save one person from injury, then it will not have been written in vain. If it helps orient the movement in Korea to possible courses of action in "democratic," industrialized societies, then it may prove helpful.

On some level, I do consider the social conditions from which European autonomous movements sprang to be similar in rough outline to those that prevail in Korea. Neither European nor Korean societies are predominantly peasant societies. Both are industrialized and increasingly mobile. Formal, representational democracy defines the public face of the political order; substantive democracy has yet to be won. Korea, Italy and Germany all house important US military bases.

Even if we reject entirely the notion that European movements have anything worthwhile to offer to Koreans, then surely one could make the case that Vietnam's struggle for independence might inform Koreans. After all, Vietnam is unified while Korea remains divided, even though both countries experienced brutal wars in which millions of people died as a result of the "Cold" War. No better authority on Vietnam's victory over the US can be found than General Vo Nguyen Giap, military commander at Dien Bien Phu and during Tet 1968). In his account of how the Vietnamese defeated the US, the role of progressive Americans in the anti-war movement figures prominently. Thus, a reason to understand European movements can be found in the possible gains that might result from alliances between Koreans and European activists (to say nothing of American activists). I describe one such victory when Korean textile workers were aided by the Red Zoras in Germany (see chapter 4). Future possibilities are quite worth considering.

The existence of a worldwide movement against globalization no doubt makes more apparent and urgent future possibilities for cooperation between activists in different countries. Unfortunately few people outside Korea are aware of the rich history of struggle here against the IMF, World Bank and WTO. After the battle of Seattle, many people identify the US movement as the point of origin of the movement against globalization when, in fact, alongside Koreans, German activists, Venezuelans, and the Zapatistas in Mexico were in the forefront of this struggle.

In part to mitigate the tendency to put the US at the center, my current book project is to write an English-language history of South Korean social movements since World War 2. Part of the reason for the unexpected success in Korea of my book on 1968 and intuitive identification with the "eros effect" is no doubt the rich history of spontaneous uprisings and movements. I am seeking to interview Korean activists and uncover dimensions of Korean movements unknown to non-Koreans, and I would welcome contact with activists and historians. (My publisher E-who will forward messages to me or I can be contacted directly at katsiaficas@wit.edu.)

I wish to acknowledge a few of the people whose energies have created the Korean translation of *The Subversion of Politics*. My friends Yoon Soo Jong and Lee Jae-Won have critically inspired me. Members of the May 18 Institute at Chonnam National University and Kwangju Citizens'

Solidarity have helped me begin to understand the magnitude of Korean social movements. Last but not least, the E-Who collective has forged a connection from me with Korea.

All Power to the People!

Georgy Katsiaficas
August 8, 2000
Boston

PREFACE TO THE FIRST EDITION (1997)

As we approach the end of the twentieth century, the pace of history accelerates to velocities previously thought impossible. In the last two generations, world population has increased more than in all the rest of our species' life. Not only is history's speed today extraordinary, but its direction is wild and unpredictable. At the beginning of the 1980s, who could have foreseen that by that decade's end, there would be fifteen nations where one Soviet Union had existed and one Germany—not two? Looking back on the end of the Cold War and the immense geopolitical transformations thereby accomplished, nearly all observers give credit for these changes to Mikhail Gorbachev or to impersonal forces such as the expense of the arms race, the Chernobyl disaster, or the crisis in the Soviet Union's political economy. Left out of our understanding is the role of popular movements—grassroots initiatives like the disarmament movement, which grew from locally defined problems. Searching for direct solutions, thousands of people constituted themselves as social forces, which helped stimulate world leaders to act by providing them with a sense of the necessary and a glimpse of the possible.

One of the claims to greatness of the United States is its freedom of the press, yet for over two decades, European autonomous social movements have been practically invisible in both the mainstream and much of the alternative press. As a result, Americans' understanding of European politics is largely confined to the arenas of parliaments and guerrillas, to votes and violence. After the dispersal of New Left social movements of the 1960s, media coverage on this side of the Atlantic included the electoral successes and failures of socialist governments in France, Spain, Portugal, and Greece; the rise and fall of Italian governments; and the emergence of the Green Party in West Germany (ecologists whose victories in elections could not be ignored). Occasional space was given to the spectacular actions and subsequent arrests of armed groups such as the Red Brigades in Italy, Direct Action in France, and Germany's Red Army Faction. After the Cold War ended and neo-Nazi violence erupted, extensive airtime was granted to it.

Left out of the news about Europe, however, were popular, direct-action movements in Italy, Holland, Denmark, Switzerland, and West Germany; movements composed of thousands of activists who refused to be confined to the ranks of mainstream politics or marginalized as guerrillas. They were a motor force driving both the parliamentary upsurge of the Greens and the armed struggle that has plagued German political life for more than two decades. Besides being a driving force of others, their militant resistance to the arms race, nuclear power, patriarchy, and the housing shortage transformed single-issue struggles into an autonomous movement whose aspirations were to transform the society as a whole. These social movements—known today as the Autonomen in Germany—are independent of political parties, and their adherents will have nothing to do with established forms of politics. They seek the subversion of nation-states and their representative structures of government and seek to replace the existing world system with anti-systemic forms of participatory democracy that they believe will facilitate greater individual and community control over everyday life.

I cannot help but wonder if some form of censorship was partially responsible for the lack of attention paid to these movements. When neo-Nazi and skinhead violence broke out throughout Europe, the media afforded fascists wide coverage, and their electoral parties regularly received attention in the pages of daily papers. As my readers will discover, the German police often turned a blind eye on neo-Nazi violence, while the U.S. media made it seem almost typically German. The opposite was true with respect to the Autonomen: the German police brutally attacked them even when they tried to protect victims of skinhead violence, while the U.S. media ignored them. Many significant events, including massive and militant demonstrations against high-ranking U.S. officials, were never reported in the U.S. media in any detail. To give just two examples: When President Ronald Reagan visited Berlin in June 1987, the autonomous movement mobilized fifty thousand people in militant demonstrations that were restrained only through illegal police actions, such as cordoning off entire sections of West Berlin. The U.S. media reported next to nothing about the demonstrations or the state of emergency approved (some say ordered) by the U.S. military officials who then governed West Berlin. When twenty-five thousand people assembled to support Reagan—half the number that had demonstrated against him—U.S. television viewers were shown prime-time footage of the president's speech to a crowd of cheering Berliners, hardly an accurate image of what had transpired. In November of the same year, two policemen were shot dead and nine were wounded by a breakaway group during a demonstration against a new runway (called Startbahn West) at the international airport in Frankfurt. The news media sensationalized the story of the shootings, carrying it widely without providing any context. It was never mentioned that one of the key reasons for the runway being built was to meet North Atlantic Treaty Organization (NATO)—that is, U.S. Cold War—needs. Six years to the day before the shootings, there had been hardly any mention of the 150,000 people who marched peacefully against Startbahn West, nor did the media cover the subsequent building of a village of huts from the trees that had been felled in preparation for the new runway. When the police brutally attacked this village after hundreds of people had lived in it for months, thousands of people defended it from the police onslaught, but Americans heard nothing substantial about it. As I followed these events through phone calls and sporadic bits of information in the alternative press, once again the media's relative silence was a second story.[1]

The difficulties that the media have in discussing the Autonomen are matched by the incapacity of some political analysts to comprehend the reasons for or meaning of autonomous movements. Many Americans find it incomprehensible when German young people portray the new world order as nothing more than a more efficient and seemingly democratic version of Hitler's thousand-year Reich. It is taken for granted that Germans want national unity and that they are loyal and obedient citizens. Nothing could be further from the truth with regard to the Autonomen: they prefer regional autonomy to national unity and would rather live as human beings in a world community than as citizens of the German state. Americans with the interest and ability to write about postwar European politics ignored extra-parliamentary movements in part because of their conception of politics as electoral. Parliamentary campaigns are of more interest than demonstrations because the former deal with power, whereas the latter often revolve around marginalized youth. The U.S. mass media, relying as they do on foreign celebrities and government officials for much of their information, made guerrilla actions into spectacles, turned them into Hollywood movies, CNN sound bites, and front-page headlines, simply because events such as the kidnapping of a U.S. general or the murders of wealthy bankers make good copy, whereas social movements composed of homeless young people taking over abandoned buildings and fixing them up apparently do not.

Governments expend tremendous energy denying popular movements legitimacy rather than heeding their emergence as a sign of an outdated social order in need of transformation.[2] In Europe, the states' strategy has been simultaneously to criminalize and co-opt extra-parliamentary movements, and to some extent, this strategy has paid dividends in the form of the semblance of stability. But as I rediscovered during each of my trips to Europe, the Autonomen were far from neutralized, and in Germany at least, new generations of activists have taken over from previous ones. Social movements are a window through which we can glimpse the essential nature of society. My experiences in the New Left taught me this. The civil rights movement illuminated racist aspects of U.S. society that no one wanted to look at; the antiwar movement and counterculture revealed the imperial arrogance of power and the ways it constrained our freedom; the feminist and gay movements showed how much our everyday lives are conditioned by unconscious structures of power and brought these structures into question. Like the earlier workers' movement, these movements posed an alternative path for society to take. Although they failed to change society as much as they hoped, they nonetheless altered prevailing customs and institutions. No one would be more surprised than I if the Autonomen were able to help radically transform Germany in the next decade or two. No matter what their future may be, however, their history provides us with sometimes startling insights into German culture and politics.

This book is not a comprehensive history of autonomous movements. Seeking to portray them in their own terms, I have relied on my all too infrequent trips to infuse my understanding, and my presentation is unsystematic, almost a snapshot picture of the movement's continental character. From 1979 to 1981, I lived in Berlin for eighteen months and wandered extensively on both sides of what used to be called the Iron Curtain. I returned to Berlin in 1988, 1991, and 1993, each time traveling around from my base in a *Wohngemeinschaft* (group house) with friends in Kreuzberg. Contained here are impressions of a social movement whose identity defies the increasing incorporation of all aspects of our lives within a unified framework (the modem world system). Although the latter may sound abstract to those unfamiliar with radical critiques of one-dimensional society, I hope that by the end of this book, readers will understand what Jurgen Habermas has called the "colonization of the life-world"—as well as the Autonomen impulse to resist that dynamic. All too often, we accept the superiority of the American way, and one of my goals is to provide North American readers with an understanding of the autonomous critique of American-style democracy and consumer society.[3]

With the publication of this book, the sequel to *The Imagination of the New Left: A Global Analysis of 1968,* the project I began there is brought into the contemporary period. My interest in spending so much of my life writing about social movements has developed out of my own involvement in them. My participation in movements has been crucial to my analysis and choice of topics. Although I sometimes feel part of the European movements I discuss, there are other moments when I feel quite alien to them, since their construction of racial identity is so different from that in the United States. As children, we all eventually learn that we belong to a particular race. As adults, few of us have the opportunity to experience a change in this aspect of our lives, yet that is precisely what happens to me every time I go to northern Europe.

For those who are unaware of it, racial identification in Germany depends more on hair and eye color than skin hue. Despite my being

Greek-American, many Germans take one look at me and think that I come from Turkey, a country that provides Germany with hundreds of thousands of immigrants who all too often are discriminated against, attacked and, since the reunification of the country in 1990, murdered. For me, Germany's system of racism means that I am periodically denied service in restaurants and occasionally encounter verbal assaults in the subway, on the streets, and in the Tiergarten (particularly when accompanied by German women). It means being careful when alone, being wary of the mean-spirited mindless for whom brutalizing foreigners has become a new national sport.

Having grown up within the U.S. Army, I had the opportunity to travel the world while I was a child, and the experience was so pleasurable that I have never stopped. Throughout much of the world—the Middle East, Mexico, and most of Europe—I blend in quite easily and experience public space from the inside. In Germany, however, I am necessarily an outsider because of my Mediterranean features. I lived in Germany for over five years as a child, but I first became aware of how racial identity is constructed there while checking into a hotel in Luneberg in 1979. When the two clerks asked me where I was from, I produced my U.S. passport and answered "California." With quizzical looks on their faces, they huddled together to inspect my passport. "Oh, you're Greek," they announced. "No," I responded, "I was born in Texas and live in California." "But your name is Greek," they replied, and insisted that I was from Greece. I let this incident pass, writing it off (along with the hotel clerks) as weird. But over the next eighteen months while I studied at Berlin's Free University, I was regularly harassed on the street, told to go back to Turkey, and once attacked when I was with a Swiss woman. Even among Germans who were sympathetic to foreigners, I felt patronized on a regular basis.

My strategy for dealing with overt racist intrusions evolved from confrontation in the beginning to sheer avoidance, until I finally hit upon a gambit suited to my own temperament. Whenever I was accosted by a German chauvinist, I would find a way to tell long and involved stories about the beauty and hospitality of my "native Turkey" and how much I longed to return. My stories always succeeded in arousing the interest of my would-be assailants, and by the time I had finished, these fellows were enraptured by my tales. When I then proceeded to invite them to come to my home in Izmir and experience for themselves the hospitality of my family, their gratitude was worth my patience, and I felt that my time had not been wasted, since I had thoroughly deceived and simultaneously neutralized would-be hooligans.

Not all potential confrontations were so easily defused. Although I was lucky in avoiding violence, once I was compelled to face down two would-be attackers by standing my ground while a Swiss friend stood behind me. She had given some retort to their verbal harassment and had run off when they came at us. I caught up with her and put her behind me, instructing her not to run any further. Turning to face the onrushing attackers, I invited them to a beating and stood my ground. After several minutes of circling, inane profanity, and taunts designed to draw me away from my friend, they finally backed down and took off into the night. I happened to run into one of them a few weeks later in Moabit, the neighborhood where we both lived. He invited me into his house, and as we sat together smoking in his room, he gave me a gift to "welcome" me into the neighborhood where I had lived for nearly a year. Never did physical violence visit me, not in 1981 nor on my more recent trips. What is new in the 1990s, however, is my friends' insistence on walking me to the subway late at night, lest I meet unwelcome company on my way home.

Despite my luck, plenty of others have not been so fortunate. After the fall of the Berlin Wall in 1989 and reunification of Germany in 1990, racial attacks dramatically increased. The outbreak of neo-Nazi violence claimed over eighty lives and caused thousands of severe injuries, developments that dramatically changed the context and focus of the autonomous movement.[4] In many instances—such as during the pogrom in Rostock in 1992—they were the only ones ready to confront the neo-Nazis in the streets, and the casualties and arrests they suffered are one indication of the price they pay for failing to conform to the more accepted norms and values. Although I will not attempt to predict the future, I do insist in this book that progressive Germans be accorded their proper place in history. Without their risks and sacrifices, there is no doubt that German political and cultural life would be even more repressive than it is today.

To be sure, we in the United States have our own brand of racism that grew out of our history of slavery and genocide, and many African-American friends have commented on how much they feel freed from oppressive racial apartheid when they go to Europe. More African-American men today languish in jail in the United States than attend colleges, and inner-city African-American communities are impoverished islands amidst a sea of plenty. Yet there is little doubt in my mind that we are far ahead of Germany (and, I dare say, much of the rest of Europe) in at least talking about these issues. One could point to both trivial and sociological facts to verify this assertion. In any German variety store, packages of chocolate cakes sandwiching whipped cream are regularly referred to as "nigger kisses" *(Negerkussen)*. European notions of national identity are themselves archaically racialistic. The boldness with which Germans flaunt their racial categories and assume their correctness is nothing short of astounding. More than once, progressive Germans have explained to me that I am a different race than they. There is such a widespread belief that Mediterraneans are a mixture of the "pure" African and "pure" Aryan races that I assume that this idiotic notion is part of the outdated school curriculum in Germany. In my view, there is only one race, the human race, and our diverse appearances derive from thousands of years of adaptation to various environments, from accidents and chance—but not from the mixing of originally "pure" races. Race is a socially constructed category: what better proof could there be than my changing races when I arrive in Germany?

In 1993, when there were daily attacks on innocent people and frequent murders of immigrants and activists, Germany felt like Mississippi during the summer of 1964 (when civil rights workers were murdered for trying to help southern blacks register to vote). Fascists were again being worshipped by a sizable minority in Italy, the racist National Front in France had become a fixture, and neo-fascist groups grew in importance from one end of Europe to the other. In Anglo-Saxon England, the *New York Times* of October 25, 1993, reported a Gallup poll that found that two of three Britons did not want Gypsies as neighbors, one of three rejected Arabs and Pakistanis, and 27 percent of those surveyed did not want to live near West Indians. Slightly fewer (24 percent) rejected Africans as potential neighbors. A similar poll in the United States found that 12 percent of people preferred not to share a neighborhood with blacks.

Although this relatively progressive character of the United States may come as a surprise to some, it should not. Over a century ago, German philosopher G. W. F. Hegel and his most famous student, Karl Marx—despite their immense differences on religion, politics, and most worldly matters—agreed that the United States was the land of the future. So much of the world today is affected by U.S. corporations and culture (particularly our music and cinema) that we often lose sight of how important the United States has been to progressive politics. May 1 is celebrated throughout much of the world as the international day of workers, and although few people celebrate it in the United States, its origins as a modern holiday are in the struggle for the eight-hour day in Chicago. For most people, our Black Panthers are a distant memory, but groups in India, Palestine, and Israel (as well as the senior citizen Gray Panthers) have appropriated the name for themselves.

As the Americanization of the world proceeds at a pace more rapid than anyone understands, anti-Americanism has been one response. In Germany in the early 1980s, when U.S. and Soviet troops still occupied the divided country and short-range nuclear missiles threatened to obliterate it, anti-Americanism was widespread. At times, it became obvious in painfully important ways, yet it was also a great source of comic relief when it appeared out of ignorance or simply as fashion. I could not help but chuckle when Germans hostile to me because they thought I was Turkish would turn around and welcome me with open arms when they learned that I was from the United States or, conversely, when some of those most friendly to me when they thought I was from Turkey, a foreigner whom they wished to put at ease, became noticeably unfriendly when I told them that I was an American. In the 1990s, as U.S. troops left Germany, anti-Americanism largely disappeared among its previous advocates but was adopted by the extreme Right, whose dreams of Germany as a world military power are frustrated by the new world order ruled by Washington.

The foregoing personal observations give some indication of the obstacles that exist in relationships between Germans and Americans, obstacles that help account for Americans' lack of interest and knowledge about Germany—with the notable exception of its Nazis—as well as for many Germans' reciprocal ambivalence about the United States. I hope that this book serves as a bridge between the two countries. As will be obvious, it grows out of collegial relationships and trusting friendships, without which it would never have been written.

ACKNOWLEDGEMENTS

I would especially like to thank Uwe Haseloff, Teodros Kiros, Billy Nessen, Susanne Peters, and Victor Wallis for their comments on earlier drafts of this manuscript. Wolfgang Kraushaar and Bernd Rabehl helped orient me in the unfamiliar world of Germany. Without the friendship and direction provided by Herbert Marcuse, I never would have started this book eighteen years ago. Hundreds of students in my social movements courses at Wentworth Institute of Technology commented on versions of this book and its ideas, as did dozens of participants in various discussions following the more than two dozen presentations I made in the course of writing it. As noted, previous drafts of various chapters appeared as articles in *Monthly Review*, *Zeta*, and *New Political Science*.

Much of my research would have been impossible without the patient explanations of activists involved in autonomous movements, especially Dorothea Z., MaMo, Schorsch, and Andre K. I was lucky to have access to a wide variety of archives. Besides personal ones and those in information shops, I also was able to use ones in the Hamburger Institut für Sozialwissenschaftliche Forschung, the Zentralinstitut für Sozialwissenschaftliche Forschung at the Free University of Berlin, the Wissenschaftszentrum Berlin, and the Institute for Social History in Amsterdam. I am grateful for grants from the Deutscher Akademischer Austauschdienst and the Fulbright Commission, which made it possible for me to live and travel in Germany. Translations from German texts, except when otherwise noted, are my own.

Finally, despite the invisibility of the autonomous movement in the United States, activists in Boston, New York, Seattle, San Francisco, and elsewhere provided me with motivation to continue and with concrete proof of the relevance of my project.

CHRONOLOGY

March 11, 1972	First national women's convention in Frankfurt
June 1974	First national feminist congress in Italy
February 1975	Twenty thousand people occupy Wyhl nuclear construction site
October 1976	Women's Liberation Movement occupies vacant courthouse in Rome
February 1977	University of Rome occupied; Communist Luciano Lama expelled by Metropolitan Indians and autonomists
March 12, 1977	Tens of thousands of people march in Rome; street fights in Bologna, Rome, Turin, and other cities
September 1977	Metropolitan Indians call gathering in Bologna; 100,000 attend
September 5, 1977	Hanns-Martin Schleyer kidnapped by Red Army Faction
February 1978	Tunix gathering of twenty thousand people in Berlin
March 16, 1978	Red Brigades kidnap Aldo Moro
March 30, 1979	100,000 march against Gorleben in Hannover
April 1979	Extraordinary repressive measures enacted in Italy
April 30, 1980	Riots in Amsterdam during Queen Beatrice's coronation
May 1980	Struggle for autonomous youth center in Zurich
May–June 3. 1980	Free Republic of Wendland (Gorleben site occupation)
December 12, 1980	"Black Friday" in Berlin; barricade fighting
February 28, 1981	100,000 protesters attack police barricades at Brokdorf
September 13, 1981	U.S. Secretary of State Haig in Berlin; fifty thousand protest
September 22, 1981	Eighteen-year old Klaus Jürgen Rattay killed in Berlin
Fall 1981	Huge peace marches in Europe; hundreds of thousands at nuclear disarmament demonstrations in Bonn, Paris, Rome, Helsinki, Athens, Madrid, Amsterdam

November 1981	150,000 people march against the Startbahn in Frankfurt
June 11, 1982	Reagan visits West Berlin—riots and repression
May 1985	Hans Koch murdered in Amsterdam
December 14, 1985	Forty thousand demonstrators at Wackersdorf construction site; *Hüttendorf* built
April 28, 1986	Chernobyl disaster
September 1986	Ryesgade occupation in Copenhagen; nine days of street fights
June 1987	President Reagan visits Berlin; fifty thousand protest; ban on demonstrations; Kreuzberg cut off from city
November 1987	Two police shot dead, nine wounded at Startbahn
November 13, 1987	Hafenstrasse defends itself from police attacks
September 1988	International Monetary Fund and World Bank conventions in Berlin; seventy-five thousand protest
November 1989	Berlin Wall broken down
October 3, 1990	German reunification
November 1990	Battle for Mainzerstrasse
September 1991	Pogrom in Hoyerswerde; four thousand Anti-Nazis gather to protect foreigners
August 1992	Pogrom in Rostock; twenty thousand Anti-Nazis assemble
September 1992	Tens of thousands of Roma (Gypsies) deported to Romania
November 1992	Lichterketten: 350,000 people march to protest racism in Berlin (Chancellor Kohl pelted with eggs); three Turkish women burned to death in Molln
December 1992	Hundreds of thousands of people march in Munich, Frankfurt, and Hamburg against racism
May 1993	German constitution changed to restrict immigration; Blockade of *Bundestag*
May 29, 1993	Five Turkish females burnt to death in neo-Nazi arson attack in Solingen

ABBREVIATIONS

AD	Direct Action (France)
AO	Workers Autonomy (Italy)
AL	Alternative List (Germany)
ANC	African National Congress (South Africa)
Antifas	Antifascists (Germany)
APO	Extraparliamentary Opposition (Germany)
BBU	Federal Association of Citizen Initiatives for Environmental Protection (Germany)
BZ	Occupation Brigade (Denmark)
CDU	Christian Democratic Union (Germany)
FEDS	Federal Employees for a Democratic Society (U.S.)
FR	Female Revolt (Italy)
FRG	Federal Republic of Germany
LC	Continuous Struggle (Italy)
MI	Metropolitan Indians (Italy)
MLD	Women's Liberation Movement (Italy)
NATO	North Atlantic Treaty Organization
NOW	National Organization for Women (U.S.)
PCI	Communist Party of Italy
PL	Front Line (Italy)
PO	Workers' Power (Italy)
PSI	Socialist Party of Italy
RAF	Red Army Faction (Germany)
RA RA	Antiracist Action (Holland)
RB	Red Brigades (Italy)
RZ	Revolutionary Cells (Germany)
SDS	Students for a Democratic Society (U.S.)
SDS	German Socialist Student Federation
SNCC	Student Nonviolent Coordinating Committee (U.S.)
SPD	Social Democratic Party (Germany)
UDI	Union of Italian Women

LIST OF ILLUSTRATIONS

MAP

Federal Republic of Germany   xxvi

TABLES

May 1981 West Berlin Election Results   98
How Germans View Foreigners and Minorities   161
Green Votes in Federal Elections   199
Forms of Democracy   211
Occupational Structure of West Germany   241
Colonization of Everyday Life   246
Opposing Values: System and Counterculture   247

FIGURE

Structure of Autonomous Movements   192
Federal Republic of Germany

FEDERAL REPUBLIC
OF GERMANY

FROM 1968 TO AUTONOMY

The now legendary 1960s movements did not die; they never existed, at least not within the temporal confines of a decade. After all, it was in 1955 that Rosa Parks refused to give up her seat in the back of the bus and in 1977 that the Italian counterculture crashed head-on into the forces of order. These examples could be regarded as atypical. More often than not, the civil rights movement and Autonomia (the Italian autonomous movement of the 1970s) are not described as part of the New Left, however globally it is defined. They were not contained by the 1960s and are usually thought to have existed independently of other movements that continued to build from the New Left: feminism and ecology, as well as the anti-intervention, peace, and gay liberation movements. In my view, despite the common definition of these popular upsurges as single-issue or national movements, their discourse and actions were often systematic and universal, and they were part of the world historical social movement of 1968.[1]

The year 1968 was a pivotal one in world history. In nearly every country of the world, spontaneously generated movements erupted that profoundly changed their societies, despite the movements' relatively rapid dispersal. Although understood as national movements, they existed as much in relation *to each other* as to their native contexts. Taken as a whole, they constituted a lasting period of global transformation, marking the crisis of industrial capitalism and its passage to what can be called its postmodern phase.[2] Like 1848 and 1905, 1968 was a year when emergent global movements were apparently defeated only to have a long-term impact of immense significance. The animating principle of the world spirit of 1968 was to forge new identities based on the negation of existing divisions: in place of patriotism and national chauvinism, international solidarity; instead of hierarchy and patterns of domination and submission, self-management and individual self-determination; in place of patriarchy and racism, egalitarian humanism; rather than competition, cooperation; rather than the accumulation of wealth, attempts to end poverty; instead of the domination of nature, ecological harmony.

Within the movement, certain organizing principles distinguished New Left movements from previous ones. These principles marked the break between modern and postmodern social movements. Although the heroic period of the movement, roughly comprising the two decades from 1955 to 1977, is over, the unfolding of its process continues today. Even considered in isolation, severed from their roots in the 1960s, the feminist and ecological movements base themselves on the New Left impulse to change everyday life. Precisely because the New Left of the 1960s was where this logic first developed, I consider it world historical—as ushering in a transvaluation of norms and values. As Umberto Eco put it in 1986:

> Even though all visible traces of 1968 are gone, it profoundly changed the way all of us, in Europe at least, behave and relate to one another. Relations between bosses and workers, students and teachers, even parents and children, have opened up. They'll never be the same again.[3]

If he had considered the effects of the New Left in the United States, Eco could just as well have said the same thing about the relationship between the races, between men and women, and between gays and straights.

I do not mean to imply that the process of social change is linear. At the beginning of the 1990s, the pendulum of history swung in the reverse direction of 1968. Rather than an integrating principle animating the broad strokes of world history, its opposite appeared: a segregating impetus to recapture identities based on blood ties, a validation of historically determined hierarchies and divisions. Although isolated clusters of activists continued to be painting fine brush strokes according to the logic of the New Left, the New Right patterned the major images. Whether observed in skinhead violence internationally and the anti-immigrant sentiment sweeping the globe, in the sexual counterrevolution and the stigmatization of people with AIDS, in ethnic violence in Bosnia, or in Operation Rescue's attempt to restore male control over women's bodies, we could find the negation of the 1960s liberatory impulses. In the gang violence in U.S. inner cities, we could see the social cost we all pay for the government's suppression of the Black Panther Party. In the struggle by some gays and women for the right to participate in combat, we could see the near antithesis of radical feminism and gay liberation. Their political orientation was once formulated within a gender-based critique of violence and a discussion of sexual repression as one of the root causes of war. Reconstituted as a "new" social movement, some varieties of feminism and gay liberation demanded women and gays in combat, not the abolition of war.

THE EUROPEAN CONTEXT

Although Europe and the United States are both subject to the same segregating world spirit of the 1990s, upheavals associated with the end of the Cold War in Europe have no counterpart on the U.S. side of the Atlantic. German reunification profoundly transformed that society, certainly changing much more than the context and trajectories of opposition movements. In addition to this difference, there is a longer-term divergence between the societies. The consolidation of a post-New Left opposition that occurred in Germany—a movement visible in the spectrum of groups from the Greens to the Autonomen and the Red Army Faction (RAF)—did not occur in the United States. Despite thousands of activist groups within the antiapartheid and Central America anti-intervention movements, the environmental movement, the campaign for the equal rights amendment, gay organizing, and the Rainbow Coalition, fragmentation defined each of these formations, and it could not be accurately said that there was "a movement" in the United States. In Germany there was. Part of the reason for this was undoubtedly German identity. In Europe, nationalism plays an entirely different role than in the United States. There, it divides the continent into distinctive zones; here, it unites an even larger region than all of Europe.

In Germany, the question of whether there is continuity between the New Left and the Autonomen is not as easily answered in the affirmative as it is from a distance. Many activists from 1968 experienced a profound break between the 1960s and the more radical autonomists of the 1980s and 1990s. At the end of the 1970s, political scientists Martin and Sylvia Greiffenhagen maintained that "the history of the protest movement is ruptured, there appears to be no continuity with the activities of present-day extraparliamentary groups."[4] Slowly but surely after the decline of the New Left, new types of popular opposition groups formed. Activists from the 1960s were influential in some of the groups, but for the most part, they were veterans of a university-based movement, and their issues of concern—the war in Vietnam, reforming the universities, and the buildup of the state's repressive forces (the Emergency Laws of 1968, as well as the *Berufsverbot* and *Radikalenerlass*) were far different from what motivated the next wave of activism. By 1980, a movement existed that was clearly more radical and bigger than that of the 1960s. The new movement was more diverse and unpredictable, and less theoretical and organized than was the New Left. Despite their differences, they shared a number of characteristics; antiauthoritarianism, independence from existing political parties, decentralized organizational forms, emphasis on direct action, and a combination of culture and politics as a means for the creation of a new person and new forms for living through the transformation of everyday Life. As in the 1960s, the regional differences in German society were reflected in the new movement's character in various parts of the country. In the early 1980s, thousands of people built barricades and fought police all night in Frankfurt to demonstrate their support for the national liberation struggle in El Salvador. A call for a similar demonstration in Hannover drew more than two thousand people—including many leftwing Turks—but fewer than fifty interested people turned out to march for El Salvador in West Berlin.

Most younger activists looked upon 1960s people as having accommodated themselves to the existing system or even gone over to the other side. Daniel Cohn-Bendit, star of the May 1968 revolt in France and later a Green government minister in the city of Frankfurt, had his speeches disrupted and his life threatened by members of the autonomous scene because of their perception that he had sold out. To be sure, prominent Greens have established comfortable niches as professional members of a loyal opposition, and some of their former national leaders have been rewarded with university professorships in a society where such positions are rare and require high-level political approval. Even within the Greens, some people looked on the "monoculture of the '68ers"[5] as having excluded younger activists from the party. Many Autonomen regard the 1968 generation as no different from all the rest of the dead weight of the past, "weighing like a nightmare on the brains of the living." They laugh at the outraged innocence of the New Left symbolized by the flowers put into the barrels of National Guard rifles in Berkeley and of Russian tanks in Prague. For the New Left, the whole world was watching as the modern epoch, one of expanding democracy and rising expectations came to an end. More than anything else, the new radicals are distinguished from the New Left by their orientation to themselves—to a "politics of the first person"—not to the proletariat or to the wretched of the earth.

Many of those who personify the 1960s for younger generations regularly fail to comprehend the changed context, preferring instead to denigrate the Autonomen, referring to them as "agents provocateurs" (as Petra Kelly told me in 1985) or even worse—as neo-fascists and anti-Semites. Hostile to the Autonomen, the German media pay sympathetic attention to the older generation of activists. During commemorations of the twentieth and twenty-fifth anniversaries of 1968, the media (which once vilified and Red-baited the New Left) celebrated its activists' paternalistic pronouncements regarding the younger generation of activists, for example, that their violence had nothing to do with the "decent" protests that occurred in the 1960s. Outrageous and seemingly unjustified Autonomen attacks on restaurants, movie theaters, and passenger cars—actions I call "civil Luddism" because they seek to break the engines of everyday life—render the revolt "other" in unexpected ways.

However we frame the debate about continuity in Germany, both sides regard the Autonomen as a movement—whether or not it is continuous with 1968. Unlike in France, the United States, or Japan, in Germany a radical opposition movement was able to regenerate itself among new generations of young people in the 1980s. The autonomous movement first appeared in Italy in the 1970s (the topic of Chapter 2), but after it was defeated, activism there largely ceased. In the 1960s, riots regularly accompanied the visits of U.S. presidents to Latin America, whereas in the 1980s, it was in Germany that appearances by Reagan and Bush caused such conflicts to break out. Despite their mobilizations against U.S. presidents, autonomous movements emerge from the New Left critique of totalitarianism of both the Left and the Right; they flow from a cultural and political rejection of society in the United States, Western Europe, and what used to be the Soviet Union. A facile reading of the movement posits its negativity as a handicap: many observers argue that because autonomous movements can never become a majoritarian movement or grasp power, they are a lunatic fringe and therefore of little interest and even less importance. The assumption contained in such a view is that power—not its disintegration—should constitute the goal of social movements.

In my view, the importance of social movements in the new epoch we have entered since the demise of Soviet Communism, far from being determined by an ability to wield national power, will be more a function of a capacity to limit the powers of nation-states and to create free spaces in which self-determined decisions can be made autonomously and implemented directly. At best, the existing system offers a facade of popular input into state agencies or allows space for cooperative groups to function within a larger context of obedience to the state and market profitability. Although it provides unprecedented consumer wealth for a majority of people in the advanced capitalist societies, the world system is founded upon unprecedented misery for tens of millions of people at its periphery—as well as an increasingly marginalized strata in its core. Powerful nation-states and mammoth transnational corporations are essentially products of the modern world—that is, the epoch between the industrial revolution and World War II. As the behemoth powers of governments and corporations expanded, popular control over significant decisions of life were eroded. Privacy continues to be invaded, family life destroyed, job security made nonexistent, environmental conditions degraded, water made unfit to drink, and air made poisonous to our health. In short, the conditions of life are being destroyed at the same time as previously independent realms of everyday life are increasingly subsumed by the commodity form and criteria of profitability. This "colonization of the life-world" shifts the sites for the contestation of power by social movements from politics to everyday life.

In contrast to the centralized decisions and hierarchical authority structures of modern institutions, autonomous social movements involve people directly in decisions affecting their everyday lives. They seek to expand democracy and to help individuals break free of political structures and behavior patterns imposed from the outside. Rather than pursue careers and create patriarchal families, participants in autonomous movements live in groups to negate the isolation of individuals imposed by consumerism. They seek to decolonize everyday life. The base of the autonomous movement in dozens of squatted and formerly squatted houses reflects a break with the established norms of middle-class propriety in their everyday lives: communes instead of traditional families; movement restaurants and bars where the "scene" can have its own space, as opposed to the commercialized world of mass culture; an international community defined by its radical actions, in contrast to the patriotic spectacles so beloved in Europe.

In this context, the Autonomen represent a paradigm shift in politics that began with the New Left but has become increasingly well defined. Unlike other movements of the twentieth century that have been preoccupied with seizing national power they seek to dissolve it. Their subversion of politics means a complete reorientation of our understanding of the role of nation-states and individual obedience to their laws. In place of massive systems of representative democracy and majority rule, they live according to principles of direct democracy and self-government. They do not seek to create mammoth structures of power, nor are they interested in participating in existing ones. Although their numbers are small, their actions often have a significance beyond what quantitative analysis would indicate. Autonomous movements have been called "postpolitical" because of their lack of regard for elections and political parties. I prefer to think of these movements as subverting politics, as transforming public participation into something completely different from what is normally understood as political.

THE MEANING OF AUTONOMY

Clearly, autonomy has a variety of meanings. Western philosophy since Kant has used the term to refer to the independence of individual subjectivity, but as I use the term in this book, autonomy refers mainly to collective relationships, not individual ones. In my analysis of social movements, several meanings of autonomy emerge: first and most saliently, the independence of social movements from political parties and trade unions. Thus, movements for regional or national autonomy are not autonomous movements in the sense in which I use the term if they are aligned with established political parties. The Irish independence movement, for example, struggles for Ireland's autonomy from Great Britain, but I do not consider it to be an autonomous movement, because it is controlled by hierarchically organized parties and traditional conceptions of politics. Separatist movements of all kinds abound today, but few, if any, are autonomous movements. National and regional autonomy has long been a central issue for movements in peripheral areas of the world system. In the current period, the demand for autonomy is present within movements in Kurdistan, India, the Basque country, and many parts of the former Soviet Union. Subcomandante Marcos of the Zapatistas in Chiapas, Mexico, presented the major demands of the peasants as "food, health, education, autonomy, and peace."[6] In Brazil, the United Black Movement, founded in 1978 when blacks gathered to protest the murder by the police of a black man accused of stealing an apple, considers political autonomy for blacks to be one of its main goals. Aspirations for greater regional autonomy for Native Americans in Chiapas or Afro-Brazilians in Bahia, although not precisely the same type of autonomy as is present in European movements, nonetheless demonstrate the formal similarity of these emergent movements. They all call for "Power to the People" and decentralization of decision making concentrated in nation-states.

In Italy in the 1970s, thousands of factory workers participated in Autonomia, and the meaning of autonomy extracted from their experiences was sometimes defined exclusively in workerist terms. According to Johannes Agnoli, the concept of autonomy in northern Italy had two dimensions: class struggle made itself autonomous of the circulation of capital; and the class struggle was not led by traditional organizations of the Left (Communists and their trade unions).[7] Although widely propagated, workerist definitions of autonomy are but one of its many forms, even in reference to the movement in Italy. As I portray in my case studies of Italian and German social movements, the autonomous women's movement in each country was vital to subsequent formations, because of feminists' innovative internal procedures as well as their capacity to act separately from men in accordance with their own autonomously defined needs and aspirations. These autonomous feminist movements set an example of a "politics of the first person," as opposed to traditional notions of revolutionaries leading the nation or the working-class. Within these movements, moreover, individuals did not take orders from higher-ups but voluntarily acted according to their own will (thereby preserving the original Kantian kernel of autonomy within an enlarged meaning and collective context). Many feminist groups operated according to self-managed consensus, making decisions independently of central leaders and implementing them according to their own self-discipline. This organizational model remains vitally important to the definition of autonomous movements.

A final meaning of autonomy emerged in the course of prolonged popular struggles against nuclear power in Germany in the mid-1970s. Activist groups began referring to themselves as autonomous to establish distance from party-oriented Marxist-Leninist groups within the antinuclear movement that denied the value of spontaneous forms of militant resistance. As radical clusters also appeared within the peace movement and the counterculture and among squatters, they merged into a multifaceted formation that eventually became known as the Autonomen. By creatively synthesizing direct-democratic forms of decision-making and militant popular resistance, the Autonomen embody what I call "conscious spontaneity."

The Autonomen do not subscribe to the belief that there is one overriding truth or one true form of autonomy. There are, nonetheless, a number of principles that provide coherence: they see their ideas as a revolutionary alternative to both authoritarian socialism (Soviet-style societies) and "pseudodemocratic capitalism." Unlike Communists, they do not believe in the need for one true revolutionary party or revolutionary sector of society. They believe in diversity and continuing differentiation. Nowhere written down, this principle emerges in the actions of thousands of people in their everyday lives. They believe in self-management and the need for individuals and groups to take responsibility for their own actions. Although these notions may be contradicted in the actions of some, they materialize in the enduring patterns of movement activity. The Autonomen seek to change governments as well as everyday life, to overthrow capitalism and patriarchy.[8]

In Portugal and Spain in the mid-1970s, social movements critically impacted these countries when they suddenly seized power. I do not analyze them in this book in part because they were not oriented toward the transformation of everyday life. At the end of 1995, a wave of strikes lasting twenty-four days suddenly brought France to the brink of a repetition of the events of May 1968 (when ten million students and workers suddenly went on strike). Despite the volatile character of the strikes in 1995, they were contained within the government: the strikers were "almost all public-sector employees, their actions were in response to the prime minister's attempt to change national policies, and their union leaders sought negotiations with the government as one of their main demands. Like nearly everything related to social movements in France, these strikes occurred within the realm of established politics. Creating contested domains outside arenas normally regarded as political is practically inconceivable there.

If movements' attempts to transform civil society were the sole criterion for inclusion in my analysis, I would also have written about Great Britain. In London, squatters have continued to take over buildings since the early 1970s, and an antifascist movement is also quite militant. The anarchist newspaper *Class War* grew out of the miners' strike and presents a unique synthesis of militant action and tabloid journalism. Historically, Britain has been part of Europe while simultaneously cut off from it, and it would not be entirely inaccurate to characterize Britain's relationship to Europe's autonomous movements in similar terms. My decision to focus on contiguous countries of central Europe (Italy, Germany, Holland, and Denmark) was predicated in part on my organic connections with activists there.

Although my focus is on central Europe, particularly Germany, autonomous politics is increasingly relevant internationally. Viewed from the perspective of how they constitute a determinate negation of the structural imperatives of the world system, the Autonomen should be understood as verification of my prognosis that the cultural-political character of the New Left would continue to define the long-term form of antisystemic movements. As autonomous movements find adherents in places such as Prague, Athens; Lyon (France), Moscow, San Francisco, and New York, it becomes increasingly apparent that, though often invisible to the mainstream, they define the phenomenal form of contemporary radical activism.

THE AUTONOMEN: AN INVISIBLE MOVEMENT

Relative to the voluminous literature on France and England in print in the United States, few books exist about Germany, and those in print deal mainly with the Nazi past, the rise and fall of Communism, or the neo-Nazis of today. It is no wonder that prejudice against Germans is not uncommon among Americans. So long as Germans are characterized as orderly and obedient, we Americans feel secure in our superior democratic values and cultural pluralism. After all, the Allies liberated the German people from their Nazi overlords, we Americans gave them their first democratic constitution, and we also financed the postwar reconstruction that made possible their current prosperity.

To the extent that Americans are aware of progressive Germans, it is generally the Greens. Taking advantage of the proportional representation rule governing German elections,[9] the Greens quickly established a presence within local and national governments and became the third largest party in Germany in the mid-1990s. In 1983, they got over two million votes in the federal election. When they took their seats in parliament, their long hair and casual attire signaled a larger change in German society and politics. On both sides of the Atlantic, mainstream analysts worried about the "threat" constituted by German pacificism to the Cold War. Due to the media's focus on them, it was commonly assumed that the Greens created and led Germany's progressives.

One of the purposes of this book is to dispel that myth. Often considered by outsiders to be identical with Left radicalism in Germany, the Greens are but the most prominent organization to emerge from a broadbased and diverse social movement. Since there is so little information in the United States concerning the Autonomen, the assumption is often made that this invisible movement is irrelevant or even nonexistent.* As I discuss in Chapter 3, long before the Green Party was founded in 1979, an autonomous women's movement had waged a militant campaign for the decriminalization of abortion and created dozens of women's centers. Other extraparliamentary direct-action movements arose and challenged the conservative spell that had gripped German national politics from Hitler to the *Berufsverbot* (government decrees in the 1970s that effectively stifled dissent by civil servants). Grassroots groups (*Bürgerinitiativen*) first thawed the frozen political terrain when they began a process of publicly challenging unpopular policies such as the construction of nuclear power plants, the expansion of the gigantic airport in Frankfurt, and the continuing housing shortage.[10] As local communities organized to protect their surroundings from encroachments by the industrial-political behemoth, their initiatives slowly gathered supporters seeking greater democratic input into significant social decisions. The country's heavy reliance on nuclear fission as a source of energy became a key issue. Confrontations against nuclear power projects posed the need for a parliamentary presence within the system that could articulate the aspirations of the emergent antinuclear movement, whose popular support was clearly greater than anyone had anticipated. As the Greens began to run for office, radicals squatted in hundreds of abandoned houses in the inner cities and used them as a base from which to radicalize the peace, ecology, and feminist movements.

---

* In 1989, after I made a detailed presentation at MIT to several hundred people on the Autonomen, which included slides and copies of their magazines. One member of the audience confronted me with the charge that I had invented the whole movement, contending that the events I had described were simply part of the Greens.

The Green Party was formed to fulfill needs dramatized by these extraparliamentary impulses—to clean up Germany's environment; to make its governing structure more democratic; and to break the hold of the patriarchal, small-town mentality that encroached upon women's freedom, denied gays the right to be themselves, and crippled the capacity of young people to live according to their own ideas. In the crucible of years of struggles, direct-action movements galvanized the radical Autonomen. Employing militant confrontational tactics against the police in the 1980s, the Autonomen played a major role in defeating the government's plans for a nuclear reprocessing plant at Wackersdorf in Bavaria that would have provided Germany with bomb-grade plutonium. Their noncooperation campaign caused the government to cancel a national census, and they helped undermine Berlin's bid to host the Olympics in 2000. These victories of autonomous movements are arguably more important than any gains won through the parliamentary system in the same period.

At first glance, the different levels of political action on which direct-action movements and the Greens operate appear to complement each other. Within the German movement, however, the contradiction between building domains autonomous from the government and participating in parliamentary activity within it animates a complex political discourse all but unknown in the United States. On the surface, since the Autonomen and the Greens both seek to achieve similar goals, such as the end of nuclear power, it appears that they differ only in their tactics. The divergence between these two wings of the German movement is actually much greater than that, encompassing organizational forms as well as differences of strategy (building self-governing centers of dual power versus transforming the society from within parliament). Although militant actions and electoral activity often provide reciprocal benefits to each other, they can also generate bitter conflicts.

For many Autonomen, the Greens are not the movement in the government but the government in the movement. They are that part of the establishment that has penetrated the radical opposition, another mechanism used by the state to extend and legitimate its authority. As such, the Greens represent the latest example of co-opted movement groups following in the historical footsteps of the Social Democratic party (with whom the Greens have formed state and local coalition governments). For some readers, it may be disconcerting to read that the Greens are on the fringe of a radical egalitarian movement, but it would be less than honest for me to present them in any other manner.

To many Greens, the Autonomen are guilty of "blind actionism" (and worse); they substitute "the struggle for their goal instead of liberation."

The Autonomen are "violent anarchists" who throw tomatoes and eggs at high government officials rather than engage them in rational debate. They are often linked to guerrilla groups such as the RAF, a group that has kidnapped and killed some of the country's leading bankers, industrialists, and political leaders.

I see these approaches (Green and autonomous, within and outside the system) as complementary. They require each other for their continual elaboration and historical impact. In Chapter 6, I discuss this issue in more detail. From my perspective, the Autonomen exist in a political terrain lying between the reformism of the Greens and the adventurism of the RAF. Most Autonomen would vehemently disagree with my characterization of the Greens as even a part of the movement. They perceive the Greens as more of a threat to the movement's vitality than any other established political force, because the Greens are able to gain access to so many movement activities, blunt their radical potential, and even aid the police in isolating the movement. During preparations for a planned demonstration against the Brokdorf nuclear power plant in 1986, for example, many of the more than fifty thousand people going to protest refused to submit to mandatory police inspections of their automobile caravans before they went on the autobahns. Green organizers, however, agreed to allow their vehicles to be searched for helmets and other materials that might be used to confront the massed police defenders at Brokdorf. Naturally, the police simply waved the Greens through their checkpoints and then bloodily dispersed the remaining protesters before they could even assemble (as occurred in Berlin). Near Hamburg, hundreds of people were brutally attacked while stopped in their cars. Many of those injured in the police attack blamed the Greens' cooperation with the police for effectively identifying those who refused to submit to the searches.

A less severe example of the Greens' distance from the Autonomen came in September 1988, when the Autonomen prepared demonstrations against the international conventions of the World Bank and the International Monetary Fund in Berlin. Thousands of militant demonstrators tried to stop the top finance ministers of 150 countries and over ten thousand world bankers from planning their future exploits (since the protestors blamed them for poverty and starvation at the periphery of the world economy). For their part, the Green Party and its affiliates attempted to defuse the planned confrontation by calling for a convention of their own to discuss the possibility of an "alternative world banking system." Unlike the Greens, the radical Autonomen would have little to do with banks—alternative or not—or any kind of system. The type of world they seek to create and to live in is as far removed as possible from money, centralization, government, and ownership in all their forms.

The autonomous framework of action constitutes a promising realm of politics that is not generally considered by analysts of social movements and activists outside Europe. Contained within my history of autonomous movements are many of their most salient points of departure from other types of politics. There are several main threads in the discourse of this book:

1. The tension between working within the system and working entirely in opposition to it, and the, relative advantages and liabilities of each approach.
2. The importance of establishing alternative humane lifestyles right now, not only challenging power at the collective political level.
3. The formulation of a universal species interest and the transcendence of exclusive identities that delimit the aspirations and vision of groups.
4. The psychological disposition and Nazi heritage of the German people and the potential for these to affect radical social movements.

The first three are certainly enduring questions, and the fourth can also be understood in a more general form: how can we prevent decentralized popular movements from attracting and incorporating hateful elements, particularly those drawn from ethnic chauvinism?

MEDIA AND MARGINALITY

Unlike the Greens, autonomists do not seek publicity—indeed, they are known for their hostility to and attacks on photographers who show up at their events. Activists have several reasons for preventing the mainstream media from broadcasting news of their movement. Most obviously, the police use photos and video footage from the media to identify and arrest people. More subtly, activists consciously wish to prevent the media from artificially creating leaders (which they view as one of the shortcomings of the New Left). In order to maintain the integrity of their own groups, they shut out the media as intrusive forces that undermine the autonomous identity they have created. They seek to control media productions about them, something that the U.S. media, unlike their European counterparts, do not permit. In 1981, for example, a CBS film crew showed up at one of the many squatted houses in West Berlin to shoot a story on the movement. Although the squatters were aware that they were dealing with a potential audience in the tens of millions, they opted not to speak to CBS because they were not guaranteed the right to approve the final segment.

Additionally, once outsiders have knowledge of their existence through the media, many activists fear that they are doomed to be invaded by tourists.[11] Typical U.S. media coverage is oriented precisely to voyeurism. After German reunification and the Bundestag's decision to move the capital to Berlin, the editorial pages of the *New York Times* paternalistically described the movement there as part of the city's touristic allure: "Hair tints tend to be polychrome, women dress to be dramatic rather than chic, and youngsters in Kreuzberg wear their anarchist politics on tattered sleeves."[12] A year earlier, the *Times* had referred to the Autonomen as "anarchic thugs,"[13] and the *Washington Post* described them in less than glowing terms: "They are a bedraggled bunch, dressed mostly in black, their hair painted in bright streaks of color, their noses and ears pierced by multiple rings." There could be no better impression of the scene, at least from the point of view of those who believe that the inner meaning of the movement is best left incomprehensible to outsiders.

Another motivation for the movement's marginality is to defy the modern propensity for uniformity and the preoccupation with neat and orderly systemization. That is one reason that there are so few written histories of the Autonomen by its members. Of what use is overarching analysis to those who seek to mitigate the entrapment of individuals and communities in the global web of commodity relationships and standardized versions of truth? Autonomous movements seek to break the stranglehold of uniformity and integration into consumer society. Even if the movement were to constitute a majority of the population, it would be an assortment of groups with different lifestyles, dress codes, political conceptions, and self-constructed norms—a majority of marginalized people from the perspective of the control center and its satisfied supporters. Their presence on the margins of German society—replete with scorn and other signs of low status—guarantees that they serve as a reminder that freedom is freedom to live differently. Particularly in Germany, where conformity of small-town life is rigidly inculcated and enforced, the continuing existence of a marginalized movement of urban nonconformists is vitally important to individual liberty.

Pursuing the issue of marginality further, we could question whether "marginal" people are on the edge of society or are central to social change. Social movements of the "second society" (unemployed and marginally employed people, youth, minorities, and women), those left out of what the Germans call the "two-thirds society" (*zwei-drittel Gesellschaft*), produce astonishingly important social changes: they usher in new values (feminism, sexual liberation, equality for foreigners) and new forms of social organization (group living, self-directed programs of work and study, cooperative working relationships) that transform the larger society over time. Although their dress codes and appearances may seem superficially outlandish, many of their essential qualities are quite reasonable. From this perspective, perhaps "marginals" are actually central to social change. The sudden proliferation of movement names, tactics, and ideas, what I consider the "eros effect,"[14] occurs so quickly in contemporary societies in part because of the media. The capacity of human beings to grasp instinctually the gestalt of a movement and to adapt it to their own context connects our species at essential levels of life. Although small groups of autonomists may currently be isolated, they can quickly reproduce in the right situation.

Despite the difficulties in conceptualizing antisystemic movements, I situate the emergence of autonomous movements in the material conditions of late capitalism, specifically in the extension of power and production from the government and factory to arenas of everyday life. The thorough penetration of civil society by capitalist social relations and hierarchical structures of authority has been accompanied by the partial incorporation into the established structures of old social movements—the traditional forces of opposition such as unions and political parties based in the working class. Under these new conditions, different types of social movements (feminist, youth, and ecology) have arisen that reveal the changed character of society and simultaneously challenge the new constellation of power. In Chapters 2 to 4, I trace the new wave of movements from Italy to northern Europe. In the course of my historical analysis, I weave in threads of discussion about the relationship of parliamentary and direct-action forms of resistance, the importance of neighborhood base areas, and the changing character of autonomous movements. As I discuss in Chapter 5, following the breakup of the Soviet Union and its allies, the Autonomen developed along the trajectory of antifascism in response to the neo-Nazi upsurge. By also paying attention to some of the movement's German attributes that are internal obstacles to their own professed goals, I seek to filter out specifically national characteristics in order to understand their more universal qualities. Chapter 6 is devoted to a discussion of the changed notion of politics introduced by autonomous movements. Drawing from documents of the Autonomen as well as my history of them, I contrast them with traditional tendencies on the Left (social democracy and Leninism) and also portray their differences from the Greens. In a critical examination of the work of Antonio Negri, I show how his workerism is an inadequate interpretation of the meaning of autonomous movements.

Given Negri's prominence in the Italian movement, my critique might help explain why Autonomia failed to regenerate itself. In contrast to Negri, I call for a "rationality of the heart" and a fresh understanding of the roles of passion and militance in social transformation. The invisibility of autonomous movements is shaped in part by the inability of major social theorists to understand them. In Chapter 7, I analyze some of the reasons for this lacuna and pose the decolonization of everyday life as an urgent need. Although much of the book is narrative history, in the last chapter, I provide the reader with an analysis of postmodern capitalism and ground my presentation of autonomous movements in a larger context. I also discuss identity politics and new social movement theory to clarify my own interpretation of them and their relevance to autonomous movements. Yet another detailed textual criticism—this time of the feminist theory of Seyla Benhabib—shows the inadequacy of traditional categories of Western philosophy for comprehending the expanded forms of autonomy possible today. With the critiques of Germanity in Chapter 5, Negri's workerism in Chapter 6, and Benhabib's feminism in the last chapter, I demonstrate how even the best ethnic, class, or gender politics falls short of a universal critique of society as articulated by autonomous movements at their best. The questions posed by contemporary industrial societies and subversive movements within them are at the level of the human species as a whole, and no partial identity is capable of reaching the species level of discourse. By the end of the book, I hope the reader glimpses the outlines of the potential for enlarged democracy and freedom prefigured in the practice of autonomous movements.

My presentation begins with Italy in the 1970s, the most meaningful postwar movement in advanced capitalist countries outside the events of May 1968 in France and May 1970 in the United States. Once the turmoil of the late 1960s subsided, most countries returned to less stormy times as grassroots movements either disappeared or became integrated into the system. In Italy and Germany, however, social movements in the 1970s continued to build from the student and worker struggles of the late 1960s. The Italian movement's broad appeal to a popular base deeply impressed German activists, some of whom moved there and later returned to Germany, where they helped prepare the ground for the subsequent emergence of the Autonomen. Just as the civil rights movement in the southern United States served as a crucible for many white and black activists who went on to facilitate and lead struggles outside the South, Italy provided many Germans with their initial involvement in popular struggles.

ITALIAN AUTONOMIA

Like nowhere else in Europe, Italy experienced a wave of protests in the 1970s that drew millions of participants and challenged the control mechanisms of the entire social order. The long wave of Italian social movements began with sporadic student protests that reached a high point in 1968. Unlike most countries, however, as campus protests subsided, Italian students found support among factory workers. During the Hot Autumn of 1969, intense labor conflicts paralyzed industry, and for four years, workers and management battled for control of production and profits. Simultaneously, feminism and a countercultural youth movement transformed social relations. In the mid-1970s, outdated laws governing divorce and abortion were challenged and changed by an autonomous women's movement. Massive strikes and "red terrorism" punctuated factory life, and a cultural revolt against patriarchal paternalism and poverty was so intense that the rebels were called a "second society."

Amid all this turmoil, the nation's government proved unable to provide even a semblance of stability to the country. Indeed, in formerly fascist Italy, there were forty-eight different governments during the first forty years after World War II. After 1968, as social movements defined the agenda of public discourse, no government was able to satisfy the conflicting demands being made by workers and management, by women and the Vatican, or to amass a clear enough majority of parliamentary deputies to rule without intense opposition. Between 1968 and October 1974, there were eight different administrations, each no different from the others in its lack of clarity and leadership, leading many Italians to believe that the political system was inherently unreliable.

In this chapter, I discuss Autonomia, as the diverse cluster of autonomous groups in Italy in the 1970s collectively became known. Beginning with the workers' Hot Autumn, I discuss the sources of Autonomia from movements of workers, women, and youth. Although relationships among these three constituencies were often strained and contradictory, when taken as a whole, they constituted a movement whose militant opposition and autonomy from established political parties lend their actions continuing historical significance. In 1977, the combination of systematic political crisis, rapid economic change, and growing popular opposition culminated in a militant revolt against the established system and its loyal Communist opposition. Subsequent guerrilla actions of organizations such as the Red Brigades (RB) helped foster massive government repression and led to the withdrawal of many people from activism, but not before autonomous movements had transformed the political landscape of Italian society: women won greater legal protection and social freedom; workers saw their standard of living rise and free time expand; and young people were increasingly liberated from the remnants of patriarchal feudalism and benign neglect in universities, schools, and families.

WORKER ROOTS OF AUTONOMY

The first phase of the Italian New Left reached its high point during the Hot Autumn of 1969. Sixty national labor contracts were due to be renewed, and in the contest between labor and management, class struggle became acute and protracted. Five and a half million workers (more than 25 percent of the labor force) struck in 1969, and hundreds of thousands of workers demonstrated, occupied factories, and committed sabotage. The government and corporations struck back, arresting thirteen thousand people and firing or suspending thirty-five thousand workers.[1] When all was said and done, mammoth wage increases had been won, but even more significantly, the working class had reconstituted itself as a historical force. Their new demands and aspirations fell outside the traditional purview of unions. While unions negotiated wage increases, the workers fought speed-ups, piecework, merit pay, production bonuses, and salary differentials; they wanted the elimination of poisonous fumes, unhealthy working conditions, and much more: "We Want Everything!" is what they screamed in the huge Mirafiori Fiat plant in Turin, where over sixty thousand workers were concentrated. For the first time, many migrants from southern Italy, historically used as strike breakers in the factories of the industrialized north, were in the forefront of these struggles.

White-collar workers joined the strikes, and in some cases, they were the initiators or sole participants. Since office workers had been mostly excluded from agreements made between unions representing factory workers and management, concessions won by manual laborers were not passed on to the "new working class" (professionals, technicians, and off-line office and service personnel such as clerks, secretaries, accountants, and engineering workers). The new workers sometimes called for wage equality with their blue-collar counterparts in the factories. They also produced new types of demands. In 1968, telecommunication workers in Milan called for "a human and anti-authoritarian way of working that enables the valorization of professional capacities." A women's study group at the same Siemens facility wrote:

> At the end of eight hours in the factory, women work at home (washing, ironing, sewing for the husband and children). They are therefore further exploited in the role of housewife and mother, without that being recognized as real work.[2]

Such insights had rarely appeared among grassroots activists, but after they were articulated, they resonated among broad segments of the populace. When a strike was organized at this same plant, the first strike at Siemens in more than twenty years, the action drew the participation of over 90 percent of the office workers. Their autonomous committee clashed with the union over tactics and demands, arguing that struggle is "for abolition of wage labor and against the system of the bosses."[3] Over the union's head, they introduced the general assembly as a decision-making body.

The combination of newly activated strata, new aspirations, and the leadership of the movement by semiskilled factory workers was unforeseen. During the Hot Autumn of 1969, unrest spread explosively, and the type of dissent was qualitatively new: the movement had clear revolutionary intent. Factory workers by the thousands took over their factories, not for the purpose of running them but to turn them into bases for organizing in conjunction with their new allies—ex-students experienced in the struggles of the previous year and office workers. "The factory is our Vietnam" was one popular slogan. New types of strikes—hiccup and checkerboard—were autonomously organized forms of creative resistance through which workers controlled production. (Hiccup strikes involved whole factories suddenly coming to a standstill. When management composed itself and workers were ordered back to work, the workers complied, only to repeat the scenario every half hour. A checkerboard strike involved one section of a factory downing tools and walking off the job until ordered to return—at which point another sector took its turn in a prearranged sequence designed to stop production. Sometimes workers with last names from A-L took the first shift of the strike. At other times, the formula was reversed.)

As the struggles in the autumn of 1969 intensified, fifty thousand engineering workers took part in a national demonstration on September 25.[4] At the beginning of October, the city of Milan was brought to a standstill by roadblocks organized by workers from hundreds of factories and joined by thousands of students. In the province surrounding Milan, 100,000 engineering workers struck simultaneously on October 7, and an estimated 71,181,182 total hours of work were lost in 1969 to unrest in the engineering sector alone.[5] As strikes spread throughout the country, they enjoyed overwhelming public support, and the minister of labor was compelled to sign an agreement with the unions that included all their major demands. Nonetheless the workers were not quieted. The frenetic pace of work, long a source of agony that the unions had been incapable of changing, was slowed by workers' concerted campaigns to reduce the speed at which they worked. The length of the workweek was similarly reduced through absenteeism or by simply leaving work early, and workers were protected from aggressive bosses by bands of "red handkerchiefs," named for the attire they wore to mask their identities when they were called on to intimidate foremen and management.

Such actions undermined the traditional hierarchy in the factories through which management ruled, and they also made the unions' claim that they controlled the workforce spurious. Particularly when workers called general assemblies during work hours and used these occasions to organize themselves, sometimes making free use of foremen's telephones to communicate inside factories, it was apparent that the Italian working class had reconstituted itself as an autonomous force controlling the factories. One commentator understood the process as one in which "the workers...learn to make the bosses dance to the rhythm of their music." Another compared it to "an orchestra [that] had managed to play a difficult symphony harmoniously without the conductor and at a tempo agreed upon and regulated by the players of the single instruments."[6] The president of Cofindustria, the organization of private employers, complained that the hiccup strikes "cost the industrialists a lot and the workers nothing.... It is useless to come to agreements between generals [i.e., between union leaders and management] if subsequently the troops do not respect them."[7]

Italy's Communist-controlled trade unions were surprised by the intensity and demands of workers during the Hot Autumn. They had the loyalty of skilled factory workers but not of white-collar employees and assembly-line workers from the south, leaders of the new struggles whose dialects were strange and who cared little about the Communists and their slogans regarding the "dignity of work." Once the resolve of these workers to fight for their demands was understood, both management and the unions, hoping to pacify the young hotheads, negotiated mammoth wage increases: 23.4 percent from 1969 to 1970, and 16.6 percent a year later.

Inflation, however, quickly ate up workers' gains in wages, and housing and services such as public transportation were outmoded and increasingly expensive. Alarmed by the prospects of future struggles, fascist groups began a "strategy of tension" designed to put Italy back on the road to dictatorship (then the rule in southern Europe from Greece to Spain and Portugal). Hoping to create the public impression that the Left was assaulting the government, the fascist strategy of tension began with the bombing of a bank in Milan that killed fourteen people on December 12, 1969. Two anarchists were arrested and accused of the action, one of whom died while in police custody—a "suicide" that "proved" his guilt, according to some daily papers. The ruse worked. Years later, this bombing was shown to be the work of fascists connected to the Secret Service and protected by important Christian Democratic politicians, but during the heat of the moment, the media blamed the Left, causing it to lose public support at a critical moment, especially since it was under severe attacks from the government.[8] While thousands of activists were arrested between October 1969 and January 1970, scores of fascist attacks on movement activists were allowed to occur without police intervention.

In this context, it was only a question of time before the "years of lead" began, when Italians shot at one another with alarming frequency. When the fascists began their strategy of tension, no distinctive left-wing guerrilla organization of any consequence existed in Italy. A decade later, the Red Brigades had kidnapped and killed former Prime Minister Aldo Moro, and the armed struggle between guerrillas and government agents overshadowed all other aspects of Italian politics. In the ten-year period from 1969 to 1979, politically motivated violence laid claim to 415 lives, and an additional 1,181 persons were wounded.[9] Although more than thirty-five thousand Americans are killed by gunshots every year, making the numbers in Italy seem minor by comparison, it should be remembered that these refer only to overtly political violence in Italy.

For four years after the Hot Autumn, intense popular struggles continually reappeared as the working class responded to decades of unprecedented economic expansion based on assembly-line production (Fordism). After World War II, immense social and economic changes constituted the Italian "miracle." From the ashes of postwar ruins, the country rebuilt itself into the world's seventh leading industrial power. Urbanization and industrialization transformed Italy, and millions of people's lives were altered unexpectedly. As agriculture was mechanized, over ten million people were forced off the land. From 1951 to 1971, the percentage of the workforce in agriculture plummeted from 43.9 to 18.8 percent. Four million people left the south and moved from the countryside to northern cities. Between 1951 and 1966, the population of the country's largest cities grew by more than five million people.[10] In the same period of time, little was done to improve social services or to build the infrastructure needed to accommodate such massive migration. Rome, Turin, Milan, and Naples had grown so rapidly that many families could not find decent housing. People slept in groups in a single room, and as shantytowns spread, so did occupations of vacant buildings by squatters. One estimate placed the numbers of squatters in Italy between 1969 and 1975 at twenty thousand.[11] In Milan alone in 1977, about fifty buildings consisting of "2,000 hard-core squatters and 35,000 occasional participants" were occupied.[12]

Events in Milan, Italy's cultural capital, often set the tone for the nation in clothing, ideas, and advertising. Beginning in 1969, Milan was also in the forefront of the impetus to housing reform, a struggle that produced a national general strike, and bloody battles that resulted in the death of 2 policemen. In 1971, as these struggles continued, two thousand police were confronted by barricades and riots when they arrived to evict seventy immigrant families who had occupied empty houses. Workers from nearby factories also mobilized to defend the squatters. When the protesters regrouped at the Architecture Faculty of the University of Milan the next day, even more police met such determined resistance that they retreated. The struggle expanded to include the Polytechnic and tens of thousands of people.[13] Rent strikes and squatters' struggles in Rome, Taranto, Palermo, Messina, Salerno, and Naples represented a new type of grassroots resistance, often led by women. Neighborhood committees, previously affiliated with political parties, became involved in popular struggles for parks, schools, clinics, and day-care facilities.[14] Unable to pay their rising bills, many people autonomously set prices at more acceptable levels. The massive character of this *autoriduzione* (self-reduction) movement made it hard to contain. In many cities, public transportation fares were set by what commuters would pay rather than what the companies charged. In Turin and Piedmont, about 150,000 families reduced their electrical bills; in Milan, about 10,000; and in the rest of Italy, tens of thousands more.[15]

Declaring "workers don't break the law," the Communists stood against the self-reduction movements and squatters. Unlike immigrants from the south, unionized factory workers had something to lose: their unions had skillfully negotiated higher wages and benefits for the organized working class, and the Communist Party of Italy (PCI) had consolidated its hold over millions of votes, growing to become the largest communist party outside the socialist countries. As it gained respectability among established politicians and industrial leaders, the PCI took over the newly formed workers' councils in the factories that had been created during the Hot Autumn as autonomously constituted organs unconnected to party politics. Italian workers belonged to three different unions, each of which was affiliated with a particular political party. By 1972, a survey showed that autonomously constituted councils existed in about one-third of the workplaces sampled.[16] The bureaucratization of the councils proceeded in two steps. Instead of a general assembly being the decision-making body, delegates were chosen. As these delegates became increasingly affiliated with the PCI, their allegiance shifted from the shop floor movement to the party.[17]

With Communists in control of their councils, workers in the factories had no one to turn to.[18] Older skilled workers loyal to the PCI were retiring, and Italian industry was modernizing. Management set a wage ceiling and told the unions that it was their role to deliver a compliant working class, leaving the PCI to enforce discipline among the young hotheads. On the one side, management was imposing Taylorism (the time management of tasks), while on the other side, workers demanded control of production and less work, raising the entire issue of how society should make basic decisions such as how to allocate its resources. Since the PCI now controlled their informal councils as well as their unions, workers had no choice but to organize autonomous strikes and work slowdowns to fight the tightening economic noose. Influenced by the Vatican and the traditional values of the ruling Christian Democrats, Italian cultural conservatism also permeated the parties of the Left (whether the PCI or the PSI—the Socialist Party of Italy, an organization that had accommodated itself to the existing system and become part of its ruling apparatus). The new aspirations of the Hot Autumn were not part of the understanding of these parties. Divorce, abortion, and other crucial questions of everyday life were simply outside their discourse. As a result, many activists joined one of the newly organized groups that had appeared after 1968.

For the most part, the plethora of radical (or even self-described "revolutionary") parties and tendencies on the far Left differed with the reformist PCI over tactics and strategy, but not vision and structure. Despite their promising beginnings, they too proved unable to comprehend that noneconomic issues were vital to their politics. The largest of the groups to the left of the PCI was Lotta Continua (LC, or Continuous Struggle). LC emerged as a major organization from the worker-student assemblies in Turin during the Hot Autumn and subsequently developed many adherents among Fiat workers. At its peak, it had about fifty thousand activists, a hundred full-time paid officials, branch offices in all ninety-four Italian provinces, and twenty-one neighborhood offices in Rome alone.[19] First published during the Hot Autumn of 1969, LC's newspaper slowly gained circulation, selling an average of thirteen thousand copies a day in 1976, and by the end of 1977, thirty-five thousand.[20] Il Manifesto (which was expelled from the PCI in November 1969) also published a newspaper with a wide readership. Manifesto had about six thousand members in 1972 and reached a high point of about eight thousand at its 1975 congress. They advocated council communism, an alternative to the PCI's notion of the party ruling society in the name of the working class. Council communists believe that workers can make their own decisions regarding how society should be run without any assistance from vanguard parties. Despite its radical veneer, Manifesto's style of politics was hierarchical, and its analysis remained bounded by traditionally defined categories. Many of the movement's leading theorists were members of Potere Operaio (PO, or Workers' Power). In addition to LC, PO, and Manifesto, there were a variety of other parties and groups. In the elections of 1972, all these groups together received more than a million votes. Significantly, several Maoist organizations rejected electoral politics, moving instead toward armed struggle. In 1970, one of them first used "Red Brigades" as its signature.

Less formally structured than any of these parties was Autonomia Operaia (AO, or Workers' Autonomy). Born in the 1950s from the needs of Italian workers in northern factories to assert their grassroots independence from both management and unions controlled by the Communists, AO became a significant force after the Hot Autumn because of its success in organizing within individual factories and its influence over regional assemblies of activists. In 1972, workers and students in Rome organized a headquarters for autonomous workers' committees, and AO existed in an informal network and series of conferences attended by various collectives, organizations, and individuals. AO believed in "raising the level of struggle within the state apparatus" and thereby initiated head-on conflicts with the government at a time when the Communist-controlled trade unions were moving in precisely the opposite direction. Although it was often criticized for its forceful methods, many workers approved of AO's efforts against the PCI and its trade unions—organizations that AO regarded as class enemies (and that considered AO to be fascist).

In September 1972, as new contracts were being negotiated, a general strike broke out in Turin. Inside the factories, militant demonstrations enforced strike discipline, and over the next months, autonomously organized tactics escalated the workers' sense of power. On February 2, 1973, an occupation at the Mirafiori plant by twenty thousand workers led to a wave of factory occupations. On February 9, nearly half a million workers marched in Rome, the largest gathering of workers since World War II, shouting "Power to the Workers!" and "Factory, School, Community—Our Struggle Is for Power!" Workers' demands were not limited to higher wages. Many worked in excess of fifty hours a week, and they wanted to limit the workweek to forty hours. Even more significantly, many workers articulated their desire not to remain stuck in the factories, with lives whose sole purpose was to make money to pay bills. On March 29, ten thousand militant strikers blocked entrances at Mirafiori, and by the next day, most of Turin's factories were in the hands of their workers. Both unions and companies rushed to reach an agreement to defuse the situation, but even when a new contract was quickly signed, more than half the workforce at Mirafiori was absent the next day.

The struggles in this period were potentially revolutionary. Workers wanted more than what the Communists aimed for (the material benefits of consumerism). They wanted to cease being factory workers, to live lives of their own collective making, not ones determined by decisions in corporate boardrooms and government ministries. As one observer put it: "More than a struggle for a new contract, this has been a rage against work." A Mirafiori worker put it this way:

> This occupation is different from the one workers did in 1920. In 1920 they said let's occupy but let's work. Let's show everyone that we can run production ourselves. Things are different today. In our occupation, the factory is a starting point for the revolutionary organization of workers—*not a place to work*.[21]

None of the Left organizations played a central role, nor were there charismatic leaders in control of the movement of 1973. Despite histories that construct their roles as crucial, the myriad organizations and publications such as AO, LC, and Manifesto were themselves transformed by the energy of the autonomous movement. It appears that tens of thousands of people were capable of self-organization and direct action. In factories, the plethora of traditional Left groups was relegated to the sidelines when workers went on strike. The movement of 1973 even prompted PO, a major presence in Padua, the factories of Portomarghera, and the University of Rome, to dissolve so that its members could become an organic part of workers' struggles. According to Franco Berardi (a prominent autonomist in Bologna known as Bifo), during the 1973 occupations:

> Revolutionary groups such as "Lotta Continua" and Potere Operaio were a marginal presence in this occupation. Thus within the takeover itself was contained the possibility of transcending those vanguard organizations that had come near to assuming the role traditionally played by the workers' movement: a role of authoritarian leadership, of bureaucratic intransigence in the face of the passions the new types of needs expressed, above all, by the young.[22]

The spontaneous character of the continuing struggles meant that by 1974, Fiat's largest factories were considered ungovernable.[23] Foremen were regularly intimidated, and hated supervisors were often roughed up by militant groups that formed to protect workers' rights. Shop-floor conflicts in Italy led annually to 227 unofficial strikes and a loss of 134 million working hours—not including absenteeism, which ran as high as 28 percent in a given week. The workers' desire to escape the drudgery of assembly lines was accommodated by new programs, especially the fulfillment of their demand for 150 paid hours of schooling. First won in 1972, this program became a vehicle for Italian workers to connect with student radicals and feminists. In the first three years of the program, 474,000 metalworkers participated, encouraging other workers to include the 150 hours in their negotiated agreements.[24]

The movement within Italian factories was undoubtedly a key part of the autonomous movement. The workerist bias permeating many interpretations of the Italian movement, however, has precluded discussion of its nonfactory dimensions.[25] In particular, there has been a failure to note the significant contributions of students, women, and artists—constituencies not traditionally conceived as "proletarian."[26] When compared with the women's liberation movement and the Metropolitan Indians (MI, a countercultural youth group), even the most far-seeing of the factory-based parties appears today to have been mired in outmoded ideologies and actions. As I discuss in the next sections, movements of women and youth, sometimes conceptualized as autonomy to the second power (or "creative autonomy") because of their independence and cultural distance from autonomous workers' groups, showed the rigidity of even the most "revolutionary" of the autonomous factory-based groups. Indeed, the distance of the latter from the daily needs of women and youth helped stimulate the development of the women's movement and the youth movement.

AO, MI, and radical organizations of the women's movement are representative of the three main strands of what I regard as the Italian autonomous movement. More than a slogan or the name of a single organization, Autonomia became the name for movements that acted in their own right. Their language was in the first person, a departure from the language of established political parties, which preached their message as if it were best for all Italians or the entire working class. Not only were these movements outside the factories (where they would have been the recipient of the Left's theoretical tutelage), but they developed their idea of autonomy from their own needs and experiences rather than adopting them ready-made from vanguard parties.

More than anywhere else, the concept of autonomy that unified and animated the movement of 1977 was developed by feminist movements. As early as 1966, the feminist Demau group (acronym for Demystification of Authority) clearly drew a line of demarcation between themselves and the culture of consumerism. Calling for "the search for a new autonomy for women," they opposed the integration of women into modern society as simply a form of the "masculinization of women." When they wrote their manifesto, there was no activist New Left, but within a decade, their ideas had profoundly influenced thousands of people's lives."[27] As I discuss in the next section, women were critical to the eruption of 1977. They brought a new, more egalitarian style of interaction into being, and their autonomous organizations provided a model for others to emulate.

THE WOMEN'S MOVEMENT

If Hegel was right when he said that to know Italy one must understand its origins as a den of thieves, he should have specified that it was a den of male thieves. The mythological origins of Italian women in the abduction and rape of the Sabine women refer to more than unfortunate fable. Over the centuries, blatant and brutal patriarchal customs have remained intact throughout much of Italy, particularly in Sicily, Sardinia, and the rural areas. Violence in the family was often used to enforce male domination, and few legal sanctions could be invoked to prevent it—including in cases of murder if the wife had committed adultery. Even in the cities in the 1970s, women walking alone after dark could easily be in real danger; hence the need to be accompanied by a man. Although rape was a crime in Italy, it was a crime "against morality" (unlike murder and assault, which were considered crimes against "personal integrity"), and it was extremely difficult for a woman to press charges. She had to go to the police within twenty-four hours, get a doctor to examine her, and prove that she had been raped. If convicted, the maximum sentence a man could receive was five years, although at the beginning of the 1970s, he could have the crime annulled by offering to marry the woman.

In this context, it would be amazing if rigid patriarchal attitudes did not penetrate emergent movements. During the student movement and Hot Autumn, women who later formed the nucleus for the women's movement gained valuable experience. From the very beginning, many females were active in student protests, and some began to meet in women-only groups. Within the New Left, however, women were often relegated to roles as secretaries inside the movement, a situation reflected in the ironic slogan "From the angel of the hearth to the angel of the copying machine." In 1970, Rivolta Femminile (Female Revolt, or FR) groups were created in Rome and Milan, and Lotta Feminista

(Female Struggle) collectives were formed in Rome and Padua.[28] In the next years, influenced particularly by U.S. feminism and the defeat of a 1974 referendum that would have banned divorce, feminism gathered momentum. Women formed consciousness-raising groups and initiated collective projects such as bookstores, journals, and women's centers. In their discussions, they began distinguishing liberation from emancipation, the former dealing with the radical transformation of everyday life, whereas the latter was seen as having a more limited focus on public life, including the workplace.[29] Taking up significant issues of everyday life that established political parties (including the Left) ignored, this first wave of feminism soon gathered wide-ranging support. Their alternative health centers became popular sites for women to find information on mothering, questions of female health, and birth control. (Contraceptives had been illegal in Italy until 1971.)

Of special importance was the issue of abortion. Fascist laws still on the books dictated that only in cases of rape or incest would abortions be allowed, an obsolete ruling that meant that well over a million illegal abortions were performed in Italy every year, and an estimated twenty thousand women died annually as a result of improper procedures.[30] In January 1974, 263 women in Trento were charged with having had illegal abortions. Since no political party called for a lifting of all restrictions, women took to the streets to demand full abortion rights. On December 6, 1975, twenty-five thousand women marched, the first time a separatist feminist movement had made itself nationally prominent. Unable to accept the autonomy of feminism, the PCI-dominated Unione Donne Italiane (Union of Italian Women, or UDI) refused to participate in the march, but the appearance of so many marchers apparently helped change its mind. A few months later (on April 3, 1976), it joined with the feminists, and some 100,000 women took to the streets to support abortion rights. As organizers lobbied parliament, 800,000 signatures were presented in support of a new referendum to extend the rights of women to include abortion.

Significantly, in some parts of the country, women organized illegal abortion clinics, an autonomous enterprise which was supported by doctors who had been students a decade earlier.[31] In 1976, a coordinating group for self managed clinics in Rome grew out of the needs of such groups in and around the city. Their platform articulated their relation to a feminist movement, not simply by providing a service to women but also by involving them in attempts to transform society.[32] By establishing their own clinics, these women acted according to autonomous decisions—not on the basis of law but on what they considered to be right. Abortion was a mortal sin in the eyes of the church, and it was also a state crime punishable by a five year sentence. To thousands of feminists, however, morality and justice were defined by their own standards. To them, the issue was power, and their autonomous abortion clinics were a step on the road to independence from the established patriarchal system. As numerous groups formed and initiated a variety of actions, discussions elicited many disparate views on women's liberation. Although all agreed on the need to reform existing laws, the radical wing of the movement, especially groups such as FR, criticized the waste of feminists' energies on the patriarchal system:

> Asking the male for legalized abortion has a sinister aspect, since both legalization of abortion and free abortion will be used to codify the pleasure of passivity as an expression of female sex, thus reinforcing the myth of the genital act, which is concluded by male orgasm in the vagina.... Let us try and think of a civilization in which free sexuality does not appear as the apotheosis of free abortion and the contraceptives adopted by women; it will show itself as the development of a sexuality which is not specifically procreative, but polymorphous; that is free from vaginal finalization.... In this kind of civilization, it would be clear that contraceptives are only for those who want to have procreative sex, and that abortion is not a solution for free women, but rather for women colonized by a patriarchal system. [33]

Within statements like this, we see the emergence of an erotic sensibility not tied to performance nor dictated by biology: we see the freedom to act according to self-determined values.

Of course, given the reality of Italian politics, other women argued that such utopian thinking was futile and that the movement should devote itself to improving the lives of women endangered and degraded by illegal abortions. The ugly reality of male brutality intervened as well. In 1975, the rape and murder of Rosaria Lopez in Circeo and the trials of the rapists of Christina Simeoni in Verona the following year produced large demonstrations against male violence. In 1976, Claudia Caputi, a teenager who had migrated to Rome, was gang-raped by a group of pimps who apparently wanted to keep her from breaking away from their control. She later recognized some of them and, in an unusual move in Italy, called for police intervention. As her case came to trial at the beginning of April 1977, she was gang-raped again and slashed with razors over much of her body in a blatant attempt to prevent her from continuing with the case. Within a few hours, radio announcements on Radio Futura and telephone chain calls led to fifteen thousand women marching through the neighborhood where Caputi and her rapists lived.

Despite police intimidation, the women even marched past the fascist party's headquarters.

Caputi's case was not isolated. Like other women, she had answered an ad for baby-sitting and moved to Rome, where she was inadvertently caught up in a prostitution ring. The men who raped her each testified that she had been his girlfriend—and therefore that he had some sort of sexual entitlement to her. Unbelievable as it may seem, the judge accepted what they said, adding: "A woman lying in a field is like after a battle.... What is a man supposed to do when he sees her lying there?"

The first of the Reclaim the Night marches was held in Rome in November 1976. Many of the ten thousand women dressed as witches and carried broomsticks. Jettisoning their usual chants such as "Divorce Now," their slogans reflected a new mood of anger and determination: "No longer mothers, no longer daughters, we're going to destroy families."[34] Sensing the need to reform its outmoded laws, the country's governing elite finally acted. In 1978, after much debate, the PCI brokered compromise legislation in parliament that left the decision up to the doctor, not the woman. The Movimento di Liberazione della Donna (MLD, or Women's Liberation Movement, affiliated with the small Radical Party) saw this compromise as "kicking us in the teeth," and it insisted on the need to simply repeal all laws regulating abortion.[35] Feminists conducted a vigil outside parliament to protest the new law, and a few months later, parliament passed one of the most progressive laws in Europe governing abortion.

Even before they had reformed the country's law, the mobilizations for choice spread feminism throughout the country, transforming conditions of everyday life for millions of women by providing them with a new-felt sense of self. Inspired by the massive numbers at their marches, the MLD took over the abandoned district court building in Rome's Via del Governo Vecchio, setting an example for a new wave of militancy. In January 1977, eighty-one feminist collectives joined the occupation, and as the movement consolidated itself, the MLD left the Radical Party (and the UDI left the PCI) in order to be true to principles of autonomy.

As feminists were becoming more radical and convinced of the need for their autonomy, members of the Left failed to comprehend what was happening. Lotta Continua provides a powerful case in point. Although it had been gradually losing members, LC dissolved itself after a crisis caused by its toughest security marshals in November 1975. Entrusted with protecting demonstrations from fascist and police attacks, the marshals themselves attacked an all female pro-abortion march because men were not allowed to join. The fallout from the attack was immediate. Some female LC members demanded an explanation from the leadership, but many more simply left the organization. Over the next months, an internal struggle ensued. Finally at a congress in Rimini in November 1976, it was decided to dissolve the organization (although the newspaper continued to be published). Exchanges such as the following typified discussions at Rimini. Ciro, a worker for Fiat, explained:

> The idea of workers' centrality expresses the fact that only the worker, as a worker, expresses what is expressed by the proletariat. Women, as women, do not express what is expressed by the proletariat. They can be women, just women, even bourgeois women. They can be reactionary women and not express the proletarian point of view.... The same thing applies to students. The student, as a student, is not a proletarian. A student can be a proletarian, as can a woman, but simply as students and as women, they do not express the proletariat. It is very different for the worker, because the conditions of his existence in society force him to be a proletarian, because he has no alternative, while the woman is not forced to be a proletarian.

Donatella from Catanzaro responded:

> As regards the "centrality of the workers," I would like to point out that there are workers among the women as well! ... In Catanzaro, a girl of 15 was raped by someone who fancied her. The rapist was charged with obscene acts in a public place—but so was the girl! That girl comes from a village where the land has been occupied, where 800 farm workers have joined the Farm Workers Union. And yet, in a village where the class struggle has been so fierce, that girl is looked on as a prostitute. Men stop her in the street, as if they can use her as they want. I believe that these farm workers are not carrying out a real class struggle and will never make the revolution.[36]

Many feminists attempted to maintain a "double militancy"—simultaneously working in the autonomous women's movement and an organized political party or mixed radical group. Their initial orientation was revolutionary, often Marxist, although as their deliberations deepened their analysis, many became increasingly critical of LC, the PCI, and the Left's acceptance of middle-class norms and values—especially the split between public and private domains of life.[37] As activists experienced in direct-action movements, they had begun with slogans such as "There is no revolution without the liberation of women and no liberation of women without revolution." Disappointed by the failure of their organizations to address specifically the oppression of women, they developed their own theories. Even when Left organizations were not hostile to feminism, it appeared that they could not deal with its autonomy. As Valeria Boccio realized, sympathetic organizations of the Left reacted to feminism by trying to incorporate it into their own hierarchies:

> The principal preoccupation was that of adapting well-known categories to a new situation, introducing a new "object" of discourse without dispensing with existing categories, as in the case of the specificity of women's struggle within class struggle. The protagonists who spoke did not reveal themselves in what they said, made very little use of the first person, and frequent use of impersonal forms or the equally impersonal "we." The interlocutor was generally an opponent—men, the institutions, the patriarchal order. It was rare for there to be a metadiscourse. Irony and ambiguity were entirely lacking.[38]

Within the movement, Italian feminism concerned itself with issues of everyday life, prompting a "crisis of the couple." Thousands of women, particularly those active in the movement, began to be more assertive in their relationships with men and began to explore alternatives to traditional patriarchal monogamy.

The feminist movement had developed when urbanization, the loss of women's jobs in agriculture, the advent of Fordism, and the concomitant consumer society built by the economic "miracle" of the 1960s all meant that women were increasingly required to work the equivalent of an unpaid mechanized job at home within the patriarchal nuclear family. Women's marginalization during the economic expansion of the 1960s was indicated by the fact that the number of women in the workforce dropped by nearly a million.[39] As Italy modernized, the transition from rurally based extended families to urban nuclear families did not mean greater freedom for many women. In response, groups such as Lotta Feminista and Autonomia Feminista called for wages for housework to dramatize the way women were exploited in arenas outside the factory.[40]

Developing step-by-step with the campaigns to keep divorce legal and to decriminalize abortion was women's insistence that housework be paid. They refused to accept their nonpaid status at the margins of society, and this demand was a way to show how much they wished to change everyday life. In 1973, when workers' struggles were reaching their high point, Lotta Feminista's anticapitalism was evident in its reformulation of Marx's economics to include housework:

Housework is done by women. This work is never seen, precisely because it is not paid.... As for the *workers,* we acknowledge their hard struggle over pay, at the moment of production in the factory. One part of the class with a salary, the other without. This discrimination has been the basis of a stratification of power between the paid and the non-paid, the root of class weakness, which movements of the left have only increased. Just to quote some of their commonplace accusations, we are "interclassist," "corporative," we "split the class," and so on, and so on.[41]

As with the issue of abortion, theoretical differences opened within the feminist movement. Some feminists argued that wages for domestic work would continue to relegate women to the home—to split private and public spheres along gender lines. For them, women's liberation meant smashing this division, it meant freeing women from the gilded cage of home and hearth.

Besides rejecting hierarchy, feminist equality was a radical departure from traditional notions of equal rights. Within the movement, strong sentiment rejected equality with men as an ideological attempt to subject women even further. Although freeing women from the stereotypical role of mother, formal concepts of equality impose an asexual identity that reduces them to the political categories developed by patriarchal governments. Becoming equal within such systems, it was argued, meant becoming more manly. It meant, as earlier defined, emancipation, not liberation. As Carla Lonzi, a key member of FR, wrote in 1970: "Equality is what is offered as legal rights to colonized people. And what is imposed on them as culture.... Equality between the sexes is merely the mask with which women's inferiority is disguised."[42] (As I discuss in the next chapter, similar debates took place in Germany.) The energies of radical feminists went into other arenas.

Within factories, women trade unionists organized female collectives to discuss their experiences as workers and activists. Beginning in Milan and Turin, such groups spread to Genoa, Padua, and Rome.[43] Whereas women constituted 30 percent of the workforce (and PCI-affiliated trade union membership) in 1977, they accounted for only 6 percent of full-time union officials and 1 percent of the national leadership. Influenced by the feminist movement, they uncovered the reproduction of patriarchy in the unions and posited the need for social revolution:

According to the militants' analysis, the difference between men and women should not be denied but, on the contrary, recognized and built upon. Picking up the message of the new feminism, they saw women not only as victims of discrimination, but also the embodiment of an alternative approach to life and politics.... "Equality of opportunity" was dismissed as a goal; the solution, instead, was to change the rules of the game for both men and women.... The result of this analysis was that women confronted women with a request for autonomy.[44]

By 1978, coordinating committees at both local and national level's existed that orchestrated thousands of women into separate contingents at union demonstrations and raised their feminist consciousness, particularly in seminars designed for the 150 paid hours of schooling. Largely excluded from the universities, women created a network of women's cultural centers "as separate and autonomous sites of sexually connoted research in order to preserve, produce culture as/for women."[45] Within ten years of the founding of the first cultural center in Turin in 1976, about one hundred existed in Italy. In 1979, the "Virginia Woolf" (also called the Women's Union) was established in Rome. Hundreds of women attend courses there every year, and many of Italy's leading intellectuals have participated. The synergy of women's centers and feminist unionists produced a convention of six hundred women in 1983. After a year's preparatory work, the resolutions adopted called on women to strengthen their autonomous cultural and political work within unions and to build up women's centers. (At the beginning of the 1990s, there were still no women's studies departments, chairs, or degree programs at Italian universities.)

By the end of the 1970s, the momentum gathered in the campaign for abortion rights dissipated, and the first wave of militant feminism subsided. Left behind, however, were millions of women whose lives had been changed and who continued to act in accordance with their feminist ideals. Women continued to struggle against sexual violence and succeeded in altering legal and normative regulations. In 1981, a rightist counteroffensive against the new abortion law failed miserably. Only 32 percent of the voters wanted to repeal the 1978 reform won by women. And in 1982, the UDI adopted the principles of autonomy and nonhierarchical relations and formally dissolved itself as a centralized organization affiliated with the PCI, embracing instead the autonomous women's movement.[46]

Italian feminists leave a legacy rich in strategic innovations. In the short run, the feminist explosion profoundly shaped the character of the movement of 1977, particularly in their reworking of organizational questions. In 1970, Carla Lonzi wrote a pamphlet entitled "We Spit on Hegel" as a manifesto for FR that showed that they were opposed to all forms of hierarchy. "We are seeking," wrote Lonzi, "an authentic gesture of revolt and we will not betray it either to organization or to proselytizing."[47]

Feminist groups emphasized the importance and autonomy of small groups through which women could raise their consciousness rather than central committees that issued directives. The feminist movement's structure was composed of numerous small groups loosely linked together horizontally. Decisions were often made in open general assemblies, and an interactive style involving listening rather than the talking-at-people style of the male Left was the norm.[48] Polemically charged and eloquently critical of one-dimensional Marxism that subsumed the "feminine problem to the classist conception of the master-slave struggle," Lonzi's essay was also vehemently anticapitalist and posed questions of strategy in such a way that they had a significance far beyond the feminist movement. For her, the woman who rejects the family and the young man who rejects military service were partners on the path of refusing to participate in patriarchal structures. In the hippie movement, Lonzi located an antipatriarchal impulse:

> The hippie movement represents a flight in disgust from the patriarchal system, the rejection of the politics of power and of political patterns of predominantly male groups. Hippies no longer split the public and the private, and their lives are a mixture of the masculine and the feminine.[49]

Like the autonomy of feminism and its collective structure, Lonzi's analysis of culture was to become crucial to the formation of a countercultural youth movement. Influenced by feminist commitments to integrate the personal and the political, politics was no longer conducted in the name of someone else—that is, the working class or the nation. It had to flow directly from the needs of participants. Moreover, feminist conceptions of organization were not hierarchical and leader oriented. As Antonio Negri summarized:

> The feminist movement, with its practices of communalism and separatism, its critique of politics and the social articulations of power, its deep distrust of any form of "general representation" of needs and desires, its love of differences, must be seen as the clearest archetypal form of this new phase of the movement. It provided the inspiration, whether explicitly or not, for the new movements of proletarian youth in the mid-1970s. The referendum on divorce (1974) itself gave a first indication of the "autonomy of the social."[50]

In many of the most significant dimensions of the meaning of autonomy, feminist currents were the most significant single source of modern autonomous movements.

STUDENT AND YOUTH ROOTS OF AUTONOMY

Still struggling to move beyond their fascist heritage, Italian universities, like the country's political system and gender relations, were sorely in need of change in the 1960s. Nowhere in the country at the beginning of the decade was there even a faculty of sociology, a fact tied as much to Italy's regional disparities as to the legacy of Mussolini. (Interestingly, it was at the country's first sociology faculty in Trento that the student movement subsequently found its epicenter.) As in many other countries in the 1960s, the Italian student movement was militant and spirited and sparked wider social conflicts. One of the first reforms won by the movement was open admissions, but without a commensurate expansion of university faculties and facilities, open admissions meant that few students or faculty even bothered to attend overcrowded classes. In 1968, there were 400,000 students in Italy; by 1977, a million were enrolled. In 1968, the economy was growing rapidly; by 1977, the aftermath of the oil shock of 1973, combined with runaway inflation and unemployment, meant that the economy was on the brink of bankruptcy. Estimates placed the number of job seekers at a hundred thousand students and half a million technical-school graduates (accountants, draftspersons, and so forth).[51] High youth unemployment, an inadequate educational system, a lack of housing, feudalistic family relations, and an increasingly repressive government all conditioned the emergence of a countercultural youth movement that fought for a new way of life that did not depend on the existing system. The lack of faith in the system was reflected in graffiti at the university in Rome: "When even shit becomes marketable, then the poor will be born without an ass."

As far back as November 1968, the central concern of Italy's student movement was the need for autonomous self-government of student affairs. The demands of students who occupied the Catholic University were first and foremost:

- the recognition of the autonomy and self-government of the student movement.
- the withdrawal of disciplinary proceedings against activists.
- freedom of speech.
- provision of facilities and timetabling for student movement activities.
- the recognition of the power of the student general meeting over all important decisions concerning administrations, teaching, etc.[52]

The idea of democratic self-management was not confined to the Catholic University (nor to Italy in 1967–68), but it was crucial there because of the paternalistic attitudes of that school's administration.

In 1968, when the student movement erupted throughout the country, Italian universities were transformed from careerist sites to revolutionary base areas, and high school students joined in the movement. In March, only six high schools experienced protests, but by November, the majority of high schools in Milan had become involved. The action committee at one of the schools, Liceo Berchet, understood the movement's goal as:

> the control and eventual elimination of marks and failures, and therefore the abolition of selection in school; the right of everyone to education and to a guaranteed student grant; freedom to hold meetings; a general meeting in the morning; accountability of teachers to students; removal of all reactionary and authoritarian teachers; setting of the curriculum from below.[53]

High school students not only *demanded* their political autonomy, they *acted* independently, meeting and producing leaflets during school hours without bothering to ask permission from teachers or administrators. Their capacity for self-organization started in their classrooms and extended to citywide coordinating groups. Their final decision-making body (as in the universities and later in factories and offices) was the general assembly. As Robert Lumley observed:

> The movement in the schools rapidly developed its *own organizations*, which started in the class and extended to the city-wide coordinating body. As in the universities, the key unit was the general meeting. A statute of the Cattaneo Technical Institute sets out the standard organizational structure; the general meeting was the sovereign body, and from it were elected commissions and study groups with special functions. Thus, there was a press commission, an administrative commission and so on, and study groups on subjects decided by the general meeting. Each class had a monthly meeting to plan and decide on teaching questions. There was also a paper, which was directly accountable to the general meeting.[54]

Not being content to confine themselves to issues of formal control, student groups queried methods of learning and developed innovative proposals that helped change Italian higher education. In the decade after 1968, the movement's demands bore fruit. Educational reforms in 1969 permitted working-class students (not only those graduating from a "classical high school") to attend universities. Besides open admissions, also implemented was the idea of "150 hours," a national program that provided thousands of factory workers with paid study leaves. Even as these reforms helped defuse the student movement, they also prepared the groundwork for the new type of worker-student who became the constituency of the next phase of the movement and created a context that influenced feminists, unionists, and others. As one observer noticed:

> The influence of the student movement was evident in both the form and the content of unions' political action: against authority and the division of labor; for equality; for direct action and participatory democracy. The influence was not only cultural; interactions between workers and students (and later, the New Left) took place at the factory gates, in the streets, in meetings, and in various organizations of students and workers.[55]

As the student occupations of 1968 came to an end and the general assemblies that had provided them with identity and coherence dissolved, the movement was increasingly defined by Marxist-Leninist groups. Their democratic centralism and sectarian behavior effectively reversed the countercultural style, antiauthoritarianism, and democratic self-management of the popular movement. Although sometimes credited with planting the seeds of autonomous thought in Italy, these Marxist-Leninist sects also helped kill the popular impulse, substituting for vital engagement in a popular movement the idle and stale prattle of the living dead.[56] The idea of autonomy and the capacity to realize it were spontaneously present among young people who had not read any of the obscure sectarian journals. They had no need for vanguard parties proselytizing them with the revolutionary truth or the correct line. The alphabet soup of Trotskyist, Maoist, and anarchist sects replaced the movement's autonomy with a coterie of cadre whose hierarchical politics changed the *form* of the mobilization from participatory spontaneity to programmed ritual. In the name of the working class, they trivialized student issues vis-à-vis the "real" world of the factory. Although their organizations occasionally were able to recruit workers, the resulting relationship was usually one in which, paradoxically, masochistic intellectuals hid their own intelligence and education at the same time as they sadistically defined workers exclusively in terms of production. More often than not, they steered workers using their 150 study hours away from cultural courses (through which they might transcend the world of work) into courses such as economics, which they expected workers to find interesting. If anyone had bothered to ask, they would have discovered that many of the workers were often more interested in youth culture than in studying the dynamics of production, and many women gravitated toward feminism rather than traditional leftist theory. In Turin, over thirteen hundred women took part in fifty-four courses on women's health, medicine, and politics.[57] In and around Milan, over thirty-four hundred women participated in seventy-six similar courses from 1977 to 1980.[58]

In reaction to the appropriation of the student movement by sectarian ideologues, youth activists became increasingly countercultural. Caught up in traditional ideologies, the various "New Left" parties were irrelevant to the political struggles of tens of thousands of proletarian youth. By 1977, when a new generation of activists synthesized culture and politics in a liberatory movement that was a product of both working-class origins and youth culture, these parties proved impotent when compared with collectives and spontaneously generated action groups. The most spectacular such group among the dozens that made up this wing of "creative autonomy" was the Metropolitan Indians (so named because they often painted themselves and dressed like Native Americans). Having grown up under conditions very different from those of their parents (depression, war, and foreign occupation), the MI were working-class youth whose expectations of material and social freedom were dashed against the reality of the austerity measures of the 1970s. Socialized according to the logic of a consumer society as opposed to the logic of a producer society, they developed group identities that were based not on massive hierarchical organizations with authoritarian leaders but on circles of friends who formed fluid and egalitarian collectives. Like the Yippies in the United States, they developed and reacted mainly to the media. Negating the cowboy mentality of the spaghetti westerns Italian cinema churned out in the 1960s, the group adopted the costume and aura of the "other" because they themselves were marginalized outsiders.

As time went on, they developed a position on self-defense similar to that of the Black Panther Party—except that in Italy it was the P38 handgun, not the shotgun, that was embraced. Their manifesto, published on March 1, 1977, called for:

- All empty buildings to be used as sites to establish alternatives to the family.
- Free marijuana, hash, LSD, and peyote for anybody who wanted to use them.*

---

* At the Black Panther Party's revolutionary people's constitutional convention in 1970, the same drugs were called life drugs, as opposed to death drugs such as cocaine, speed, and heroin. After 1978, the wide availability of heroin and the simultaneous dearth of life drugs in Italian cities (most of all in Bologna) were blamed by many on the Mafia and the

- Destruction of zoos and the rights of all animals in the zoos to return to their native lands and habitats.
- Destruction of the altar of the Fatherland, a memorial sacred to fascists in Rome.
- Destruction of all youth jails.
- Historical and moral reevaluation of the dinosaur Archeopterix, unfairly constructed as an ogre.

Their first communiqué was released after the storming of a jazz festival in Umbria and noted that the "weapon of music cannot replace the music of weapons." The June 1975 issue of the magazine *A Traverso* reported the explanation offered by the MI:

> Music as spectacle is the attempt to reduce every collective moment to "free time." Between the organizers of the concert and the mass of proletarian youth is an objective contradiction, which is not simply a question of administration, of whom music serves. The problem for us is that the concert serves up a spectacle just like the ritualized demos and rallies serve up politics as spectacle. In both cases, we're reduced from a public to spectators.[59]

As news of the jazz action spread, groups of young people began to do the same thing in movie theaters. Entering as a group, forty, fifty, or more people would simply refuse to pay or pay something reasonable for movies. These were not "spoiled children of the rich," as film director Bertolucci had referred to the students of 1968. They were children of workers lacking money to live as full members of society. For them, *autoriduzione* was a necessity. Calling them the "illegitimate child of a secret mother and a Marxist father," the media focused on trivial things such as their painted faces or their failure to show up as promised at demonstrations but said little about their propensity to plunder record albums, liquor, or clothes from expensive stores—or to feed themselves at the best restaurants and refuse to pay. The media and police ignored the posters of hard drug dealers that the MI put up in their neighborhoods, but when they arrived at the opera in Milan with leaflets criticizing "noodles for the proletariat and caviar for the bourgeoisie," the police attacked them, arresting 40 and injuring 250.[60]

The MI carried irony and paradox to their political limits, and even in circumstances that would have been taken seriously by most people, the group avoided fetishizing their own importance. In March 1977,

---

CIA. The ill effects of this situation on the movement were obvious.

they broke into armories to steal guns to defend themselves from police attacks, but they also made off with tennis rackets and fishing poles. By putting play and joy at the center of political projects that traditionally had been conducted in a deadly serious manner, the MI did to Italian cities what Dada had done to the European art world at the beginning of the twentieth century. As Dada's anti-art scandalized the world of galleries and parodied the seriousness of artists, the MI's anti-politics broke with traditional conceptions of political conduct and revealed a wide gulf between themselves and previous generations of radicals.

Artists also contributed to the development of the concept of autonomy. Playwright Dario Fo, for example, asserted the autonomy of culture by bringing his plays directly to unconventional sites such as bowling alleys, plazas, and factories. After his first year, Fo estimated that he performed in front of 200,000 people, 70 percent of whom had never before attended a play. Fo reminded his audiences that for centuries popular culture had been autonomous from the rulers of society. Modern mass culture, increasingly centralized and regulated by giant corporations, restrained the autonomy of popular culture, thereby necessitating the political development of a counterculture.

At the end of 1975, legislative decisions had voided the government's monopoly of the airwaves. Within a year, there were eight hundred "free radio" stations and one hundred new television channels (about 20 percent of which were left wing, the rest being special-interest groups, minority groups, and, in the case of radio, non-commercial twenty-four-hour rock 'n roll).[61] None of these were run by the PCI, since the Communists believed that their loyalty to the government would gain them access to the mammoth state-controlled broadcasting system. The women's movement established its own network of radio and television stations in the 1970s, a network that grew out of a proliferation of feminist writing and the setting up of a daily feminist newspaper.[62] Radio Futura was set up in Rome with funds from two of the small parties to the left of LC, and in Bologna, Radio Alice reflected that city's vibrant countercultural radical scene. In addition, about one hundred leftist magazines were regularly published.

By the mid-1970s, Left groups such as LC and Manifesto had begun to lose membership to the PCI, whose electoral successes brought it a share of power. In the local elections of June 1975, the PCI won stunning victories with over ten million votes (almost exactly one-third of those cast), enough to form governments led by Communists and socialists in vast areas of Italy: in the States of Piedmont, Liguria, Tuscany, Emilia-Romagna, and Umbria, as well cities such as Naples, Rome, Milan, Turin, Genoa, Bologna, and Florence. Left coalitions governed more than twenty-seven hundred cities, accounting for more than half the country's population.[63] At the same time, Italian cities were alive with housing occupations by poor families, spontaneous community struggles, and "Mao-Dada" happenings in which small groups of friends disrupted official ceremonies and demonstrations. A wave of mini-Woodstock music festivals swept the country. In Milan's Lambro Park, eighteen thousand working-class youth danced a giant sun dance, "blowing everyone's minds," and then were compelled to fight the police for several hours.

In the 1976 national elections, no single party won a majority, and if the Communist Party had not subsequently endorsed a "historic compromise" with the conservative Christian Democrats, no one would have been able to form a government. With over 34 percent of the popular vote and the country's major trade unions firmly under its control, the PCI agreed to abstain from defeating Christian Democratic initiatives.[64] When the latter embarked on a program of cutbacks designed to make industry more profitable, it fell to the PCI to discipline the working class and deliver social peace to the national effort. Participating as a junior partner in the Christian Democrats' austerity program meant justifying wage cuts, reduced cost-of-living subsidies, cancellation of public holidays, rising prices, and closed factories; it meant explaining why university fees were raised and why poor families living illegally in vacant houses were evicted when a severe housing shortage existed. Last but not least, it meant controlling the vibrant youth scene. In places such as Bologna, the PCI government paid more attention to the complaints of wealthy merchants about hippies than to the social needs of working-class youth. In February 1976, the Communist city government of Bologna sent bulldozers to demolish the building in which one of the city's autonomous youth groups, the "Red Berets," met and partied. Given these dynamics, is it any wonder that the popular movements to challenge the government's austerity programs would be autonomous of existing political parties?

In May 1975, the Christian Democrats and their allies had passed an act (the *Legge Reale*) giving Italy's police legal authority to fire their weapons at unarmed demonstrators whenever they felt that "public order" was threatened. Going beyond laws remaining on the books since the days of Mussolini, the act criminalized possession of handkerchiefs, ski masks, and helmets at demonstrations. Licensed to shoot, the police went on a rampage between May 1975 and December 1976. A 1979 study put the number of innocent people killed by the "forces of order" since the *Legge Reale* was adopted at 53.[65] Another estimate put the number of victims of the new law at 150.[66]

Now that the Communists were part of the forces of order, the movement would have only enemies among the major parties. In 1968, 1969, and 1973, while trade union leaders and PCI members had been heckled and abused, the movements and their spontaneously formed organizations had tolerated an uneasy dialogue with the Communists and other organizations of the Left. The events of 1977, however, revealed a much more radical mood among activists, many of whom were working-class youth who would have been expected to be sympathetic to Communists.

1977: A YEAR OF CRISIS

The escalating spiral of repression and resistance in 1977 marks a turning point in the history of Autonomia. In Rome and Bologna, major confrontations were ended by the use of overwhelming police force. The provocative cycle of violence and counterviolence began on February 1, 1977, when about one hundred armed fascists attacked the university in Rome, shooting unarmed students protesting the government's educational reform bill. The next day, when thousands of youth protested in front of the office of the neo-fascist Italian Social Movement, the police opened fire with submachine guns, wounding four people (as well as a policeman caught in the crossfire). In response to these attacks, thousands of people occupied the university, and their ranks swelled to an estimated thirty thousand by February 9. To guard against any new fascist invasion, students patrolled the campus and created checkpoints at all gates. All over Italy—Palermo, Bari, Milan, Turin, Venice, Bologna, Florence, Pisa, Cagliari, and Naples—students occupied university buildings in solidarity with Rome. The striking students joined the ranks of hundreds of women who had occupied the old district court in the Via del Governo Vecchio since October 1976. Within the occupied universities, feminists, hippies, and autonomists based in factories came into intense discussions, and a new set of issues vital to the movement became defined.

At this point, the most famous scene from the movement of 1977 transpired. On February 17, Luciano Lama, chairman of the Communist-controlled trade unions, went to the University of Rome to convince students to end their occupation. To guard against possible disruption of his talk, he entered the campus on a flatbed truck with his own sound system and hundreds of handpicked security men. He also brought about two thousand union members who were told that they were needed at the university "to liberate it from fascists." Communists regularly referred to students as "petit bourgeois" (a derogatory term meaning unreliable and money loving), but Rome's university was the world's largest (over 300,000 students), and students were largely children of the proletariat. To call them fascists was certain provocation.

The night before Lama was to come, the general assembly of those occupying the university finally agreed to let him enter but to try to defeat him politically, and they adjourned to watch a film about the 1968 student movement. The next morning, between five and ten thousand people gathered to hear Lama speak. The Metropolitan Indians, armed with rubber tomahawks, streamers, and water balloons, surrounded his platform, and began to chant "Lamas belong in Tibet!" "More churches, fewer houses!" and "We want to work harder and get paid less!" Referring to the military coup in Chile, they shouted "In Chile, tanks; in Italy, the Communists!"

Soon after Lama began his talk, cries of "Idiot, Idiot" arose when he referred to students as "parasites at the expense of productive labor."[67] As shoving began near the stage, a brawl ensued between the security forces and the autonomists, many of whom quickly donned masks and unceremoniously threw Lama and his entourage out of the university. During the full-scale battle between Communists and autonomists, Lama was spat on, and the platform where he had been speaking was destroyed. In the fighting, at least fifty people were seriously injured. After Lama and his entourage were expelled, the rector called in the police. Hundreds of Communists stood and cheered the police on as they went through the gates. To the students, the Communists shouted "Fascists, Blackshirts, your place is in the cemetery." A Communist sociology lecturer was heard to remark: "I think the police were quite right to clear the university. After all, there weren't any real students in there, only hippies, queers and people from the slum districts." In describing what it dubbed a "little Prague," Lotta Continua put it this way:

> You could imagine you're hearing the voice of the KGB thundering against the dissent movement in the USSR. Only this time what they are attacking is a mass movement, not just of students, but of thousands and thousands of young people who are jobless. This is a movement that is reacting with organization and struggle against a regime that is devastating our social life and forcing poverty and unemployment upon us.[68]

Two thousand police roamed the university, using their tear gas and clubs against anyone in sight. They injured dozens of people, many of whom were uninvolved in the movement. Later that day, thousands of people gathered to discuss the events and plan their next actions. Two days later, more than fifty thousand people marched through Rome against the police, the unions, and the PCI. They shouted slogans such as "They've kicked us out of the university, now let's take over the city." Minister of Interior Cossiga went on television to announce new repressive measures against the movement, and the Metropolitan Indians quickly responded to his warlike language. Here is their entire text:

Dear Big Chief Paleface Minister,
Hail Paleface of Teutonic design. How happy we were to see you on the Magic Box. Your forked tongue hissed wondrously; and your metallic voice spat Poison on the human tribe. You said:

"We are telling these gentlemen that we will not allow the University to become a hide-out for Metropolitan Indians, freaks and hippies. We are determined to use what *they* call the forms of repression, and what *I* call the democratic forms of law and order."

We continued to stare in silence at the Magic Box. Our silence contained all the Hatred that the human tribe can muster against your Vile Brood, all the Hatred that hundreds of thousands of young people from the ghettos of the inhuman Metropolis will howl against a Monstrous Society that tells us to swallow our suffering.

But "swallow your suffering" are words that only exist in *your* language, in *your* putrid social relations, in *your* eyes that are lifeless and without humanity.

No, Minister Cossiga, *we will never "swallow"!*
Because our will to live is stronger than your thirst for death. Because, in the bright colors of our warpaint we wear the red of the blood of hundreds of comrades, of young people murdered in the streets by your "democratic" law and order, murdered by heroin in the desperation of the ghettos, and murdered at police roadblocks Just because they didn't have a license for a moped!

You have built the Reservation for us, and now you want to chase us back into it, into the ghettos of marginalization and despair. No more is this possible! Because it is precisely out of the ghettos that our Rebellion has exploded. Today Human Beings have found themselves again, have found their strength, their joy of collective living, their anger, and their thirst for communism.

Your police-goons, dressed up like Martians, have chased us out of the University. They thought they could smash our dream, our desire to transform ourselves and transform the world. But you have not understood. Your Tin Brains can only think up hunger, repression, violence, special laws and death. You have not understood that you will Never Again be able to destroy us. Because our anger and our imagination howl more loudly than your thirst for vengeance!

Minister Cossiga, we accept your Declaration of War, so that the battle may be turned into a War for the total defeat of your Vile Brood.

As long as the grass grows on the Earth, as long as the Sun warms
our bodies, as long as the Water bathes us and the Wind blows through
the hair, *We will never again bury the Tomahawk of War!*

The Metropolitan Indians of North Rome

For Autonomia, Lama's expulsion marked a crucial turning point. As
the news about the expulsion of Lama and the fighting in Rome spread,
students went on strike throughout the country. As both the government and the movement gathered their forces and planned the next steps,
contradictions appeared within the autonomous movement, particularly
between what have been called its "creative" and its "organized" wings.
For example, during the occupation of the university in Rome, women
had to close their meetings to men after some "comrades" attacked wom-
en. At a national conference called by striking students on February 26
and 27, over five thousand people showed up, including more traditional
Left groups such as LC. At one point, feminists and the Metropolitan
Indians walked out of the meeting to discuss what to do in their own
circles. Only after prolonged discussions did they agree to come back to
the meeting, where they insisted on confronting the traditional groups
that were trying to assert their leadership over a movement that had little
to do with traditional politics. After much discussion, all those present
united in a call for a national demonstration on March 12.

The intense drama surrounding March 12 was overshadowed by events
the previous day in Bologna, however. An activist and former member
of LC, Francesco Lorusso, was shot in the back and killed by the police
after a scuffle broke out between a fanatic Catholic youth group and
other students at the University of Bologna. Bologna is in the center of
Italy's most progressive region, and with Radio Alice quickly notifying
its listeners, the murder produced an immediate reaction. That same
night, crowds set two police stations on fire, wrecked the Catholic sect's
bookstore, and occupied the main train station.

The next morning, although many people boarded buses to head for
the national demonstration in Rome, thousands more marched through
Bologna. In the afternoon, while Francesco's brothers and friends were
holding a press conference, news reached them that the police were attacking the university. Thousands of people spontaneously counterattacked,
liberating the city center and setting up barricades and beating back the
police. In the enthusiasm of the moment, one participant wrote:

> The police have gone away. Tiredness. Anger. Joy. The whiff of rebellion
> after years of cringing submission. The faces of comrades are smiling;
> their eyes are all red from the tear gas. Bottles of good wine taken from

the bars are passed around. Champagne, joints, Molotovs.... A piano is playing Chopin. It's in the middle of the street. Somebody brought it out of a bar. Right behind a barricade.... Nobody's giving orders today. Tomorrow? Tomorrow they'll come with tanks. They'll crush us again. But today, for a few hours, this land is free. Chopin. Wine. Anger and Joy.[69]

With the city liberated from the police, the university became a free space where general discussions about strategy and goals took place. While the movement formulated its options, the police raided Radio Alice and shut it down. At dawn the next day, three thousand *carabinieri* and police accompanied by armored cars moved into the university, which they found deserted. Dramatically illustrating once again which side it supported, *L'Unitá*, the PCI's daily newspaper, smugly reported: "As regards the role played by Radio Alice as an organ of subversion, it is worth saying that the repressive measures inflicted on it have come rather late in the day."

Like the expulsion of Lama, the murder of Lorusso was an event of national significance. Clashes broke out again in Rome, Turin, Padova, Lecce, and Messina, and a veritable state of siege was imposed on "Red" Bologna by its Communist authorities. Video cameras were installed on the main streets so the police could keep constant watch; activists were whisked off the street by police if recognized as leaders, and groups were forbidden to congregate. Some activists were charged with "conspiracy against the democratic state" and accused of being paid agents of foreign governments (both Moscow and Washington). Autonomists who attempted to leaflet factories were prevented from doing so by PCI goon squads. Perhaps the greatest affront to the movement, however, was the PCI insinuation that Francesco had been shot by provocateurs inside the Left—an insinuation made despite many eyewitnesses who testified that a uniformed policeman had shot him in the back.

The PCI did its best to repress the new movement, pressuring doctors not to treat those wounded (many of whom would not go to hospitals for fear of arrest) and lawyers not to defend the 216 people arrested on serious charges. The feminist center, a former café that had long stood vacant before women squatted it, was cleared out and boarded up. The Communist mayor of Bologna mobilized 200,000 to march against violence (in a city whose population was only 600,000). At the same time, about ten thousand autonomists demonstrated; notably, many were young people who had been brought into the movement. Although some of the PCI's demonstrators exited to go with the younger militants, events in Bologna portrayed graphically the generation gap that was tearing Italy apart.[70]

Interior Minister Cossiga refused to grant a permit for the autonomists' March 12 demonstration in Rome, and he called on the government to use the army against the marchers—something that had not happened since 1898, when cannons were used against workers in Milan. The police raided bookstores, newspapers, and magazines in Rome, Milan, Bologna, Verona, and Mestre, shutting them down, confiscating materials that were being printed, and arresting many people. Despite the government's intimidation tactics, more than 100,000 people turned out on March 12, one indication that the movement, far from being isolated (as the Communists and the government insisted), was growing stronger. In other cities—including Bologna, Milan, and Iglesias—there were also large demonstrations. Delegations of marchers arrived in Rome from as far away as Sicily, and there were contingents of hospital workers, construction workers, white-collar workers, steelworkers from Naples, high school students, and women (who were forced to bear the brunt of the subsequent police attacks). Worried that the marchers would reach their national headquarters, the Christian Democrats ordered the police to attack while many people were still crowded together waiting to begin marching. In Piazza Venezia, the fighting was particularly heavy. Clouds of tear gas reduced visibility to zero, and firearms were used to scatter the demonstrators. Once the marchers regrouped, the police opened fire again.

After the violence of the police, the PCI was used to justify it. On March 23, the PCI mobilized 100,000 people in Piazza San Giovanni. On the same day, twenty-five thousand autonomists staged a demonstration that took the wind out of the PCI's sails. Early in the day, high schools emptied and bank workers, public employees, and even many PCI members assembled for Autonomia's march. Some people linked arms, others danced in the streets, and the Metropolitan Indians marched in arrow formation. Despite government threats designed to intimidate the autonomous marchers, this was the moment in which Autonomia upstaged the new party of order. Overwhelmed by the huge throng that approached, the ranks of PCI marshals (who had been instructed to keep the "700 savage autonomists" away from their rally) had to let them through.

In this poignant moment, when these two disparate, political forces stood face-to-face, the autonomists used irony and paradox as their weapons. Entering the piazza at the same moment as Luciano Lama began speaking, dozens of autonomists kneeled on the ground before the podium, sarcastically imploring "Lama, forgive us!" while others waved cardboard replicas of 38-caliber pistols in his direction. At one point, they chanted "Liberate your tongues! Use them for making love, not licking the boss's ass!" Rhythmically repeating what was said from the podium, they made Lama's message appear ridiculous. Even normally conservative engineering students began to chant slogans against the PCI's support of the government, and the PCI crowd begged for unity with chants such as "workers, students, unemployed—organized together, we shall win!" Many people joined the autonomous march as it filed past the podium. When they reached their final destination for the day in the Piazza Santa Croce, the autonomists entertained themselves with guerrilla theater and spontaneous raps from various unannounced participants, not prolonged monologues from recognized leaders.

For a few months, it appeared that ever-larger sections of the working class might break loose from the Communists' control. On April 6, over three thousand workers representing 450 factory councils gathered in Milan to discuss how to oppose both the government's and the unions' collusion in their wage reductions. Adopting the language of the Metropolitan Indians, they referred to the unions as "palefaces who speak with forked tongues." Women articulated the need to confront discrimination against them inside the unions and argued passionately for cultural revolution—to fight against the family as the "kernel of unpaid labor and oppression of women."[71] To some, a revolutionary moment had arrived. As disenchanted workers mobilized, they joined with students already in the middle of two months of strikes at major universities. On April 21, a general assembly of students at the University of Rome demanded the expulsion of the police, who continued to patrol the campus since the Lama incident. Several faculties were occupied in support of this demand. The rector again called for the police to clear out the student protesters, and in the ensuing battle, the police used armored cars and tear gas while students overturned buses to build barricades, and hurled Molotovs. As injuries mounted on both sides, the police began to use their pistols. This time, the students shot back, killing a policeman.

That night, heated discussions took place at the mass meeting in the Architecture Faculty. The free-flowing discussion contained a diverse range of reactions to the shooting. Some advocated adopting further violence in self- defense, but others warned of the consequences of such a decision. More than a few called for full-fledged guerrilla warfare as the next step. Lotta Continua summed up its position:

> The movement is being driven towards its self-destruction today by the theorization of "armed struggle now," by the search for "higher levels of struggle." ... It is possible to assert the movement's right to

mass self-defense only on condition that the movement has the right to defeat positions inside which are adventurist and suicidal. Thousands of young people have been in the forefront of the struggles of the last few months, and have reaped some very rich experiences. The issue now is to let these experiences bear fruit. We must...prevent the suffocation of the mass initiative of the students which, over the last few days, has seen a fresh upsurge in towns all over Italy.[72]

This same tactical division (guerrilla warfare versus popular movement) had already spelled the end of the New Left in the United States. Few people in Italy were aware of that history, nor would it have mattered much even if they had been, since the situation was not controlled by anyone. The movement was trapped in a deadly spiral of confrontation with the government. Each time a demonstrator was killed, some activists thought that a policeman should also die. That is precisely what happened again three weeks later on May 12 and 13, the third anniversary of the successful referendum defeating the attempt to outlaw divorce. Despite Minister Cossiga's ban on all demonstrations in Rome until May 31, civil rights and feminist activists decided to celebrate peacefully the anniversary of their victory. Without any provocation, heavily armed police went on a rampage in the city center. Journalists and members of parliament, elderly women and passersby, were all savagely attacked with truncheons and leather gloves. Later, the police opened fire on unarmed demonstrators, killing nineteen-year-old feminist Giorgiana Masi and wounding another woman. The next day, demonstrations took place throughout Italy. In Milan, twenty people broke away from the march and fired on a squad of police, killing one.

It mattered little that the bulk of those involved in the movement disapproved of the shooting. Indeed, in Milan right afterward, two AO members were beaten up by other demonstrators, and even the AO publicly distanced itself from the use of firearms. Nonetheless, the government used this killing as a pretext to enforce even more ruthlessly its ban on demonstrations. The curtailment of public space for protests drove many activists underground (into a guerrilla struggle), thereby intensifying the government's use of force: police provocations aimed at depoliticizing the movement, at ending the involvement of hundreds of thousands of people, began to succeed. Dynamics internal to the movement, particularly the patriarchal legacy inherited from the society, wreaked havoc on the movement's ability to act an its own initiatives.

Some activists welcomed the intensification of the struggle with the government, believing that they—not the forces of order—would win a civil war. In retrospect, their shortsightedness is evident, although at that time, no one could have been sure of such a judgment. The police killing Giorgiana Masi sent a clear message that peaceful demonstrations would no longer be allowed. When the movement responded in kind to the police violence, the prospect of a continually expanding popular mobilization was dissipated. Caught in a vise between the police and gun-toting radicals, the movement was denied public space vital to its existence. Squeezed between the violence of the police and the small-group actions of armed militants, the popular movement came to an abrupt end, and the drama of guerrilla warfare (as I discuss in a moment) began in earnest. What is most problematic is how a movement hoping to create a more democratic society can defend itself from armed attacks while simultaneously strengthening popular participation. One activist expressed this dilemma:

> When the act is secret, calculated, it still needs to be thought "elsewhere," somewhere other with regard to the consciousness of the person who lives, struggles, makes demands, achieves, changes and is changed, who doesn't make weighing up in advance the life of others, be it an enemy or even an army of enemies, the be-all and end-all of his militancy. To fight with a gun is like taking it upon oneself to think for others, not only for the moment of rupture, of revolt, but holding hostage an ideal of life which lay behind the rupture, bringing it about.[73]

Two developments merit special attention here. First, the tragedy of heroin sapped the life forces of the counterculture. At that time, many people blamed the Mafia and the CIA for its abundance on the streets of most cities, but simply blaming the suppliers cannot explain why so many activists substituted the thrill of death drugs for the erotic bonding of a liberatory movement. Simultaneously, government repression became the major fact of Italian politics. Historically, fascism has short-circuited liberatory impulses, as with Hitler's destruction of Germany's political movements and cultural avant-garde. From the strategy of tension beginning in 1969 to the five attempted fascist coups after World War II, Italian fascists had conducted an elaborate strategy aimed at curtailing civil liberties and forcing the government to the right. The government's ban on demonstrations was a small victory for the fascist strategy compared with subsequent ones.

REPRESSION AND RESISTANCE

In the final phase of Italian Autonomia, government repression became the main focus of the movement's energies, and small groups of guerrillas took center stage in the country's dramatic political upheaval. On September 22, 23, and 24, 1977, at least 40,000 people (some estimates were 100,000) responded to a call from the Metropolitan Indians to attend an antirepression gathering in Bologna—the center of creative autonomy. As the streets became jammed with people, parks, squares, and any public spaces were made into campsites. Hundreds of small groups involving thousands of people discussed heatedly what the next steps of the movement should be while others made music, performed theater, and danced in the streets. In Bologna's soccer stadium, thousands of people (mainly those affiliated with organized groups) debated the question of armed struggle. Some used prearranged cards from their seats to create mammoth images of P-38s and slogans advocating armed struggle. One after another, sectarian groups paraded their members and slogans, finally deciding to exclude various groups for their lack of revolutionary resolve or incorrect beliefs. One participant related:

> This part of the Movement, about 8000 people, was divided and clashed among themselves, smashing chairs over one another's heads and failing to arrive at any solution (generally, a political solution is represented by written motion approved by a majority). Another part of the Movement, the majority, entered the city, sleeping anywhere in the streets, under porticoes, creating an enormous curtain, exploiting a few upright sculptures in a small square, conveying furniture and chairs outdoors, conducting discussions and seminars in thousands of small groups, passing out the little legalities that had been produced for the occasion (fake train tickets, drugs, keys to open telephone coin boxes and traffic lights, etc.).[74]

Perhaps the outcome of the conference would have mattered more if there had been no centralized Left parties intent on seizing the center of political attention through spectacular actions. The powerful eruption of 1977 convinced incipient guerrillas that the time for armed insurrection had arrived. Since the movement was not permitted to assemble in the streets, armed actions provided an outlet for those who were not content to exist as political spectators. Clandestine actions reinforced their group identity, and there was no shortage of supportive communes, collectives, circles of friends and acquaintances.

So many actions were claimed by groups in this period that it is possible to speak of "armed autonomy" in terms similar to "workers' autonomy" and "creative autonomy" as describing a tendency composed of the independent choice of action made by thousands of people. Of the more than five thousand armed actions attributed to left-wing groups from 1970 to 1982, over five hundred different signatures were used to claim credit for them, a number that reflected both the decentralization of decision-making and the growing role played by armed small-group actions. Although there were many groups that followed this strategic choice, the majority of actions were attributed to two, the Red Brigades (RB) and Prima Linea (PL, or Front Line).[93] Between 1974 and 1981, bank robberies attributed to those two organizations alone grossed over $3 million, and kidnap victims paid them an additional $4 million.

The RB emerged from currents of dogmatic Maoism present in 1968 at Italian universities. Their earliest action was in 1970, when they abducted two managers at Fiat. Organized hierarchically along Marx-ist-Leninist-Stalinist lines, the RB consisted of base groups of three to five individuals in a factory, school, or neighborhood. In the larger cit-ies, several base groups capable of acting together formed columns. The central committee directed these columns, and a group of ten to fifteen met yearly to set the organization's strategic direction. The man destined to become its overall commander and most important media personality, Renato Curcio, was a veteran of the student struggles in Trento, where he married a brilliant local student, Mara Cagol. Although there is evidence that very few of the RB's hundreds (some said thousands) of members actually went underground and abandoned their identities, Curcio and Cagol were compelled to do so, particularly after she led a group that broke Curcio out of jail in 1975. Cagol was killed by *carbonieri* later that same year, an action that some believed was deliberate murder, since she had been captured alive and, like Che Guevara, was executed after falling into enemy hands. Unlike RB, PL's internal structure and actions were decentralized and spontaneously organized. Whereas the RB believed that the heart of the state could be struck by a dedicated military cadre, PL thought that a longer-range civil war could be won only if the armed struggle spread to involve hundreds of thousands of people. PL publicly attacked feminists, labeling separatism a "petit bourgeois" tendency. It insisted that "genuine" revolutionaries become part of the organizations of the armed struggle. A third guerrilla group, Armed Proletarian Nu-clei, formed in 1974 in Naples. Its membership and actions reflected the mobilization of Italy's lumpen proletariat.[76] Not surprisingly, the writings of George Jackson and the Black Panther Party were a major influence on its members. When one of them was killed, he was buried with a page from Jackson's book, *Blood in My Eye*, in his hands.

The many individuals and groups constituting "armed autonomy" acted independently of one another. There was no central organiza-tion, no central committee in control. All that changed on March 16, 1978, when the RB abducted one of the country's leading politicians, Christian Democratic President Aldo Moro, after ambushing and killing his bodyguards. For fifty-five days, the media made Moro into Italy's most famous man, and the RB became the central concern within the established political system. Their demand was straightforward: release members of their organization who were in prison. After nearly two months of negotiations, it became obvious that the government would not make any concessions, and the group carried out its threat to kill their captive. All that was left was to have a state funeral attended by ten thousand people without Moro's corpse present, a clear sign—a necro-simulacrum—of Italy's transition to postmodern politics.

The armed guerrilla struggle had begun as an outlet for continuing resistance to police violence and fascist attacks, but it ended up serving to highlight the central importance of the political system. More than any other single event, Moro's kidnapping and murder constricted the possibilities of autonomous political engagement. By kidnapping Moro, the RB reproduced the values of the system, helped turn thousands of former activists into spectators, and made the popular movement seem unimportant. After Moro's execution, the country witnessed the capture of one after another of the RB's main columns. When new laws were passed allowing those who had committed criminal actions to be granted immunity if they would testify against others, former comrades turned against one another, and the organization completely collapsed.

As government repression against the popular movement continued to mount, fascists broke into the studios of Radio Donna, an independent women's radio station in Rome, and shot and wounded four of the women who worked there. Denying the movement opportunities to exist publicly, the government enacted a variety of laws enabling the forces of order to seize control of the situation. The period of time a person suspected of "subversion against the state" could be held prisoner before a trial was lengthened to an incredible twelve years. On April 7, 1979, the government imposed an iron fist. Over three hundred activists were arrested on such charges, including many workers and students, as well as several prominent intellectuals (among them Professor Antonio Negri, who was accused of the ridiculous charge of being the secret leader of the RB). These arrests were the beginning of a wave of repression that sapped the remaining strength of the movement. All that was left was to demand justice for the prisoners. In July, a prominent group of French intellectuals, including Jean-Paul Sartre, wrote a public letter of protest demanding the immediate release of these political prisoners:

> Italy has been shaken by a revolt—a revolt of young proletarians, the unemployed, students, and those who have been forgotten in the politicking of the Historic Compromise. Faced with a policy of austerity

and sacrifices, they have replied by occupying the universities, by mass demonstrations, by casual labor, by wildcat strikes, sabotage, and absenteeism in the factories. They have used all the savage irony and creativity of those who, ignored by the powers that be, have nothing more to lose.... When they are accused of plotting and conspiring, and of being financed by the CIA and KGB, those whom the Historic Compromise has excluded reply: "Our plot is our intelligence; your plot is to use our rebellion to step up your terror campaign."

In 1980, new antiterrorist measures were implemented, and at least three thousand activists were incarcerated in maximum-security prisons, incommunicado without normal legal rights. Many complained of mistreatment and torture.[77] The trials faced by members of the autonomous movement were not trials in any normal sense of the word. It was unclear in many cases what charges individuals faced, and the prosecution was allowed wide leeway in fishing for violations of the law. At the same time, defendants were required to answer all questions. Many gave eloquent public testimony, even swaying the justices before whom they were brought.

Despite the differences between guerrilla groups and popular movements, both the government and the Communists equated the RB and Autonomia, considering them to be neo-fascists because they did not respect the norms of democratic dialogue nor operate within the forms of parliamentary democracy. Apparently, the PCI could not understand a distinction made by one of the chief justices of the Italian court system. In the words of this magistrate: "The *Autonomia* groups refute in principle every rigid, verticalizing, hierarchical structure; are not of a coordination among diverse, associated organs but of a spontaneity which has very little in common with the character of professional crimes" (such as the RB). He went on to distinguish RB attacks—aimed at the "heart of the state"—from Autonomia's attempts to create its own independent life.

In contrast to the RB attempts to attack the government directly and diminish its sovereignty, Autonomia aimed to choke off the legitimacy of the government among the citizenry, to undermine its popular support while building new sources of dual power. The RB went for the jugular, whereas Autonomia sought to clog up the capillaries by creating nonhierarchical organizational forms as part of a political culture that had little to do with parliamentary policy and elected representatives. The RB prematurely posed the question of power, attempting to take over the central government themselves, not to dissolve its powers and make room for autonomously constituted forms of self-government. In contrast to a system that produces politics as spectacle, in which citizens are little more than powerless spectators, autonomous movements sought self-govern-ance. The political intuition of activists within Autonomia understood that any attempt to change the government from within was corrupting, since it involved traditional politics. That was one motivation to remain autonomous—to have nothing to do with established politics.

In the 1960s, the movement's demand for autonomy of the universi-ties had reached a dead end in a practical realization of its social limits: a free university is not possible in an unfree society. Unlike the repression suffered by the youth movement, feminists saw abortion conditionally legalized and the major parties accommodate women's voices. A similar fate befell the workers' movement of 1969–73. It was used by the PCI to improve union contracts and to give Communists greater political power. If there had been a workers' revolt in 1977 on the scale of the ones in 1969 or 1973, a revolutionary situation might have resulted, although it is doubtful that insurgent forces could have won an armed contest for power.

The Italian movement was defeated by government repression, but its inability to maintain momentum and continuity can also be traced to internal dynamics, particularly the widespread reliance on traditional analysis used to understand society and to formulate movement strategy. Despite its break with traditional political parties, Autonomia failed to understand itself in nontraditional ways. Instead, activists relied on previously formulated notions and ideas (see Chapter 6 for a more spe-cific analysis). Publicly available for the first time in the 1960s, Antonio Gramsci's theories—penned when Mussolini was in power—seemed new to activists in 1977. Despite thousands of factory workers and office workers uniting against the unions, obsolete politics, workerism, and the failure to connect with the youth culture and feminism spelled the end of any hope for the continuation of the autonomy. The death of the factory movement was obvious in the disastrous failure of the Fiat strike in 1980, during which assembly-line workers and office workers joined to march against the unions.[78]

Although remnants of the RB continued to act, kidnapping NATO General James Dozier in December 1981, their actions were of little con-sequence. Dozier was rescued in January 1982, and even though renamed elements of the RB continued to act for the next six years, they were marginalized players in a political game of little interest to most Italians. The feminist movement continued long after the campaigns of violence and counterviolence came to an end. Women led popular movements against NATO's stationing new nuclear weapons in Sicily and continued to build their autonomous cultural centers and counterinstitutions.

Even if the RB had never existed and government repression had not been so intense, could Autonomia have won over a majority of the country? Or was this movement doomed to be a transient expression of a militant minority, like the factory councils of the 1920s or the American Wobblies? Despite political crises and economic dislocations, the affluence of consumer society was an option for far too many Italians for them to follow the lead of autonomous movements. Only when faced with no acceptable alternative will most people choose the path of revolution. Although it failed to provoke the revolution it advocated, Autonomia's impact helped reform Italian universities and workplaces. The workweek was shortened, housing modernized, universities brought into the modern era, and women's status improved. Emergent popular aspirations expressed in social movements prefigure the future, and the impact of movements is often directly proportional to their militancy. Although the Italian movement was dispersed, its lessons and legacy were powerful influences further north, as I discuss in the next chapter. Both the reality and the myth of Autonomia helped inspire and provide direction to the next generations of activists.

SOURCES OF AUTONOMOUS POLITICS IN GERMANY

Largely forgotten in both the popular media and scholarly accounts of the end of the Cold War is the peace movement. Millions of people in Europe and the United States protested the irrationality of nuclear weapons, particularly the instability introduced with medium-range missiles (Pershings and SS-20s), which made it possible for Europe to be devastated in a nuclear war but the United States and the USSR spared direct attack.[1] In the fall of 1981, hundreds of thousands of people participated in marches with distinctly anti-American overtones in Paris, London, Brussels, Bonn, and Rome.[2] The upsurge in Europe erupted very suddenly and gained momentum quickly. Caught by surprise, U.S. policy makers had few clues where this movement came from. If its origins were in the liberal policies of the governing Social Democrats, as European conservatives maintained, it would not have contained such a strong dosage of skepticism toward all political parties.

Politicians and intellectuals contributed, but peace initiatives in Europe were linked to a militant extraparliamentary youth movement. Through their attacks on nuclear power and weapons and their defense of squatted houses, a new generation of radicals helped delegitimate the authority of national governments and NATO at a time when the postwar division of Europe into hostile zones of East and West had yet to lose its rationale in the minds of many Europeans. Within West Germany, the youth movement, at times violent and tempestuous, became a driving force that made peaceful marching an acceptable course for many people who otherwise might not have risked getting involved. As a movement, these activists cared little about established forms of politics, but their actions caused the mayor of Hamburg to resign and precipitated the downfall of the national Social Democratic government in Bonn and the city government in West Berlin. At the end of 1979, widespread disenchantment with the policies of the two major parties—both the Christian Democratic Union (CDU) and the Social Democratic Party (SPD) supported nuclear power and NATO missiles at that time—gave rise to the ecologist and antimilitarist Green Party, which won a number of local and national elections soon after its founding. The left wing of the governing SPD was long courted by the Greens, and the growing influence of ecology together with direct confrontations of the nuclear power industry and the atomic military worked together—despite the absence of any formal ties or professed allegiances between the militants and the ecologist politicians—to help spark heated debates in the highest circles of government. In 1982, Chancellor Helmut Schmidt was forced to resign, but he had long threatened to do so if groups in his Social Democratic Party did not cease their opposition to U.S. missiles. He issued a stern warning to his party not to consider the possibility of aligning themselves with the Greens.[3] In posing the milieu of blue-collar industrial workers against that of "new social movements," he miscalculated the significance of the impetus from below, and his government fell.

A more historically significant effect of the popular movement was the initiation of a process of questioning the rationality of the Cold War. As is today clear, the division of Europe into two warring zones, although accepted by most people for nearly forty years, had become politically unnecessary and ecologically destructive, and it posed an all-too-frightening potential catastrophe. "The people make history"—little more than an empty rhetorical device for political leaders holding the reins of power—clarifies the driving force behind the Cold War's end. For a few years, governments were perceived as the problem: in the language of the European Nuclear Disarmament Appeal of 1980 (signed by millions of people), its signatories should not be "loyal to East or West but to each other." The construction of a transnational civil society unanchored in any state or political party proceeded slowly at first. Long before nuclear disarmament developed massive support or Gorbachev considered perestroika and glasnost, grassroots citizens' initiatives against nuclear power and other megaprojects of the state-industrial behemoth galvanized locally based opposition movements, sometimes across national borders. As bottom-up initiatives proliferated, Gorbachev was encouraged to act by the electoral successes of the Greens, and Western leaders were compelled to respond because of the pressure of the peace movement. Moreover, although the massive peace movement had a militant wing, it was essentially a single-issue movement backed by mainly middleclass people using traditional tactics.

As I discuss in this chapter, the autonomous women's movement, the movement against nuclear power, and youthful squatters all became springboards for more generalized resistance involving militant tactics. As citizens' initiatives and new social movements followed their own internal logics, the radical Autonomen were created and expressed fundamental opposition to the existing world system. Unlike many specialists in European affairs, those of us involved in these movements were not surprised by the hundreds of thousands of people who subsequently marched in the streets of Europe. In this chapter, I recall the history of how localized struggles against nuclear power plants and isolated squats helped create the possibility for the massive mobilizations against NATO plans to deploy new nuclear weapons.

No doubt the Allies made a wise decision at the end of World War II when they chose to rehabilitate rather than humiliate Germany through another Versailles treaty. It was hoped that the emergence of a new Hitler would thereby be precluded, and a buffer against Soviet expansionism would be created. With a few minor adjustments to the U.S. Constitution (such as the deliberate exclusion of a strong executive and the creation of a system of proportional representation designed to ensure the inclusion of small parties in the government), American-style democracy, complete with the promise of affluent consumerism for a comfortable majority, was adapted to and adopted by a compliant West German citizenry. Part of the new social contract tacitly agreed to by all but a few protesters after the founding of the Bundesrepublik (Federal Republic of Germany, hereafter FRG) was to support the new democratic state.

During the 1960s, as occurred nearly everywhere else in the world, opposition in Germany crystallized based upon the norms, values, and actions of young people. The most important German New Left group was SDS, Sozialistischer Deutscher Studentenbund (German Socialist Student federation), a unique blend of dissident refugees from communist East Germany, left-liberal student activists, and a few nascent bohemian counterculturalists. Originally the youth wing of the SPD, SDS became fiercely independent of political parties after the two fell out. During campaigns for an open university, freedom of the press, and peace in Vietnam, SDS grew in national importance. The country's two major parties, the CDU and the SPD, ruled together in a "grand coalition," so opposition was necessarily confined to the streets. In conjunction with a variety of groups, SDS participated in a loosely aligned extraparliamentary opposition (Ausserparlamentarische Opposition, or APO). The APO included SDS, a few trade unions, and religious groups active in the peace movement, whose Easter marchers mobilized hundreds of thousands of people.[4] As the first massive opposition to the Cold War consensus in West Germany, it took up the long-abandoned revolutionary tradition of the German working class, a heritage betrayed at the outbreak of World War I when Social Democrats voted to support the Kaiser's war.

The 1960s in Germany produced an extreme reaction to the Nazi past. Young Germans questioned why their parents' generation had participated in the horror of Nazism. When they realized that many ex-Nazis were part of system whose police were attacking their demonstrations, sometimes with deadly force, many lost all faith in the political order's democratic potential and initiated an armed struggle designed to overthrow it. Weakened by the male chauvinism of its members,[5] German SDS eventually succumbed to dogmatic Maoist and adventurist Guevarist forces within the organization, and after it dissolved, it spawned an assortment of "Marxist-Leninist" parties and cadre groups, whose appearance signaled the end of the first phase of the APO. Besides providing recruits for new communist parties (whose members totaled approximately fifteen thousand in the mid-1970s),[6] the APO's dissolution also sent many people into the SPD, which acquired about 100,000 new members from 1969 to 1973.[7] A variety of independent activists continued the "long march through the institutions," a strategy originally charted by SDS leader Rudi Dutschke that called for radicals to enter the existing system in order to demonstrate its practical incompatibility with a free society while simultaneously winning as many reforms as possible. Hundreds of activists went into German factories to organize, and in 1969 and again in 1973 (coincidentally, also when Italian labor unrest peaked), waves of wildcat strikes rolled through industry. Along with German laborers, these struggles involved immigrant Turkish workers in automobile plants, women working on assembly lines, and, for the first time in half a century, workers in the chemical industry. In 1970, negotiated wage increases averaged 10.6 percent, the highest in the history of the FRG.[8] In 1973, 275,000 workers in at least 335 factories struck for better working conditions and higher wages.[9] For the first time, Volkswagen workers went on strike. Only after numerous police attacks, headlines in *Der Spiegel* blaming a Turkish invasion for the unrest, and mammoth wage increases (totaling almost 30 per cent from 1969 to 1973) did things quiet down. Hundreds of radical activists were quickly dismissed from their union positions and lost their jobs.[10] In 1974, public employees struck for the first time. As economic crisis set in during the mid-1970s, however, German unions were able to discipline the workforce and win it Europe's highest standard of living.

Finally, a tendency of the New Left that grew after SDS dissolved was the antiauthoritarian counterculture. At the end of the 1960s, the German New Left discovered rock 'n roll around the same time that the Kreuzberg Hash Rebels came into existence, and guerrilla groups such as the RAF and the June 2 Movement began their armed attacks and bombings. Needless to say, these developments transformed a highly intellectual movement whose everyday life had reflected the cultural conformity of the society from which it had developed. As I discuss in the next section, feminists became increasingly autonomous of German society. Currents of sexual liberation and cultural revolution clashed with the dogmatic ideology of cadre groups and the stern disapproval of parents and authorities.

The counterculture became a source of political activism that had little to do with the Left or mainstream concerns.[11] At the beginning of the 1970s, activists organized the first squats in Munich, Cologne, Hamburg, and Göttingen. In Frankfurt, squatters' struggles in the early 1970s were especially strong, and the city became the center of the *Spontis* (spontaneit-ists who engaged in direct actions and street fights without belonging to formal organizations). In Bremen, Göttingen, Munich, Marburg, Kassel and Berlin, regionally organized *Sponti* groups were active.[12] Like the Metropolitan Indians in Italy, *Spontis* loved to poke fun at their more serious "comrades" and used irony rather than rationality to make their point. In 1978, *Spontis* in Münster helped elect a pig to a university office, and in Ulm, a dog was nominated to the Academic Senate.[13] Reacting to the holier-than-thou position assumed by many leftists vis-à-vis the general population, *Sponti* spokesperson Humphrey Tse Tung was quoted widely as saying, "The revolutionary must swim among the masses like a fish on a bicycle." Regarding the dying German forests, *Spontis* quipped: "Acidity makes jovial—the forest laughs itself dead."

During the early 1970s, feminism and the antinuclear power move-ment slowly awakened alongside thousands of *Bürgerinitiativen* (citizens' initiatives or independent grassroots groups that arose to protest local issues such as pollution problems, rising fares for public transportation, or the need for playgrounds and parks). From about a thousand such groups in 1972, the number grew to over four thousand by 1975, when it was estimated that they involved anywhere from 60,000 to 160,000 people.[14] By 1982, another estimate claimed that the BBU (Bundesver-band Bürgerinitiativen Umweltschutz, or Federal Association of Citizen Initiatives for Environmental protection) represented over a thousand groups, with a total membership between 300,000 and 500,000.[15] As these new groups formed, eventually they constituted a movement far larger than anything in the 1960s. During the same period, all but a few New Leftists, particularly the old membership of SDS, became integrated into German society.

German SDS never had more than two thousand members,[16] and even though the New Left created quite a stir in West Germany, it never at-tracted the widespread participation so essential to the larger movements in France or the United States.[17] For the most part, members of the New Left became part of the university "establishment" and filled other pro-fessional positions. The most public examples of New Leftists who were not absorbed into the middle class were imprisoned members of guerrilla groups, some of whom were incarcerated in sunless, constantly videotaped isolation cells. Solidarity with these prisoners became an important rallying point within the movement, despite severe legal sanctions against writing or even publicly speaking in favor of "terrorists."

During the 1970s, the government's counteroffensive against "terrorists" and remnants of the New Left that were busy with the "long march through the institutions" led to widespread repression of public employees, teachers, and anyone who protested, making it difficult to find ways to dissent publicly. In 1972, Willy Brandt implemented a ministerial decree aimed at curtailing "radicals" employed in the public service. Known as the *Berufsverbot* by its critics and *Radikalenerlass* by self-described neutral observers, the decree resulted in loyalty checks on 3.5 million persons and the rejection of 2,250 civil service applicants. Although only 256 civil servants were dismissed, the decree had a chilling effect. By criminalizing such mundane actions as signing petitions and speaking openly against government policy, the decree went beyond its intended effect. Although more members of extreme right-wing groups were employed in the public sector in 1972, the Left became the target of government officials entrusted with carrying out the terms of the new law. About half of the right-wingers employed by the government were in the military, compared with a similar percentage of leftists in the post office. One observer noted that the historically vital "anti-Left syndrome encourages rightist groups to become active against the Left, a development that is only too reminiscent of the Weimar period."[18] According to a Mannheim survey, 84 percent of university students there refrained from regularly checking leftist materials out of public libraries for fear of being blacklisted.[19] So many people were concerned that the FRG was self-destructing that when the Sozialistisches Büro organized an antirepression conference in June 1976, twenty thousand people attended.[20]

In 1977 (when the revolt in Italy reached a boiling point), West Germany suffered through its "German Autumn," a time of both armed attacks on the country's elite and intense political repression. For some time, the hard core of the guerrillas—then called the Baader-Meinhof group, today the RAF—had been robbing banks, setting off fires in department stores, killing local officials, and outrunning police in high-speed chases on the autobahns. On September 5, the RAF kidnapped one of the country's leading industrialists, Hanns-Martin Schleyer (whom they insisted had been an SS man during World War II). As police checkpoints appeared around the country during the six weeks that the RAF held Schleyer before they killed him, the fascist state that many Germans feared would rise like a phoenix from the ashes of Nazism appeared to be real. Overwhelmed by the deadly force brought to bear by the state, *Spontis* helped intervene by organizing a giant convention they called *Tunix* (Do Nothing). In the deadly serious atmosphere of an apparent police state that was the German Autumn, the *Sponti* response was to turn utopian. They called on all "freaks" to "sail off to Tunix beach... beneath the cobblestones of the country."[21] Using the conference against repression in Bologna as a model, organizers drew an estimated twenty thousand young people to Berlin in February 1978. The strong and vibrant turnout surprised even the conference organizers. As freaks participated in theaters of the absurd and other happenings, looming in the background were the twin ogres of Italian repression and the German Autumn. By the time *Tunix* ended, many people felt that they had gone beyond the reality of repression, and the subsequent activation of thousands of people spelled an end to the repressive atmosphere that had so endangered German democracy.

More than anything else, what fired the imagination of the new activist impulse at the end of the 1970s was the autonomous movement in Italy. Discussing the existence of "autonomous groups" in Germany after *Tunix*, one theorist, Johannes Agnoli warned that the Frankfurt *Spontis*, like the West German Left in general, felt so isolated and powerless that they identified too strongly with the Metropolitan Indians and Italian Autonomia. In the same year, a book about the Metropolitan Indians was published in Germany, and some of them traveled the country seeking to spark similar formations.[22] We can trace the trajectory of the autonomous movement from Italy to Zurich and Amsterdam, then to German cities, especially Berlin and Hamburg, and finally, in the summer of 1981, to British cities.[23]

In Switzerland, a massive struggle for an autonomous youth center broke out in Zurich in May 1980, transforming that city's conservative social landscape. In many European cities after 1968, struggles for autonomous youth centers had been waged, but the contest in Zurich was so intense and assumed such innovative and imaginative forms that it became the point of origin for subsequent actions.[24] Using a combination of tactics, including nude marches and "roller commando" demonstrations, a radical youth movement opposed to the complacency of middle-class culture challenged Swiss society to make the lives of its youth more fulfilling. Their struggle for an autonomous youth center was, in their own words, to create a place "where new forms of living together can be found and our own culture developed" as a step toward a "society in which humanity, freedom of opinion, and the unfolding of human personality can be made real."[25] The movement in Zurich originally formed around circles of proletarian youth. Upset with the high cost of concerts and having nowhere to hang out, bands of youth stormed concerts. Eventually they wanted their own space for concerts, and they created Rock as Revolt, modeled on the English Rock Against Racism and the German Rock Against the Right. The Swiss group did not see racism or Fascism as the main problem, but the generally boring and alienated conditions of their everyday lives.[26] Beginning with a small protest against the lavish renovation of the opera house, a Dadaist movement erupted, turning the city upside down. They alternately won support from the city's government for their youth center and fought police and drug dealers for control of it. Using slogans like, "Turn the government into cucumber salad" and "We are the cultural corpses of the city," the movement expressed its desire to transcend the "death culture" of work and consumerism and to overturn the whole society, not just the state and institutions.[27] But the authorities would not allow them their own space. At the end of 1980 (when the squatters' movement was first consolidating itself in Berlin), more than eleven hundred youth faced criminal charges in Zurich, and thousands of people at general assemblies debated the movement's next steps. In eighteen months, there were more than sixty confrontations with the police and over twenty-five hundred arrests.[28] Despite Swiss prosperity (there were more jobs available than workers willing to take them), a cultural crisis was evident in statistics such as the suicide rate for young men (it more than doubled from 1970 to 1980).[29] The lack of free space was compounded by a painfully stark housing crisis. Rent increases sparked by inflation were resisted by a wave of occupations of vacant buildings, and a shantytown named Chaotikon was built on one of Zurich's fashionable lakeside parks to dramatize (and partially solve) the problems young people had in finding places to live. Chaotikon was cleared out and destroyed by riot police only one week after it was built, but it was repeatedly reconstructed, like the autonomous youth center that was temporarily won, lost, and won again. The movement spread to Basel, Bern, and Lausanne. In 1981, two people were killed by police, and the polarization of Swiss life reached unexpected extremes. In 1982, the youth center was finally demolished in Zurich. Hard drugs had helped sap the movement's strength, turning imaginative action into quiet resignation. Nonetheless, the myth and reality of the struggle in Zurich became a model for others.

From Italy via Zurich, the idea of an autonomous movement was carried to Hamburg and Berlin, where, merged with the practice of Dutch squatters, the Autonomen were consolidated. Not a concept that fell from the sky, autonomous politics developed from many sources, all of which stemmed from practical experience in struggles to transform the social order. As I discuss in the remainder of this chapter, it would take years of popular direct actions in Germany before the Autonomen would appear, and several sources flowed together to create them: the autonomous women's movement, the antinuclear movement, squatters, and the alternative movement.

Like the counterculture, feminism transcended national boundaries and played a significant role in transforming German social movements. The women's movement in Germany zealously maintained its autonomy from the rest of the Left, setting an example for emergent movements. Although groups from the militant antinuclear power movement around Hamburg used the term "autonomous" to describe themselves early in the 1970s, they might as well have used the word "independent," since they were not using the term to link their identity to the idea of an autonomous movement.[30] The feminist movement that appeared in Germany was the main source of continuity between the 1960s and the 1970s, although as I discuss later, feminists initially negated the strident style of SDS. As in Italy, women injected a "politics of the first person" into movement discourse, and in so doing, they realized an enduring meaning for the concept of autonomy.

THE AUTONOMOUS WOMEN'S MOVEMENT

As the APO and the popular upsurge of the 1960s faded, feminism in Germany went from the margins of a student revolt to become an enduring movement that affected German society far more profoundly than any postwar social movement. In 1988, twenty years after the appearance of militant feminism, Alice Schwarzer, one of the autonomous women's movement's most important spokespersons, declared, "We feminists have made a cultural revolution! The only real one since 1945."[31] Although her optimism may have been exaggerated, her point was not incorrect.

The direct impact of feminism was clear enough in the newfound political power enjoyed by women, as well as in new opportunities in other domains previously reserved for men. Most importantly, in the transvaluation of the subtle and overt demeaning of women that centuries of patriarchy had produced, everyday life had been transformed for millions of women. Indirectly, the women's movement prefigured what would later become the Autonomen. Feminists were the ones who made "autonomy" their central defining point, and they passed it along to the next generations of activists. Their counterinstitutions were visionary and, like their illegal occupations of vacant houses that were then fixed up (*Instandbesetzungen*), subsequently became examples for larger movements. Before others did so, they began to work with immigrant Turkish women, and well before the Greens developed the slogan that they were "neither Left nor Right but in front," the women's movement had labeled Left and Right as patriarchal concepts having little to do with feminism.

On September 13, 1968, a critical date in the history of the German New Left and of German feminism, Helke Sander, a member of the Berlin Action Council for Women's Liberation, gave an impassioned speech at the national meeting of SDS in Frankfurt calling an her male comrades in SDS to remove "the blinders you have over your eyes" and take note of their own sexism.[32] As expected by some, the meeting returned to business as usual as soon as she finished speaking. But when SDS theoretician Hans-Jürgen Krahl was in the middle of his speech (having nothing to do with the feminist appeal for support), another female delegate from Berlin screamed at him: "Comrade Krahl, you are objectively a counterrevolutionary and an agent of the class enemy!" She then hurled several tomatoes in the direction of the podium, one of which hit Krahl squarely in the face.

Many of the women in SDS were embarrassed by the action, but the deeds of the Berlin Action Council for Women's Liberation electrified feminists and are considered to be the beginning of the autonomous women's movement. Although it had formed while organizing among mothers with young children trying to cope with the scandalous lack of day care (Kinderladen), the Berlin Action Council's roots in the antiauthoritarian New Left defined its overly critical understanding of motherhood. In January 1968, it wrote: "The function of the mother is to internalize forms of domination and treat them as love." As many of these women were compelled to bring children to meetings and interrupt their own participation while their male comrades gave speeches about the "repressive nature of monogamy" and the need to negate (Aufheben) the "fixation of the children on their parents," women's self-critical comments were transformed into a mothers' movement around the issue of day care. While their subservience in SDS was initially ignored by their male counterparts, after they successfully organized kindergarten teachers, their groups began to be taken over by men.[33]

Initially, women saw their withdrawal from mixed groups as temporary, "to bring us to the point where we can come to our own self-understanding without hindsight and compromises. Only then will we be capable to unite with other groups in a meaningful fashion."[34] Like their male counterparts in the New Left, they believed that the class struggle was primary and women's liberation a "secondary contradiction." As women mobilized, crass male domination propelled militant feminists into ever more radical theory and practice. In November 1968, a group of SDS women from Frankfurt attempted to read a prepared statement at an SPD celebration of the fiftieth anniversary of women's right to vote, but they were physically prevented from doing so by SPD officials. They then formed a "Broad's Council" and prepared a now legendary leaflet for the next national SDS meeting a few weeks later. Entitled "Free the Socialist Eminences from Their Bourgeois Dicks!" the leaflet pictured six mounted penises with the corresponding names of male SDS leaders beneath them and a reclining female figure with an axe in her hand.

Nothing was more important to the new movement than the campaign to liberalize the abortion laws. Statutes criminalizing abortion had been on the books since 1871,[35] and at the turn of the century, intermittent struggles had failed to win significant reform. The specific statute that the second wave of feminists sought to repeal was paragraph 218 in the Basic Laws that outlawed abortion. On March 8, 1969, International Women's Day, the first of many demonstrations for deletion of paragraph 218 took place. The number of illegal abortions in West Germany was estimated at anywhere from half a million to a million (although the government's figure was only 1,005 for 1969). In the same year, a poll showed that 71 percent of German women (and 56 percent of the entire population) were against paragraph 218. As demonstrations and public pressure mounted, a shock wave hit Germany on June 2, 1971, when 374 women publicly declared, "I have had an abortion" in *Stern*, one of the country's main magazines. Initiated by Alice Schwarzer (who copied the action from the Women's Liberation Front in Paris, where 343 French women had published a similar declaration two months earlier), this public confession made abortion rights the country's number-one issue. Within two months of the *Stern* article, more than 2,345 more women signed on, 973 men admitted their "complicity," and 86,100 solidarity signatures were gathered.[36]

Women's movements in the United States, Holland, and Denmark were similarly engaged in feminist campaigns, and the international diffusion of action and thought was a noteworthy feature of this period. Forging connections with women's movements in other countries, feminism in Germany helped negate national chauvinistic tendencies. At a time when anti-Americanism was a growing force among leftists, women translated and read numerous texts from the United States. They also rediscovered the existence of a first wave of German feminism, a vibrant movement dating to the mid-nineteenth century whose history had largely been hidden.

As the campaign to decriminalize abortion gathered momentum, 450 women from forty groups came together in Frankfurt on March 11 and 12, 1972, for the first national women's congress. In plenaries and four working groups, women accelerated their pace of activity. The working group on families developed concrete demands, including division of domestic chores between men and women, equal pay for equal work, an end to traditional roles in the family, a year with pay for new mothers and fathers, unconditional twenty-four-hour kindergartens, and large dwellings at cheap rents to counter the isolation of the nuclear family. Working group "Action 218" prepared a new offensive against paragraph 218. Between twenty and thirty of the forty groups participating in the conference had originally been formed to legalize abortion, and the working group served to coordinate their future activities. The conference as a whole resolved that the women's question would no longer be subsumed beneath the question of class and that they would expand their autonomous organizations. Declaring their opposition to becoming an isolated "women's island," they promised to "struggle against the existing system."[37]

After the national congress, action groups against paragraph 218 intensified their efforts. In Frankfurt, over a hundred women staged a "go-in" at the cathedral during Sunday services to protest the church's antiabortion policies. With the slogan "The unborn are protected, the born are exploited," the women shouted down the priest as he tried to read the latest church letter on abortion. Feminists also stormed a disco having a "Miss Disco" competition and threw pigs' tails at the jury. At another "go-in," this time at a meeting of the mainstream medical association, women handed out leaflets and threw red-stained tampons at the doctors, a majority of whom declared their support for the government and made statements that they would not perform abortions even if they were legalized. In Köln, a two-day tribunal against opponents of abortion was held.

In Berlin, less confrontational actions were planned. Articulating a new style they called "feminist realism," three women artists organized an exhibition entitled "From Women—For Women—With Women." These artists developed a medium to portray clearly what they perceived to be the position of women, but even that tranquil act was too much for city officials, who promptly withdrew their funding, forcing cancellation. Nonetheless, the women hung their work at movement meetings and on billboards. Bread ♀ Roses, a Berlin feminist organization, produced the first women's handbook containing information on birth control and abortion. They declared the need for women to understand their own bodies rather than relying on male doctors' expertise. Self-help groups formed to teach women how to do self-exams. That same year, from within the Homosexual Action Center of West Berlin emerged the first public lesbian group.

Feminist euphoria was everywhere in 1973. In February, hundreds of women met in Munich and planned a new set of national actions. After the Munich gathering, consciousness-raising groups adopted from the United States spread throughout the country, symptoms of an inward turn in the movement. As the first divisions within the movement between socialist feminism and radical feminism appeared,[38] women's groups coalesced in the strategy of creating women's centers, self-managed autonomous spaces in which men were not allowed. Although there were more than a hundred active feminist groups and a few thousand activists in Germany, in only two cities (Berlin and Frankfurt) were there such centers. All over the country, women began to create them. On January 17, 1974, in Heidelberg, women occupied a house that had stood empty for a year. Using money collected from their supporters to fix it up, they worked on it for six days. In the middle of the night, the police broke down the door and arrested them all. In their court appearance, one of the women spoke for the group:

> We women are generally not self-reliant and are regarded as helpless. And so it is that we have never learned to step forth and take matters into our own hands.... Our experiences have shown that groups that deal with apparently private problems like family, raising children and sexuality are in the position to activate women, to open their horizons, to activate them to change their situation... that's why we need public space available to every woman... to free our time and energy.[39]

By the spring of 1974, a dozen autonomously financed (and managed) centers were open, and by the end of the year, there were seventeen.[40] These centers were places where the old organizational forms were questioned and nonhierarchical and decentralized action points were created. In these group contexts:

> The solitary woman experiences differences and other women that radiate more security and formulate autonomous goals. Every solitary woman brings with her desires for emancipation, and the group can start making demands for emancipation very quickly—with the result that the solitary woman in a discussion group soon feels she is living a lie (because of the discrepancy between reality and demand).[41]

Isolated housewives and students went from the margins to the center of German social life, reformulating their identities in the process of creating a vibrant set of autonomous women's institutions: women's bars, newspapers, magazines, presses, bookstores, film festivals, and rock bands (such as the Flying Lesbians).

Although at least eight different women's political parties were founded in West Germany after 1950, none was able to become a forum for the women's movement. There was never a centralized organization like the National Organization for Women (NOW) in the United States, yet Germany's feminists prided themselves on being the "best organized of all."[42] Within the women's centers, differences emerged, particularly between leftist bureaucrats and anarchists. Conflicts between weak and strong personalities were the topic of many discussions. There was frustration at constantly having to return to a zero point when new women had to be oriented, particularly as to the reasons that men were not allowed. Nonetheless, the centers thrived, organizing the campaign against paragraph 218 and initiating other projects as well, notably an annual feminist summer university in Berlin.[43]

On March 16, 1974, a national day of protest, thousands of women went into the streets. Using street theater and puppet parades, they sought to pressure the governing Social Democrats to end their ambivalence on abortion. "Action Last Attempt," born from a small group from the Berlin Women's Center, had several parts: In *Der Spiegel*, 329 doctors risked losing their professional licenses by admitting having helped women obtain illegal abortions. Two days later, the television newsmagazine *Panorama* scheduled a sensational program: fourteen doctors were going to perform an illegal abortion using the vacuum method (widely practiced outside Germany, but hardly known inside the country). Shortly before it was to be aired, the program was banned, and all that viewers saw during prime time was a blank screen. The ugly hand of censorship reappeared in Germany.

These actions brought thousands of new women into the women's centers, people who had read about the centers in the wake of the *Panorama* scandal and sought advice and shelter as well as ways to get involved in the movement. In April 1974, when the *Bundestag* passed a new law permitting abortions in the first trimester, it seemed that the movement had won a victory. Thousands of women danced all night at a party in Berlin in May, but on June 21, the Supreme Court suspended the new law. Pressure mounted from all sides, and finally, on February 25, 1975, the court declared the new law unconstitutional. A week later, the Red Zoras, a feminist guerrilla group, bombed the court's chambers in Karlsruhe. Numerous police searches were unable to locate anyone tied to the Red Zoras, but they disrupted networks of activists working against paragraph 218. A year later, a new law was enacted that remained in effect for over a decade: if a woman underwent counseling, she would be able to have an abortion.

The struggle to decriminalize abortion was exemplary in its organizational forms and militance. After decades of invisibility, women suddenly gained a massive following and made their agenda a national issue. They were exemplary in another less positive way as well: the fate of millions of women was decided by a handful of male judges, an all too painful reminder of who held power. As one woman put it:

> Once again it was not whether to abort or not, but how one could abort: namely that it was not the responsibility of the woman, but the guardianship of men—doctors, psychologists, judges. The real function of the law, namely the intimidation and tutelage of women, was preserved.[44]

Difficult as it was for the movement to be unable to change the law despite majority support and militant confrontations, it was only the most blatant example of female subordination to patriarchal power. Is it any wonder that women reacted by creating their own autonomous domains?

Berlin was clearly the avant-garde city for the German autonomous women's movement. Berlin's Republican Club, an informal New Left discussion group, was where women first came together to discuss women's issues.[45] The first women's center was in Berlin's Hornstrasse, the first women's bar (the Blocksberg) opened there, and the first self-help groups originated within the Berlin Women's Health Center. In 1976, Berlin's feminist magazine *Schwarze Botin* considered the women's movement "the only group in this moment at all capable of performing a radical and critical critique of society that... is anticapitalist, but primarily antiphallic and antipatriarchal."[46] As the women's movement turned into the "women's projects movement," the concept of autonomy was made real: taken together, the projects created a "countermilieu" in which women would be free to build their own forms of life without having to deal with men.

Limits on feminist utopianism intervened in the mid-1970s, as violence against women escalated in response to the movement's strident actions and contestation of power relations in everyday life. The issue of violence against women became the central action point of feminists around the world. In Portugal, two hundred women, who took to the streets to demonstrate against pornography and the oppression of women, were attacked by a crowd of over five thousand men who screamed, "Burn them! Women only in bed!"[47] In Spain, women had to celebrate clandestinely on International Women's Day. In 1977, the case of Italian Claudia Caputi and Italian feminist marches also had a significant impact in Germany.[48] Statistics showed that a woman was raped every fifteen minutes in Germany, yet there was no social consciousness about violence against women, no shelters for battered women and children. The first such shelter was founded in Berlin, and within two years, dozens of others had been created in the rest of Germany.[49] On April 30, 1977, feminists took to the streets to "take back the night," the first of what became an annual Walpurgis Night march against pornography and rape. As illustrated in the previous chapter on Italy, male activists were surprisingly callous to their sisters. When the leftist magazine *konkret* had a cover story on feminism featuring a man's hand holding a woman's breast, its doors were plastered shut by a group of women. This instance illuminates a continuing problem in the Left. While the Left was mobilizing against increasing repression from the government (something feminist groups also faced), women were also repressed in everyday life by men. As one group tried to explain it:

> From childhood on our capabilities are throttled. We have a permanent Berufsverbot. Our identities have been stolen, from early on we learn to find ourselves through men only. Our bodies are permanent sites (*freiwild*) for glances, for fondling and for comments. The streets are for us enemy territory. We don't feel safe alone in the streets at night. For us there's always a curfew.[50]

Discussions focused on the colonized soul of women, on lives that were barraged with male violence and repression; the need for autonomy continually resurfaced. The concept of autonomy had several meanings for feminists. On an individual level, women were concerned with their personal autonomy. As Alice Schwarzer put it: "A women has no existence as an autonomous being—only in relation to a man."[51] But individual autonomy, the most common way the term is understood in our society, because it refers to individual distance taking, is often linked to male behavior. For the women's movement, autonomy referred to the need for female collective autonomy—for women to have shelter from male violence and male dynamics, for spaces of women's own making and design. Within the movement, local groups used the term in yet another sense: to refer to their independence within a nonhierarchical framework that did not create a division between leaders and followers. Finally, and most importantly, the meaning of the term autonomy was political and referred to the feminist movement's independence from established political parties, As Ann Anders summarized: "The first principle of autonomy is the lack of any hierarchy and alignment with state, party or any other rigid political-social structures."[52] Another activist summarized the many meanings of autonomy:

Above all, autonomy of the women's movement means its self-organization, separation from the male-dominated Left and men generally.
Moreover it refers to the relationship of the movement to the government
and its institutions, which because they are recognized as patriarchal and
system stabilizing, are rejected, resulting in a complete detachment from
state and institutional connections. Within the movement, autonomy
means primarily decentralization, autonomy of every single group. In
existing groups, it means the self-determination of working structures
and content, within which hoped for antihierarchical structures allow
affected individuals the widest possible space for their autonomous
development.[53]

Besides helping illuminate the multifaceted meaning of autonomy, these
definitions illustrate the continuity between the autonomous women's
movement and the extraparliamentary opposition of the 1960s. Both
formations were deeply suspicious of the co-optive consequences of entering into the established system. By definition, being autonomous for
both feminists and the APO meant refusing to go into these institutions
in order to change them. On the one side, the women's movement was
on the offensive against paragraph 218, but simultaneously it created its
own counterinstitutions "out of the extraparliamentary Left, that began
in 1968 to build alternative structures, to live in group houses and to
have its own presses and meeting places."[54] These two dimensions, opposition to the domination of the existing system and construction of
liberated spaces within it, define the universe of discourse of autonomous
movements.

   In comparison to its counterpart in the United States, the German
women's movement emphasized autonomy rather than equality.[55] After
the U.S. movement was able to win abortion rights, its energies became
focused within the established political arena. One result was that liberal
feminists led thousands of activists into pouring millions of hours into
an unsuccessful campaign for the equal rights amendment. Despite de
jure equal rights in Germany, the failure of German feminists to obtain
commensurate abortion rights preconditioned their greater emphasis
on autonomy. No central organization exists there, and liberal feminists
have little influence. Identified primarily with radical feminists, the
autonomous women's movement refers to local projects, a network of
bookstores and presses, women's centers, and publications.

   Courage, the first national women's magazine, was founded in 1976
with a press run of five thousand copies. Although it began as a West
Berlin magazine, it soon was circulated throughout West Germany and
by November 1978 had a circulation of seventy thousand.[56] In February

1977, Alice Schwarzer and a group of radical feminists that included many professional journalists published *Emma*, with a first issue of 300,000; it regularly printed 100,000 copies. Both magazines were controlled by nonprofit feminist groups and were produced exclusively by women. Having two feminist magazines with different perspectives helped stimulate probing exchanges and sharp polemics among women. Although the debates sometimes resulted in personal attacks,[57] they provided thousands of activists with ongoing forums for political education and discussion. Two key issues German feminists have continually returned to over the last quarter century are women's work in the home and motherhood. Deep divisions opened in the movement in response to the problem of unpaid domestic drudgery and the confinement of women to the home.

In 1973, Alice Schwarzer published her book *Women's Work—Women's Liberation*, and a few months later, a German translation appeared of the classic text by Mariarosa Dalla Costa and Selma James.[58] If the personal is political, as these theorists maintained, then the unpaid domestic labor performed by women (estimated at various times to be in the billions of hours) should be considered part of the economy—counted in the calculation of gross domestic product and compensated in dollars. They insisted that if women were paid for what is now unpaid work, the division between the world of paid work and that of unpaid labor would be rendered meaningless. This would lead to a complete revaluation of women's role and an end to their relegation to the home and the private sphere, where they serve as unnoticed appendages to men. Other feminists, however, had a different perspective. They believed that enacting a system of remuneration for household work would only further institutionalize women within these spheres, thereby reproducing barriers to their entrance into other institutions—politics, corporations, universities. Since the ghettoization of women is the material product of a patriarchal division of labor that privileges men in terms of careers and jobs, they believed that sharing the burden of domestic chores and child-raising responsibilities was the only way to overthrow this patriarchal structural imperative.[59] Radical feminists complained that wages for housework glorified the place of women in the home rather than seeking to involve men in household chores.

The Left generally tried to organize women at the site of production, "at the side of the working class," where women were consistently underpaid.[60] As one woman expressed the relationship between these two dynamics: "Above all, unpaid housework turned up again as underpaid work outside the home: since women's work is worth nothing in the home, it is worth less outside the home."[61] Hannelore Mabry called the double and triple burden of women "patriarchal surplus value." Noting the Left's and unions' antipathy—or at best ambivalence—toward women's issues in the past, Mabry maintained: "Women and mothers did not split the labor movement, but rather male workers have from the beginning betrayed and plundered women and mothers—*because for them too, the patriarchal right of the mighty prevailed!*"[62]

As the debate over wages for housework receded, a new dispute emerged in the form of debates about the "new motherhood" and equal rights. Radical feminists argued that "equal rights (more women in politics, etc.) are blind demands insofar as they do not question the underlying issue of whether we should accept the structures of manly domains, whether we should become part of manly politics and science."[63] They understood motherhood as something that society expected of women, and they sought to revise the definition of a full life for a woman as not necessarily including having children. They simultaneously regarded the conditions of motherhood (being overworked, living on the margins) as oppressive. These ideas were contradicted by a text in *Courage* that contained notions such as the "natural wish for children" of all women that came deep from within the belly, a naturally given "peaceful mother-child relationship," and a "psychically/physically anchored preparedness of mothers to be victims."[64] Taken with New Age ideas, some women began celebrating "women's intuition" and found tarot cards to be a way to divine the future.[65] This inward turn in the movement signaled "a new femininity" and celebration of motherhood that verified the feelings of some women that their femininity—including their motherly intentions (or actuality)—was not to be denied. These developments raised objections and bitter responses (particularly from lesbians, who saw it as an "acceptance of heterosexuality within the women's movement").[66]

Since the birth rate in Germany was lower than the death rate, all political parties, the CPU most strongly, were doing what they could to encourage women to become mothers. Some feminists supported the mothers' centers that were then being created with government money to help new mothers learn new skills, earn money, and put their children in play groups. They argued that mothers' feelings of self-worth had been cracked, and called on women to validate mothers and support them. Courage called for at least one year off at full pay for new mothers, guarantees that mothers could return to their jobs, the creation of jobs to which mothers could bring their children, higher child-subsidy payments for nonworking mothers, and more publications about breast-feeding. Insofar as these ideas overlapped with some of those discussed by the government, they were subjected to relentless criticism by radicals.

In contrast to the position of a genetically defined female nature (a position called "essentialist" in the United States), radical feminists sought to raise the possibility that male and female traits are products of social-historical forces that have molded our identities in particular ways. As early as 1975, Alice Schwarzer had articulated this position in what became a classic text of German Feminism, *The "Little" Difference and Its Great Consequences*. In it she posed a future where

> gender would no longer be destiny. Women and men would no longer be forced into role behavior, and the masculine mystique would be as superfluous as the femininity complex. Sex-specific divisions of labor and exploitation would be suspended. Only biological motherhood would be women's affair; social motherhood would be men's affair just as much as women's. People would communicate with each other in unlimited ways, sexually and otherwise, according to their individual needs at any given time and regardless of age, race, and gender. (There would be no class system in this liberated society.)[67]

According to this logic, what has been culturally determined can be remade, in contrast to the absolutely unchangeable character of naturally given inner nature. Even naturally given abilities such as breast-feeding were deconstructed and critically examined by radical feminists. They perceived the government's support for mothers as little more than a liberal version of Hitler's limitation of women to the three "K's" (kitchen, children, and church). They saw the new femininity as "part of the counterrevolt coming out of our own ranks" and posited the possibility of a third way in which "we would no longer be reduced, no longer cut in half. A way that would allow us to be strong and weak, emotional and rational, vulnerable and daring."[68]

In 1979, at the fourth Berlin summer university for women, the theme was "Autonomy or Institution: The Passion and Power of Women." For the first time, there were long discussions about the peace movement, and a public demand was made to the SPD to oppose the new U.S. missiles or face a vote boycott. At the same time, the long-standing debate about motherhood and pay for domestic work continued. A new element was injected by Vera Slupic. Using irony to accentuate her point, she called for wages for lesbians, since they also worked around the home. Slupic also turned her critical eye on lesbians.[69] As the women's movement felt increasingly isolated, its projects taken over by government monies or turned into established ongoing businesses whose subversive cutting edge seemed blunted, many women felt disenfranchised by the turn toward motherhood and a new femininity. As many women turned further inward, limiting themselves to their private spheres of lovers and close friends, radicals felt that the slogan "The personal is political" had been turned on its head—to the point where the political was irrelevant. It was not even included in the women's movement's own publications, where the new interest in sadomasochism took up more space than the missile crisis.

Even in this context, few women felt the need for a centralized organization. Indeed, one activist wrote in 1981: "The autonomous groups have enabled women to focus on creative, cooperative work structures. They have also prevented women from getting caught up in the wheels of cooptation and compromise."[70] Many politically oriented women became active in the Greens, but they were often disappointed. At the party's 1980 Baden-Württemberg state convention, a platform including abortion rights was narrowly defeated. Women were determined to swing the Greens around, and by 1983, an exclusively female leadership, the so-called Feminat, held all four major leadership posts in the party from 1984 to 1985. They led an offensive against those in the party unable to support repeal of paragraph 218.[71] Within the party, women won the right to vote separately on issues related to them, and when they were not with the party majority, their vote functioned as a kind of veto. A strict 50 percent quota was established for all electoral slates, and the party sponsored national meetings for only female members to discuss problems of the autonomous women's movement, as well those within the Greens. The first of these conferences drew a thousand women. Women pressured the trade unions to sanction autonomous mobilizations of women, they compelled the second largest union in Germany (ÖTV, the Public Services, Transport, and Communications Union) to advocate repeal of paragraph 218 in 1983, and their votes helped dislodge conservative governments in state and local elections.

Some women began to get involved anew in mixed groups, signaling a new phase of feminism—one in which the autonomous women's organizations and the newly forged self-confidence of women provided a background from which women could draw strength and participate in mixed groups.[72] As feminism went from an obscure margin to a mainstream movement, millions of women internalized a new consciousness, transforming the political culture of West Germany. All political parties had to incorporate women's issues into their programs. Within the radical movement, women took part in house occupations for women only, and within mixed squats, others organized women's evenings.[73] The autonomy of feminism gave women a power base at the same time as it provided a political concept that galvanized other new social movements (squatters, peace activists, alternatives, and the antinuclear power movement).

THE ANTINUCLEAR MOVEMENT

In contrast to Italy, which Aurelio Pecci (president of the prestigious Club of Rome that sponsored studies such as *The Limits to Growth*) considered "not well behaved enough for nuclear technology,"[74] German order and stability meant that nuclear power was intensively developed after World War II. In 1976, when Italy was suffering through its chronic political instability, an article published in the London-based magazine *New Left Review* maintained that Germany was "the last stable fortress of reaction in Europe."[75] A few years later, the movement against nuclear power became increasingly militant, and Germany provided a textbook example of the volatility of social movements in the industrialized core of the world system.

The "economic miracle" in Germany after World War II was predicated upon capital-intensive industries such as steel and automobiles. Economic development played a major role in the country's physical reconstruction and also in its psychological rehabilitation. As one journalist put it:

> There was no way to express German national feeling after the war. This would have been interpreted as a Nazi attitude. West Germans instead constructed their new national identity around economic growth and power. Nothing better symbolized this than the nuclear industry. Nuclear power is the sacred cow of a new German nationalism. If you are against it, the establishment considers you anti-German—a traitor.[76]

Postwar West Germany enjoyed unprecedented economic growth for nearly three decades. In 1945, no one expected that the country, devastated by war and occupied by the Allies, would become one of the world's leading economic powers. As a critical part of the Cold War, the FRG received huge amounts of U.S. aid. After the building of the Berlin Wall, subsidies to West Berlin were increased dramatically, and the city was made into a showcase in the fight against Communism. Political stability in West Germany was based on economic prosperity. In 1973, per capita economic output was more than double that of Italy, and exports per capita were triple those of Japan.[77] Only about the size of the state of Oregon, West Germany became the world's leading net exporter.

Of all industrialized countries, Germany had the highest percentage of factory workers, yet compared with Italy, German workers never joined the movement en masse, and in notable cases, they opposed the antinuclear movement. Traditional issues of the workers' movement—wages, benefits, and working conditions—had long since become negotiable within the welfare state's institutional apparatus, and union bureaucracies were substantially identical to established political parties. Indeed, in Germany and Italy, they often overlapped and were indistinguishable. With the integration of the SPD into the governing elite and workers sitting on corporate boards of directors under the FRG's codetermination system, a smoothly functioning institutional apparatus was the envy (or fear) of much of the world.

In the mid-1970s, although the economic miracle turned into economic crisis, the majority of the country had never had it so good. Despite the gradual breakdown of the historic accord between capital and labor, German workers remained relatively quiet (a continuing dynamic in the 1990s, indicated partially by the fact that the Autonomen, unlike Autonomia in Italy, have never been able to attract widespread participation by workers). From the perspective of radical autonomists, there was a fundamental problem with unions: the workers should decide for themselves the kind of goods they produce and the kind of society they live in rather than leaving such decisions up to their unions and to whoever happens to sit in the seats of power. In the early 1980s, some unionized workers showed signs of movement. Even though the national executive committee of the German Federation of Trade Unions forbade its members to participate in the 1981 peace march in Bonn, for example, over three hundred locals endorsed the march, and large contingents of predominantly young unionists were present among the 250,000 demonstrators. Within the antinuclear movement, a coalition of farmers, students, and youth was increasingly joined by some workers and middle-class people, especially residents of small towns in the vicinity of nuclear power stations. In the 1980s, many students were active, but the movement was no longer primarily campus based, as it had been in the 1960s.

The antinuclear power movement initially developed as an antidote to the lack of democracy in the country's political decision-making process. Although Germany spent billions of marks on nuclear research and development beginning in 1956, only in 1975 did the Interior Ministry finally present an overview of nuclear policy to the *Bundestag* (Germany's parliament). Six months passed before the policy was first discussed, and when it finally came before the country's elected representatives, only 50 of the 518 members of parliament even bothered to be present.[78] The country's political class may not have been concerned, but many Germans were. Beginning in 1972, opposition emerged among the local population to a proposed nuclear plant in Wyhl (in the area where Germany, France, and Switzerland border one another).[79] In February 1975, the day after construction began, hundreds of protesters occupied the construction site, but they were brutally dispersed by the police. A few days later, twenty-eight thousand people demonstrated against the facility, and many protesters stayed on in the encampment. Hundreds of people built huts from felled trees on the construction site and established a "people's college" dedicated to stopping the nuclear plant. The police failed to clear them out, and they spent the next eleven months organizing national (and international) opposition to nuclear power. Wyhl became a global symbol of resistance. (After a film about Wyhl was shown in New England, for example, people organized the first meetings of the Clamshell Alliance, a group that went on to lead years of resistance to the Seabrook nuclear power plant in New Hampshire.) At the "peoples's college," more than fifty diverse courses were offered, including some taught by respected pro-nuclear scientists.

One effect of the movement was to make public the antidemocratic character of the government's nuclear policies. Immediately after Wyhl was occupied, the prime minister of Baden-Württemberg (governor of the state) smugly announced: "There can be no doubt that Wyhl will be constructed." His declaration was quickly followed by revelations in the media that the state's minister of economics was also the acting vice-chairman of the utility company's board of directors. Such an interlocking relationship between a high government official and the nuclear industry was not unique: in Lower Saxony, government officials conducted secret negotiations with the nuclear industry for more than a year before publicly applying for a construction permit for a plant in Esensham. In Brokdorf near Hamburg, although 75 percent of those questioned opposed the construction of a nuclear power plant, plans for its construction went forward.

Beginning in 1974, protesters had targeted the proposed fast breeder reactor at Kalkar. On September 24, 1977, an estimated seventy thousand Europeans converged on Kalkar to demonstrate their opposition to it. Twenty thousand of the protesters never made it to the demonstration because the police blocked highways and stopped and searched trains, checking over 147,000 identity cards that day.[80] In the midst of the repressive atmosphere of the German Autumn, these popular movements appeared to many people as the last chance to defeat nuclear Nazism and to save any remnant of democracy in Germany. The desperation felt by many turned into bitter confrontations. In northern Germany, resistance to nuclear power went far beyond the mild-mannered protests at Wyhl and were often labeled a "civil war" because of the intensity of the fighting. Describing the situation at Brokdorf, Markovits and Gorski commented:

Before construction began, "Fort Brokdorf" emerged—complete with moat, fence, and barbed wire—in order to prevent a repetition of the Wyhl occupation. Four days later, some 30,000 to 45,000 protestors appeared for a rally.... Following the obligatory speeches, 2,000 demonstrators pressed through the police lines, bridged the moat, tore down a segment of the wall under the barrage of water cannons, and occupied a section of the construction site.[81]

Generally speaking, when thousands of people protest so vehemently, they represent a far larger base of discontented people and indicate the future direction in which public opinion will swing. This was clearly the case in the FRG. Although the SPD had missed the antinuclear boat in 1977, grassroots protests shook up the country and gradually brought a majority (including the SPD) into the antinuclear camp.[82] Although it would take a decade of protests and the nuclear catastrophe at Chernobyl to cement the new consensus against fission power, the modest beginnings at Wyhl, Kalkar, and Brokdorf produced major policy changes. In 1977, even some trade unionists defied their own organizations and created an autonomous antinuclear group, Action-Circle for Life.[83]

The first victories won by the antinuclear movement were in the courts. In the climate of public scrutiny of nuclear power caused by the direct-action movement, an administrative court found the Wyhl reactor design to be flawed and banned its construction in March 1977. Similar administrative rulings delayed construction of nuclear installations at Grohnde, Kalkar, Muhlbach-Karlich, and Brokdorf Significantly, the court withdrew the Brokdorf construction license on the grounds that the issue of disposal of the highly toxic nuclear waste had not been adequately addressed. To many people, the administrative decisions seemed like a response to the decisive resistance mounted by the antinuclear movement.

The country became bitterly divided over the issue of nuclear power. In Dortmund, forty thousand trade union members (many from corporations engaged in building the power plants) marched in favor of nuclear power in October 1977 as part of a campaign directed by a public-relations company aimed at preventing the ruling Social Democrats from voting for a temporary moratorium on nuclear power.[84] On the other side, one activist, Hartmut Grundler, burned himself to death the day before the Social Democrats were to decide their energy policy to dramatize his opposition to their waffling. Finally, in November, the SPD voted to accept the pro-nuclear position, but with the proviso that the problem of waste disposal would be dealt with before any further expansion of nuclear power.

Building a nuclear dump site then became the top priority of the nuclear industry. When Gorleben (in the eastern most part of West Germany, jutting into what was then East Germany) was chosen as its location, stopping the project became a unifying focus for the well-developed and experienced antinuclear movement. Gorleben was supposed to be the largest industrial complex in West Germany, and opposition to it quickly generated a huge movement. The mobilization against the construction at Gorleben was initiated in 1977 by local farmers, and on March 31, 1979, they drove hundreds of tractors and marched more than 100,000 strong on the nearby city of Hannover.[85] After the accident at Three Mile Island in the United States, construction was temporarily halted, but when it began again, antinuclear activists from all parts of the country (and many other nations as well) gathered together as Wendlanders. For one month, from May 3 to June 6, 1980, five thousand activists staged a live-in on the grounds where the German nuclear industry had already begun constructing a huge underground waste disposal site for radioactive by-products from reactors in Germany and other countries served by the transnational German nuclear industry. A city was built from the already felled trees—a wonderfully diverse collection of houses—and dubbed the Free Republic of Wendland (a name taken from the region's traditional title). Local farmers, about 90 percent of whom were against the nuclear dump yard, provided the thousands of resident-activists with food and materials to help build their "republic." Passports were issued bearing the name of the new republic, imaginative illegal underground radio shows were broadcast, and newspapers were printed and distributed throughout the country. Speaking personally, Gorleben was one of the few places I felt at home in German public life. Unlike in normal everyday life, I did not feel like an outsider. No one approached me as a Turk nor reproached me for being an American. Indeed, national identities were temporarily suspended, since we were all citizens of the Free Republic of Wendland and owed allegiance to no government. We became human beings in some essential meaning of the term, sharing food and living outside the system of monetary exchange. An erotic dimension was created that simply could not be found in normal interaction.

Wendlanders lived together not only to build a confrontation but also to create a space for autonomous self-government through political discussion. Nearly everyone joyfully participated in the heated debates, whose main topic was how best to prepare for the inevitable police assault. At the same time, there was wide discussion of the future direction of the movement. Wendland was a time and space of openness, of sharing and friendliness. It contrasted sharply with everyday life in Germany, which was characterized by the hierarchy of patriarchal families, the uniformity of small-town life, the authoritarianism of the modernized Prussian bureaucracy, and the competition of corporate culture. After seemingly endless discussions, the Wendlanders democratically agreed on a tactic of passive, nonviolent resistance to the police, a tactic that served its short-term purpose remarkably well.

On June 3, 1986, when the largest deployment of police in Germany since Hitler—some eight thousand strong—violently attacked the sitting Wendlanders (as well as numerous reporters and photographers), thousands of people around the country were outraged. Once the site was cleared of people, the huts were razed and barbed-wire fences erected around the construction zone. But the police brutality against nonviolent demonstrators did not slow the movement or intimidate people; it radicalized thousands of people who had lived at the Free Republic of Wendland and their growing ranks of supporters. That same day, well-organized, peaceful protest marches occurred in over twenty-five cities. In six cities, churches were nonviolently occupied by small groups of protesters. More than fifteen thousand people gathered at Savigny Platz and marched in Berlin, and at the end of the march, speakers from the Free Republic of Wendland called for the occupation of parks and empty buildings as a base to continue the struggle. Although only a few people immediately did so (and were soon cleared out by the police), the Gorleben struggle had created a radical core of resistance that had a national membership. A motley assortment, including ecologists, feminists, students, alienated youth, and farmers, galvanized themselves into an extraparliamentary cultural-political movement of resistance not only to nuclear power but also to the system that relied on it.

The changed character of the movement became obvious on February 28, 1981, at Brokdorf. Building of the Brokdorf plant had been delayed after bitter confrontations in 1976, but when construction began again at the beginning of February 1981, it took less than a month for the movement to respond. Although the state government and Federal Constitutional Court prohibited demonstrations, over 100,000 protesters converged on police barricades around the construction site of the nuclear power station. About ten thousand police and soldiers were mobilized to protect the construction site. At and around Brokdorf, however, the assembled forces of law and order were unable to beat up passive, nonviolent resisters as at Gorleben. This time, the police themselves were under attack. Their heavily fortified bridges over icy streams were quickly cleared by foolhardy demonstrators who braved the waters in extremely cold weather and went on to beat back the "bulls—as police are sometimes referred to in Germany. Even though many of the buses carrying demonstrators had been stopped by police miles away, and concentric rings of police defense guarded the approaches to the construction site, thousands of people managed to converge on the last circle of fences around Brokdorf and attack it with sticks, rocks, and Molotov cocktails. The police responded with massive blasts of tear gas fired from within the construction compound, and (in a tactic modeled on U.S. search-and-destroy missions in Indochina) groups of twenty to thirty police were sporadically dropped from thirty-five helicopters to beat back demonstrators until a counterattack was organized, and then relifted to safety in the skies. By the end of the day, the construction site itself was still intact, but a new level of resistance had been reached by the movement against nuclear power. The passive nonviolence of Gorleben had given way to massive active confrontation.

For many people, it was all but impossible to embrace tactics of active resistance or violent confrontation, to do more than risk arrest and accept the violence of the police. Even for many people who were heavily involved in *Bürgerinitiativen*, nonviolent tactics such as voting or attending peaceful marches were as far as their consciences (or fears) permitted them to venture from their patterns of political participation. Based on the teachings of Gandhi and Martin Luther King, pacifism should have been a welcome phenomenon in Germany, where militarism is so near the core of cultural identity. Instead, NATO generals and German politicians echoed each other's deep concerns that postwar prosperity and permissiveness had produced a generation incapable of resisting Russian aggression.

The dialectical tension between pacifism and its militarist opposite was at the core of both inner movement discussions and dynamics of the world system during this period. From 1981 to 1983, antinuclear weapons marches involved millions of Europeans. For a century, German pacifists had been opposing war, and as late as 1968, they had helped organize huge Easter marches for nuclear disarmament. After the demise of 1960s protests, the first sign of a renewed peace movement came from a women's group in 1975, and as church groups joined in, mobilizations against nuclear weapons exceeded anyone's expectations: 300,000 marched in October 1981 in Bonn; 400,000 people protested when President Reagan addressed the *Bundestag* the following summer. At rejuvenated Easter marches, 500,000 people turned out in 1982 and more than 650,000 in 1983.[86]

The new peace movement combined many levels of organization and action. Besides a Communist-dominated coalition and a variety of committees linked to churches and political parties, radical activists organized their own independent coalition in 1982. Although all these groups united, for example, in a national petition campaign that gathered more than two million signatures, the uneasy alliance among vastly dissimilar activist formations became unmanageable in the summer of 1983, when hundreds of rock-throwing demonstrators attacked the limousine carrying Vice President George Bush in Krefeld. For many people in the peace movement, the legacy of German militarism was seen as responsible for such confrontational currents.

As their militant actions became attacked even by their allies, radicals became increasingly autonomous—some would say isolated—from mainstream protesters and came to constitute their own source of collective identity. As a tactic, militant confrontation may have helped make peaceful marches seem a more acceptable course of action for many people who were afraid to be photographed at a peace rally, but violence also helped the government make its case that protests were dangerous and counterproductive. Radicals from the peace movement merged with similar tendencies in movements against nuclear power, resurgent militarism, and the expansion of Frankfurt's airport.

During late October and early November 1981, an action similar to Gorleben occurred near Frankfurt as thousands of people attempted to stop a new runway from being built at the international airport. This time, however, when the police attacked the massed protesters in their *Hüttendorf* (village of huts), a majority fought back. They had lived in their structures since May 1980 and had built a remarkable movement based in the local towns that would be most affected by the runway.[87] Early in the morning on November 2, police brutally cleared out the sleeping inhabitants of the huts, indiscriminately beating women, children, and senior citizens as they fled through the forest. Despite the police savagery, people tried to rebuild the huts the next day, and for two straight weeks, a spontaneous movement involving tens of thousands of people at all hours of the day and night refused to accept Startbahn West's construction. Besides small groups practicing active nonviolence by disrupting train stations, sponsoring strikes at school, and occupying offices, there were huge mobilizations. On November 7, 40,000 people demonstrated at the building site, and a week later, 150,000 people assembled in Wiesbaden at the state capital to deliver over 220,000 signatures calling for a popular referendum.[88] People simply refused to stay home. Risking police violence, they continually reconstructed the *Hüttendorf* only to experience further brutality on November 25 and January 26.[89] Every Sunday for the next six years (until the shooting deaths of two policemen on November 2, 1987), hundreds—sometimes thousands—of people took a "Sunday walk" along the runway to dramatize their opposition. Despite having to accept a defeat after over two decades of action against the runway, activists from the Startbahn West struggles played critical roles in the peace movement and later in the successful campaign to shut down a nuclear reprocessing facility at Wackersdorf, and the local Greens made tremendous headway in the state parliament.

In other parts of the country, comparable radical groups emerged. In 1980, hundreds of helmeted demonstrators attacked the annual induction ceremonies of the *Bundeswehr* (the army of West Germany) at the soccer stadium in Bremen. Part of the stadium and many empty buses that had been used to transport the new recruits to their induction were set in flames by Molotov cocktails. In Bonn and Hannover, similar ceremonies were laid siege to, part of the wave of militant demonstrations against NATO plans to deploy medium-range nuclear missiles. The radicalization of so many people in various parts of the country grew out of a militant squatters' movement that had occupied hundreds of houses in inner cities. These collectives infused the radical movement with its cutting edge and provided a core of thousands of activists capable of focusing the diverse energies of the radical movement. Nowhere were the group houses more important than in West Berlin, center of the punk scene, feminism, and anti-authoritarian revolt that had suddenly become internationally visible through the peace movement.

MÜSLIS AND MOLLIS: FROM THE NEW LEFT TO THE PUNK LEFT

In 1980, the dependence of local politics and economics on the world constellation of power was nowhere more clear than in Berlin. Then a divided city with occupation troops from the United States, Great Britain, France, and the Soviet Union in control, Berlin was home to hundreds of thousands of immigrant workers and their families from Turkey, the Middle East, and southern Europe. The "economic miracle" of postwar West Berlin—the city's gross national product increased tenfold from 1950 to 1973—owed much to national and international assistance and to the foreign workers who traveled far from home to take jobs that were too hard, too monotonous, too dangerous, too dirty, or too low-paid for Germans to have even considered. In 1931, West Berlin had the fifth largest Turkish population of any city in the world, and according to government statistics, more than two million foreign workers and their families resided in West Germany, a country with a population of 61.4 million.

By 1975, the economic miracle seemed to have a hollow ring as a deep recession set in. Many foreign workers went home as the number of unemployed in Germany topped one million for the first time since 1954.[90] In 1980, unemployment rose to include about two million Germans. West Berlin was particularly hard hit, not only as a result of the international economic downturn but also by a series of financial scandals as well. The magazine *Der Spiegel* put it succinctly: "The city is being made poorer because financial capital is plundering the government's bank account." The Berlin construction industry operated with a profit rate around 120 percent, but greedy developers and their politician friends were the subjects of three major scandals. At the same time, a housing crisis of immense proportion was touched off by an informal capital strike by big landlords after the passage of rent control and tough protection laws for tenants, which coincided with the beginning of the recession in 1974. The construction of new housing had peaked in 1973 because it was extremely profitable for landlords to abandon their buildings and thereby become eligible for low-interest city loans to build condominiums for the upper middle class. Seventeen thousand people without anyplace to live were registered with the local housing authority as cases of "extreme emergency," but well over fifty thousand Berliners were looking desperately for somewhere to live, even though estimates showed that there were between seven thousand and seventeen thousand empty houses and apartments,[91] and an additional forty thousand apartments were expected to be cleared out for renovation or destruction. Under these conditions, is it surprising that people without places to live simply moved into some of the scores of abandoned buildings?

The movement spontaneously constructed a base in Kreuzberg. Adjacent to the wall separating East and West Berlin, Kreuzberg had a sizable Turkish population and countercultural scene. Hundreds of abandoned buildings along the wall were an invitation for squatters, and beginning in the late 1970s, organized groups of fifty or more people successfully seized many buildings. At its high point, the squatters' movement in Berlin controlled 165 houses, each containing more than a dozen people. They restored abandoned buildings to liveable conditions, giving birth to a new word (*Instandbesetzen*, or rehab-squat). When their actions were construed as an attack on private property, the squatters responded: "It is better to occupy for restoration than to own for destruction." In March 1980, they formed a squatters' council (*Besetzerrat*) that met weekly. In the 1980s, thousands of adherents of an "alternative scene" established themselves in Kreuzberg, and by the end of the decade, they constituted approximately 30,000 of Kreuzberg's 145,000 residents. One estimate of Kreuzberg's composition was 50,000 "normal" Berliners, 30,000 to 40,000 from the alternative scene, and 40,000 Turks.[92]

For decades, young Germans had moved to Berlin. Since the city was not formally a part of West Germany (but governed by the Allies), young German men who lived in Berlin were exempt from mandatory military service. The city's radical tradition and comparatively liberal nature also attracted many youth, as did the Free University and the Technical University, two of Germany's best and largest universities. Out of the congruence of these various conditions, a radical Berlin "youth" scene appeared, largely composed of people who were either unwilling or unable to become integrated into middle-class German society. The city government estimated that this stratum of marginalized youth comprised at least 150,000 people in all of Berlin, and it expressed concern that many of them were not only opposed to the established parties, to the government, and to nuclear power and weapons, but were also unable to accept as legitimate the middle-class values of their parents.[93] According to another government study, 20 percent of the squatters in Berlin in 1980 were marginalized people looking for an alternative lifestyle, and the other 80 percent were evenly divided between students and poorly paid industrial apprentices. Although viewed as a problem by government officials, the squatters actually fixed up their buildings and the neighborhoods they lived in. They helped turn sections of Kreuzberg from largely deserted ghost towns and no-man's lands alongside the "Iron Curtain" into vibrant multicultural enclaves.

The squatters' movement began where the APO had left off—with the fusion of a cultural politics. But this time, punk rock became the music of the movement. Punk was part of the breaking free of established routine and the constraints imposed by the cultural order. After mainstream rock 'n roll had become big money, punk was fresh. Because it was a marginal phenomenon, bands played for their friends at private parties, not in amphitheaters filled with masses. Punk music was a means of unleashing aggressive reaction against the dominant circumstances of conformity and consumerism.[94] If there was something hard-core about punk, the most hard-core of the new generation of activists felt dutybound to defend imprisoned guerrillas. Rather than being rejected as sterile and counterproductive, the commando tactics that contributed to the New Left's demise were supplanted by anarchy and disorder as the specters raised by the movement's militant fringe. "No power to anyone," a popular slogan in 1981, sharply contradicted all brands of established politics, whether that of the young social democrats who ran for student government or that of the cadre of the new communist parties. The black leather jackets worn by many people at demonstrations and the black flags carried by others signaled less an ideological anarchism than a style of dress and behavior—symbols of a way of life that made contempt for the established institutions and their U.S. "protectors" into a virtue, on an equal footing with disdain for the "socialist" governments in Eastern Europe. Black became the color of the political void—of the withdrawal of allegiance to parties, governments, and nations. Nude marches and an unwillingness to communicate with politicians were facets of this phase of the movement, causing order-addicted German authorities more than a little consternation. When Hamburg Mayor Ulrich Klose invited the staff members of the city's high school newspaper to city hall, five of the students came and stayed only long enough to reveal circled "A"s painted on their bare behinds.

Such flagrant violations of the social code testified to the delegitimation already suffered by the nation's institutions, but a nihilistic moment of the opposition was reproduced within the movement. When a virtuous contempt for the social order is carried over into activist circles, it becomes highly destructive, especially when there are many deep divisions within the multifarious new movement. Of all the internal differences, the most commonly named one was between punks and hippies, or, as it was known in Germany, between *Mollis* (people who might throw Molotovs) and *Müslis* (a reference to a breakfast cereal that is a little softer than granola). Generally, the Müsli Left referred to long-haired, ecology-oriented activists who were into passive nonviolence, large-scale educational projects, communal living, and the development of a harmonious, liberated sensibility in relation to all life. The Müsli Left was considered "soft" in contrast to the Punk Left's cultural rebellion and professed affinity for violent confrontations, a politics quickly dubbed the "hard line." To generalize once again, the Müslis gravitated to the country (especially the area around Wendland, where scores of organic farms sprang up); the punks were inner-city dwellers. Punks were harder and colder, dressed in black, and were male centered, whereas Müslis were warmer, rainbow, and female oriented. These two strands were intimately woven together in the movement's political culture.

The squatters defied simple classification: from rockers with working-class roots to feminists, recent immigrants from Turkey to the elderly, students to single mothers, and born-again Christians to ideological anarchists, they were more a motley collection than a self-defined collectivity of mainly students like the New Left was. As living behind barricades became a way of life for many squatters, the illegality of their everyday lives radicalized their attitude toward the state and hardened their own feeling of self-importance.

When they moved against the squatters, German authorities adopted a course of action that sought to criminalize and punish hundreds of people whose only "crime" was having nowhere to live and moving into a vacant house. This hard-line approach further radicalized large numbers of young people, pushing many into desperate acts of resistance to perceived injustice. Beginning in December 1980, police attacks on squatted houses in West Berlin touched off an escalating spiral of mass arrests, street fighting, and further occupations. Over a hundred persons were arrested and more than twice that number injured there when barricade building and heavy street fighting lasted through the cold night of Friday, December 12. The squatters' movement quickly spread throughout West Germany and collided head-on with Bavarian order.

The conservative Christian Democratic government in southern Germany had long been critical of attempts to "compromise" with the squatters by its scandal-ridden Social Democratic colleagues in Berlin. The Christian Democrats showed their own method of governing when 141 young people attending a film about squatters in an occupied house in Nürnberg were rounded up by police after the building was surrounded. Even though many of those arrested were under sixteen years old and guilty of nothing more than going to a movie, they were held incommunicado for seventy-two hours or more, and in many cases, the police refused to tell concerned parents whether their missing children were under arrest. The resulting outrage among generally conservative middle-class Germans became the prime story of the nation's television stations and newspapers, but it did not stop the Christian Democrats from bringing criminal charges against some arrested minors and defending the largest mass arrest in Germany since World War II. As the number of house occupations continued to climb, police in southern Germany surrounded another squatted house, the "Black Forest House" in Freiburg, and again conducted mass arrests.

The Freiburg squatters called for a national day of solidarity demonstrations against the police attacks, and on Friday, March 13, 1981, rallies and demonstrations were held in every major city in West Germany, as well as in many other towns that had not seen a political protest for more than a decade. The biggest demonstration in the history of Freiburg—twenty-one thousand people was a festive affair; more than a thousand showed up in Bremen and Tübingen, and more than two thousand people marched in Stuttgart. In Hamburg, a peaceful demonstration of five thousand people was viciously attacked by police with dogs. On the same day, street fighting and trashing broke out in many cities. On "Black Friday," as that day was dubbed in Berlin, the downtown Kurfürstendamm (which caters to the shopping whims of chic, mainly upper-class customers) was heavily trashed, as it had been many times before. Unlike previous confrontations, the number of people in the streets reached fifteen or possibly twenty thousand, rather than the usual two to three thousand militants. There was a nude march at the same time as small, organized groups of marauders attacked at least thirty-nine buildings. They even set the Reichstag on fire—an ill-conceived attempt to replicate its 1933 destruction through arson, which touched off the Nazi reign of terror.

(Although George Dimitrov and other Communists were blamed for the arson in 1933, it has long been suspected that the fire was set by the Nazis themselves as a pretext for seizing power.)

Die Tageszeitung (*Taz*), the independent radical daily newspaper, estimated that the widespread violence and massive participation in the squatters' movement of Friday the thirteenth greatly exceeded any high points of the late 1960s. Indeed, the defense of Kreuzberg was coordinated by the squatters' council, whose members developed elaborate plans for erecting which barricades to hinder the police's ability to cross canals and main thoroughfares leading into the neighborhood. After the street fighting of December 12, 1980, *Taz* had celebrated the barricades in the spirit of the barricades of 1848, 1919, 1929, and 1967. But on Black Friday, the newspaper's office in Berlin was raided by police and its new issue confiscated from kiosks throughout the country. To top it off, criminal charges were brought against its editors. For some, the political scenario became more reminiscent of the Nazi terror of 1933 than the democratic movement's temporary victory in 1848.

The December barricades and savage street fighting in Berlin set off a political whirlwind. The city's housing crisis was brought into the limelight of the nation's media, scandals rocked the city government, and what to do about the squatters became one of the major political questions in the country. Faced by the strong resistance of the squatters' movement to police attacks, the governing Social Democrats in Berlin put forth a plan to allow the squatters to remain in their occupied houses on the condition that they pay a minimal rent. This offer of compromise brought the Social Democrats under heavy criticism from conservatives, who accused them of condoning illegal occupations of vacant buildings. Within the squatters' movement, the compromise proposal drew the usual yawns, but it also caused a few sharp debates between those who saw it as a way of simply integrating the movement into the system and those who welcomed the opportunity for a short-term solution to their individual housing problems. Although a few groups of squatters collectively decided to begin paying rent, the vast majority did not.

As the number and frequency of occupations continued to grow, the police were instructed to raid only those houses occupied by activists who were suspected of being part of the leadership of the squatters' movement, particularly organizers of demonstrations or publishers of radical periodicals. A few people from each house overrun by the police were then charged under paragraph 129 with membership in a criminal organization—a legal statute carrying a possible life sentence that previously had been used to prosecute only suspected "terrorists." The government attempted to stop the movement's internal discussion and decision-making capacity. On April 7, 1981, the entire squatters' Council (128 people) was arrested. By August 1981, over three hundred people had been brought up on serious charges, the equivalent of conspiracy indictments in the United States.[95]

The squatters had prepared elaborate telephone, radio, and word-of-mouth communication networks through which hundreds of people could be instantaneously mobilized when the police gathered for their attacks, but because Berlin is so spread out, those who would have helped resist the police attacks arrived at the scene too late—long after the barricades inside the occupied houses had been broken through and the residents taken away by the police. With no other alternative in sight, the response of the movement was to begin a new round of street fights by late afternoon on the same day that the police had attacked. This escalating spiral of attacks and counterattacks culminated in the massive outbursts of Black Friday.

After the confrontations of Black Friday, German authorities launched a major national propaganda offensive against the squatters, attempting to isolate and criminalize them by linking them with guerrilla groups. Roman Herzog, then minister of the interior in Baden-Württemberg (and, beginning in 1994, president of the republic), charged that the RAF was infiltrating and recruiting from the squatters' movement. The West German interior minister, Gerhard Baum, claimed to be able to tie seventy of the thirteen hundred known squatters to armed groups. The media pointed out that Knut Folkers, serving a life sentence for terrorism, had been arrested in 1974 in a squatted house, and Susanne Albrecht (whose Face adorned the "Wanted for Terrorism" posters that hung in every post office and many other places in West Germany) had been part of a group that had moved into a vacant house in Hamburg in one of the first occupations in 1973. Positing links between the squats and armed groups was one of the government's chief means of trying to isolate the movement, which in turn refused to ignore the plight of the imprisoned "terrorists." During April 1981, another wave of riots was touched off in Berlin, this time in response to the death of an imprisoned RAF member on a hunger strike.

Although the German movement was under attack and its major daily news source was momentarily silenced on Black Friday, local calls for action aroused mobilizations that surpassed even the most optimistic expectations. After Black Friday, the number of occupied houses jumped from 35 to 160 in West Berlin and from 86 to at least 370 (possibly as many as 500) in all of West Germany.[96] The number of squatters was estimated at between five thousand and eight thousand.[97] Besides vacant apartment buildings, empty factories, breweries, and other commercial spaces cleared for demolition were taken over. These larger buildings provided even more room for groups to create regional cultural and action centers. At the KuKuCK in West Berlin, fifty people lived in a complex that included three stages, performance areas for ten theater groups, practice rooms for five bands, a studio, a café, and an auto repair shop.[98] Besides providing room for larger groups to live near their projects, such spaces were also ways for the movement to involve people at many levels. As one observer noted:

> Creating cultural centers—the Kukuckcentrum, Spectrum Cafe, Bobby Sands Café, [they] took it with the help of alternative mechanic collectives, printing collectives, plumbing collectives, took it with money collected from habitues of alternative cafés, with the help of "Patenschaften," literally "Godparent" groups, support groups of teachers, union members, artists, doctors, lawyers who created a moat around occupied housing, keeping the alligators at bay, pledging to sleep in when police came.[99]

The movement had moved into a new phase: instead of demanding alternative youth centers from the government (as in Zurich), they took matters into their own hands, defied the authorities, and defended their centers. Autonomy had become real, not simply an abstract aspiration or phase of rebellion against parental control trips. On March 29, over one thousand people converged on Münster for the first national congress of squatters. Vowing to fight the state's criminalization of their movement, the assembled squatters promised to spread the occupations further. In October, the squatters' council in Berlin wrote an open letter to the city's citizens. Asserting that without police attacks, there would be no riots, the letter provides an insightful exposition on the meaning of autonomy as it explains the motivation for squatting houses:

> When we occupied them, it was not only for preserving living space. But we also wanted to live and work together again. We want to put a stop to the process of isolation and destruction of collective living. Who in this city is not aware of the torturing loneliness and emptiness of everyday life that arose with the growing destruction of the old connections through urban redevelopment and other kinds of development of the city? This has driven more people out of their apartments than the war.[100]

The governing Social Democrats' inability to stop the new occupations led to a new hard-line Christian Democratic government in Berlin, but its offensive against the squatters proved of little value. The movement's response to an ultimatum issued by the new mayor demanding that the squatters clear out of eight houses was a poster of ten people mooning the government and an international call to *Tu Wat* (Do Something). Although some optimistically estimated that fifty thousand Autonomen from all of Europe would converge on Berlin to defend the squatted houses, at the appointed hour, less than five thousand people took to the streets—not an insignificant number when we remember that there were no more than a couple of hundred Weatherpeople in the streets of Chicago during the Days of Rage in 1969.

In 1981, the government's inability to defeat the squatters in the streets led to a tactical innovation: legalize the squatted houses in the large cities, thereby depriving the movement of a focus for action and, more importantly, of a sense of fighting against the existing system. Legalization meant that those who were previously living an everyday existence of resistance to a repressive order were suddenly transformed into guests of a tolerant big brother who provided them not only with low-rent houses but also with money to repair them. On the one side was the carrot—but the state continued to alternate its use with the stick, hoping not only to split off the movement's hard core from the marginal supporters but also to drive more militant activists into underground actions that would alienate and depoliticize the popular movement. As long as the struggle was between the forces of law and order and militant street fighters and "terrorists," the vast majority had little choice but to sit on the sidelines and take in the spectacle.

Of course, in the smaller cities and towns, places where the movement's activist base was small, the government's tolerance was never known. Squatted houses were simply cleared soon after they were occupied, and the local authorities were able to contain what militant opposition there was. In the larger cities such as Berlin, Hamburg, and Frankfurt, however, legalization was an important factor in the depoliticization of the movement. Even when the new city government in Berlin brought massive police power to bear against the squatters, they were not able to force the movement out of existence. Over a year of legalizations and intense police attacks succeeded only in reducing the number of squatted houses in West Berlin from 162 to 123, but the continuing crisis refused to disappear. The government estimated that only 25 of these 123 houses were active squats, the rest being composed of either "drop-outs" or peaceful squatters ready to negotiate. The hard-core squats were targeted by the police, while the rest were brought to the bargaining table.[101]

Despite the severe repression, the political impact of the squatters on the established system was far greater than anyone imagined. Although often overlooked, the relationship between extraparliamentary movements and the political system is worth exploring, particularly in the case of West Berlin, since its constellation of direct-action movements and establishment politics prefigured the alignment of national political forces a few years later.

THE ELECTIONS IN BERLIN

At the beginning of 1981, the West Berlin city parliament was forced to resign in scandal, when state-insured loans to the firm of architect Dietrich Garski became due. Already rocked by similar scandals, the city was forced to shell out 115 million marks (at that time, about $60 million) when Garski's company ran out of money while building two military academies in the Saudi Arabian desert. Insult was added to injury when it became publicly known that Garski had personally designed what *Der Spiegel* joined others in calling "the ugliest new buildings in West Berlin" (Aschinger at Bahnhof Zoo).[102]

As continuing political violence polarized the city, the radical Alternative Liste (AL) ran candidates for office claiming to represent the squatters. A conglomeration of ecologists, squatters, Turks and other immigrants, radical pacifists, women's groups, theoreticians, and activists from the New Left of the 1960s, the AL also included a few ideologues from the small 1970s new communist movement (generally Maoists who had been active from its origins). The AL also coalesced with more than thirty-five citizens' initiative groups (who previously confined their energies to putting issues—not candidates—on the ballot), with some senior citizens' groups, and with the local Greens. (West Berliners were not eligible to vote in elections in West Germany because the city was governed by Allied occupation forces.) The local Greens—themselves plagued by scandals—joined the more radical AL, which then became, in effect, the local arm of the national Green Party. Much to the credit of the AL, foreign workers residing in Berlin—although legally barred from voting or holding office—were also run as candidates on the AL ticket.

AL members were highly intellectual, and they did not use charisma, huge amounts of money, or celebrities to win votes. Rather, they attempted to involve hundreds of people in creating a radical political force within the government as part of a larger movement. The AL succeeded in attracting Berlin's leftist intelligentsia, and in its formative years, the organization often had all-night meetings where global questions such as East-West relations and the divided status of Berlin were debated. Hundreds of position papers on a vast range of issues were written and discussed in the course of the AL's preparation for its first electoral campaigns. Its platform included strong positions against NATO and

TABLE 3.1

MAY 1981 WEST BERLIN ELECTION RESULTS

	SEATS	PERCENTAGE	COMPARISON WITH 1979
Christian Democrats	60	47.3%	+2.8%
Social Democrats	49	38.4%	-4.3%
Free Democrats	7	5.5%	-2.6%
Alternative List	9	7.9%	+4.2%

advocated reducing the garrisons of the Allied powers to purely symbolic forces. In 1981, when no one seriously considered the possibility, the AL came out in favor of the reunification of Germany as a way to establish a nuclear-free zone in central Europe.

The AL rode the wave of popular unrest in Berlin. In March 1981, when the squatters' movement was fighting with the police, polls gave the AL as much as 15 percent of the vote, and it did not back away from this noncoincidence; the AL publicized the fact that one of its offices was located in a squatted house and particularly pushed its candidates who lived behind barricades. (The Christian Democrats responded in kind, vetoing the nomination of one of their candidates who was accidentally discovered to have a residence in a squatted house and, in the name of law and order, calling for no compromises with the squatters.) Because of its strong stand against nuclear power and weapons, the AL pledged not to coalesce with the pro-nuclear power and antisquatter Social Democrats, a position that helped garner votes for the AL from many people who generally boycotted elections.

On May 10, 1981, the ruling Social Democratic-Free Democratic coalition government was voted out by West Berliners. The number of votes received by Berlin's Social Democrats fell to the lowest level since before the Nazi putsch. Table 3.1 summarizes the results of the election.

In absolute numbers, the Social Democrats' losses were not so great, but the relative balance of power within the parliament was altered. The Free Democrats barely received enough votes to survive (a minimum of 5 percent was needed to be part of the government), and they continued to "govern" the city, but with a more conservative Christian Democratic partner. On the one hand, the liberal coalition SPD government collapsed, but on the other hand, the AL, which some regarded as an arm of the movement, entered the senate for the first time. Although the mass media called the vote a shift to the Right, the real winner was the radical AL, which nearly doubled its tally from two years before and won seats in the government for the first time.

In alliance with the Free Democrats, the Christian Democrats were in a position to form a new majority coalition with a clear mandate to force an end to the mushrooming squatters' movement. The first step taken by the new conservative Berlin government was to break off all negotiations with the squatters and call in the police against them. The CDU was determined to make the Berlin squatters into a national example. Twice after the elections—on May 26 and June 25 to 26—police attacks were met by street fighting of the intensity of Black Friday. Even after the media called it a "civil war," the Christian Democrats continued to believe that they could accomplish through force what the Social Democrats had sought at the bargaining table, and they vowed to clear out ten of the key squatter strongholds during the last week in August. In response, the squatters put out the *Tu Wat* call, inviting activists to come to Berlin and defend the movement.

On September 13, 1981, amid a flurry of guerrilla attacks on U.S. personnel and bases in West Germany, over seven thousand riot police were needed to guard Secretary of State Haig from at least fifty thousand demonstrators in West Berlin, and in the ensuing turmoil, hundreds were arrested and over 150 police injured.[103] When the street fighting returned to more "normal" levels, the police were vicious. On September 22, Klaus-Jürgen Rattey, an eighteen-year-old squatter, was killed (run over by a city bus) during the melee after two thousand riot police charged eight occupied houses in Winterfeldplatz. The next night, heavy rioting broke out in ten West German cities (as well as in Amsterdam), and there were over fifty attacks on corporate and government targets in West Berlin.[104] Only then did the Christian Democrats back off. On September 26, the stalemate was formally announced; no more attacks on squatters—the *Bundestag* would debate the housing question.

The crisis in Berlin had an immediate national impact, and the results of the elections there were replicated in other places. In 1982 in Hamburg, for example, the electoral forces aligned with the radical movement did even better: the Free Democrats were unable to stay in the government when the Green Alternative List (Hamburg's equivalent of the AL) won more than enough to be represented, and the SPD won a majority. Although the numbers varied a little, the Berlin and Hamburg election results of 1981 were duplicated in the national elections of March 1983, allowing the entrance of the Green Party into the *Bundestag* for the first time. By receiving over two million votes (5.6 percent of the total), the Greens captured twenty-seven seats in the *Bundestag* and became part of the electoral opposition to Chancellor Helmut Kohl's new Christian Democratic national government. In local elections the next year, the Greens surpassed their national performance: one estimate placed the number of Greens elected to local government entities by 1984 at between five and seven thousand.[105] Having lost hundreds of thousands of voters to the Greens, the SPD shifted in the direction of Green positions. While the Greens called for the end of the Cold War division of Europe into blocs, SPD politicians quickly took up the movement's call for a nuclear-free zone.[106] A former Social Democratic mayor of West Berlin was heard describing himself as a German patriot, and representatives from the Free Democrats also spoke out for a "German nationalism of the Left."

Although the Greens' success is most often understood as a reaction to NATO's new missiles or to the abysmal state of German rivers and forests, it was no coincidence that it accompanied the growth of extraparliamentary movements that militantly contested government control of cities and national policies regulating nuclear power and weapons. As the call for the demonstrations at Brokdorf put it: "Who still believes that even a particle of the corrupt politics in Berlin would have become known if not for the house occupations and the street fighting—that there would be a discussion about the Bundeswehr and NATO, without the resistance in Bremen, Hannover, Bonn?" Despite its political impact, the extraparliamentary Left in Berlin emanated from a source of politics that had little to do with elections, nor could the political establishment greatly affect it. Strata of marginalized youth developed a way of life that stood in opposition to the established system. As I discuss in the next section, their spontaneously generated forms of organization provide significant and innovative ways of generating popular opposition.

THE STRUCTURE OF SPONTANEITY

Parliamentary groups operate according to the logic of the established political system. The first rule of any party must be to obey the law. To ensure members' compliance with existing rules for participation in the government, a structure must be maintained that is compatible with the state. Insurgent social movements aimed at limiting the power of government and creating autonomy seek forms of decision-making of a qualitatively different kind. The organic structures of the popular sources of the Autonomen (feminists, squatters, ecologists, and alternatives) were loose tactical organizations within which many people with diverse viewpoints could debate differences and democratically participate in formulating programs and making decisions. General assemblies open to all were the final decision-making bodies of the Berlin squatters, as were similar gatherings at Gorleben. Within these general assemblies, decisions were reached as often as possible through the consensus of hundreds of people, a process that sought to maximize participation and nurture the expansion of activists' political consciousness. Sometimes smaller groups were delegated by the general assembly, but only to carry out the will of the larger group.

In Berlin, the individual houses were the building blocks of the movement, serving as its eyes and ears. Democratic self-discipline among the squatters made it possible to avoid an overdose of centralism. Composed of representatives from each house who shared information and made strategic decisions, the squatters' council functioned as a forum where rumors and news were discussed, and it also linked the movement with its counterparts in other cities and countries. Self-discipline was evident in the special care taken not to produce media stars or individual leaders. More often than not, television crews could not find anyone willing to speak with them.

The antinuclear movement was similarly decentralized and bottom-up. Locally organized action committees put out the calls for both the Gorleben occupation and the actions at Brokdorf. Although national coordination existed for both mobilizations, there was no centralized antinuclear organization that developed a national strategy or steadied the movement's ups and downs. Apparently, such centralization was considered superfluous, since the antinuclear movement continued to build its mobilization capacities and popular support without it and ultimately stopped the construction of all new plants. As antinuclear weapons demonstrations grew more massive, two large national coalitions formed, one composed of independents, and the other dominated by Communists.

In the mid-1970s, autonomous groups first came together as vehicles for activists who were not organized into Marxist parties to discuss practical issues of tactics and strategy. By creating spaces in which fresh perspectives on militance and spontaneity could be articulated, these small autonomous groups helped steer the antinuclear and alternative movements clear of the ossified thinking of the traditional Left (although the same was not true of the disarmament movement and the Greens). Few if any Marxist groups showed up at Gorleben, a blessing in disguise that allowed the movement there the space to develop its own analysis and experiences (from which many people were further radicalized). The squatters' and antinuclear movements similarly constructed space in which popular initiatives governed by democratic forms of decision-making and wide-ranging debates were possible. Even within these free forums, however, rigid thinking appeared, as illustrated in the following example. At the same time as the Free Republic of Wendland was in its first week of existence, over a thousand socialists, ecologists, activists from alternative institutions, and "nondogmatic" leftists gathered at a conference in Kassel to discuss "Ecology and Socialism." In one of the keynote speeches, Green member Rudolf Bahro (formerly an imprisoned critic of the regime in East Germany) maintained that the workers' movement could not and should not continue to be separated from the ecology question. This statement brought on hours of debate with the conference's orthodox Marxists, who expressed strong reservations about the "value of environmental politics as a part of the workers' movement."

Another source of the Autonomen was the alternative movement: a collection of self-managed institutions built up to serve the everyday needs of the movement. Bookstores, bars, free schools, ecology centers, food stores, cooperative living groups *(Wohngemeinschaften)*, and day-care centers were created by activists throughout West Germany. In West Berlin, where the alternative movement was particularly strong, the movement entrenched itself in the Kreuzberg neighborhood. *Die Tageszeitung*, grew to a daily national circulation of over fifty thousand.[107] According to government statistics, in February 1982, anywhere from thirteen hundred to fifteen hundred new "self help" groups in West Berlin involved 15,000 volunteers in projects affecting 80,000 to 100,000 people.[108] These alternative institutions spawned a self-help network (*Netzwerk*). Each person put a small part of his or her monthly salary into the network, and these funds were then given or lent to various projects and new or needy alternative institutions. In its first year of existence beginning in October 1978, *Netzwerk* assembled a membership of over thirty-six hundred people and distributed about 300,000 marks (then over $150,000).[109] It quickly grew in membership and resources, and it served as a model in more than thirty-six other cities.[110]

Like the feminist movement, each of these sources of the autonomous movement (squatters, the antinuclear movement, and the alternatives) shared a similar decentralized, bottom-up form of organization as well as a common belief in immediate action decided upon by participants, not by commanders. In the contemporary world, is there a need for a Leninist centralized organization to bring scientific consciousness to the masses? Or does the conscious spontaneity of the Autonomen contain its own transcendental universality? The organized spontaneity of the squatters' council and other organically generated groups seems to prove that rigidly centralized organizational models are superfluous and even destructive. By creating forms of direct democratic decision-making that necessitate popular involvement, autonomous movements unleash a process that, when allowed to proceed according to its own logic, continually enlarges its constituency and further radicalizes its adherents. Unlike the epoch in which Leninist centralism was formulated, we live amidst jet planes and global news broadcasts, developments that make international connections intuitively obvious to the most casual activist. Fax machines, tape recorders, and e-mail help integrate time and space, facilitating the sharing of experiences and making it possible to overcome regional isolation. Free radios and independent print shops make informational ties globally possible from the base.

Without centralized organization, however, political discussions at public meetings were seldom coherent enough to produce unity or to have an effect on anyone other than those who happened to show up at a given time and place. Despite clear similarities among the various incarnations of the decentralized impulse for autonomy (feminism, peace, squatters, alternatives, ecology), few attempts were made to understand their shared political content. Since there was no centralized organization of the movement, a fragmentation of the movement's consciousness and theory accompanied its multifarious activism. Worst of all, in the midst of escalating mobilizations and confrontations with the police, the movement's energies were often directed by the most militant activists, whose presumably higher level of commitment and sacrifice gave them the moral high ground from which they pontificated on the need for armed resistance and on the facilely criticized tendencies from which they were distanced.

Ideally, the movement would have found a process whereby each of its parts would be strengthened by criticism. Instead, each wing of the movement considered itself in isolation from the others. All too often, spokespeople and articles sought to legitimate the "correct" nature of their position. In December 1980, for example, Wolfgang Pohrt wrote a review in *Der Spiegel* of the book *Wer Soll das alles Ändern?* ("Who Should Change It All?"), a portrayal and analysis of the German alternative movement by Joseph Huber. In a scathing attack on Huber and the alternatives, Pohrt accused them of having Nazi tendencies and of succumbing to what Adorno had named the "authoritarian syndrome." Rather than examining the sectarian character of Pohrt's attack on the alternatives, many militants in Berlin greeted the harsh rebuff of the alternatives as further proof of the rightness of their contempt for the "petit bourgeois" alternative institutions. *Radikal*, Berlin's local underground newspaper, whose editors were among those facing criminal charges, reprinted the review from *Der Spiegel* without even soliciting a response from Huber. A movement whose internal process involves glib slander of individuals without simultaneously providing means of discussion of such allegations is no more democratic than established politics. The coarse form and politically insulting content of Pohrt's review are examples of the paltriness of the inner life of the movement, a process in which friendly disagreements are turned into major antagonisms.* But Pohrt is only one example among many. At one point, the squatters' council was unable to continue meeting because fistfights broke out among the diverse participants.

Pragmatic activism and decentralization are certainly healthy qualities when counterposed to the totalitarianism of the Nazis, and they testify to the grassroots strength of the movement as well. However, the fragmentation and atomization of the youthful movement's theory and practice can also be seen as reflections of the centrifugal force of corporate capitalism and German culture. From this point of view, the anti-intellectualism and aggression of some activists are a spontaneous carrying over of some of the worst characteristics of present-day Germany, not the self-conscious or collective creations of a liberatory movement. In the contemporary context, self-defeating tendencies (what Herbert Marcuse called "psychic Thermidor") are extraordinarily important problems of social movements, and later in this book, I return to the issues of organization and internal reaction.

Another question posed by the forms of interaction discussed above is that of the movement's self-definition. Because some of the alternative institutions received financial support from the state, for example, some people questioned whether these groups were actually part of the autonomous movement. A few critical voices went further, asserting that the alternative institutions and the West Berlin scene (including the squatters) were nothing more than "political Disneylands" where young people could go through their adolescent rebellion, after which they would "come to their senses" and fill the niches of the bureaucracy and the offices of big corporations. Other autonomists responded that the building of a new society is not an abstraction or to be reserved for the distant future and that the abandoned inner cities were precisely where free space to begin building a new society was created. Because many radicals bitterly condemned the alternative institutions as "the middle class within the movement," it was difficult to even argue the possibility that alternative institutions (such as the distrusted and often spurned Greens) could have either liberatory or co-optive functions, in part depending upon their relationship to a larger social movement. So long as the movement is defined solely by its oppositional moments,

---

* Pohrt's own contradictions were reflected years later in his advocacy of the use of nuclear weapons against Iraq during the Gulf War. He moved from attacking mild-mannered Joseph Huber as a Nazi to calling the antiwar movement in Germany "brownshirts." It was not only in Germany that "left-wing" personalities advocated such extreme positions. Problems such as these are universal and human in scope and are not contained within national boundaries.

it fails to offer alternative forms capable of sustaining it over the long term. Activists opposed nuclear power and weapons, housing policies based on profits for speculators, hierarchy, and patriarchy, but they did not develop to the point where they could offer a socially legitimate alternative that a majority of people could join. The alternative movement is positive insofar as it provides some activists with nonalienating jobs, creates nonhierarchical institutions, and provides a sense of community rooted in friendship. But the alternative institutions can serve as mechanisms of integration when they lead to the commercialization of previously uncommercialized needs, fulfill unmet needs within an oppressive system, help to fine-tune the established system by mitigating its worst excesses, and provide a pool of highly skilled but low paid social workers within "alternative" institutions. The criticism of alternative institutions by activists often helped depoliticize and isolate the alternatives, giving rise to individual and group power trips, greedy takeovers of their resources for individual ends, and authoritarian attempts to control their political content.

Despite their apparent shortcomings, oppositional moments were increasingly transformed from single-issue struggles into a coherent and vital movement. Besides being the driving force behind larger social movements and political adjustments, these militants succeeded in forging a new synthesis of theory and practice. Unknown in Europe since the heady days of Russia's Bolsheviks and Germany's Spartacists, a synthesis naming both capitalism and patriarchy as the structures to be destroyed galvanized itself across national and continental boundaries, as I discuss in the next chapter. More than a decade after the New Left, newly developed youth movements continued to question fundamental premises of industrial civilization. In this questioning was hope for a new kind of society based not on the accumulation of wealth and hierarchical politics but on the improvement of the quality of life for all.

EUROPEAN AUTONOMOUS MOVEMENTS

Within massive mobilizations, whether those of the peace movement, the contestation of nuclear power plants at Brokdorf, or the prolonged attempt to stop the Startbahn West runway in Frankfurt, the role of the Autonomen was to provide the militant cutting edge to popular struggles. By the mid-1980s, they consolidated themselves and served as an organizing base separate from single-issue campaigns and locally defined groups. As I discuss in this chapter, they built urban bases in Berlin, Hamburg, Amsterdam, and Copenhagen. After the high point of autonomous "dual power" of the squatters in Kreuzberg in 1983, activists moved on to other projects and campaigns. By 1984, all the squatted houses in Germany had been legalized, and the antinuclear power and weapons insurgencies were momentarily quiet, but the Autonomen, galvanized in the crucible of years of militant struggles, helped create a "renaissance" of resistance.

The most significant victory won by the autonomous movement occurred at Wackersdorf, Bavaria, the site where a nuclear reprocessing facility was being built that would have had the capacity to provide Germany with bomb-grade plutonium. Twice in 1985–86, Autonomen initiated the occupation of the construction site.[1] Demonstrations of between forty thousand and eighty thousand persons were pulled together with regularity, often despite police bans on such gatherings.[2] On December 12, 870 persons were arrested when the first *Hüttendorf* was cleared out, and on January 7, another 700 people were taken into custody at a nearby encampment.[3] Impressed with the sincerity and determination of the Autonomen, Bavarian farmers and middle-class people became involved in the protracted campaign to prevent Wackersdorf from ever opening. Every weekend for months, thousands of people gathered at the site, and when confrontations occurred, autonomous groups received support from the local population. As one unsympathetic observer put it: "Stunned Germans watched unprecedented scenes on their TV screens as old ladies led masked Autonomen away to hide them from the police, and farmers wielded shovels and pitchforks against police."[4] The response of the authorities was to forbid public events (even the performance of Haydn's *Creation* in June 1987) and private meetings (as when antinuclear groups were prevented from having a national meeting in Regensburg at the end of November 1986). Nonetheless, the movement continued its mobilizations and militant actions, eventually winning closure of Wackersdorf (although the government claimed that it was for technical reasons).

As exemplified at Wackersdorf, autonomous movements synthesized a new militance—neither armed guerrilla actions nor passive civil disobedience. Their conscious spontaneity provided an alternative to party membership that facilitated activism and provided a new means of impacting political developments. Besides Wackersdorf, Autonomen also played a critical role in a victorious campaign against a national census that would have authorized half a million bureaucrats to pry into the private lives of West Germans.[5] During the same time that the Common Market unified European planning and production, autonomous movements resisted world economic developments that impacted cities and regions without taking local needs into account. Opposition to gentrification and capital-intensive building projects, exemplified in the struggles against Startbahn West and Wackersdorf, is part of the defense of localized life—worlds being destroyed by the giant governments and global corporations.

Despite conservative interpretations of autonomy as meaning isolation from the rest of the world—or worse, autonomy at the expense of others, as in the case of Serbia—the type of autonomy practiced by the transnational Autonomen was in harmony with the downtrodden. In solidarity with the "wretched of the earth," they acted according to ethical and moral imperatives of international solidarity. In June 1987, the day before Ronald Reagan paid his second presidential visit to Berlin, more than fifty thousand people went into the streets to protest, and ten thousand riot police mobilized to protect him.[6] The next day, in order to prevent a disruption of Reagan's speech, the city fathers and their U.S. military governors issued an order banning three scheduled demonstrations. To make sure that their will prevailed, they sealed off the Autonomen stronghold in the Kreuzberg neighborhood of Berlin, claiming that "technical difficulties" caused the subways there to stop running. Promised replacement buses never appeared, and anyone trying to leave Kreuzberg was stopped at one of nine checkpoints ringing the neighborhood. Despite all these precautions, when a spontaneous demonstration erupted in the middle of the city, the police quickly surrounded it and held over five hundred people in a "kettle" (an encirclement of police) for over five hours. Several of these measures violated existing laws, causing a legal crisis of no small proportions. But the shooting deaths of two policemen at Startbahn West on November 2, 1987, soon overshadowed the government's abuse of power in Berlin.

In September 1988, the autonomous movement moved to the next level of confrontation against the world system. Using the international conventions of the World Bank and the International Monetary Fund (IMF) to dramatize the contradiction between internationalization from the top and the destruction of autonomy at the grassroots, they were the motor force behind a broad mobilization on Berlin. While the Greens met to discuss alternatives to the existing world financial system and dozens of other groups organized events, the Autonomen declined to cooperate with reformists vis-à-vis the IMF.[7] Der Spiegel quoted one radical as saying: "A death machine can only be combated."[8] Acting on their understanding of the imperialist role of the IMF, the Autonomen mobilized thousands of militants from across Germany as well as from England, Italy, Holland, Denmark, Austria, and the United States. When eighty thousand protesters arrived to demonstrate against the conventions of these globally decisive organizations, thousands of bankers were compelled to cut short their meetings and leave Berlin a day earlier than they had planned. During the convention's first four days, the twelve thousand police and and four thousand private bodyguards were able to maintain order only by banning demonstrations and viciously attacking hastily assembled groups of protesters. As members of the international press corps and local residents were brutalized by roaming police snatch squads, public sympathy for the Autonomen grew. On their side, the Autonomen enforced a strict ban on alcohol at movement bars. In preparation for their confrontations, they tried to drive heroin users and dealers out of Kreuzberg in a campaign dubbed "Fists Against Needles." Most importantly, rather than inviting riots into their neighborhood, they took great pains to make sure that street fights would happen in the fashionable sections of Berlin, indicating that the movement had built a base area that it was now protecting from police invasion.

As their international links developed, the Autonomen in many countries paralleled one another more than they conformed to mainstream politics or even to countercultural values in their own countries. Activists converged in conferences, friendships, and internationally coordinated campaigns, and a loosely linked network of "info-stores" or libertarian centers sprang up, functioning as the movement's eyes and ears.[9] For years before anyone dreamed of anything resembling the Autonomen, regional movements sprang up that punctuated local scenes with creative tactics and ironic interventions. In Holland, the Provos released chickens at rush hour in Amsterdam to have fun with traffic, and squatters were a huge presence. Copenhagen's flowerful counterculture was the darling of all Europe. By the end of the 1980s, however, the movements in these cities had adopted the features of the Autonomen, an intuitive and practical unity that transcended or even negated the nationalistically defined conceptions of self still inculcated in many young Europeans. As I discuss in this chapter, a remarkably coherent autonomous movement developed in Europe out of many disparate struggles. Their uniformity and unity had both positive and negative features. In Holland and Denmark, countries that, for a variety of reasons, had largely avoided violence of the German variety, the movements adopted tactics from Germany and became increasingly militant—to the point where their isolation hurt their own existence.[10] In Hamburg, Amsterdam, and Copenhagen, the central thrust of local autonomous movements was to create free spaces for everyday life—and there have been long and bitter struggles to defend these liberated territories. These two sides of Autonomen activism—campaigns against what they view as the system's irrationality and the buildup of their own "revolutionary dual power"—define complementary (and sometimes contradictory) dimensions of their existence. The former can easily lead to isolated small groups and prison, and the latter poses the dangers of integration and accommodation.

As European radicals became increasingly violence-prone, police actions were also internationally coordinated. In one month, police destroyed an Autonomen stronghold in Switzerland (the Zaffaraya encampment in Bern); evicted squatters in the German cities of Göttingen, Freiburg, Düsseldorf, Bochum, and Kiel; and mounted an unsuccessful assault on the Hafenstrasse squatters in Hamburg. The kettle tactic they used in Berlin was copied from earlier kettles in Hamburg and Mainz.[11]

In the 1980s, the "economic wonder" of postwar Europe turned into economic crisis, a continually developing erosion of economic prosperity that has not turned around in the 1990s. This economic downturn worried the guardians of *Pax Americana* long before their attention turned to the possibility of limited nuclear war or a breakdown in Western Europe's military and political alliances. During Jimmy Carter's presidency, the word "recession" became widely used in the United States, but in Western Europe, "depression" was how the economy was commonly described. In the period 1980–81, unemployment in Common Market countries rose 30 percent. After Margaret Thatcher came to power in May 1979, Great Britain's unemployment rate more than doubled to over 12 percent (about three million people), the highest unemployment rate there in over fifty years. Dutch unemployment rose to a postwar record of over 350,000. The expected turnabout never materialized, and unemployment remains the main economic problem of Europe.

An above-average—and climbing—unemployment rate for young people was a new phenomenon. Over the next decade, as these trends only intensified, unemployment among youth in Germany climbed to 9.6 percent in 1982 (over 20 percent in both France and the United Kingdom), and it remains above 9 percent into the 1990s.[12] Since the postwar baby boom in Germany was delayed until after reconstruction, the number of Germans between fifteen and twenty-nine years old in the workforce did not reach its apex until 1987.[13] The economic dimension of the crisis of youth is told in statistical surveys of shortages of housing and jobs, but another moment of the crisis accounted for the emergence of autonomous youth movements—a cultural-motivational dimension obvious in the unwillingness of young people to integrate themselves into what they considered to be the "middle class." The legitimacy of the family, the hegemony of the state, and the desirability of an everyday existence predicated on material comforts in exchange for hard work (the Protestant ethic) all became questioned. The new radicals were less concerned with material comforts for themselves than with creating a new relationship between humans and nature, with finding a way of life free from both capitalist exploitation and bureaucratic domination. Their aspirations for a nuclear-free, fully housed society seemed unattainable within the existing system: their aesthetic fight defied the logic of large-scale capitalist efficiency, and their notion of freedom as more than freedom from material want seemed incomprehensible in a world where starvation and war were still remembered by many older Europeans.

AMSTERDAM

From the 1960s into the 1990s, imaginative and playful countercultural movements in Amsterdam and Copenhagen connected with each other in a synchronous continuum of issues and tactics. Not burdened with the weight of reacting to nationalistic militarism, activists in these two cities shared a political culture of immediate actionism, and their actions often had direct national effects. In the 1980s, Amsterdam was a city being (post)modernized through a massive infusion of capital. Billions of guilders were pumped into urban revitalization programs, and as Holland became part of the homogenization process (widely perceived as the scourge of Americanization) sweeping Europe, its movement underwent a transition from a purely Dutch phenomenon, one replete with *provos, kabouters,* and *kraakers,* to a wing of the international Autonomen. In 1986, during a three-hour battle against police guarding the nuclear power plant at Borssele, the first Dutch group formed that referred to itself as Autonomen.

At its high point in the early 1980s, the *kraakers of* Amsterdam fired the imaginations of young people all over Europe. Between 1968 and

1981, more than ten thousand houses and apartments were squatted in Amsterdam, and an additional fifteen thousand were taken over in the rest of Holland. Many of these squatters (or *kraakers*—pronounced "crackers") were organized into a network of resistance to the police and the government. In squatted "People's Kitchens," bars, and cafés, food, and drink were served at affordable prices. In occupied office buildings, neighborhood block committees set up information centers to deal with complaints against police and landlord brutality. A *kraaker* council planned the movement's direction, and a *kraaker* radio station kept people posted on new developments and late-breaking stories.

The single most important event in the life and death of the *kraakers* (and the most internationally publicized one) occurred on April 30, 1980, when riots marred Queen Beatrice's lavish coronation. *"Geen woning—geen Kronung"* ("No place to live, no coronation") was the slogan for the demonstrations, but it was meant more as a mobilizing call than a physical threat to the ceremony. The *kraakers* had originally hoped for a peaceful party day, although, like any other day, they had also planned to occupy a few more empty dwellings before beginning to party. They were against a coronation so lavish that it cost 56 million guilder (about $25 million). When mounted police attacked some of the street parties, people fought back, unleashing a storm that the police were unable to control. The police were so badly beaten that day that the next week, the police commissioner complained that many of his men could not continue to fulfilll their duties for psychological reasons.

In Amsterdam, a city with fewer than 800,000 inhabitants, more than 50,000 dwelling places were needed. When polled, a majority of the Dutch people repeatedly expressed sympathy for the squatters because of the dearth of reasonably priced places to live. Given the widespread sympathy enjoyed by the squatters, local authorities attempted to divide the movement by proclaiming only a few to be dangerous radicals who "led astray" thousands of "honest" squatters. Intense police attacks were then mounted on houses perceived to be the central leadership, but hastily assembled throngs of squatters, about one thousand within the first half hour, blocked the way to besieged houses in the Vondelstraat on March 3, 1980, and the Groote Keyser after the queen's coronation.

The *kraakers* were able to control the streets in the early 1980s, but their victories exacted a high cost: Dutch tolerance was tempered with a new edge of legal reprimand and revengeful violence. Citizens' committees formed to support the police, and football teams were recruited by landlords to clear out occupied buildings. These groups often did their dirty work dressed in American football gear (helmets and shoulder pads) and steel-tipped boots. In response to *kraaker* self-defense, the

Dutch parliament reconsidered laws governing the vacant buildings. As previously liberal social security payments to students and young people were curtailed, the police were granted more money and more power. New laws were enforced to make it easier for landlords to evict squatters. Property owners had needed the names of specific individuals in order to obtain authorization to call in the police, and because no self-respecting *kraaker* used his or her full name, it was all but impossible to evict them. The new laws waived the name requirement to obtain eviction papers and speeded up the time for actions to be sanctioned by the courts to less than a month. Also introduced were temporary rental contracts under which landlords did not have to show grounds for annulling contracts. When compared with laws in the United States and other European countries, Dutch law remained quite liberal in terms of squatters' rights.[14] Once a table, a chair, and a bed have been moved into a vacant apartment, the occupant is legally permitted to stay.

Although there continued to be new squats (in Amsterdam, a new squat per week was recorded), public opinion had turned dramatically against the squatters, and the police had inflicted a series of major defeats on them. One of the first battles lost by the *kraakers*—for the *Lucky Luiyk* (the Lucky Luke) in 1982—was fought against the police and members of one of the small but increasingly violent neo-fascist parties in Holland. The squatters repelled the fascists who assaulted the house, but they could not hold out against the police. When a streetcar was set on fire in this fight, schisms began to appear in the ranks of the movement, since many people questioned this extension of militant self-defense.

In truth, some *kraakers* were not interested in the radical transformation of society but merely needed individual solutions to their housing needs. To them, fighting the police was unnecessary, especially when it was possible to negotiate with the government and obtain a reasonable solution to their housing problems. From their point of view, the simultaneous existence of thousands of empty apartments and tens of thousands of people in need of housing was a technical problem that could gradually be solved by the existing system. Other *kraakers*—the radicals—saw the housing crisis as another example of the system's irrationality, an irrationality also evident in the increasing starvation in the Third World, the production of nuclear waste, and the transformation of cities into concrete jungles. From their point of view, using crowbars to occupy vacant buildings and barricades to defend them was part of the same struggle being waged with stones and slingshots in occupied Palestine and with AK-47s in Nicaragua. They felt that being afforded the luxuries of Dutch citizens was part of their national privileges as members of an affluent society in a corrupt world system. These *kraakers* understood the atomization and standardization of their lives as part of the price exacted by the world system, and they hoped to contribute to its global transformation.

By 1983, this division among the *kraakers* was no longer an internal matter. After doing all they could to distance these two wings of the movement from each other, Dutch authorities moved resolutely to eradicate the radicals. At the battle for the Groote Watering, the police used armored vehicles and construction cranes to evict the squatters. The cranes were used to hoist metal containers filled with half a dozen police onto the roofs of the building, where they could penetrate the elaborate defenses. At first, the *kraakers* were able to repulse these rooftop attacks, but the police used their imagination and loaded a police officer dressed as Santa Claus into one of the containers. His emergence so surprised the *kraakers* that the attack succeeded. The next police target was a building on Weyers, a huge stronghold with art galleries, coffee shops, and a concert hall. Despite five hundred defenders in the building and thousands of people in the streets, the massive police concentration and their use of overwhelming quantities of tear gas, armor, and cranes won the day. Today the new Holiday Inn at Weyers is a painful reminder of the police success, and February 1984 is remembered as a time when the movement was split beyond repair.

Despite these setbacks, the *kraakers* were not yet defeated. When the pope visited Amsterdam in May 1985, millions of guilders had to be spent on his defense. Anonymous individuals offered a hefty reward to anyone who reached the pontiff, and in the riots that ensued, severe damage was inflicted on the city. The government reacted quickly. Using a specially trained unit, the police illegally evicted a woman and her child from a squatted house in a working-class neighborhood known as a *kraaker* stronghold. When hundreds of people attempted to resquat the house, the police panicked, shooting one person in the arm. The house was retaken by squatters. As riot police arrived to bolster the forces of order, hundreds more *kraakers* reinforced the ranks of their opponents. After the police took the house for the second time, they badly beat all thirty-two people inside and put them in jail without bedding, food, or medical care. The next day, Hans Koch, one of those who had been beaten, was found dead in his jail cell. For the next three nights, angry groups of *kraakers* attacked police stations, torched police cars—some in front of police headquarters—and smashed city offices. City authorities stonewalled any response to the death of Hans Koch, and even a year later, the government still had not completed its inquiry into his death. In December 1986, when the report was finally released, it blamed the victim, claiming that his drug addiction had caused his death. Although the *kraakers* swiftly responded by firebombing more police stations, the government had chosen a violent solution in the struggle to reclaim Amsterdam.

The next month, when the new law governing housing went into effect, the balance of forces shifted. With yuppies on the ascendancy, the movement moved underground, and those committed to a vision of change developed new forms of resistance. Alternative institutions, previously incidental offsprings of a vibrant popular movement, were compelled to tie themselves more intimately to their only remaining constituency: the international Autonomen. Increasingly cut off from the younger generation in Holland, the *kraakers* replenished their ranks with activists from England, Germany, and as far away as Australia. The internationalization of the movement only intensified the reaction of the Dutch Right. Portraying the *kraakers* as foreigners, they recruited Dutch football teams to join with neo-fascist groups and attack squatted houses, often in full view of police. In one such confrontation, a team known as the Rams arrived in full American football gear, and although the occupants tried to surrender peacefully, they were severely beaten, to the point where one of them had to spend two weeks in the hospital with multiple fractures of the legs and arms and severe facial lacerations.

With the intensification of the attacks against the movement, a greater commitment to practical resistance seemed needed. With a declining popular base, secretive small-group actions, particularly by people using the signature of RA RA (Anti-Racist Action Group), became more common. RA RA grew out of the *kraaker* movement, and like the squatters, it became part of a wider European movement. By the late 1980s, RA RA was part of a militant anti-imperialism movement on the rise in European circles. In 1985, RA RA began its most successful campaign—to force MAKRO supermarkets, a chain owned by one of the largest corporations in Holland, to divest its investments in South Africa. After a series of firebombings caused over 100 million guilders in damages to these supermarkets, the corporation withdrew its money from South Africa. Emboldened by success, RA RA then attacked Shell, Holland's largest corporation, one of the world's largest multinationals, and the Dutch queen's main source of income. In one night, thirty-seven Shell stations were torched in Amsterdam alone. Despite more than a hundred such attacks on its gas stations, Shell increased its investments in South Africa and simultaneously launched an extensive public-relations campaign against the domestic "terrorists."

The Dutch royal family is one of Shell's largest stockholders, and the police were eager to show their loyalty. On April 11, 1988, Dutch police raided ten houses, seizing address books, diaries, and computers and arresting eight people on suspicion of belonging to RA RA. Although the press immediately declared that the hard core of RA RA had finally been apprehended, five of the eight were quickly released for lack of evidence, and the cases against the remaining three were undeniably weak. Moreover, in response to the arrests, Shell stations were sabotaged in Utrecht, Apeldoorn, Tilburg, Baarn, Almere, and Haaksbergen, a clear sign that the infrastructure of RA RA remained intact. At the same time, the popular movement declined. We see here a stark subcycle within the better-known synergistic dynamic of repression and resistance: secretive conspiratorial resistance helps minimize the possibility and impact of open popular forms of resistance; guerrilla actions replace massive mobilizations; and the impetus to increasing democracy is lost as the bitterness of confrontation becomes primary. In such contexts, the forces of order thrive while popular movements become weakened and vulnerable.

In Holland, the police first crushed the *kraakers* in Nijmegen, their second greatest redoubt. A large vacant building owned by Shell—the Marienburcht—had been resquatted on April 24 by over a hundred people wearing masks, helmets, and gloves, and armed with clubs. They quickly scared away the few policemen at the scene and barricaded themselves inside the building. At 5 A.M. the next day, hundreds of riot police retook the building, arresting 123 people. Three weeks later, another building, originally squatted by a women's group in 1980, was also attacked by police enforcing the city council's declaration of the city as a "*kraaker*-free zone."

The government's success in Nijmegen encouraged the police to take action in Amsterdam, where the squatters were strongest. On July 18, hundreds of riot police launched a combined assault from the canals and the streets on the last big *kraaker* bastion in Amsterdam on the Konradstraat. Hundreds of people defended the building, an old textile mill used for years as an alternative workplace for artisans and home for 140 people. At one point in the battle, the building caught on fire, causing a giant cloud of smoke to rise ominously over the city. In the aftermath of their eviction, one of the *kraakers* expressed his frustration: "We were disappointed not because we didn't carry our own plan of defense, but because the police came at us much harder than we anticipated." At the time, homelessness and unemployment were severe problems in Holland, and the Dutch state was throwing money at them. Few people expected the huge attack on the Konradstraat, particularly because its occupants had put forth a proposal to renovate the building at a low cost. The squatters' plan would have provided double the number of apartments and jobs that eventually were created, but the fate of that building revealed that the Social Democrats governing Amsterdam had another priority: destroying the *kraakers*.

By 1990, massive police attacks and modification of the laws covering squatters succeeded in displacing thousands of them from the center city, areas that were reclaimed by yuppies and sanitized for tourists. In 1993, fewer than a thousand apartments and houses were occupied in the entire country. What had been a feeling of empowerment in 1980 had been transformed into marginalization and paranoia. Whereas conflicts with the system had once been paramount, as with all movements in decline, the most pressing problems became internal ones. Such splits were so severe that a "traitors" list was published, a booklet entitled "Pearls Before Swine" containing the names of about two hundred people found guilty of informing to the police, negotiating with the government for their own personal gain, or becoming yuppies.[15] The movement had cut itself off from its own membership. One of the participants explained: "Once paranoia sets in, every new person is suspect, and you're left with 200 militants in your friendship circle. Then the rest of society has been insulated from the movement, and the 200 gradually become 150, then 50."

COPENHAGEN

In September 1971, a former army base on Christiania Island in Copenhagen was occupied by fifty activists, and during the years since, a diverse group of nearly a thousand inhabitants has made the 156 abandoned army buildings into homes. Christiania has long been a focal point for a cultural-political opposition in Denmark, and its residents have repelled attacks from police and an invasion of bikers in 1976. They have created more than two hundred jobs in self-managed institutions and provided foreigners and Danes alike with a countercultural haven.[16] The Christiania squat grew out of the same 1960s impetus that produced the "children's power" movement in Copenhagen. Danish society took care of every Dane's needs, but left out of the smoothly functioning system was any consideration of young people determining how to live their own lives. To create alternatives for themselves, teenagers squatted several empty houses in the late 1960s and were heard to shout: "Free us from our parents!" In March 1972, they established the Children's Liberation Front, a decentralized organization that had groups living in several parts of the city. They dedicated themselves to providing a sanctuary for battered, abused, and bored young people. In response to complaints from concerned parents, the police raided some of the houses in the summer of 1973. Trying to maintain a safe refuge, the group kept its campaign going by squatting one of the buildings in Christiania.[17]

In the Free Republic of Christiania, hundreds of people illegally live in an alternative community where no authority counts except that of the *Ting*, an ancient Danish form of consensual decision making. One of the central buildings is known as the *Tinghus* (Ting house). Sitting in a circle at meetings of the communal council, each resident may go to the center and speak, and decisions are made by the eventual agreement of all through consensus rather than a majority vote. Direct democracy within the Danish movement does not have to be explained—it is almost second nature—nor is it limited to occasional gatherings of political groups who use it as a formal method of decision-making. In other free areas besides Christiania, the *Ting* has been the way of life for over a thousand people since 1971.

Social atomization in the United States has advanced far beyond Europe, and our cultural heritage is young and diffuse. Consensus often means that dissenting individuals exercise veto power over a group, making it impossible to formulate a common will and fomenting internal strife. In contrast, the bonds between those who live in Christiania are reinforced by the *Ting*. As one communard explained Christiania's structure to me:

> If a problem comes up, it is first discussed in the house where it originates, where it hopefully will be resolved. Only if the issue is still not taken care of will a neighborhood meeting be called to discuss it. This way, the house and then the neighborhood must fail to deal with the problem before it becomes necessary to have a community meeting, and by then, most people have already heard about the matter and considered the various options. We never vote at community meetings nor do we have a council, because then some people make decisions for others. We only have community meetings when we need to—sometimes not for years, other times once a week.

Although Christiania is squatted, rent is collected for community projects and utilities. Every neighborhood has a person who collects a minimal payment (about $100 per resident per month, or 400 kroner, in 1990), and each of the bars, restaurants, and shops pays something to the "big box," as the community fund is known. "Little boxes" for each neighborhood spend about half of the collected money, a structure that keeps decision-making at the base and also guarantees the availability of funding for grassroots ideas and initiatives. Residents have created a variety of shops: blacksmiths and metalworkers produce ecological ovens and a unique Christiania-designed bicycle; jewelers, potters, candle makers, and shoemakers labor side by side in other workshops; and there are numerous alternative healers and restaurants. The hundreds of people who work in Christiania's shops have a workers' council with regular meetings open to all who labor in the alternative institutions. The council also funds a child-care center.

Although many people live in Christiania for only short periods of time, some have stayed together through the years. At a particularly tense moment in their relations with the authorities, the long-term residents formed a "Rainbow Army" (committed to nonviolence) designed to deal with repeated threats by the authorities to evict them, to keep the collective buildings in good repair, and to meet other communal needs. The call in the Christiania newspaper, *Ugespejlet* (Daily Mirror), read:

> By creating a Rainbow Army of nonviolent, hardworking people who all collaborate with each other, every individual in his or her own way, we can stand united, one for all and all for one, and overcome the threatening situation we are facing. Because we love each other, we can organize ourselves practically, in spite of our differences.[18]

On April 1, 1976, Danish authorities had promised to clear out the communards, but the imaginative campaign mounted by the Rainbow Army brought twenty-five thousand supporters to Christiania on the appointed day. Some of the best bands in Denmark had produced a Christiania record, and the Christiania Action Theater had toured the country with a production of *April Fool's Day*. Evidently, the Rainbow Army won a decisive victory, because the planned eviction was first postponed and finally canceled altogether in favor of legalization. Christiania thereby was transformed from a free space in which laws did not exist to a charming village throwback to feudal Europe, where autonomous principalities existed only with the consent of the lord.[19] In this case, Christiania pays the Ministry of Defense over $500,000 annually for water, electricity, and other services and has been recognized officially as a "social experiment."

Like any community in formation, Christiania has problems, particularly drugs and police incursions. Over the years, the most severe internal issues Christiania has faced have been profit-hungry heroin dealers who moved into the "liberated" zone and refused to leave, even though at every entrance to Christiania, signs posted by the residents read: "Speed, coke, heroin etc. are forbidden to be sold, used or possessed in Christiania." Christiania's position on drugs is the same as that of the Black Panther Party and the Metropolitan Indians: life drugs (marijuana, hashish, mushrooms) should be cheap and legal, and death drugs (speed, cocaine, heroin) should be unavailable. Not only does this sensibility contradict mainstream understanding of psychopharmacology, but its realization represents the de facto enactment of dual power regarding everyday life. Outdated, hypocritical regulations governing individual decisions on drug use are a revealing dimension of the obsolete character of the existing criminal justice system. Christiania's existence as a center for life drugs is civil disobedience in everyday life. In this context, being a dealer should not simply be understood as individual criminal behavior. Since the community tacitly accepts the use of life drugs, making them available at a reasonable price is part of the process of living according to self-determined norms and values. The existing government's laws are at best, a nuisance, and at worst, a giant conspiracy supporting corporations that manufacture alcohol and market tobacco. Between January and October 1975, over a thousand people were arrested in police sweeps aimed at hashish dealers and petty thieves.[20] These police intrusions come in waves, but the Christiania communards are left to fend for themselves when confronted with death drugs. Twice they used the *Ting* to convince motorcycle gangs who were dealing heroin to leave Christiania, although several people suffered injuries while persuading the bikers to leave.[21] Unless the movement is able to deal with the drug issue collectively, Christiania will be destroyed from within like Haight-Ashbury in the 1960s. Despite public support for an "Amsterdam solution" (i.e., turning a blind eye to hashish as—long as heroin is not sold), in the summer of 1987, there were fourteen days of fights with the police, numerous searches, and many arrests before the authorities finally relented. The threat of renewed hostility remained, but the police returned to their old policy of tolerating hashish dealers as long as the quantity they carry is less than 100 grams.

In the mid-1980s, RA RA's anti-Shell campaign spread throughout Europe. In Denmark, on November 23, 1986, twenty-eight Shell stations were simultaneously attacked, causing damages of about $200,000. Although the international cycle of repression and resistance was not yet fully synchronized, these actions were one indication that the targets and tactics—particularly the turn toward small-group destruction of property—were increasingly coordinated across national borders. Years earlier, the struggle in Switzerland for an autonomous youth center had profoundly affected emerging Danish movements. In August 1981, thousands of people signed a petition requesting the use of a vacant bread factory to create a youth house "managed by those using it through direct democracy." For two months, the group raised money, canvassed the neighborhood, and negotiated with the city council. When they were unable to achieve even the slightest positive response from Copenhagen's politicians, the *Initiv-gruppen* decided to take matters into their own hands—they squatted the factory. But within two hours, the police evicted them.

A week later, after hours of meetings with city officials and debates among themselves, the *Initiv-gruppen* squatted an abandoned rubber factory in the same neighborhood. This time the police response was quite violent. The hundred or more people in the building, ranging in age from ten to twenty-five, were shelled by massive quantities of tear gas, the first time gas had been used against demonstrators in Denmark since the 1930s. The police violence led to an intensification of the struggle. Five days after the gassing, hundreds of people converged on an abandoned convent and barricaded themselves inside (and made preparations to repel even a heavy gas attack). Public support was with the squatters, and the police could do little more than encircle the building and await the outcome of neighborhood elections, which happened to be scheduled for that week. The Left Socialists, a small radical party that grew out of the New Left of the 1960s, won control of the borough and quickly sanctioned the use of the convent for a youth house. During the next four months, however, the dream of a youth center turned into a nightmare. Drug addicts from the neighborhood used the convent as a shooting gallery, and a biker club, the Black Panthers, beat up the youthful occupants on several occasions without having to worry about police intervention. After months of such problems, the *Initiv-gruppen* disbanded themselves in disgust, leaving behind only twenty activists, who were soon evicted without incident.

Despite the disappointing outcome, a new group emerged—the BZ (Occupation Brigade)—and a month later they squatted a vacant music museum, the Mekanisk Musikmuseum, in an upper-middle class neighborhood. This time the police were unprepared to deal with the escalation of the confrontation. For the first time, the squatters fought back when the police arrived, throwing anything and everything—including a toilet—out the windows. The stubborn resistance mounted by BZ was initially successful, but after several hours of fighting, the police retook the building and arrested all 147 people inside. The ground rules of confrontational politics in Denmark were forever changed. After the battle for the music museum, a militant squatters' movement emerged in Denmark's cities, and although it was never as massive as the one in Holland, it forged significant ties to groups of retired elders and linked up with the "free areas" of Christiania and Thy camp in northern Jutland.

Christiania provides a living example of the fusion of work and play—of the organizing principles for a new society—and its effect on Denmark's movement has been unmistakable. As one communard explained, in much of Europe, political activists generally emerge from the tough punk rock milieu, whereas in Denmark, many people who become active were first hippies whose earliest experiences with self-determined actions were in Christiania. Christiania is a safe back area to which evicted squatters can escape and from which new actions can emanate, it provides a respite from the turmoil of urban repression and stress; and it also acts as a brake on the reduction of popular movements to small-group actions and martyred heroes. In one such example, a BZ base of four squatted houses in one block was under attack. As the police massed for their final assault, the squatters saw the handwriting on the wall and made use of an elaborate network of tunnels to escape. After the police had battered down door after door in the adjoining squats, much to their public embarrassment, they found no one in the buildings: the BZers had vanished. Although no one would say for sure where they went, Christiania was a common guess.

Perhaps the most well-organized single action of the international Autonomen was accomplished by BZ in September 1986, when hundreds of people took over part of the Osterbro neighborhood in Copenhagen and held it for nine days despite repeated attacks by police and fascists. The fight for the Ryesgade, as this action became known, grew out of the housing crisis but was also an extension of the politics of anti-imperialism. Inside the "cop-free zone," one of the first acts was to torch a building owned by Sperry Corporation, a U.S. multinational involved in the production of Cruise and Pershing missiles. As one BZ activist explained: "It's not enough to talk. Love is a battle. We are fighting homelessness and gentrification, but also the USA, South Africa, and capitalism to show our solidarity. Many of us have been to work in Nicaragua. Now the battle comes home."

To call the Ryesgade action a battle is a slight misstatement. Actually, it was a series of street fights, all of which were won by the squatters. It all began on Sunday, September 14, when a thousand people gathered in the center of the city for what was supposed to be a march to a park. The demonstration suddenly broke away from the "planned" route, and following a prearranged scheme, hundreds of people ran to the Ryesgade area, completely fooling the police. In the words of one of the participants, when the police finally massed and marched on the barricades: "It was a vicious fight. As hundreds of riot police attacked, we threw Molotovs, fireworks, bricks, and slung catapults, driving them back." When the police counterattacked from the other side of Ryesgade, hundreds of masked Autonomen repulsed them. When the police retreated for the final time that day, the barricades were reinforced and a huge street party began. Hundreds of people slept at the barricades in preparation for the next attack. In the morning, the police were again greeted with "concrete rain" when they charged, but this time the police attacked on two sides simultaneously and broke through on one. As someone described the scene: "All seems lost, then at the last moment, over a hundred supporters from the city come charging in from the rear, attacking the police from the rear and forcing them to flee! The riot cops run away and don't try to break through again. We reinforce the barricades."

Even though the situation in the neighborhood resembled martial law, the local residents remained supportive of the BZers. During the nine days of fighting, BZ members went food shopping for elderly residents of the neighborhood who were afraid to venture out beyond the barricades because of possible police reprisals. As the city government met in emergency sessions, the Danish autonomists discussed their options. They easily reached a consensus that reformist solutions—such as the offer of a Danish rock star to buy the buildings and give them to BZ—were out of the question. BZ did not recognize the legitimacy of the government, and BZ members resolved to prove that they were beyond its powers. In Amsterdam, a solidarity demonstration attacked the Danish consulate, and there were marches in Aarhus (Jutland) as well as in Germany and Sweden. The network of free radio stations in Denmark provided support for the four hundred people in the Ryesgade by sponsoring open mike debates and calling for food, blankets, and supplies to be delivered to the "liberated area." After nine days, the city finally called on the army for help, and a bloody finale seemed imminent. The squatters called a press conference for 9 A.M. on Monday, September 23, but when the media arrived, they found the houses deserted, prompting the two negotiators working for the city to ask: "Where did the BZers go when they left? What did the town hall learn? It seems the act can start all over again, anywhere, at any time. Even bigger. With the same participants."

After the Ryesgade action, the police tried unsuccessfully to locate the leadership of BZ. At the same time, the movement began to attack targets related to South Africa. Besides an increasing number of small-group sabotage actions, particularly against Shell, another tactic became widely used: "compulsory relocations." A large group of people would suddenly arrive at a corporate office, bank, or travel agency guilty of some wrongdoing, such as having ties to South Africa. People would quickly remove everything, piling typewriters, computers, desks, and furniture in the street while others handed out letters of explanation to the workers and to onlookers. Finally, as quickly as the action began, everyone vanished, leaving the office relocated. These quick and peaceful compulsory relocations enjoyed wide public support and, because they were accomplished so quickly, afforded little opportunity for the police to attack. The same could not be said of the attacks on Shell. In the fall of 1987, activists accidentally damaged a gas station's underground tanks and caused hundreds of gallons of fuel to leak into the earth. Taking advantage of the movement's apparent blunder, Danish police raided homes, offices, and the youth house, arresting people and confiscating property.

Internationally, the Autonomen borrowed tactics and targets from one another, and in May 1988, Danish BZ copied a page from their German counterparts and put together an action week like *Tuwat* in Berlin and *Tag X* in Hamburg. The actions began on May 12, when the door of city hall was painted with the word *Amandla* (African National Congress' slogan for victory) and Israeli, NATO, and Confederate flags were burned from a makeshift gallows. On Friday the thirteenth, small groups carried out attacks throughout Copenhagen. Supermarkets carrying Israeli produce were spray-painted to remind shoppers of the boycott of Israeli goods; a street was barricaded and a house quickly squatted; spontaneous demonstrations fought off police attacks. Although such tactics helped activists feel good, they did little to help broaden their base of support. Prior to the action week, it was already clear that the autonomous movement was increasingly isolated. The meager number of votes garnered by the Left Socialist Party when it used a slingshot as its campaign logo was one such sign. (It failed to receive even the 2 percent needed to gain parliamentary representatives.)

Like their counterparts throughout Europe, the more the Autonomen relied on militant small-group actions, the less popular support they got and the more they came to rely on a small circle of people. As the rise of anti-imperialist politics created a set of priorities focused on the Third World, many activists did not care whether they received popular support within their own societies. As the movement became increasingly violent, it lost whatever sympathy it had, making it an easy target for the forces of repression to hit. Finally, on May 18, 1993, militant isolationism reached its climax when several hundred demonstrators, reacting to the Danish electorate's approval of closer European union, went on a rampage in Copenhagen. As cobblestones and bricks were thrown at police, the order was given to fire on the crowd, and that night ten people were wounded by police gunfire.[22] During the subsequent trials, riot participants received little public support, and long sentences were meted out to many activists.

HAFENSTRASSE: INTERNATIONAL SYMBOL

By 1988, the international focal point of the Autonomen was undoubtedly the set of houses first occupied in 1981 in Hamburg's Hafenstrasse.

At the same time as the squatters' movement reached its high point in Berlin, several empty houses in the St. Pauli district of Hamburg were quietly taken over. These eight houses on the harbor gradually became the single most significant focal point of the struggle waged by autonomous movements in Europe. Repeated attempts by the city government and police to dislodge the squatters failed as the Hafenstrasse squatters mobilized thousands of sympathizers and hundreds of street fighters to protect their liberated space. They enacted elaborate defense plans in the face of repeated police assaults; put together lightning-like retaliatory raids on city offices and corporate targets after assaults on the squatted houses; dealt with severe internal problems; and walked a thin line between the state's programs of legalization and criminalization. Moreover, they hosted international Autonomen gatherings in their houses, thereby strengthening the movement's international vitality by providing a forum where the movement could discuss its options and plan its actions.

When the squatters' movement elsewhere suffered a series of defeats, the Hafenstrasse's capability to remain intact made it a symbol of almost mythic proportions among Europe's Autonomen. As one leaflet put it: "Everything is present in this struggle: militant resistance, the fight to live together in communes, internationalism, the struggle for self-management and collective structure. The Hafenstrasse has shown that resolute struggle can become the path for many." Unlike their counterparts in Berlin and elsewhere, who were often ex-students or of respectable working-class origins, the Hafenstrasse drew heavily from the lumpen proletariat (the criminal element and blackmarket entrepreneurs). Part of the squatters' murals painted on the side of one of the houses transformed the famous call made by Karl Marx ("Workers of the World, Unite!") into "Criminals of the World, Unite!"

Klaus Dohnanyi, then mayor of Hamburg, was unable to control the Hafenstrasse *Chaoten*. He sent his police to clear out these houses four times without success. In 1986, after the Hamburg electrical utility documented the yearly "theft" of more than $50,000 worth of services by the squatters, hundreds of police were called in and were able to clear out a few of the buildings, although eight houses clustered together in three large buildings remained in the hands of the Autonomen. In response to these attacks, the movement unleashed its own counteroffensive, marching more than ten thousand strong around a "black block" of at least fifteen hundred militants carrying a banner reading "Build Revolutionary Dual Power!" At the end of the march, the black block beat back the police in heavy fighting. The next day, fires broke out in thirteen department stores in Hamburg, causing damages estimated at almost $10 million. Over the next months, while the city government floundered, the movement kept the pressure up.[23] On "Day X," April 23, 1987, small groups of Autonomen again retaliated, attacking houses of city officials, court buildings, city offices, and radio Hamburg. In all, more than thirty targets were hit in a fifteen-minute period.

The city then declared the occupied houses "Public-Enemy Number 1," and the squatters braced themselves for fresh attacks. Steel doors were installed, bars were mounted in the windows, and barbed wire was hung on the sides and roofs of the buildings. In early November, the city promised to clear out and tear down the houses within fourteen days. The squatters painted a new slogan on the side of the one of the houses—"Don't count our days, count yours!" —and barricaded the houses. Rumors spread that a network of underground tunnels had been dug for resupply or escape. Netting was hung on the second stories of the houses to ward off the use of ladders, and patrols on the roofs guarded against helicopter landings. Four thousand police arrived from all over Germany, and the country's borders were closed to suspicious-looking tourists headed in the direction of Hamburg.

On Friday, November 13, 1987 (less than two weeks after the shootings at Startbahn West), the squatters' radio station began broadcasting for supporters to join the fight. Police helicopters were chased from the rooftops by a few shots from flare guns, and loudspeakers blasted the song "It's war, war in the city," as the fight began in earnest. After a night of fighting, the barricades were still standing, and rush-hour traffic had to be rerouted because part of a nearby bridge had been borrowed to help build them. Adopting a Spanish Republican and Sandinista slogan, the banner hung on the outside of the houses said "No pasaran!"

Over the next week, as the Autonomen celebrated their victory, two thousand police reinforcements arrived, posing an even uglier confrontation. Mayor Dohnanyi, however, had had his fill, and he succeeded in averting a final battle by mobilizing support for a new plan: legalize the Hafenstrasse squatters by creating a corporation composed of liberal city council members and some of the squatters. The building would then be leased to the squatters, and the city would provide funds for renovations, thereby creating needed "alternative" housing. Most importantly, by providing government approval, these measures would have the effect of ending the illegal occupation of the Hafenstrasse. Although Dohnanyi's plan gave the Hafenstrasse and their supporters a victory, he vowed to clear out any new squats in Hamburg within twenty-four hours (Berlin's solution to militant squatters).

At first, conservative politicians resisted Dohnanyi's plan, but they reluctantly agreed to support it in order to defuse the crisis. After the approval of Dohnanyi's proposal by the city government, the jubilant

Autonomen dismantled their street barricades, stripped the houses of their defenses, and even sent the mayor a bouquet of flowers. For his efforts, Dohnanyi was awarded the prestigious Theodor Heuss medal. After six months of peace, however, conservatives in the city government blocked the new corporation in May 1988. Rather than participate in a new round of fighting, Klaus Dohnanyi resigned as mayor, leaving the future of the Hafenstrasse in doubt. Years of negotiations led to a long-term agreement under which the former squatters can remain in the buildings, and in the early 1990s, residents drew up blueprints for major renovations rather than for militant self-defense.[24]

Although they were victorious, the Hafenstrasse's residents paid a high price for their years of continuous resistance to state assaults. Among the earliest occupants, children were driven out, and the internal relationships among those remaining were strained. One of the lowest points was reached in June 1984, when three squatters (two women and a man) beat and raped a visitor in one of the buildings.[25] The collective decided to take matters into its own hands: the three were beaten up, their heads were shaved, and they were thrown out in the street. In a leaflet explaining their actions, the residents wrote: "It was clear that we could not work with the bulls [the police] and the judges in order to deal with the problem. If we had, that would have meant going to precisely the same forces that never missed an opportunity to trick us, and with them in control, they would have tried to do us in." Because they exercised their own brand of revolutionary justice, the squatters were accused of creating a space outside the law, a common conservative charge employed over the following years to justify the use of massive police force.

The psychological price paid by those who lived in the Hafenstrasse was all too evident in their paranoia and crisis mentality. As Hamburg's eight-hundredth birthday celebration approached and more and more new construction was completed along the waterfront, the future of the Hafenstrasse remained contingent upon constant alertness and the willingness of hundreds—possibly thousands—to fight for their free space. Although the Autonomen's continuing resistance to anything approaching middle-class respectability should have resulted (at least by U.S. standards) in a decisive offensive against them, the costs of clearing out the houses would have been unacceptably high by European standards.* For more

---

* Many Americans find it hard to understand how the Hafenstrasse could resist the police. After all, around the same time (on May 13, 1985), a similar group in Philadelphia (MOVE)—as well a the entire neighborhood in which they lived—was wiped out by a massive police firebomb, and squatters in the United States are routinely evicted brutally by overwhelming police force. Unfortunately, the delicate nature of authorizing deadly force in Europe finds no parallel in the United States.

than a decade, the squatters' stubborn refusal to accept the inevitable succeeded in transforming the idea that the imposition of the system's will is inevitably the outcome of the popular contestation of power.

The Hafenstrasse inspired the conscious spontaneity of the autonomous movement. Their continuing existence symbolized militant resistance, and they were the cutting edge of an autonomous movement that existed in a series of militant confrontations. To be sure, the Autonomen remain a diffuse collection of militant counterculturalists who assemble sporadically and whose identity is far from fixed. Their strength is not in their overwhelming numbers. In June 1987, for example, when President Ronald Reagan visited Berlin, the autonomous "black bloc," identified by their black ski masks and militant disposition, numbered only three thousand of the fifty thousand anti-Reagan demonstrators. And in 1988, when seventy-five thousand protesters gathered at the meeting of the International Monetary Fund and the World Bank in Berlin, only a small fraction could be counted as Autonomen. In both cases, however, the initiative of the Autonomen resulted in larger actions, and they were the militant organizers creating a context in which other forms of participation (signing petitions, attending programs and rallies, publishing informational leaflets, and so forth) had meaning.

After the shootings at Startbahn West in Frankfurt and the wave of arrests throughout Europe in November 1987, however, public opinion dramatically swung over to the states' side. Criminalizing the autonomous movement, as had been done a decade earlier in Italy, caused many people to drop out of political activism altogether. Yet the structure—or, to be precise, the lack of formal structure—of the autonomous movement made it difficult to obliterate the movement. No matter how many times the police raided offices or arrested people, they could not seize the leaders of the movement—since there were none—or destroy its organizations—since they were fluid and changing. The Autonomen occupy a nebulous territory of oppositional forces located somewhere between the clandestine red underground and green corridors of parliament, and the counterculture nourishes and creates a context out of reach of political repression.

THE GUERRILLAS AND THE MOVEMENT

Whereas the declining opportunities for young people in Europe and the movement's diffuse structure were conditions for the continued existence of the radical opposition, internal dynamics continually cut the movement off from a larger constituency. Visible in the arrogance of "anti-imps" (anti-imperialists), the self-righteous, holier-than-thou mentality reaches its most extreme expression in guerrilla groups such as the RAF.[26] Since the mid-1970s, when it kidnapped and killed Hanns-Martin Schleyer, one of Germany's leading industrialists, the RAF has waged a deadly campaign against the country's rich and powerful. In the process, it has repeatedly exhibited disdain for legal methods of struggle and set a standard of "commitment" that essentially invoked its own members' deaths as a superior form of political activism when compared with others whose risks are not as extreme.

Although all the original members are either dead or in jail, the group has repeatedly been able to regenerate itself, and it remains capable of taking daring initiatives. In 1972, only about forty people associated with the RAF were wanted by the police, but by 1974, one estimate placed the number at three hundred.[27] The group's low point was reached in 1977. In a daring series of actions, one RAF team kidnapped Schleyer and held him at a secret location, demanding the release of RAF prisoners—including its founder, Andreas Baader. (The Red Brigades in Italy would copy the technique used to kidnap Schleyer six months later when they kidnapped Aldo Moro in Rome.[28]) While negotiations were under way with the authorities for the exchange of prisoners, another team composed of RAF members and Palestinian allies hijacked a Lufthansa jet and took its eighty-six passengers and crew to Mogadishu, Somalia. The demand to release prisoners was increased to include two Palestinians. While waiting for word that their imprisoned comrades had been freed, the hijackers were subdued and all but one killed by a special commando unit. That night, all three of the main imprisoned RAF leaders died in what the authorities maintain was a suicide pact. A few days later, Schleyer's body was found in the trunk of a car parked in France near the German border.

It took a few years for the next generation of RAF to emerge, but when it did, its actions were vengeful. In 1979, RAF members tried to kill Alexander Haig when he visited NATO headquarters in Belgium, but the bomb exploded after his car had passed. In 1981, a RAF bomb wounded twenty people at the NATO air base at Ramstein, and a RAF rocket hit the car of Frederick Kroesen, U.S. commander in Europe.[29] In 1982, over six hundred bomb attacks were recorded in West Germany, many of which were tied to the RAF.[30] By 1984, the third generation of RAF publicly formed a working relationship with its French counterpart, Action Directe (AD). Numbering no more than a few dozen people, the two groups moved ahead with their action agenda. In 1985, a joint RAF/AD group killed an American enlisted man simply to steal his identity card (which they used to plant a bomb on a U.S. base that killed two people). In 1986, the RAF killed a prominent foreign ministry official in Germany, and AD assassinated Renault chief Georges Besse. After all AD members and many RAF members had been arrested, the remaining RAF formed an alliance with a revived Red Brigades, then called the Fighting Communist Union.[31] In 1988, the two groups held a series of meetings and eventually issued a joint communiqué in which they declared:

> Western Europe is the cardinal point in the conflict between the international proletariat and the imperialist bourgeoisie. Because of its historic, political, and geographic character, Western Europe is the area where the three lines of demarcation intersect: State/Society, North/South, East/West.[32]

Within a few days of the communiqué, police in Rome arrested most of the Italians involved in this alliance, and the German RAF was left without significant international ties or resources.

By the end of the 1980s, only about two dozen imprisoned RAF members were left in Germany, but their symbolic importance far exceeded their numbers in the media and for the movement. On February 1, 1989, some of the RAF prisoners began a hunger strike (their tenth in a series) to demand that political prisoners be allowed to serve their time together in groups and that they be permitted to receive visits and mail from a range of people. Despite their being held in isolation, many imprisoned guerrillas regularly write letters to movement magazines. Within a few weeks, more than forty-three prisoners throughout Germany were refusing food, and thousands of people mobilized to support them. Small groups attacked government buildings and the Frankfurt stock exchange. On April 8, thirty-five hundred people protested in Berlin, and on April 29, more than five thousand people marched in Bonn, after which hundreds of people occupied government offices. Even the Greens, normally reluctant to say anything supportive about "terrorists," called for the imprisoned members of RAF to be recognized as political prisoners. As support groups formed around the country, in three states where the Social Democrats governed, they offered to put the prisoners in small groups of four to six. Determined to live in one large group and to get a national settlement, the hunger strikers refused the offer. Like the Hafenstrasse and others, collectives defined the way the imprisoned members of the RAF wished to live. Unlike their Irish counterparts, the German prisoners did not fast to death but orchestrated their hunger strikes in stages. On May 12, 1989, after it was clear that there was no hope of obtaining their demands, they temporarily ended the fast, calling for a renewal of the anti-imperialist struggle by supporters. On November 30, in the first attack linked to the RAF in three years, a bomb exploded under the limousine of the chief executive of the country's largest bank, killing him and his chauffeur. According to police, the first car in the three-car convoy was allowed to pass before the bomb was detonated.

After the demise of East Germany, many RAF members gave themselves up, and others were arrested. Newly released information showed that the group had received aid for years from the East German *Stasi* (secret police). Although reported by the police to be nearly finished, the armed struggle continued to haunt the country's elite in the 1990s. On March 31, 1991, the head of *Treuhand*, the government agency overseeing the economic transition of eastern Germany, was shot and killed in his home in Düsseldorf. In 1993, a few days before a new $153 million prison was scheduled to open, RAF bombs were so precisely exploded that four cell blocks and the administration building had to be razed, adding a cost of over $60 million to the project and delaying its opening for years.[33]

Neither the government nor the guerrillas appear ready to acquiesce. In Italy, the Red Brigades were effectively destroyed through a government program of amnesty for informants, and in the United States, there are few (if any) remaining underground groups. As yet another new generation of guerrillas emerges in Germany, there appears to be little chance for an end to the armed struggle. Although the group made one offer to cease its operation in exchange for leniency for the remaining prisoners, no deal was struck. Part of the reason is that the German authorities refuse to adopt a lenient position even toward those who agree to turn state's evidence. One woman who fully cooperated with the authorities was nonetheless given a "relatively light sentence" of twelve years. Those who remain underground fare much worse. In what many regarded as an assassination, on June 27, 1993, Wolfgang Grams, a RAF leader, was killed during a shoot-out with an elite antiterrorist team. Eyewitnesses, including one of the government's commandos, claimed that Grams had been captured alive and finished off at close range.[34]

Could part of the reason that the German authorities refuse to negotiate an end to their guerrilla war be that it serves their needs? The climate created by the armed struggle conditions an all-too-easy acceptance of the use of violence within the movement and gives the state an easy excuse for increasing its repressive powers. The issue is complicated, because small groups' use of force has had results. Squatters in one house related the story of how their landlord finally relented in some of his demands after his house had been attacked by unknown persons. Another group described how it had "persuaded" the dentists who owned the building housing the neighborhood bar to rescind a large rent increase that would have driven the bar out of business. Apparently, the mere presence of scraggly autonomists in the sanitized waiting room of a medical practice is enough to bring landlords to their senses. In a case made infamous in the United States by a *New Yorker* article, an upscale Kreuzberg restaurant owned by a former activist was driven out of business by unfriendly autonomists bent on resisting the gentrification of their neighborhood.[35] On at least two occasions, a small group ran into the restaurant and threw excrement at customers. Although these actions were easy to chastise, some acts were focused on more clearly appropriate targets. Perhaps the most successful of the various guerrilla groups is the autonomous feminist group called the Red Zoras.

THE RED ZORAS

In the early 1970s, after nearly every member of the original RAF had been killed or imprisoned, the Revolutionären Zellen (Revolutionary Cells, or RZ) became the newest name among groups waging small-group warfare on the established system.[36] In contrast to the Marxist-Leninist ideology and centralized structure of the RAF, the RZ consist of independently organized groups that select their targets and tactics according to specific conditions, particularly as defined by popular struggles. One estimate placed the number of RZ members at about three hundred in the early 1980s.[37] Unlike the Marxist-Leninist RAF, the RZ are organized in autonomous groups, each of which is responsible for its own actions. They parallel the Italian group Prima Linea (discussed in Chapter 2).

The Red Zoras, an autonomous part of the RZ consisting solely of women, formed from currents of feminism and anti-imperialism. They took their name from a popular novel in which young girls steal from the rich to give to the poor. It is not uncommon for autonomous groups to borrow images from the world of children to describe themselves. In a popular squatters' song, the Hafenstrasse long relied on Pippi Longstocking to help explain how the houses miraculously remained occupied. In some sense, autonomous groups refuse to grow up: they refuse to shed their dreams of a better world or to conform to existing cultural norms such as marrying, living in nuclear families, and taking on careers. Their affinity for the pleasure principle—or at least their negation of the reality principle—is a salient part of their identity.

Since 1974, when they bombed the Supreme Court building the day after the court overturned the abortion law, the Red Zoras have conducted militant campaigns against pornography, international traders in women (those who profit from importing Asian women as "brides" for German men), the Doctors' Guild ("We see the Federal Doctors' Guild as exponents of rape in white trenchcoats"), and drug companies (notably Schering, which produced the birth-defect-causing drug Duogynon). In conjunction with the RZ, they have launched over two hundred attacks on selected targets. Their most successful campaign was won in the summer of 1987, when they compelled Adler Corporation, one of Germany's largest clothing producers, to agree to the demands of South Korean women textile workers. Adler had initially fired twelve South Korean women union leaders, but after the Red Zoras and their sister group in Berlin, the Amazons, firebombed ten Adler outlets in Germany, causing millions of dollars in damages, the company rehired the twelve and agreed to meet the textile workers' demands. In a recorded interview, the Red Zoras explained: "We do not fight for women in the Third World, we fight alongside them." Looking at the massive disarmament movement whose practice has been constrained by pacifism, they commented: "When the refusal of violence is elevated to the level of an inviolable principle where good and evil are counterposed, it is not a question of disagreement but of submission and obedience."

The antiauthoritarian structure of their groups—a decentralized decision-making process for choosing targets and a lack of uniform politics or spokespersons—made it nearly impossible for German authorities to find them. In their frustration, the police resorted to massive raids on women's groups. In December 1987, hundreds of federal police conducted raids on thirty-three offices and apartments in an attempt to destroy the Red Zoras.[38] The police seized address books, audio and video cassettes, mail, and research archives relating to abortion rights, reproductive technology, and the movement against generic engineering, and took twenty-three women in for questioning. Although all but two of these women were quickly released, the cases of Ingrid Strobl and Ulla Penselin became the focal point for an international campaign of solidarity. These two women were longtime feminist activists, and their being charged with "membership in a terrorist organization"—the Red Zoras, to be exact—was designed to criminalize the women's movement.

The Red Zoras' popularity and success had to be punished, and the arrest of Ingrid Strobl and Ulla Penselin, however weak the evidence against them, was the state's avenue of last resort. Because these two activists had played significant roles in the women's movement over the past decade, the police tactic may also have been designed to exacerbate the growing differences within feminist circles. Penselin spent eight months in prison, and Strobl was released after two and a half years.[39] For over seven years, Strobl worked for the feminist magazine *Emma*, writing on topics as diverse as immigrants in Germany, Rosa Luxemburg, and witchcraft. In 1987, when women associated with the Greens issued a "Mother Manifesto" calling for a new conception of women's liberation, she wrote the autonomist response. Noting that the Greens' demands for paid child-rearing and paid housework were premised on the assumption that German women are "primarily mothers and gladly mothers," she responded angrily: "It's a proposal for a few middle-class women who are not ready to continue the struggle but prefer to return to the gilded cage of home and hearth. It is extremely doubtful if the majority of women, who aren't waiting for the gilded cage but for the nose ring of the runaway slave, will follow the Mother Manifesto on the path of betrayal." Strobl's polemic was one of the better-crafted criticisms of the Greens.

In 1981, the feminist movement was extremely critical of the "male violence" and "penis politics" of the extraparliamentary movement, and the Autonomen were still a movement in formation, clearly unprepared to deal with issues raised by feminists. Seven years later, the greater role played by women in the movement made it impossible to argue against violence solely from the perspective of sexual politics. The very existence of the Red Zoras was an indication of the transformation of this new generation of German women and profoundly affected the ground rules upon which feminism and the politics of gender in general are evaluated by men and women alike. The very notion that some inherent peacefulness in women's nature makes them naturally disposed to resist domination was viewed as part of the system of patriarchy by the Red Zoras:

> When sections of the feminist movement ingenuously return to norms of feminine behavior to find in "the nature" of women all the characteristics that find parallels in the peace movement in the form of the will to sacrifice, humility, refusal of confrontation and combat, they favor the biological theory of "femininity" which for a long time has been known and understood as a product of power.

The autonomous women's movement had long worked with Turks, but given the cultural contrast between punks and newly arrived immigrants from Turkey, feminist connections, beyond those forged by working together in cooperative food stores selling organic produce or learning German, took time to develop. When Turkish and German women first began to meet, obstacles seemed insurmountable. German women, for example, could not understand why their Turkish counterparts insisted on retaining the traditional scarfs worn by Islamic women to cover their heads in public. Turkish women could not convince the Germans that public lesbian leadership and gay banners at marches on International Women's Day made it almost impossible to justify their own participation to their communities. Despite such cultural divergence, common needs led to a women's crisis center being established. The Gray Wolves, Turkish fascists who have long attacked leftist Turks in Germany and in Turkey, issued warnings to Turkish women to stay out of the center. When these warnings were ignored, a gunman assaulted the center in 1984, shooting a Turkish woman dead and severely wounding one of her German coworkers. Along with the Gray Wolves, the police also treated Kreuzberg as enemy territory, frequently entering punk bars such as the Pink Panther and Turkish coffeehouses to arrest people.

By May Day of 1987, the stage was set for a reaction to police brutality, and when it finally came, everyone seemed surprised by its intensity.[40] What began as the traditional street party in Kreuzberg's Lausitzer Platz quickly turned into a full-scale riot. Although the police has initiated the confrontation, they quickly realized that they did not have the strength to control the crowd, and they hastily retreated. Store after store was looted—or, as some insisted, became the scene of "proletarian shopping." One of the participants jubilantly remembered: "From Heinrichplatz to the Gorlitzer Bahnhof, a liberated territory was held for most of the night. It was not just the Autonomen who participated but also 'normal' people: youth, grandmothers, Turks. It was fantastic."

A year later, with thousands of police massed on what seemed to be every side street, demonstrators formed spirited contingents of women, Turks, and a "black bloc" of ski-masked militants ready for action. The banner leading the march, "We fight internationally against capital and patriarchy," indicated the growing influence of the women's movement on the Autonornen, as well as the ascendancy of anti-imperialism as the defining content of the current generation's politics.

MAY DAY 1988: A PERSONAL NOTE

As the sun set and the full moon rose on May Day 1988, I sat with friends at an outdoor table at a Greek tavern in Kreuzberg. Police sirens began what would be their night-long wail, and a line of more than thirty police vans, each containing half a dozen helmeted riot police, pulled past the bar and headed for the street party at Lausitzer Platz. After they passed, someone strolled over to the corner and returned with a report: "The bulls [police] are going nuts. They must still be smarting from last year." We quickly discussed our options: leave the scene, go and fight the police, or stay and drink some more beer under the full moon. We chose the latter.

Given the police preparations, none of us felt any possibility of winning the streets, but we did not want to head home in case we had not evaluated the situation properly. Gunther quickly improvised a spontaneous modification of our plan. He strolled back to the corner and moved a trash barrel into the middle of the street. Udo went next, carrying a broken chair from the back of the bar, followed by Renate, who picked up a cement block and tossed it on the growing pile. Before long, the street was flimsily blockaded.

We ordered another round, and I asked Gunther if we should reconsider our decision not to move back to Lausitzer Platz. "Look," he began, "we're driving the bulls up the walls. They don't know what to expect from us. Years ago, when we were fighting them every day on the Ku'damm [Berlin's main shopping street], there were a few thousand of us ready to go at it. It was such a hot day we couldn't stand it, and you know if we were hot, it might have been hell in full riot gear. A few people took off their clothes and before you knew it, people were jumping into the Hallensee [a nearby lake] to cool off. Then we all stripped and jumped in. Thousands of us were enjoying ourselves at the beach, while the bulls stood by sweating like pigs not knowing what was happening. The city government, the media, and the bulls could never figure out who gave the order to jump in. They still can't understand our politics or our culture, especially when we don't lose our sense of humor. Right now there are hundreds of bulls looking for us and here we sit, enjoying ourselves drinking a beer. Look at that moon!"

As we sat watching the arc of the moon, I recalled my last night in Berlin in 1981. No matter where in Kreuzberg you went, vicious street fights erupted when the police savagely—and unsuccessfully—attempted to stop the squatters' movement from occupying more vacant houses. After their brutality against nonviolent protesters at Gorleben, the police had suddenly found themselves unable to maintain order in any of Germany's big cities, and Berlin, of course, was in the forefront of the movement. I will never forget the transformation of Hans. He and I had gotten to know each other fairly well in the eighteen months I'd lived in Berlin. He'd patiently explained nuances of German politics to me, while I, perhaps not so patiently, had questioned his assumptions regarding the propriety of pacifism. After a few hours of back and forth with the police in Hermannplatz one night, our roommate Anna and I had grown weary of the effort and were determined, to head home. When we found Hans, he was incredulous that we were leaving. "What?" he shouted. "You're leaving now? I'll be here until there are no bulls left in the streets or no more rocks to throw at the bulls!" Hans's radicalization was symptomatic of thousands of people who followed a similar trajectory in 1981, as the cycle of resistance and repression had intensified.

Around two in the morning, the riot was apparently over, and we headed home, taking the indirect route through Lausitzer Platz. Evidently, not all the partygoers had had time to pack up their belongings before heading home. There were many abandoned items of clothing in the streets. The city had cleared the streets of anything that looked like it could be used to build barricades, but the charred remnants of wood lying in the streets indicated that the state's preparations had not been entirely successful.

The next day, as we read the newspaper reports on the previous night's events, several people stopped by the commune looking for friends who had not made it home. Renate was quite concerned about the fate of Arnt, since he was nowhere to be found. As she searched for him in the neighborhood, we read *Die Tageszeitung*. Apparently, the police had moved against the street party when a small campfire had been lit. The ensuing confrontation involved fifteen hundred Berlin police against the remnants of six thousand demonstrators, most of whom had chosen not to participate in the resistance to the police assault. The Pink Panther had been raided again, and by the end of the night, more than a hundred people had been injured and a total of 134 people were under arrest—most of them with the equivalent of felonies that might bring some jail time.

On the bright side, Arnt was discovered sleeping in the commune next door, and among the casualties of the previous night's police riot were none other than Berlin's chief of police and two of his top aides. These gentlemen had been observing the police action from the edge of the crowd when, from another direction, they were confronted with newly arrived members of the riot squad, who proceeded to bash heads without warning. When the police officers exclaimed that they were in charge of the riot squad and that one of them was the chief of police, the response was indicative of the demeanor of the police that night: "Yeah, and we're the emperors of China!" That remark was followed by blows, which sent the three to the hospital.

When Gunther finally came downstairs and heard the news, he bellowed, "You see, who says there isn't justice in this world?" As he drank his morning cup of coffee, he continued, "This whole system is destroying itself—killing off the rivers and the forests, poisoning the air, stockpiling nuclear waste, and building the ugliest buildings imaginable. No wonder they're beating up their leaders. They can't even take care of Germany's two and a half million unemployed."

"Where's the alternative?" one of us rejoined. "It's certainly not in the anti-imps [anti-imperialists], who would just as soon see Germany go down the tubes, and the Greens are part of the system, no?" For the first time, Gunther looked serious: "The alternative won't appear ready-made overnight, my friend, but we see it growing in the Hafenstrasse, in the resistance to Wackersdorf, to Startbahn West, and in our street parties. An army of lovers cannot lose."

PHOTOS

KuKuCK: squatted cultural center in Berlin, 1982.
Photo by R. Warzecha Interglotz Visionen.

Cranes against *kraakers* in Amsterdam, 1980. Photo by Ronald Hoeben in *De Stads Oorlog* (A W Sijthoff Alphen Aan Den Rijn, 1981), p. 81.

Central gathering point in Gorleben, Free Republic of Wendland, 1980. Photo by the author.

Movement meeting in Gorleben, Free Republic of Wendland, 1980. Photo by the author.

Call for *Tiwat* demonstrations, 1981. Photo by anonymous individual.

Tuwat demonstration, August 5, 1981. Photo by anonymous individual.

Communal dinner in the resistance village at Startbahn West, 1981. Source: *Startbahn-West Fotos und Interviews*, p. 25 (produced by a collective of authors and photographers and published by Burckhard Kretschmann).

Police water canon attacking demonstrators at Startbahn West, 1981.
Source: *Startbahn-West Fotos und Interviews*, p. 89

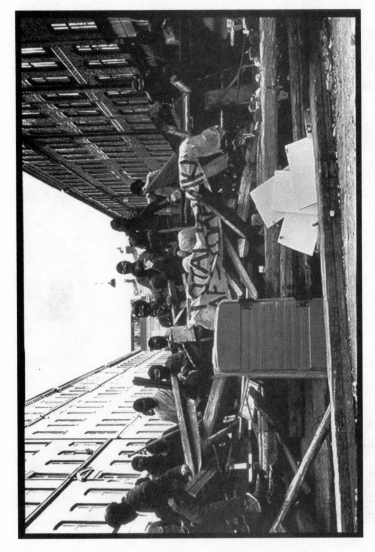

Barricades in the Ryesgade (Copenhagen), 1986. Photo by Lino Fjog.

Black block at the anti-Regan demonstration, June 12, 1987.
Source: *Berlin 1.Mai 1987–12. Juni 1987* (Berlin: Ermittlungsausschusses, 1987), p. 53.

Berlin kettle, June 12, 1987.

Source: *Berlin 1.Mai 1987–12. Juni 1987* (Berlin: Ermittlungsausschusses, 1987), p. 53.

Victory parade for the Hafenstrasse, November 1987.
Source: *Black Flag* (London)

THE AUTONOMEN IN UNIFIED GERMANY

Seldom steady, the pace of history can be wildly erratic and entirely unpredictable. Sometimes it seems that an entire decade elapses without major transformations in international relations. At other times, breathtaking changes occur in a few days or weeks, as in November 1989, when the Berlin Wall came down. Nearly everyone immediately recognized the enormity of the changes under way, but few people expected the subsequent results. In the aftermath of the heady days of the end of the Cold War, East Germans rushed through the wall to have their first experiences as Western consumers, and the government quickly jumped through the window of opportunity to unify the two countries. In the vacuum of power, two social movements emerged: as is well known, thousands of neo-Nazis violently attacked foreigners, murdering and brutalizing them in what was meant to be an ethnic cleansing of the German nation; and during the same period, the Autonomen spread their movement to the east. In this chapter, I discuss both these social movements.

The neo-Nazi upsurge after German reunification coincided with a larger shift in the political landscape of advanced capitalist societies—the international appearance of ethnic chauvinism on a level unattained since World War II. At the end of this chapter, I probe the deep nature of the problem of German identity and find that such chauvinism exists even within the views of some of the most progressive Germans. At their best, autonomous movements pose a species solidarity that transcends ethnic exclusivity. By critically exposing the failure of Germans to go beyond their Germanity, I seek to portray the need for a new species universality. To the Autonomen, neo-Nazi behavior was latently present in the personality structures of individual Germans as well as in the nation's social structures. When immigrants were violently attacked and murdered, the Autonomen came to their defense sometimes more rapidly than the German police.

At first glance, the ineptness of the political elite, tellingly revealed in its inability to manage the economic aspects of reunification, was also to blame for the latitude afforded the xenophobic Nazi minority. A realistic assessment of the actions of government officials, however, reveals less incompetence and more glaring deficiencies of four decades of de-Nazification in both eastern and western Germany. In 1990, as neo-Nazi attacks broke out throughout reunified Germany, the police bloodily repressed the Autonomen but gave neo-Nazis a green light. Judges regularly sentenced perpetrators of violent attacks on immigrants to light fines or short jail terms; government officials made a deal with a rampaging anti-foreigner mob in Rostock, permitting the pogrom to have free run of the city; the Social Democrats joined with conservatives to deport tens of thousands of Roma (as Gypsies prefer to be called) and other immigrants and changed the constitution to seal off Germany's borders to refugees seeking political asylum and economic opportunity.

German reunification occurred most dramatically in Berlin, where thousands of people tore down the wall. The wall's fate—its being sold in pieces—quickly happened to all of East Germany, as speculators from around the world bought up much of the country. Despite rosy promises made by Helmut Kohl about the economy, Germany slid into its deepest slump since the end of World War II. While construction cranes hovered on all sides of Berlin's Potsdamer Platz, the former no-man's-land along the wall now slated to be home to corporate headquarters for such giants as Sony and Mercedes (Daimler-Benz), the German parliament decided to move the federal government there. Although the *Bundestag* will probably not convene in the Reichstag until the twenty-first century, in the first day after the vote in Bonn, housing prices in Berlin jumped another 5 percent on top of the 50 percent increase since the reunification of Germany (100 percent in Kreuzberg). Very quickly, commercial rents soared as much as 900 percent in parts of the city.[1]

Despite the common expectation that the radical direct-action movement in Berlin would disappear with the opening of the wall, especially since West Berlin was run by a leftist coalition government, the reverse was true. A new wave of more than 130 squats engulfed the old eastern part of the city. Massive police attacks on the largest of these in the Mainzerstrasse made it impossible for the Alternative List to continue governing the city in alliance with the Social Democrats. As in 1981, the initiative of the squatters' movement led to the downfall of the city's government. In 1990, however, the government of a unified city tumbled and fell not because of clumsy, Cold War realities but because of the impact of local initiatives. The Social Democrats and the Christian Democrats quickly formed a grand coalition to ensure the governability of Berlin, testimony to the inability of either major party to carry through a policy of repressing the Autonomen.

Within the autonomous scene, many were convinced that the coming of the capital would leave little room for them in Berlin. They feared that rents in Kreuzberg would become so high that it would no longer be home to Turks and Autonomen but to yuppies and government officials. Rather than move out, they vowed never to surrender their base in Berlin without a significant struggle. As one group summed it up:

Since October 3 [1990—the day of German reunification], the government has been blowing a storm against the Left.... A new phase of the confrontation is now beginning. In the future, we will have to deal with even stronger repression. But repression breeds resistance, and this much is clear: We will give no quarter. If their goal is a capital city Berlin, we will build a front-line Berlin. They will gain no peace and quiet in which to conduct their disgusting behavior, and this is no empty threat!

In response to the new constellation of power, groups immediately formed to work against the existing plans to bring the Olympics to Berlin in 2000, and research collectives exposed the authorities' plans for urban renewal and gentrification. Others initiated small-group anti-yuppie actions, attacking upscale restaurants, expensive automobiles, and fancy shops.

In the old eastern part of the city in the months following the *Wende* (turn to a new epoch, as people refer to the collapse of Communism), factories closed by the dozens, rents skyrocketed, museums shut their doors and disposed of their collections, libraries threw away mounds of books, and universities were purged.[2] Cutbacks in daycare undermined the economic independence of women in the east, and stricter regulations governing abortion further impinged upon their ability to determine the course of their lives. Undoubtedly, the most odious aspect of reunification was the rise of neo-Nazis.

NEO-NAZIS AND THE STATE

With reunification, the far Right seized the political initiative and was able to consolidate and expand a considerable base of support. The Republicans, a neo-Fascist party, received nearly a million votes in the national elections in December 1990, and although they did not enter the national parliament, the far Right attracted a sizable following among German youth.[3] By waging a militant campaign against the influx of pornography and prostitution in the east (formerly forbidden except in state-run brothels), they struck a sympathetic chord among many people who otherwise would have been repulsed by their fascist politics. During times of economic hardship, the Right's attempt to channel frustration against the nearly six million foreigners living in Germany may have permanently altered the political and social landscape of Germany. In order to stop the arrival of refugees, the constitution (or Basic Law, as it is called) was amended by the *Bundestag* in May 1993.

As we have already seen in the case of the antinuclear movement, direct actions, played a central role in changing government policy, and after reunification, neo-Nazi skinheads pushed the government as hard as they could. Although they stayed out of Kreuzberg for fear of being beaten up, thousands of young Germans took it upon themselves to Germanize their newly united country. Flush with patriotic pride as their nation unified, bands of young hoodlums roamed the country, attacking Vietnamese workers, Turkish immigrants, and any foreigners—Polish tourists on shopping trips, Americans looking for a party (such as the Olympic luge team), or British schoolteachers on holiday. They brutalized Vietnamese children in kindergartens, sent Greek children on their way home from school to the hospital with broken bones, attacked disabled people in their wheelchairs, and set homeless loners on fire. Other favored targets of the skinheads included punks, gays, lesbians, and anyone who looked like a nonconformist. In the suburbs and countryside, many German youth were compelled to choose between joining the neo-Nazis and hiding. Neo-Nazi youth enjoyed themselves at football games and rock concerts. Their Oi music, a fusion of punk and heavy metal that expunged African influences from rock, was popularized by groups with names such as Destructive Force (*Störkraft*) and Evil Uncles (*Böse Onkelz*). With lyrics such as "Germany awake!" (a slogan used by Hitler) and "Turks out!" skinhead music encouraged attacks.[4]

The casualty list from one month, May 1991, is indicative of the wave of violence. Two Namibians in Wittenberg were thrown off the fifth-floor balcony of a foreigners' hostel by a gang of neo-Nazis. In Dresden, a band of drunken Republicans attacked forty Soviet children who were seriously ill from Chernobyl and were in East Germany for treatment. The house where the children were staying had its windows broken, and burning torches were thrown inside. When the police finally arrived, they saw no reason to make any arrests. On the night of May 6, there were three separate fights involving skinheads. In Hanover, fifty fascists attacked Turkish youths in the train station, and in the ensuing melee, one skinhead was injured when the Turks shot him with a flare gun. In Scheessel, after an empty house had been squatted by Autonomen, fascists attacked it. In Kiel, another squatted house was marched on by skinheads, although the squatters quickly drove them off. During May, one of the squatted houses in what used to be East Berlin was invaded by a band of skinheads in the middle of the night, and several people were badly beaten before help arrived; a bar on Alexanderplatz was also attacked.

These examples are certainly not an exhaustive list, but they convey the feeling that was so common then: that something might happen at any moment. In 1991, several Autonomen living in a squat in eastern Berlin told me that they knew four people who had been killed by neo-fascists in the last three months. Although skinhead attacks occurred throughout the country, Dresden was selected by fascist organizations to become a stronghold of the far Right. In November 1990 (as hundreds of Autonomen in Berlin's Mainzerstrasse were being evicted by thousands of police), neo-Nazis squatted an empty house that became their base of operations. Foreigners were warned to leave the city. In March, fascists threw a Mozambican worker off a streetcar and killed him. Although the police initially refused even to write down the names of witnesses who wished to see the assailants arrested, they later added that case to the more than thirty-five other attacks that were scheduled to be adjudicated in the courts. On New Year's Day at one in the morning, the Café Bronx (the city's first radical bar) was invaded by skinheads, smashed up, and then burned out. When the owner called the police, he received no response. He ran to a nearby paddy wagon, but it pulled away. When he returned to the bar, he was savagely beaten. Needless to say, the bar never reopened. That same winter, a Vietnamese hostel was attacked by neo-Nazis with axes and Molotovs. Employers in Dresden told their foreign workers to avoid walking at night, because it was "life threatening." Leipzig, Saxony's largest city, was reportedly just as dangerous. In an attack modeled on Dresden, a German longhair was killed there on June 6 after being thrown from a streetcar.

The porno dealers and pimps who moved into eastern Germany did not take the fascist attacks on them lightly. On May 31, 1991, they killed the leader of the most militant neo-Nazis in Dresden. For the German media, the killing (and subsequent days of rampage by skinheads) was simply more proof that eastern Germany was sinking into chaos, that the "wild, wild East" was destined to become home to bank robbers, neo-Nazis, and other outlaws. The killing was particularly embarrassing for the federal government, since it occurred on the same weekend that it had invited foreign ministers from the European community to come to Dresden to invest in its future.

In 1991, police estimated the number of hard-core members of neo-Nazi groups in eastern Germany at slightly more than two thousand, a figure regarded as notoriously low by most knowledgeable persons.[5] By the end of 1992, as attacks on foreigners mounted, the government estimated that there were more than forty thousand right-wing extremists in Germany, of whom sixty-five hundred were classified as neo-Nazis.[6] More than twenty-three thousand right-wing extremist crimes were investigated by police in 1993 alone. Altogether, at least eighty killings were attributed to fascists between 1990 and 1994.[7] The "brown network" of skinheads, neo-Nazis, old Nazis, and neo-fascist parties apparently includes many police as well. Among 2,426 police reserves in Berlin, 607 (an astounding one in four) had prior associations with the Right, and half of the entire force was reputed to vote for the Republicans.[8] Police have also been linked to the mistreatment of foreigners. In 1995, Amnesty International published a report accusing police of dozens of such cases. In Bremen, the police systematically mishandled, and in some cases tortured, Africans and Kurds who had had the misfortune of being arrested.[9] In Hamburg, twenty-seven policemen were eventually suspended after being accused of abusing foreigners.[10]

The upsurge of neo-fascism at the beginning of the 1990s was not purely a German phenomenon.[11] Parties such as the National Front in England and France (where Le Pen has received almost 14 percent of national votes), Fini's National Alliance in Italy (with 13 percent of the votes in 1994, enough for five cabinet seats in the Berlusconi government), Jörg Haider's party in Austria (which has drawn almost 20 percent in elections), and the Progress Party in Denmark and Norway are practically indistinguishable from Germany's Republicans. Skinheads first appeared in England, and there have been reports of them attacking people even in normally sedate Switzerland, the Czech Republic, and Belgium.

Contrary to popular belief, the violence in Germany was not mainly in the east. Government statistics consistently showed that more attacks took place in the western part of the country. In eastern Germany, however, European neo-fascists (and their American friends who supplied them with money and printed their propaganda) calculated that they had the best chance to entrench themselves, and that is where they concentrated their resources and energies. They knew well in advance that the campaign promises of an easy transition to a prosperous future made by Helmut Kohl and the Christian Democrats were politicians' jargon. At the end of August 1991, the official unemployment rate was 12.1 percent (1,063,200 out of work), and another 1.45 million people were working reduced hours or being paid simply to show up at work. Half a million more were forced into early retirement, meaning that nearly one worker in three was unemployed. Government subsidies for the transitional period paid these two million people, but the money was phased out at the same time as rents rose sharply.

The housing crisis was nearly as bad as the shortage of jobs. Under the Communists, rents in East Berlin had been fixed at 1 mark per square meter, but they quickly shot up to between 4 and 6 marks per square meter, a 400 to 600 percent hike! Over 500,000 homeless people were counted in West Germany before reunification,[12] but there were few homeless in the east, since everyone was guaranteed a place to live and evictions were constitutionally prohibited. In reunified Germany, however, homelessness grew rapidly, one of the most visible signs of the consolidation of a postmodern regime of accumulation. (See Chapter 7 for discussion of postmodern capitalism.) At least eighty thousand people in both West and East Berlin were looking for apartments in 1990.[13] Because the Communists were perpetually short of cash, many old buildings had been left empty for years—at least fifteen thousand vacant apartments in what used to be East Berlin (perhaps 200,000 in all of eastern Germany).[14] The housing stock there was in such bad shape that even conservative estimates were that thirty-four thousand of the inhabited dwellings had no private toilets and seventy-two thousand were without showers or baths. The population of Berlin is expected to rise from 3.5 million to 5 million over the next twenty years, so the shortages of decent jobs and housing are expected to get worse.[15]

As we know today, economic downturns more often result in fascism than in revolution, and the more severe the downturn, the better the chance that a severe turn to the right will occur. Despite the temptation to posit a facile economic explanation for the resurgence of Nazism, many German sociologists regard the emergence of neo-fascism as conditioned by more than economic factors. The list of causal forces includes the atomization of life, a convoluted sense of what being a man entails, and the fragmentation of what had been a relatively stable social system. Perhaps most important is the peculiarity of the German context. In plain English, once the wall came down, East Germans became second-class citizens, so pride in Germany became a means of promoting their own superiority vis-à-vis foreigners. Rather than live an obscure existence and wait for opportunity to knock, many chose to fight for the purity of German national identity as a way to be somebody. The anonymity and depersonalization of consumer society, which in the affluent West produced the New Left of the 1960s, had an entirely different outcome in the 1990s.

Beginning in 1990, neo-fascist groups such as the Republicans and the National Democratic Party joined the ongoing Monday demonstrations in Leipzig, which played a key role in mobilizing opposition to the Communist government, and it became more difficult for leftist groups to participate. In one instance, protesters opposed to the presence of neo-Nazis were spit on by other demonstrators, who called them "children of the *Stasi*"(the former secret police). Although neo-Nazis existed in East Germany prior to the fall of the Communist regime, they were unable to organize publicly, and the police were generally unsympathetic. Not so in reunified Germany. The police regularly provide them with protection and almost always attack counter-demonstrators. In July 1990, after neo-Nazis had mounted attacks on foreigners, the police moved in to do the job for them. At many train stations, police used tear gas, water, and clubs to prevent Polish, Bulgarian, and Romanian asylum seekers from getting off trains.

For more than a year, the world watched as Germany's future seemed to hang in the balance. Dozens of pogroms broke out in different parts of the country. During the first one in Hoyerswerda in September 1991, hundreds of youth attacked Angolans and Vietnamese in their houses while townspeople cheered. Through either stupidity or design, the government exacerbated nascent contradictions between foreigners and Germans. In Rostock, a building used as a youth center was taken away from local people and turned into a temporary housing facility for refugees. The resentment over this building's transfer to foreigners could have been easily allayed by allocating an alternative site, but none was provided, and in August 1992, Rostock became the scene of the next major pogrom. More than a thousand people attacked a refugee center containing hundreds of Romanian Gypsies and Vietnamese workers. Shouting "Next to us, the Hafenstrasse is nothing!" the crowd stayed in the streets for nearly a week, attacking foreigners and strutting in the media spotlight and support of the populace—and of the local police. As one observer described it: "One thousand neo-Nazis in Rostock firebombed a building housing 200 Romanian Gypsies, while demonstrators chanted 'Sieg Heil.' Onlookers applauded and chanted 'Germany for the Germans.'"[16]

The police chief made a deal with the mob: the police would withdraw from the city for four hours, during which time the rightists would have free rein.[17] When the refugee center was set on fire with at least a hundred Vietnamese inside, the fire department refused to answer the call for help, and the police were nowhere in sight. A German television crew was caught in the burning building. Using a cellular phone, they contacted their network in Berlin; from there, phone calls were made to Bonn, which eventually resulted in police and fire intervention to save the German reporters (and the foreigners). As neo-Nazis roamed the city, the pogrom spread to at least a dozen other towns and cities. Only when Autonomen converged in force on Rostock did the attacks cease (and the police appear in large numbers). After nearly a week of terror, there had been only about a hundred arrests, but on the first day of the Autonomen counterattack, the police detained more than that number of antifascist activists.

Combined with Chancellor Helmut Kohl's refusal to visit Rostock

TABLE 5.1

HOW GERMANS VIEW FOREIGNERS AND MINORITIES[19]

Group	Favorable	Unfavorable	Don't Know
Vietnamese*	59	29	15
Jews	52	24	24
Soviet émigrés	37	31	32
Turks	35	46	19
Poles	31	50	19
Romanians	28	44	28
Gypsies (Roma)	19	59	22

*Only East Germans were asked their opinions of Vietnamese.

after the fighting had ended, police and government cooperation with the neo-Nazis left little doubt that antiforeigner violence would be allowed to run its course. Emboldened by government inaction and media attention, neo-Nazis embarked upon a systematic campaign of murder: the subsequent firebombing deaths of two Turkish children and a grandmother in Mölln and five Turkish women in Solingen were neither the first nor the last criminal homicides committed by those bent on establishing a Fourth Reich, but they shocked the country. In their wake, hundreds of thousands of Germans marched with lanterns to protest the violence in processions called *Lichterketten*. In Munich, 300,000 people turned out; in Hamburg, 250,000; in Essen, 300,000; and in Nuremburg, 100,000. Besides marching in candlelight processions, progressive Germans distanced themselves from neo-Nazis by demonstrating at government offices, volunteering to work at asylum centers, and reinvigorating a militant antifascist movement.

Nonetheless, neo-Nazi attacks continued. Leftist activists were targeted, and several were murdered in different parts of the country. Without substantial opposition, the right-wing violence and murders provided impetus to the prompt passage of anti-immigrant legislation by the *Bundestag*. It then swept through the parliament with support from both major parties. On July 1, 1993, the new laws regarding asylum went into effect, and with this victory, the neo-fascists' extremist violence subsided. Under the provisions of the new law, the number of asylum seekers permitted to enter Germany was drastically reduced. Other legislation had already succeeded in deporting tens of thousands of foreigners. The first to go were the Roma. Ignoring a Helsinki Watch human rights report issued in September 1991 that detailed the mistreatment of the Roma, Germany offered to pay Romania millions of dollars to take tens of thousands of them back.[18] During the Third Reich, more than 500,000 Roma were murdered in a systematic Nazi extermination campaign, and German public opinion remains remarkably hostile to them even today, as Table 5.1 details.

Whereas a majority of those polled had a "favorable" impression of Jews, only 19 percent were so inclined to regard Roma. By 1995, as the government supervised ethnic relocations, it reportedly paid tens of millions of marks to the government of Vietnam in exchange for its taking back thousands of Vietnamese workers stranded in Germany after the end of the Cold War.

The rulings of German courts have also played a large role in encouraging the revival of Nazism and fomenting racism: Five skinheads, convicted of beating to death an African immigrant on November 25, 1990, in the eastern town of Eberswalde, were sentenced to two to four years. Three men who pleaded guilty to attacking a residence for foreigners during the pogrom in Hoyerswerda were sentenced to probation. In court, they expressed frustration at being unemployed and at failing to rob a Vietnamese street vendor. Before announcing the reason for his leniency, the judge described their crime as a common one.[20] In another case, a judge ruled that an anti-fascist group, SOS Rassismus, that had guarded a residence for foreigners in Nauen for five months would not be permitted in the house because they "disturbed the quiet at night."[21] Another judge in Hildesheim blocked construction of a residence for foreigners seeking asylum on the ground that "odors from the home might disturb neighbors."[22] In Flensburg in the fall of 1992, a judge ordered restitution of 10 percent of their travel expenses to a group of German tourists because they had had to endure the "sickening" sight of disabled people in the breakfast room of their hotel.[23] Such rulings were not confined to lower courts in small towns. The federal court in Karlsruhe, the country's highest appeals court, overturned the conviction of the leader of the far right National Democratic Party by ruling that his claim that the Holocaust never occurred did not in itself constitute incitement to racial hatred.[24] Although the ruling was later reversed, the ambivalence of judges reflected the huge base of neo-fascist sentiment.

In order to understand the context of these rulings, it should be pointed out that de-Nazification was short-circuited in West Germany by U.S. authorities whose priority (as determined in Washington) became fighting Communism, a struggle in which former Nazi enemies became valuable allies.[25] No Nazi judges or attorneys were ever convicted in the FRG's federal courts. The political and psychological structures of postwar Germany carried within them extraordinarily anti-Semitic and authoritarian characteristics. A few examples should suffice to demonstrate: On January 3, 1953, the West German patent office in Wiesbaden issued a patent to

J. A. Topf and Sons for the design of the crematorium at Auschwitz and other Nazi camps, a patent for a "process and Apparatus for Incineration of Carcasses, Cadavers, and Parts Thereof" that contained a design innovation: it used the fat of burning corpses as fuel for the furnaces.[26] Forty years later, at the end of July 1993, the commandant of the Nazi death camp at Treblinka (where about one million people were murdered, the majority of them Jews) was released from prison after serving thirty-four years, despite an appeal by state prosecutors.[27] In some parts of West Germany, Hitler's anti-Roma laws remained in effect until 1970, and the statutes used by Nazis to imprison homosexuals were not thrown out until 1969.[28] Even as late as 1995, the Bavarian town of Plattling published an official list of honorary citizens that included "Adolf Hitler, Reich Chancellor" and "Heinrich Himmler, SS-Reichsführer."[29]

The policies of the German government criminalized and reversed the communist past while turning a blind eye (or worse) to the Nazi legacy. Property in the eastern part of the country that was nationalized under the Communist regime—but not under the Nazis—was returned to its previous owners. If there was one thing that united the United States and the USSR during the entire Cold War, it was the belief that the Junkers—the old Prussian landowning aristocracy that had built up German militarism and supported Hitler—would not regain control of their estates. Nonetheless, the German government's policy was to deny Jews whose property had been confiscated by the Nazis any chance of regaining it while restoring Junkers' estates. Other prominent features that also legitimated the Nazi past include the fact that former *Stasi* chief Milke's conviction and sentencing were not for actions he committed while running the East German secret police but for the murder of two policemen who had hunted him when he fought against ascendant National Socialism in 1931.

Public opinion and small-town parochialism also served as effective barriers to an open multicultural society. In Dolgenbrodt, many of the town's 260 residents met on two occasions at an inn to discuss how to keep foreigners out of the asylum home that was being constructed. At their second meeting, they passed the hat and raised $1,200, which they paid to neo-Nazis to torch the building. Although the man arrested by police for arson was released for lack of evidence, the case was reopened after *Taz* reported the story.

After the murders in Mölln and Solingen, Chancellor Helmut Kohl refused to attend the funerals of the victims or the subsequent memorial services. When Kohl publicly declared that "Germany is not a country of immigration," he left no doubt where his sympathies lay. A senior U.S. diplomat accused the government of encouraging skinhead violence against the nearly seven million foreigners legally residing in Germany. As arson attacks on foreigners spread throughout the country, Germany was summoned before the United Nations Human Rights Commission to explain why it was not doing more to protect foreigners. The government finally moved. It banned eleven of the most militant hate groups and cracked down on Oi music, but it also deported tens of thousands of foreigners seeking asylum.[30] These measures only increased the stature of the Right, the former by adding the glitter of illegality to its appeal, and the latter by giving the impression that the goal of a foreigner-free Germany was finally being implemented by the *Bundestag*.

Although economic crisis and the political vacuum in the east are important dimensions of the explanation for the reappearance of Nazism in Germany, how identity is constructed and understood in everyday life—by Germans of all political persuasions—also needs to be considered. To put it in a nutshell: one's identity is one's blood. In the United States, an individual's descent is traced through his or her family's national origins, but in Germany, biology is destiny. One's national identification is equivalent to the national origins of one's genes. Thousands of people born and raised in Germany who speak no language other than German are not entitled to citizenship if their parents do not have German blood flowing through their veins.[31] German Americans from Texas who do not speak a word of German have a better chance of becoming citizens than do third-generation Turkish Germans.[32]

The German problem revolves precisely around this construction of identity on the basis of biology as opposed to territory. Hitler launched his extermination programs to purify the gene pool, not to reduce unemployment (and his mass murder succeeded in accomplishing that goal). To "engineer" correct genes, disabled persons were targeted alongside Jews, Roma, gays, and communists. Ironically, those who explain Nazism as Teutonic propensities toward violence carried in German genes share common assumptions with the Nazi concept of biologically determined behavior. Although their evaluation of German national character differs, they similarly conceive its roots in biology.[33]

As in past decades, the future of Germany hinges on events in Berlin. The neo-fascists predicted that in ten years, streets and squares would be named after Adolf Hitler, and shortly thereafter, the Fourth Reich would appear. Their electoral slogans were "Berlin must remain a German city" and "Germany for Germans," and they railed against the "Jewish-American conspiracy" planning the "New American World Order" (presumably one that does not allow Germany its proper role as a great power). Their demand for "equal wages for German workers in all of Germany" resonated in eastern Germany, where wages (and prices) had been kept artificially low by the Communists. At the beginning of 1989, the Republicans were elected to the city council of Berlin with 7.9 percent of the vote (enough for eleven seats), and another neo-fascist group won seats in Frankfurt. In 1992 and 1993, the Republicans had impressive vote tallies in Baden-Württemburg and Schleswig-Holstein, but they received well below 5 percent of the vote in the national elections of 1994.

AUTONOMY AND ANTIFASCISM

The German government's failure to halt the advancing neo-Nazi movement after reunification came as no surprise to the Autonomen. In their view, the FRG's governing elite contained many former Nazis, and few doubted that most police were secretly members of fascist groups. Given the failure of their parents' generation to stop Hitler's rise to power, is it any wonder that the Autonomen militantly fought resurgent Nazism? Radicals often wore *Gegen Nazis* (Against Nazis) patches, part of a wardrobe that was more than a political statement, since these patches were a defiant invitation to combat in any chance encounter with a group of skinheads. Many Autonomen interpreted the candlelight vigils as Germans' attempts to look good in the international press, not as signs of their having overcome the racism endemic to their heritage. When Chancellor Kohl and President Richard von Weizsäcker, the same political leaders who refused to crack down on neo-Nazis and debated how to stem the flow of foreigners into Germany, appeared at a huge rally against violence in Berlin, Autonomen pelted them with eggs, paint bombs, and tomatoes.[34]

Believing that the police would do little or nothing to stop attacks on foreigners, the Autonomen took it upon themselves to do so. They attacked the squatted neo-Nazi center in the Lichterfelde neighborhood of Berlin in 1990 and mobilized scores of counterdemonstrations that prevented Nazis from marching. As an antifascist movement grew out of the Autonomen, it gathered momentum. It disrupted public events sponsored by neo-Nazis and came to the rescue of foreigners under attack whom the police were unable (or, as many people insisted, unwilling) to protect.[35] The antifas (as antifascists are known) were one of the sources of support for a multicultural Germany.[36] They campaigned for voting rights for foreign residents and made special efforts (such as printing leaflets in several languages) to include foreigners in their events. From their inception, most antifa organizations grew out of the anti-imperialist (anti-imp) tendency in the movement. Significantly, antifascism was one of the key pillars of the East German government's self-definition.

Autonome-Antifa (M) was one important antifa group that was Leninist. The antifas and the Autonomen were tied together by their militance in the face of neo-Nazis more than by shared political views or cultural affinities.

The refusal of many people to be "good Germans" brought them into conflict with both the police and the neo-Nazis, and the resultant street fights added to the chaos as well as to the demands for "law and order." In March 1989 (before the wall came down), about a thousand antifas tried to evict an elected Republican from his office, but the police intervened. On April 20, 1989 (the hundredth birthday of Hitler), antifas prevented many planned fascist rallies throughout Germany, but they were brutally attacked by the police. After the usual street fights, the media turned their wrath on the antifas, accusing them of subverting the democratic principles of modern Germany. Even *Taz* justified the police attacks by saying that the antifas "were armed to the teeth." *Taz* ran daily stories warning against antifas direct actions, since the Republicans were a "democratically elected party." Apparently, *Taz*, like its counterparts in the Greens, would stop at nothing to defend the existing system of representative democracy. For them, the rights of the minorities being attacked were less important than the rights of German neo-Nazis to participate in government.

Standing alone as the sole opponents of neo-Nazi participation in government, the antifas were compelled to organize themselves more effectively. In May 1989, the National Alliance of Antifas was established, with active groups in ten cities and organizing committees in a dozen more. On October 14, sixty antifas women prevented the Republicans' chairperson from delivering a speech to another right-wing party, and he had to be escorted to safety by the police. By the time the wall was opened (November 9, 1989), the police were in no mood to show restraint to the antifas. As millions of East Berliners visited West Berlin for the first time in their lives, a neo-Nazi rally in front of the Reichstag, permitted by the authorities, was "canceled" by Autonomen, which then had to turn and face a police assault. In Göttingen on November 17, an Autonomen woman was chased by police onto a highway, where she was killed by a speeding car. In the following days, downtown department stores, banks, and government buildings were attacked by Autonomen in more than thirty cities.[37] On November 25, in a tense and emotional mood, more than fifteen thousand people gathered in Göttingen. The masked "black block" was two thousand strong, and when the peaceful demonstration ended, they attacked the police, ninety of whom were injured in the ensuing battle.

The media made the Autonomen appear to be perpetrators of violence, just like the neo-Nazis. When Autonomen and neo-Nazis clashed, the state appeared neutral and above social conflicts. For its part, the neo-Fascist movement enjoyed its new visibility, all the more so because its treasuries were augmented with millions of dollars raised in the United States. After squatted skinhead houses in Dresden and Frankfurt (on the Oder) were evicted, new ones were quickly purchased. The German government's ban on printing Nazi literature was circumvented by having most material imported from the United States. As Klansmen and right-wing racists from the United States made appearances in Germany, the far Right developed its thinking to include new constituencies. An internal memorandum of the Deutsche Allianz (one of the most ambitious of the many fascist formations that rose to prominence after reunification) ordered: "Social drop-outs and previously neglected strata have to be approached and politicized, even when this causes conservatives to turn their noses up." Targeting the constituency of the Autonomen during the Gulf War, neo-Nazis showed up as "supporters" at peace rallies, and they approached squatted houses of the Autonomen with an offer to ally against police attacks, an offer few houses would even discuss. The dangers to the Autonomen were that their base might be turned rightward, but also that the federal government was using the Right against them.

Between the fall of the wall and reunification, as attacks on immigrants spread, antifascist mobilizations were the most pressing matter for many activists. In August 1990, more than a thousand fascists were permitted to parade in Wunsiedel on the anniversary of Nazi Rudolf Hess' suicide, and when twenty-five hundred antifas showed up to stop them, the police attacked. On October 2, 1990, as midnight (and German reunification) approached, demonstrations began in many cities. In Berlin, eight thousand Autonomen marched out of Kreuzberg carrying banners reading "Never Again Germany" and "Shut Up Germany—That's Enough." As they made their way to Alexanderplatz, street fights broke out with the more than ten thousand police who surrounded them, and the fighting lasted into the night. In Göttingen, more than a thousand Autonomen marching behind a "Nazis Get Out" banner created chaos in the downtown area. Whereas most Germans were jubilant in their nation's moment of glory, the Autonomen's isolation tellingly revealed their distance from the mainstream.

As the antifas struggle intensified, it created space for foreigners to organize and gave them encouragement to defend themselves. After the murder of an Afro-German woman in Berlin in January 1990, a Black Unity Committee formed. On November 16, 1990, a twenty-year-old Republican was killed after he and his associates chased three Turks who had gotten into the same subway car. The neo-Nazis pulled pistols out and threatened the Turks, but one of the Turks quickly used his knife to wound two of the attackers and kill the third. Grudgingly, neo-Nazis were compelled to begin rethinking their attacks, although it would take years for them to admit it. Perhaps more than anywhere else in German political culture, minorities found space for themselves within the contestational universe created by the Autonomen. Beginning in 1987, Turkish youth gangs participated in radical street fights, sometimes to the chagrin of Autonomen hoping for a peaceful event. In Frankfurt and Berlin, youthful minority street gangs developed distinct (sub)cultural forms that indicated their integration into German culture.[38]

Although the harsh reality of German politics and prejudice in the 1990s demanded that the autonomous movement expend much of its energies in the antifascist struggle, the Autonomen also continued to carve out free spaces within which the movement was free to develop itself and live according to principles of its own making. Ten years after the squatters of 1980, a new wave of building occupations occurred. The cultural hegemony of the far Right and the government's capability to muster thousands of police against the Autonomen meant that the movement's efforts to build base areas would not be easy. The police had stood by while anti-foreigner mobs went on rampages, but they behaved quite differently with the Autonomen, particularly after they were ordered to assault the new Autonomen base in the Mainzerstrasse.

THE BATTLE FOR MAINZERSTRASSE

Immediately after the wall came down, hundreds of vacant buildings in East Berlin and the relative vacuum of power there presented the Autonomen with a unique opportunity to seize new buildings and spread their movement to the east. Even before squatters from what used to be West Berlin moved into empty houses in the old eastern part of the city, the first houses there had already been squatted by locals. Beginning in January 1990, two months after the fall of the wall, and continuing to April, more than seventeen houses were occupied by East Germans. In their negotiations with the interim authorities, these new squats were guaranteed the right to exist. On April 30, a group from Kreuzberg took over an entire block of twelve abandoned tenements in the Mainzerstrasse, five-story buildings that stood empty because they were scheduled to be torn down.[39] One of the buildings was occupied solely by gays, another by women, and there was enough room for a movie theater, a bookstore, and several cafés and bars. In the next few months, hundreds of squatters, many of whom had accumulated significant political experience in the west, took over abandoned buildings in the adjoining neighborhoods of what used to be East Berlin. The movement spread to Magdeburg, Erfurt, Potsdam, Halle, Leipzig, and Dresden. An activist from Berkeley, California, described the scene in Berlin:

> Over 1000 squatters here from Germany mainly but also Italy, Canada. The US, Japan, Peru etc. have taken over old, dilapidated buildings and through sheer dedication and struggle, turned them into habitable buildings with communal kitchens, libraries, cafés and more—into a real community, a vibrant and colorful community where gays and lesbians are out and strong, where anarchists argue politics, plan actions and so on. And of course, 95% of these people have no jobs, making it even more remarkable that these buildings were revived from decay.... The squatter/anarchist movement here is about autonomy, community, vitality and is not organized around violence, street fighting and so on. Clearly thousands of hours of work has gone into finding, entering, repairing, cleaning, planning, raising money, dealing with bureaucratic petty officials, painting, partying all for the squats.[40]

On July 24, housing regulations from the west became valid in what used to be East Germany. This meant that the *Berliner Linie*, West Berlin's hard-line policy of clearing out new squats within twenty-four hours and completing negotiations on the government's terms in remaining ones, would apply to the whole city. Facing imminent police action, more than eighty of the new squats organized a negotiating council that began discussions with the authorities. Their foremost demand was that the fate of all the houses be negotiated in one agreement. The city administration wanted no part of a group solution, citing confusion over ownership of property in what used to be East Germany as the reason.[41] Three months of negotiations produced nothing, and on October 8, the city abruptly broke off the discussions. Later the city's chief negotiator stated that a peaceful solution was "politically undesirable."

Over the next month, the squatters tried all available means to come up with a peaceful solution, but the authorities were determined to break the spirit of the movement. Individual contracts were acceptable, they said, but not the demand for a group solution encompassing all the houses. At 7 AM on November 12, three squatted houses were evicted in the vicinity of Mainzerstrasse. Autonomen gathered to protest the evictions and then paraded through the city chanting "Clear out the prisons, not our houses!" When the group returned to the Mainzerstrasse, hundreds of police and a water cannon awaited them. The police shot tear gas and water into the buildings on both sides of the street, although one side consisted of legally rented apartments. In one apartment, the tear gas forced the evacuation of a family with a very sick infant. The neighborhood's chief elected representative, Helios Mendeburu, implored the police to stop, but he too was shot at with tear gas and water.

The squatters feared that all the houses in Mainzerstrasse were going to be evicted, and they began building barricades and digging trenches in the streets. At the same time, they called a press conference at which they announced their readiness to negotiate, promising that the barricades would be dismantled if the police would leave and the city would provide them with a written guarantee that they would not be evicted. Without warning, the police again attacked, this time with several water cannons. Not only was normal tear gas shot, but even stronger CS and CN varieties were used. A group of prominent city politicians from a spectrum of parties (Social Democrats, Alliance '90/Greens, the Party of Democratic Socialism, and the AL) tried to form a human shield between the police and the barricades, and even though they were swept away by the water cannons, they regrouped and stood their ground for hours. Finally the police pulled back and began to talk with some of these prominent citizens (derisively referred to as "promis" in the scene). True to their word, the squatters dismantled some of the barricades and hoped for a negotiated settlement.

Throughout the next day, discussions continued. The squatters held another press conference, this time to counter the media's assertion that they were unwilling to negotiate. Documents proving that they had been engaged in discussions with the city for six months were made available to the press, and they reiterated their willingness to clear the remaining barricades as soon as the city guaranteed not to evict them by force. Neither of these statements appeared in the mainstream media.

At 5PM, alarming news reached the Mainzerstrasse. More than three thousand police were to begin assembling in twelve hours for a final assault. According to sources, the Berlin police were being joined by a wide variety of tactical police units from what used to be West Germany (*Sondereinsatz-kommandos, Bundesgrenzschutz*), as well as by the equivalent of SWAT teams (special units of federal antiterrorist troops that had been used in 1977 to kill the hijackers of a plane in Mogadishu). The former East German *Volkspolizei* (*Vopos*, or People's Police) were considered unreliable. (One of the stories told about the *Vopos* has them evicting a women's squat. After the eviction, they locked the door and stood out front. The women simply went around to the back and retook the building through a roof door. They hung a sign out the front reading "Police 1, Squatters 1." The police simply walked away. They had only been ordered to evict the squatters once.)

After the news of the police build-up reached Mainzerstrasse, the barricades were strengthened and the ditches deepened. Under banners reading "Where the state stops, life begins!" more than a thousand people prepared the defenses through the night.[42] The barricades were reinforced by car frames, beds, and floorboards, and when they were finished, they were thirty-five feet thick. In the words of one squatter: "The support from outside was super. Many who didn't want to join the fight helped us in a variety of ways. An architect explained to us how the trenches had to be constructed so that the armored cars couldn't go over them, and a construction worker showed us how to use a jackhammer and a dredger. One of the neighbors put a loudspeaker in his window so we could be accompanied by good music."

At 3:45AM, a fire of suspicious origin broke out in the basement of one of the tenements. The street was a flurry of activity as everyone gathered sand or formed bucket brigades to put out the fire. Someone tried to call the fire department, but the block's one remaining telephone had ceased to function. Finally, fire trucks arrived and the barricades were cleared by the squatters to allow them in. As if by design, when the fire was finally extinguished, the telephone worked again.

At 6AM, the police moved in behind a thick cover of tear gas. Although forbidden in Berlin, rubber bullets were fired at squatters on the rooftops. The fire in the basement broke out again, but this time the fire department refused to help, so the squatters had to use much of their energy to extinguish it. The first armored police car through the barricades got stuck in a trench and had to be towed out. One of the water cannons was set on fire and was evacuated as it burned out of control. Police snipers wearing masks continued to fire rubber bullets at squatters on the rooftops, who in turn threw Molotovs, paving stones, and metal rods at the police below. Many of the injured Autonomen were treated on the scene by movement medics wearing gas masks and white helmets emblazoned with a red fist.

Despite the determined resistance, the battle was over in three hours. More than 130 police were injured, four of whom required hospitalization. Even more squatters were wounded, particularly after the arrest of 417, nearly all of whom were severely beaten while in custody. Among the ranks of the more than two hundred people who managed to elude arrest, there were many serious injuries. Besides the destroyed water cannon, fifteen paddy wagons were also burned or destroyed, and the damage caused by the street fighting was estimated in the millions of marks.

The media sensationalized the events, reporting that it was "man against man, meter by meter, floor by floor." Berlin's mayor justified his unprecedented use of force by declaring that the squatters had been "prepared to kill." Reporters had said that the squatters were armed with Russian weapons (now cheaply available), but all that the police could say was that a pistol and a "super-molli" capable of burning a water cannon had been found in the building. The squatters had a variety of weapons for use against the police, but all denied the existence of a pistol. Moreover, despite the "man against man" headlines in the press, 111 women were among those arrested, many of whom had been in the front lines.

That night more than fifteen thousand people (the *New York Times* reported the number to be "tens of thousands") marched through Berlin to protest. The Roman Catholic bishop of Brandenburg deplored the police violence, stating that "violence of this sort, once begun, soon becomes endemic." The next day, counterviolence erupted. Autonomous groups occupied city offices in Berlin to protest the police violence, and even the Berlin police union criticized the attack: "Some 135 injured officers and untold plunder and destruction are the result of a flawed security policy," it said in a prepared statement. A student strike shut down the institutes for sociology, philosophy, political science, and psychology at the Free University. Students wearing masks and signs parodying the mayor's comment about squatters being "ready to kill" refused to allow employees to enter some of the institutes. *Neues Deutschland*, the newspaper of the old Communist regime, railed against "the brutal police terror," adding that the East German police attack in October 1989 (on the fortieth birthday of East Germany) was a "boy scout jamboree" in comparison to violence at the Mainzerstrasse. There were protests in more than ten other cities.

The defeat suffered by the movement at Mainzerstrasse dampened the spirit of resistance. The solidarity evident in the demand for a negotiated settlement including all the houses soon broke down, and the remaining squatted houses began individually negotiating the best deal they could get. For months, the squatters' council did not even meet. As people began to be sentenced to jail time for defending Mainzerstrasse, further demoralization set in. One man received a year for throwing a molli, a harsh sentence by German standards, but probably much less than the consequences he would have suffered for such an act in the United States.

After Mainzerstrasse, Berlin's coalition government could not continue, particularly because the AL's base of support included many who identified with the squatters. Indeed, two AL representatives who sat on the city council had been arrested in the occupied houses, but they were released under the rules of parliamentary immunity. In a meeting of the eleven elected representatives of the AL, they quickly agreed to end the coalition with the Social Democrats. Berlin's Social Democratic Mayor

Momper criticized them for withdrawing from the government, calling their decision "the coward's solution of stealing away from responsibility when times get tough." The AL insisted that it had not been consulted on the decision to evict Mainzer, nor had the city government even considered its offer to serve as intermediary between the police and the squatters. Since Berlin is a city-state, the city council has control of the police, and Momper's decision to use force without the approval of the AL was plainly contrary to any notion of coalition government.

In the weeks following the eviction of the Mainzerstrasse, support for negotiated settlements was proclaimed by local politicians racing to ensure that their constituents would be spared violence. Nonetheless, the police continued to evict other squats. Simultaneously, gentrification of Kreuzberg accelerated as the immense political changes associated with the fall of the East German regime revamped the cultural-political landscape of the western part of the city. Prior to the fall of the wall, Kreuzberg was at the far end of West Berlin, but in the unified city, it lies near its center, within walking distance of the Reichstag and Potsdamer Platz. Many of the neighborhood's buildings were never gut-rehabbed ("sanitized," as the Germans call it), so architecturally as well as geographically, it has become quite a desirable place to live. The mix of Turks, punks, marginally employed youth, and artists who live there are being forced out, not by police attacks but by the impersonal mechanisms of the market.

In response, autonomous groups seeking to preserve the independence and character of their neighborhoods intensified their attacks on yuppie entrepreneurs, leading to a widespread perception of the Autonomen as little more than neighborhood mafias (Kiezmafia). Seeking to create a "dead zone for speculators and yuppie-pigs," groups waged a concerted campaign against gentrification in Kreuzberg. They vandalized upscale restaurants catering to professionals—in some cases throwing excrement inside—torched luxury automobiles costing in excess of $40,000, and repeatedly damaged businesses they deemed undesirable.[43] The police were unable to stop these attacks, in part because there were so many possible suspects—"1200 violence-prone Autonomen in Kreuzberg," according to their estimate.[44] Autonomist intervention in civil society took many forms. In early February 1993, about a dozen Autonomen interrupted a speech by Alain de Benoist, whom they considered "one of the chief theoreticians of French neo-fascism." After escorting him from the lecture hall, they beat him, broke his glasses, and left him in a distant part of the city. Later that month, another group stormed Sputnik, a small movie theater in Kreuzberg, sprayed the projectionist with tear gas, and used butyric acid to destroy a copy of the film Terror 2000, which they considered "sexist and racist." They promised to return and "destroy everything" if the theater decided to show the movie again.[45]

The desperation felt by many at the perceived invasion of their neighborhood lies behind the civil Luddism they practice. Although not as acceptable as passively getting arrested, such actions are a form of civil disobedience. Many autonomists believe that in order to preserve their way of life, they must smash the machinery of consumer society and contest all the forces that seek to colonize their community. Despite continually negative press, unrepentant autonomists published a satirical year-end report, "Autonomia Inc.," modeled on a corporate balance sheet, in which they detailed dozens of neighborhood actions.[46]

THE CONTRADICTIONS OF AUTONOMY

The foregoing description of the scene in Berlin could easily lead outsiders to think that all of Kreuzberg and the squats in the east were occupied by hard-core radicals bent on fighting the police. In reality, much of Kreuzberg was comfortable, and many of the new squats were occupied by students and unemployed young people who had nowhere else to live. In a city where available housing was scant and the fee to move into an apartment was in the thousands of dollars, moving into a house with free rent was irresistible for many young people. Willing to risk little more than having to move out at the first sign of a coming eviction, they were called "opportunists" by those for whom squatting was a political act. For others, preservation of neighborhoods facing gentrification was the reason they occupied buildings. Squatters in Potsdam issued a statement that received much public support when they proclaimed the need "to prevent the destruction of the baroque quarter of the city" as one of their motivations for occupying empty houses scheduled for demolition.

Among the political squatters, a healthy and widespread skepticism toward their own importance was so strong that many refused even to characterize themselves as a movement, pointing to the opportunists among them and lamenting the new rental contracts agreed to by all but a few of the houses. As one of them told me: "This is not a movement since the opportunist dimension is so strong. If the houses were to come under heavy pressure from the state, most people would simply take off." He explained the new wave of squats in 1990 as caused by the collapse of the Communist regime and the global realignment of power ushered in by Gorbachev, not by the explosive potential of a restrained movement. The wall's opening was an unprecedented chance to squat a house and also to try to spread the movement to the east. But the cool reception they received dashed any illusions they might have had about the radical potential of East Germans.

As in 1980, for more radical squatters, the squats were a "liberated area" serving as "organs of revolutionary dual power" and a "starting-point for the destruction of the state and the system." But in 1990, activists were more modest and made less grandiose claims for their actions' importance. At a minimum, squatting actualized an attempt to live differently—to be part of a collective rather than living alone or in a patriarchal family. They were part of the resplendent "scene" that had emerged spontaneously and included cartoonists (notably Franziska Becker and Seyfried), mural painters, political bands, architects, and artists of all media. Collectives contradicted middle-class prosperity and the isolation of consumer society. Group houses served an essential function by uniting people who otherwise would suffer severely from the alienation that is so widespread today. Particularly in smaller German cities, squatted autonomous centers played a vital role in providing a critical mass for the very existence of a movement. A leaflet from Mainz written by a group announcing its occupation of a new youth center put it this way:

> We need a house in which we can build up our own non-commercial and unconventional culture and make real our conceptions of political work—without control or censure! We need immediately a center in which the possibility exists to work, to have events like movies, theater, concerts and discussions and above all to create a group living space. The high rents and lack of housing in university city Mainz are as much the reason to create living space as the isolation of apartments which are nothing more than toilets and silos in which today we are compelled to live.

Big enough to include movie theaters, practice rooms for bands, bookshops, bars, women's centers, and some of the few openly gay public spaces, group houses were the basis for autonomous culture and politics. As one of the squatters explained their significance: "Politics assumes an entirely different relation to everyday life when last night's meetings are discussed over breakfast. Not only is the movement's progress accelerated, but truly important issues, ones which are lost in the shuffle when we live in isolation, are topics of immediate concern and action." The group houses that were fought for and won in 1980 and 1990 embody a collective form of life that negates the atomization of contemporary society; their egalitarian and leaderless structures stand outside normal hierarchical relationships rather than reproducing them; and collectively determined campaigns and productions avoid alienation from the products of heteronomously determined work. As opposed to the mainstream, which views gays or immigrants as "other," within the scene, diversity is the rule, not the exception. Although German racism remains a national problem, Kreuzberg and other movement neighborhoods have more than their share of immigrants. Daily interaction and friendships create a context where objectification of others is subverted. The fetishization of commodities and the allure of individual consumerism give way to a sensibility of utility. Collectives need fewer durable goods and involve less waste than households composed of atomized individuals and couples. Automobiles are shared among several people, as are VCRs, which can easily be carried from room to room in the *Wohngemeinschaften*.

For many squatters, the desire (or even need) to live in a collective is more than a whim; it is a vital need so strong that they preferred to remain homeless rather than move into an isolated apartment. After the eviction of the Lübbenerstrasse, for example, members of the group lived for awhile in tents in Lausitzer Platz, even though the December cold was severe. One of them was pregnant, and when she was offered an apartment with a shower by a member of the city government, she declined, saying that she wanted to live with the whole group. They were one of the groups that helped occupy the largest squat in eastern Berlin (located at the Brünnenstrasse no. 7), and it was one of the few squats that included people who had lived in East Berlin before the *Wende*. Comprised of four separate apartment buildings and a large back courtyard, the squat accommodated a wide variety of people. In 1992, tired of being saddled with the chores, the women insisted on having their own building. Despite what could easily have become an acrimonious situation, the group continued to function more or less as a unit.

Of all the people I met during my first trip to Berlin after the dissolution of East Germany, Tilman left me with the strongest impression. His father had been a general in the East German army and his mother a ranking member of the Unified Socialist Party (usually referred to as the Communist Party). After the travel ban imposed by the Communists was lifted, he had been to western Germany three times: once to the occupied houses at the Hafenstrasse in Hamburg, once to an antifascist demonstration, and finally to Bavaria to "have a look at the mountains." I asked him where he would most like to go now that he could freely travel. After a moment's reflection, he replied, "to El Salvador." Incredulous by now, I asked why. "Because," he calmly continued, "a collective doing political work there could be enormously constructive." For Tilman, living in a squat was a vital need.

The uprooting of established reality's hold on everyday life should not be envisioned along the lines of an overnight insurrection magically curing all of society's ills. The cradle-to-grave manipulation of life and increasing regulation of family relations took centuries to occur. Re-creating values (or deconstructing corporate culture) will no doubt be a process involving several generations. Although supposed to be "liberated areas," squats were not free of internal problems. Some people enforced political conformity and sought to destroy differences. The oft-criticized compulsory dress code (all black) and mandatory political approval of violence against police are two common examples. Uniformity was enforced through a variety of means: defamation, isolation, and even physical confrontation. One story told of a squat consisting of two houses with a dilapidated electrical system, The people in the back house received no electricity when the band in the front house hooked up its equipment. After weeks of acrimony, one of the squatters in the back house finally took an axe to the electrical connections leading to the band's working room. No one was severely hurt in the ensuing melee because cool heads prevented the situation from getting out of control.

More serious are instances of male violence reported by Autonomen women in three cities from 1987 to 1989. In Bielefeld, an antifas was named as the man who had raped a woman. In Duisberg, one Autonomen was reported to have raped three different women over two years. As the controversy over what should be done with him raged, the public response of two of his friends was that "Micha in the first place is our comrade." As debate intensified, these same men wrote a leaflet in his defense, telling his accusers. "Stop the shit so we can get on to something else." Needless to say, such attitudes seriously jeopardized the movement's inner vitality and integrity.

In Düsseldorf in the summer of 1988, a women's group published what became known as the "green leaflet," naming five Autonomen men who had committed actions against women, including rapes and physical attacks. One man simply refused to leave a house he had helped to squat so that it could become a squat for women only. Men wrote a variety of responses, none of which dealt with the problem of violence against women. Instead, one man accused the women who wrote the leaflet of using Nazi tactics. Another leaflet parodied the green leaflet by asking for punishment of a woman who gave birth to a son, a Turkish woman who would not burn her scarf, and two lesbians who lived in a mixed commune. One of the men accused of violence worked in the city's squatted Autonomen center. In a fight with his former lover, he had hit her with a ski pole. He was defended by his group in a statement that said that the green leaflet was based on a "classical model of domination. The violence of men was not discussed, criticized and eliminated, but the perpetrators were made into victims. Men—these men—were thrust into social isolation by the publicity (as though men don't do enough to isolate themselves)." In response to the collective's failure to expel this man, five women left the group. For the authors of the green leaflet, "the response of the Autonomen center indicates that in these patterns of violence against women, all the moral pressure and consequences were put on the woman. She has to be responsible for what happens to the guy because of the publicity, but no one felt responsible to confront the men with their acts and the consequences for women."

These examples illustrate the continuing problem of sexism in the movement and indicate how much the Autonomen are a product of the social system they wish to destroy. At the same time, they raise another issue: the need for "centers of dual power" to enact resolutely alternative forums of justice. Without public hearings of all the evidence, it is conceivable that individuals could be unjustly accused without any recourse to establish their innocence. Nor will women victimized by sexist behavior find justice unless the movement develops new ways to enact its "revolutionary dual power." Clearly such a measure is imperative if autonomous alternatives to the existing criminal justice system are to be developed. In the case of a decentralized and militant political formation like the Autonomen, the specific problems and negative dynamics include the short lives of collectives, where apparently trivial matters (such as personality conflicts) develop into substantial problems. At the other extreme, groupthink too easily sets in within more stable groups, a dynamic in which individuals are singled out for punishment and irrationally treated. Elitism, self-righteousness, and hostility are all German cultural attributes reproduced in the movement. Severe disagreements between anti-imperialists and more locally oriented activists and between action freaks and counterculturalists often become rancorous and outweigh the positive aspects of any dialogue. Years of militant confrontations also helped produce a paranoia that has isolated the movement and fragmented its membership.

The political distance of Autonomen in the 1990s from the squatters of the early 1980s is one example. Although some old squatters continue to be active, publishing magazines and working in alternative institutions, others have turned against the Autonomen, even publicly attacking them as "new stormtroopers" and giving lectures to the police in which they claim that the Autonomen are fascists. Legalization, not eviction, was the solution arrived at to defuse the squatters' movement a decade ago, and the next generation of activists derided their legal and comfortable houses. Few Autonomen appreciate activists from previous waves of movement activity.

In 1980, *Taz* was under severe attack from the government (see Chapter 3). Its editors were charged with "inciting to riot." Several times, the newspaper was seized by police from kiosks around the country. In 1991, I was with squatters in the Brünnenstrasse (the largest of the new squats), and I showed them a poster from 1981 advertising *Taz*, portraying it as a weapon in the struggle alongside Molotovs, rocks, and black ski masks. They laughed incredulously. People could scarcely believe that this newspaper, by then little more than a mouthpiece for the realists in the Greens, had once identified itself as part of a radical movement. Their disdain is also illustrated by a story about the resistance at Mainzerstrasse. At the final press conference, a group of squatters appeared wearing nothing but black ski masks. The table around which they stood, nicely set as if for an elegant meal, was the same table used at Kommune 2, the second major political commune in Germany at the end of the 1960s. The table had been "liberated" from the offices of *Taz*, and after the press conference, it was spirited away to another squatted house. Despite the apparent co-optation of the Greens and counterinstitutions such as *Taz*, in what other countries do newly created "movement" parties or daily newspapers elicit hostility from a movement for their failure to live up to radical expectations? Where else is there radical disappointment with the apparent failure of counterinstitutions? Disappointment contains within it an element of belief in a promise left unfulfilled, a promise that continues to animate political action.

The distance of the Autonomen from anything resembling a movement capable of sustaining long-term activism is obvious in their failure to actualize their own new values within their groups. In relation to outsiders, additional problems exist. Attacks on expensive automobiles and yuppie restaurants in Kreuzberg are one way to respond to gentrification. By forcibly restricting individual consumer choices, however, this tactic gives the mass media grounds to transmit the message that the Autonomen are against the privacy of individuals and seek to control middle-class people whose upward mobility might allow them a few luxuries.[47] Within the scene, many criticize these attacks as leading the movement to a depoliticized struggle against atomized consumers, not against the system that produces mass consumption as a replacement for community and group membership. In a context where the extreme Right was making significant gains and attacks on the movement were increasing, I find it difficult to fault those who attack neo-Nazis and films like *Terror 2000* in which gratuitous violence and sexual objectification reproduce within the movement the very values it opposes.

No matter how heroic its members, the existence of an oppositional movement does not necessarily mean that a new psychological structure has emerged that stands in contrast to the unconscious structures of the old social order. By themselves, combativeness and a constant willingness to fight are not revolutionary attributes—indeed, they are probably the opposite. Even at a moment when the Autonomen were the only public force in Germany to oppose the fascist wave of violence that swept across the country in 1992, fights broke out among those who went to Hoyerswerda to stop the pogrom. Internal dangers are all the more real, since there are elements of the Autonomen that contain within them the seeds of aggression and destruction. "Punk rules," once a popular slogan, has counterparts today in equally absurd ideas: "Germany—all downhill now" and "Fire and Flames." The pure nihilism present to some degree in the movement is expressed in a variety of ways. The combat boots and black leather jackets worn by many militants can be disregarded as superficial, but equally obvious characteristics of the scene merit attention: a scathing anti-intellectualism, an overt and often unchallenged "male" process of events, and random violent clashes among members of the scene. To put it mildly, the movement often fails to establish a peaceful and supportive community, and it also contains a dose of German national pride. Both the Greens and the Autonomen have been widely criticized for focusing too much on the German movement's needs and not enough on the international movement. On these levels, they have not broken with some of the worst dimensions of their cultural tradition.

THE GERMAN PROBLEM

The appearance of the Autonomen as primarily a German movement clouds their international importance. Many commentators of vastly different political persuasions have long called attention to the ways in which German politics is impacted by deeply ingrained cultural forces. The reappearance of elements of indigenous cultures within modern social movements is of far greater importance than is generally realized. Frantz Fanon's analysis of spontaneity revealed how the extant remnants of tribalism and superstition blocked the revolutionary impulse in Africa. In the German context, is it possible to understand the existence of cultural remnants within the psychological constitution of Germans? If so, then in the advanced capitalist societies, Fanon's critique of spontaneity might involve understanding and negating psychological remnants such as ethnic chauvinism and patriarchy that get unconsciously reproduced within the movement. The German problem is important to my analysis for two reasons: In order to open the issue of the possible applicability of autonomous politics to other contexts, I need to filter out the German dimension. Moreover, the universal species interests upon which autonomous movements at their best act are sometimes hidden by their appearance as German movements and distorted by that particular cultural prism. To uncover this universal interest, I try to filter the German dimension in the following pages.

Fascism in Germany in the 1930s and 1940s was not merely the dictatorship of the most reactionary wing of the bourgeoisie, as Dimitrov and Soviet Marxists used to insist. Nor was it simply the rule of the feudal aristocracies in the twentieth century, as Barrington Moore so persuasively demonstrated.[48] Nazi power's roots were in the psychological structures of German everyday life. Strict child-rearing practices emphasizing stern discipline and paternal authority prepared the führer's rise to power, without which no fascist party could have dictated such murderous behavior. Despite heroic resistance by some Germans, so many supported Hitler that outside force was required to liberate Germany from fascism.

German mass psychology was not automatically altered after liberation from the Nazis. On the contrary, Cold War exigencies constrained Allied denazification programs, and shortly after 1945, as ex-Nazi Gestapo agents became Allied employees,[49] no real attempt was made to rework German everyday life. Even today, despite the feminist movement and counterculture, German society suffers from some of the same psychosocial dynamics that helped bring the Nazis to power: the authoritarian family; hatred of foreigners; and a cold, calculating disposition that basks in the unhappiness of others (*Schadenfreude*). *Kinderfeindlichkeit* (hatred of children) continues to be a major social problem, and what can be said about neo-Nazi attacks on disabled people?

All too often, German national identity continues to define realities that have little or nothing to do with national or cultural boundaries. "Typically German" is a phrase whose wide use ranges from commentary on immature male behavior to trivial observations regarding the most mundane actions of everyday life. As a phrase, it means very little, since nearly every culture has its stereotypical moments. When used repeatedly to explain so many different dynamics, however, "typically German" is used to assert the existence of a uniquely German character, presumably one that is qualitatively different from other cultures. If not for its deadly historical consequences, that mentality would be worthy of little more than contempt and ridicule. The tragic impact of German chauvinism makes it imperative, however, to examine further the internal beliefs and structure of identity that cause Germans to understand their own behavior as "typically German."

It is not only the far Right that asserts its Germanity (in contrast to its humanity). Unfortunately, references to uniquely Germanic behavior extend to nearly all Germans, even to those, like Günter Grass, who are clearly against German racism. If, as I portray below, German identity is so important even to progressive Germans, then clearly the problem for the whole society is greater than many people imagine. Considered by many to be Germany's greatest postwar writer, Grass opposed reunification of the country precisely because he was afraid of its consequences for foreigners and the rest of the world.[50] Yet his analysis of incipient neo-Nazism asserts that the phrase "traitor to the fatherland," when used in conjunction with "rootless cosmopolitan," belongs to the "special vocabulary of German history." This is no casual reference, for in that work and elsewhere, Grass continually uses the term "cultural nation" with "one history and one culture" to refer to Germany. Such an assertion flies in the face of history. In the eighteenth century, there were hundreds of principalities in what is today called Germany. One estimate placed the number at two hundred to three hundred states plus ten times as many smaller entities during the Enlightenment.[51] How can there be one history of these disparate realities, unless Grass seeks to accomplish in mind what Bismarck and his Prussian cohorts were able to accomplish in 1871 through blood and iron (German unity)?[52]

Christa Wolf, the best-known writer in what used to be East Germany and, like Grass, a progressive person clearly opposed to neo-Nazis, used a similar construction of typical German behavior to comment on the ways East Germany's history and her own role there were being critically reviewed. She complained that in place

> of an honest, blunt discussion carried out... in an atmosphere of empathy, about our personal history in the last few decades, [there is] the good old German inclination for always being right, for thoroughness in reckoning with the "opponent," the bigoted demand to fulfill an abstract, rigorous moral code.[53]

Once again, it is German behavior, German thoroughness, and German bigotry that define the situation. "Always being right," a type of personality that exists in far too many cultures, is not a human condition for Wolf, but a German one. The fact that Grass and Wolf, unquestionably progressive human beings, are the ones making reference to uniquely German behavior is an indication of how widespread the tendency to Germanize human problems is. In their own internal deliberations, members of the autonomous women's movement also referred to how their movement was not spared the "German sickness of friend/foe, black/white thinking, the widespread incapability to discuss differing ideas, and the customary habit of defaming differences."[54] During the

Gulf War, Alice Schwarzer (Germany's leading feminist) publicly declared that she was proud to be German because the country's new pacifism was superior to the U.S. militarist mentality.[55]

Like other particularistic cultures, Germans tend to regard their history (and destiny) as unique (and of superior significance to that of other nations or cultures). Expressionist painter Kirchner and the *Blaue Reirer* understood themselves as German nationalists.[56] German world maps commonly ascribe old German names to cities that have long since had other names—for example, Königsberg. One radical German claimed that Left and Right were political categories developed in the course of the German revolution of 1848 rather than the French Revolution of 1789.[57] Even in how the worst aspect of their history is understood, Germans believe in the "uniqueness of the German history of extermination" (*Einzigartigkeit der deutschen Vernichtungsgeschichte*).[58] U.S. genocide at My Lai or Wounded Knee may not be as neat, orderly, premeditated, or calculated as German genocide at Auschwitz, but it is genocide nonetheless—as were the actions of the Khmer Rouge in Cambodia, Indonesia in East Timor, and Turkey in Armenia. To consider Germany's genocide during World War II as a special case outweighing all other cases of genocide is to deny the human capacity for genocidal behavior, a denial that fails to mitigate such possibilities in the future. Whether Serbia's "ethnic cleansing," Brazil's ecocidal destruction of rain-forest life, or Germany's death factories, the effect of these monstrosities is to kill those defined as "other" and to seize their land and property.

Progressive Germans are capable of arguing for hours that the African slave trade and the genocide of Native Americans, despite their quantitative superiority to the Holocaust, qualitatively differ from the latter. Changing the subject, these same progressives will go on at equal length about the uniqueness of the German autonomous movement, the German neo-Nazis, or the German Greens, as if any of these constructions existed purely along national lines. Considering Nazism and its genocide as purely a German problem is to end up producing the same effect as that intended by Hitler: Germanization of the cultural universe.[59] Such a mechanical negation of Nazism (not a determinate negation in Hegel's sense of the word) loses sight of the human dimension of the situation, the human essence of action, and the potential for genocide of human beings. Even in our failures and horrors, we exist as a species—a dimension of our existence severed and mutilated by assertions of Germanity.

Whether their forests or their fascists, the Nazis romanticize everything German, but all too often, anti-Nazis do the same thing, albeit in a negative rather than a positive fashion. Like Israelis and Japanese, Germans take enormous pride in their uniqueness and exclusivity. Based in their final analysis on bloodlines, such constructions of identity serve to obscure the commonality of the human experience. Historically speaking, the German nation-state (the one from Bismarck to Hitler) existed for less than seventy-five years. The brevity of Germany's political life helps explain the motivation behind Germans' enthusiasm for their positive political accomplishments (and the current government's comparative lack of legitimacy can be traced to its historically transitory character).

One of the political legacies of German history is that structures of authority within the personalities of German people remain comparatively strong. One of the latest proofs of Germans' addiction to order was publicized in 1993.[60] After an American journalist joked that "*order über alles*" characterized Germany, five students at the University of Trier constructed a way to determine whether Germans would actually obey "absurd rules." At the main post office in Trier, they hung official-looking signs on telephone booths that read "women only" and "men only" and then watched the reaction. Of sixty-nine telephone users observed, nearly all the women and three-fourths of the men obeyed the instructions; only one woman and nine men were bold enough to use the phone designated for the opposite sex. On January 28, 1994, students at the University of Münster conducted an experiment to test whether German students would allow themselves to be steered into racially segregated entrances to the university's student cafeteria. Holding signs reading "Germans" and "Foreigners" at adjacent doorways, the students found that 95 percent of their colleagues allowed themselves to be steered into the "correct" entrance.[61]

Such unconscious dimensions to racism and authoritarianism are difficult to measure, but West Germans' conscious affinity with Nazi beliefs was continually documented in study after government study. One such study was conducted in 1979 and kept secret for two years (until May 1981), when it was finally given media coverage. The survey claimed that 18 percent of West Germans believed that "under Hitler, Germany had it better." The government report went on to say: "A total of 13 per cent of the voters [about 5.5 million people] have an ideologically complete frame of mind, the main supports of which are a national socialist [Nazi] view of history, hatred of foreigners, democracy, and pluralism and an exaggerated devotion to people, fatherland, and family." In 1989, *Der Spiegel* published a comprehensive analysis of Hitler accompanied by the results of a new poll in which it found that only every other German had sympathy for the Jews, whereas a total of 79.9 percent were mildly to strongly "proud to be German."[62]

These polls may not come as a surprise, but what is astounding is many activists' and militants' unawareness of the deep psychological structure on which the espousal of fascist beliefs depends. When not subject to conscious reflection and their transformation, these patterns of everyday interaction can be spontaneously reproduced even within the movement. As the Autonomen developed from the crucible of popular struggles and merged with their cultural counterparts in the youth ghettos, it was often an unprincipled fusion wherein violence and callousness went unchallenged. At the same time, the Protestant ethic so proudly claimed by Max Weber to be at the heart of capitalism continued to be a powerful force on political activists. One could begin by pointing out that the Autonomen black uniform is the same color as that of the Puritans. Even in the movement, puritanical norms are evident. Comparing the German Autonomen with their Polish counterparts (the Orange movement) or to Danish BZ people, there is a hard edge to the Germans that does not exist in these other contexts.

Even though there are severe problems within the movement, nowhere else in the political universe of Germany do the desire for a different kind of society and the necessity of building a new way of life coincide. Hope is to be found in the sublime harmony of many activists as well as in their attempts to build a supportive collectivity amid daily anxieties about police and neo-Nazi attacks. Whether or not these marginalized groups survive to live in the kind of society they want, they have to some degree already brought it into existence in their small groups. Whether autonomous movements are able to realize more freedom depends, at least in part, on a protracted transformation of the inner character of everyday life.

THE (ANTI)POLITICS
OF AUTONOMY

Almost without exception, revolutionary social movements in the twentieth century have sought to conquer national political power—either to take over nation-states through elections or to overthrow them through violence. The goal of autonomous movements is to transcend nation-states, not capture them. Since autonomists are singularly uninterested in what is normally regarded as politics (campaigns, votes, fund-raising, party formation, and so forth), is it possible to speak of the politics of autonomy? An affirmative answer rests upon a redefinition of politics, one that considers civil Luddism and confrontational demonstrations to be forms of political action. In this chapter, I compare autonomous (anti)politics with the politics of the Greens and of the Left. In so doing, I hope to demarcate the boundaries of autonomous movements and speculate on their possible applicability to other contexts. As will become clear in the course of my discussion, one of the principal weaknesses of contemporary political movements has been their tendency to adopt ready-made theories from previous waves of activism. In order to mitigate such dogmatic behavior in future autonomous movements, I develop a detailed critique of the theories of Antonio Negri, the Italian autonomist whose notions of revolutionary strategy vary widely from those I understand as most effective and relevant. In contrast to Negri's call to adopt the cyborg as a model of action, I propose a rationality of the heart and a reconsideration of the role of spontaneity and militance.

Unlike social democracy and Leninism, the two main currents of the twentieth century Left, the Autonomen are relatively unencumbered with rigid ideologies. The absence of any central organization (or even primary organizations) helps keep theory and practice in continual interplay. Indeed, actions speak for most Autonomen, not words, and the sheer volume of decentralized happenings generated by small groups acting on their own initiative prohibits systematic understanding of the totality of the movement, a first step in the dismantling of any system. No single organization can control the direction of actions undertaken from the grassroots. Although the Autonomen have no unified ideology and there has never been an Autonomen manifesto, their statements make it clear that they fight "not for ideologies, not for the proletariat, not for the people" but (in much the same sense as feminists first put it) for a "politics of the first person." They want self-determination and "the abolition of politics," not leadership by a party. They want to destroy the existing social system because they see it as the cause of "inhumanity, exploitation, and daily monotony."[1]

No doubt the Autonomen are difficult to define. Neither a party nor a movement, their diffuse status frustrates those who seek a quick and easy definition for them. They appear as the "black block" at demonstrations, in "autonomous assemblies" that are regionally organized or oriented around specific campaigns, but they have no fixed organizations or spokespersons. In an age of sound bites and instant coffee consciousness, the propensity for quick fixes on fragmentary factoids often leads the media to use (erroneously) the term "anarchist" to refer to them. Their political terrain lies somewhere between that of the Greens and the RAF, somewhere between parliamentary participation and guerrilla struggle. For *Taz*, they were the "residue of radicalism" in the early 1980s.[2] In 1986, Hamburg's police chief described the Autonomen as that part of the post-1968 New Left that refused to accept the discipline of Marxist-Leninist cadre parties. "Their development was accelerated by the new strength of the ecology movement.... They stand up for spontaneity, self-organization and autonomy." He also discussed their refusal to accept leaders and their lack of coherent theory. At the beginning of the 1990s, a sociologist referred to them as "a mixed product of different movements, like Spontis and Metropolitan Indians, neighborhood and prisoner solidarity initiatives, squatters, the anti-nuclear movement and continually appearing, marginalized and strongly apolitical youth."[3] Another definition focused on their tactics, "Autonomen is not more than a catch-all category; it stands for small, well-organized circles of goal-oriented political activists as well as for the highly diffuse ideological spectrum of militant protests, that refers, above all, to the forms of the protests (including youthful subcultures). Autonomen propagate—with and against non-violent activists—the free choice of their forms of resistance, under the difficult to guarantee condition, that endangering human life must be excluded."[4]

The Autonomen themselves have been none too eager to define precisely who they are. For *Radikal*, itself one of their more important zines, "autonomy was a notion that overnight gave our revolt a name.... Previously we understood ourselves as anarchists, spontis, communists or had diffuse, individual conceptions of living freely. Then we were all Autonomen."[5] In 1982–83, when various new social movements had passed high points (squatters', antinuclear, and peace movements), a group of Autonomen in Hamburg organized a series of national meetings for autonomists to discuss their future. In their preparatory materials, one of the clearest statements from the movement can be found:

> The aspiration for autonomy is above all the struggle against political and moral alienation from life and work—against the functionalization of outside interests, against the internalization of the morals of our foes... This aspiration is concretized when houses are squatted to live humanely or not to have to pay high rents, when workers call in sick in order to party because they can't take the alienation at work, when unemployed people plunder supermarkets... because they don't agree with the absurd demands of unions for more jobs that only integrate people into oppression and exploitation. Everywhere that people begin to sabotage, to change, the political, moral and technical structures of domination is a step toward a self-determined life.[6]

In early 1995, when over two thousand activists gathered in Berlin to discuss the autonomous movement in the twenty-first century, one of their principal themes was the concept of autonomy. Although there were numerous attempts to define it, no one even attempted to develop a rigid definition of autonomous politics that could be used with precision to explain it to the world. Apparently the indeterminacy of the Autonomen is one of their defining features, a facet of their mysterious anonymity that permits a wide range of fact and opinion to coexist alongside a diversity of action. Are they a determinate negation of consumer society, or simply its militant outsiders? Are they the long-term form of antisystemic movements in the core of the world system? Or is their civil Luddism due to become an obscure historical footnote like the original machine-breakers of England? I leave it to the reader to answer these questions.

Hundreds (sometimes thousands) of people participate in analyzing and directing autonomous movements independently of existing parties. Their theory is not that of isolated activist-intellectuals searching for academic clarity. Rather, they focus on specific problems and insist on understanding the rapidly changing character of contemporary society and its shifting constellation of power. The names of some of their more internally relevant statements reveal the decentralized and pragmatic character of their theoretical work: the Lupus paper against the ritualization of violence; the Rote Flora's (a squatted center in Hamburg) collective critique of alcohol; and the Heinz-Schenk debate, an orthodox Marxist critique of the Autonomen.[7] At the 1995 Berlin conference, preparatory materials included proposals for workshops on the relationship between punk and critical theory (especially Adorno and Horkheimer), a reexamination of the role of violence, men against patriarchy, the politics of drugs, and art and activism.

The most obvious problem associated with such an informal relationship of practice and theory, action and ideas, is that the movement might be unable to provide itself with direction and coherence, because so many divergent viewpoints exist. Resistance to centralized leadership and to uniform theory is often regarded as a weakness. Many people in the autonomous scene think of the movement's decentralization as a blessing, however, making it more difficult for police to infiltrate and easier for grassroots initiatives to develop. As the magazine *Radikal* put it: "The Autonomen movement is not a party and it consists of a minimum of organization if we make an historical comparison. This fact can be an advantage as the jailers search for structures and leaders which are not to be found." The magazine had asked local groups to send in brief descriptions of activism in their areas, and the magazine prefaced the responses from twenty-three German cities by stating that its goal in reprinting the material was not only to inform one another but also to help people think about organization at the regional and national levels. (Evidently, a dose of German pride more often than not prevents such discussions from considering international dimensions.)

Many collectives communicate with one another through magazines, newspapers, and brochures distributed in more than fifty cities by a network of informally linked information shops. Most "info-shops" have archives dealing with local struggles, and on various days of the week, they are reserved solely for women or gays. Collectives working on single issues often hold their meetings at these shops, providing connections between groups that might otherwise not meet each other. Many shops have copy machines, making the purchase of expensive books or magazines superfluous when only a few pages are needed. Information is not treated as a commodity to be bought and sold, nor is it passively scanned by spectators looking in from the outside. On the contrary, hundreds of pamphlets, position papers, articles, magazines, and newspapers are created by the users of these shops, making them less consumers in a store than part of a network within a movement. In this context, the info-shops organically connect ideas and action. A variety of other forms of alternative media also functions to integrate the movement's diverse and disconnected base. The Autofocus video collective in Berlin has helped overcome the fragmentation of the movement by collecting videos from Germany and from insurgent movements around the world. The relatively low cost of home video production allows grassroots groups to produce their own videos. Autofocus's collection can be rented for a night, copied, or reserved for public events.

International associations have linked info-shops in Germany, Norway, Denmark, Sweden, Holland, Belgium, and Switzerland, and communication at the grassroots has also been facilitated through a variety of conferences such as those in Venice in June 1992, when hundreds of people gathered to "build a Europe of social movements, not elites"; *Class War*'s (a British anarchist organization) international congresses; those at the Hafenstrasse in Hamburg; or the Easter 1995 gathering in Berlin.

In many cities, squatted and legally purchased movement centers exist to provide further space for movement networks to expand. One of the largest of the latter is Mehringhof in Berlin. A huge building and courtyard provide office space for activist groups, meeting rooms, a women's center, a theater, a bookstore/café, occasional dance parties, and a bar. The Hafenstrasse has a people's kitchen and a bar with dancing every couple of weeks, and a group of Turkish activists also has a café there. Hamburg's *Die Fabrik*, Copenhagen's *Ungdomhuis* (Youth House), and Amsterdam's Palace Revolt (a squatted bar/restaurant) are other centers where public space for activist groups exists. Like the women's centers of the 1970s, these meeting places are an alternative form of organization that provides more flexibility and decentralized networking than traditionally centralized organizations, as well as facilitating the movement's survival during periods of state repression.[8]

The horizontal—even circular—collective structure of the Autonomen facilitates discussions and actions whose sources are numerous and diverse, and whose approval depends upon the agreement of others, not directives from above. The structure of autonomous movements facilitates individual decision-making and political development. With initiative coming from many sources, collectives are able to act immediately and decisively without waiting for a central committee to deliberate and approve ideas. Figure 6.1 approximates such a movement structure.

Within the activist core can be found crystallization points whose variety is indicated by different symbols: collectives, action committees, coalitions, squatted houses, activist communes, and, when their sectarian tendencies are under control, even hierarchically organized groups with ideological underpinnings. Together with unaffiliated individuals, they constitute the base from which actions and programmatic impetus are initiated. They rely on the next level, the scene, for their everyday political-cultural sustenance. Alternative institutions with no explicit political content are part of the scene, as are cafés, music clubs, street hangouts, and parks. Active sympathizers include people who are caught up in movement mobilizations and occasional meetings. Passive sympathizers

Figure 6.1
STRUTURE OF AUTONOMOUS MOVEMENTS

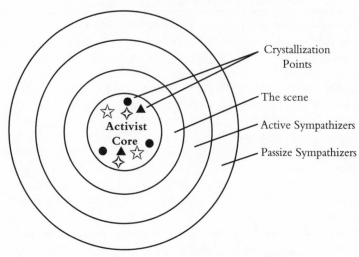

Crystallization
Points

The scene

Active Sympathizers

Passize Sympathizers

Activist
Core

Source: Adapted from Hanspeter Kriesi, *Die Zürcher Bewegung: Bilder Interaktionen, Zusammenhänge* (Frankfurt/New York: Campus Verlag, 1984), p. 213.

refer to financial supporters, readers of the alternative press, professors who discuss ideas and actions in their seminars and classes, workers who contribute ideas to colleagues, and so forth. The fluid character of these movements means that people often move between levels or even participate simultaneously at many different points.

Theoretical statements aimed at generalized explanations are not one of the strengths of autonomous movements, but increasingly, activists have sophisticated views of the history of radical politics, international economics, patriarchal forms of sexuality and gender relations, and racism and xenophobia. Although activists are generally hostile to "scientific" analysis (i.e., analysis that dispassionately discusses human relationships as though they are things), theoretical issues are debated in informal papers that get passed on and xeroxed by collectives in different cities. The variety of views within the movement makes for lively debates and continual discussions that, since there is no need to fixate on developing a correct line, are more often oriented to action than to ideology. Because no one is required to adopt certain viewpoints or read particular texts, individual consciousness is deeper and carries none of the standardization so common among members of cadre groups.

The movement's norms and values help transcend some of the worst aspects of a dogmatic reading of history. The nearly universal practice of signing articles in movement publications with pseudonyms emphasizes ideas, not personalities. Readers are thereby compelled to consider arguments on their own merit rather than for the prominence or ideological allegiance of their authors. Frozen positions based on personal feuds or rigidly "anarchist" or "anti-imperialist" positions are subverted, since it is often unclear who or what the affiliation of an author is. German activists make a concerted effort to prevent the emergence of individual leaders (*"promis,"* or prominent people). At demonstrations, speakers are either masked or sit inside the sound truck, out of public view. Although it is rather strange to hear a voice that cannot be matched to a face, individuals cannot be identified by the police or rightwingers, nor can "leaders" be made into celebrities by the media. When the media spotlight focuses on an individual, collectivity and democratic organization are obscured, sometimes even destroyed. Such attempts to forestall the creation of individual leaders reveal how much the movement not only stands against the established system of wealth and power but also opposes any sort of differential status.

For many people, the radicals' rejection of traditional ideology implies the elevation of pragmatic values and the isolation of activism from theory. Neither of these appears to be necessary consequences of autonomist politics. Theory is contained within the actions of autonomists rather than being congealed in rigid ideologies that precede action. Preparations for actions, the actions themselves, and the inevitable (and often prolonged) soul-searching afterwards involve intensive theoretical reflection. Flexibility of action means that the Autonomen are capable of lightning-swift responses to public events. When neo-Nazi gangs go on a rampage and the police are slow to respond, the Autonomen have been able to mobilize hundreds of people within a few minutes, providing immediate assistance to foreigners. The ability to contest skillfully both government policy and incipient right-wing violence as material conditions change is a great strength of the Autonomen. After German reunification, the movement redirected its energies to confront neo-Nazi groups. Nazi demonstrations allowed by the police were closed down by Autonomen, and at least four different antifascist publications provided quality exposés of the New Right, helping to skillfully direct the movement's energies.

An indication of the participatory framework for action was the wave of more than 130 squats in the old eastern part of Berlin after the fall of the wall. Despite being defeated after the mammoth battle of Mainzerstrasse and generally rebuffed by a public anxiously awaiting the advent of consumer society—not the radical politics of the counterculture—the self-directed action of hundreds of people (thousands if we include the concomitant student strike at the universities as well as the solidarity demonstrations) provides a model for political organization and action. In Italy, autonomous movements were inseparable from the working class. No doubt the relative quiescence of German workers is due, at least in part, to their materially more prosperous and politically more stable conditions of existence relative to their Italian counterparts.

Orthodox Marxists and anarchists alike have criticized autonomous decision making as "spontaneous," lacking organizational direction and the "conscious element."[9] In the dialectical relationship between movements and organizations, the question of participation is vital. Organizations that impose impersonal structures onto collective movements can short-circuit popular involvement, replacing movements with sects whose preoccupation is theoretical correctness (a contemporary version of the medieval problem of how many angels could dance on the head of a pin). Beginning with the New Left, contemporary social movements have provided astonishing evidence of the spontaneous creation of participatory forms. In the United States, four million students and half a million faculty organized a coordinated strike in May 1970 in response to the invasion of Cambodia and the repression of the Black Panther Party, with no central organization bringing them together.[10] The next year, a researcher visited 150 communes and reported that none used majority votes to make contested decisions. All used consensus.[11] When not intruded upon by traditional Left ideologies, organizations such as US SDS practiced consensual decision making that they reinvented from their own needs rather than inheriting from the Old Left or gleaning from a reading of anarchism.[12] I do not wish to suggest that their internal process was exemplary, merely that it was developed by intuition. Nor do I think that movements should fetishize intuition as their source of political insight. Looking back at the history of the New Left and radical social movements since 1968, I cannot help but be amazed at how distorted political conceptions become when political ideologies are grabbed wholesale and applied by activists. Like many autonomists, I am inspired by a variety of thinkers from previous waves of action and find their insights extraordinarily important to my own development.[13] Unlike many people in what is called the Left, however, I do not seek to construct a set of categories that serve as a prism for my friendships and alliances, preferring instead to form these on the basis of feeling and action, not ideological purity.

Action defines the autonomous discourse, not the sterile contemplation of its possibilities or the categorization of its past occurrences. Since the mass media focus on the movement's militant tactics, not its unobserved internal dynamics, the public's sole definition of autonomous politics is arrived at through deeds. This is not a trivial point. As we saw in Chapter 3, militant opposition to nuclear power and the resolve of squatters to seize and defend houses were crucibles for the galvanization of the Autonomen. Their ability to provide a confrontational cutting edge to larger movements helped radicalize thousands of people and was crucial to stopping the Wackersdorf nuclear reprocessing plant (and Germany's possession of bomb-grade plutonium).

Confrontational politics invigorated Germany's political debates, compelled the established parties to change policies and programs, and deepened the commitment of many people to fundamental social transformation. Militant resistance to local instances of the system's encroachment upon previously autonomous dimensions of life propelled many people into resistance to the system as a whole. Within broad campaigns, the role of the Autonomen has often been to extend the critique enunciated by single-issue initiatives. In its 1989 annual report, the German federal police recognized this crucial role within movements against nuclear power and genetic engineering: "As soon as protest movements develop, above all Autonomen and other 'New Leftists' press for 'direct resistance' against 'the system.'" By raising the level of discourse from specific institutions to the system as a whole, a radical critique of the entire system of capitalist patriarchy gets wide discussion and is sometimes transmitted to new sectors of the population.

The Autonomen seek to live according to a new set of norms and values within which everyday life and all of civil society can be transformed. Beginning with overt political beliefs, they seek to change isolated individuals into members of collectives within which egalitarian relationships can be created—relationships that subvert the traditional parent-child, husband-wife, couples-singles patterns that characterize patriarchal lifestyles. In place of the hierarchies of traditional political relationships (order-givers–order-takers, leaders–followers, media stars–media consumers), they strive for political interactions in which these roles are subverted. Their collective forms negate atomization; their activism transforms the passivity of consumeristic spectacle; their daily lives include a variety of people (immigrants, gays, lesbians, "others") indeed, they themselves are regarded as "other" by most Germans—thereby negating the reification and standardization of mass society; their self-determination negates the all-too-prevalent alienation from products of work. They seek a context that encourages everyone to think and act according to his or her abilities and inclinations. Of course, no self-respecting autonomist would claim to speak for the movement or to be its leader, but most people are part of groups of some sort, and horizontal linkage between collectives creates councils capable of coordinating local actions and integrating a variety of constituencies into ever-widening circles of thought and action.

AUTONOMY AND THE GREENS

Many Greens sympathize with the feminism and egalitarianism of such an autonomous vision, but others do not—nor are they required to in order to be part of a political party formally constituted to participate in government. Like all parliamentary groups, the Greens aspire to create legislation and allocate funds to meet the articulated needs of their base of support. Of necessity, they must conform to the hierarchy of the state on two dimensions: Within the context of carrying out governmental duties, they must accede to the dictates of higher officials. Within the party, some members are elected representatives and sit in parliament, and others do not; millions pay dues to or cast votes for the few who are paid to carry out party policy. These hierarchical imperatives were recognized by the Greens even before they formally organized themselves. One of the threads woven into the discourse of this book has been the relationship of parliamentary and extraparliamentary forms of political engagement. In this section, I trace the history of the Greens and analyze some of the issues that animated their development from an "antiparty party" to the third largest party in Germany. Although the Greens grew out of the same milieu as the Autonomen, as time passed, the two formations became increasingly embittered and estranged from each other, and today few Germans treat them as connected. From my vantage point, they are each crystallization points within a diffuse continuum of opposition to behemoth nation-states and multinational corporations. Whether or not their efforts are successful depends, at least in part, upon their synergistic impact.

In the category of parliamentary parties that participate in elections, the early Greens were unique. They manifested many of the same qualities as the German New Left and new social movements such as feminism, the antinuclear movement, squatters, and alternative institutions: grassroots initiative (*Basisdemokratie*), consensus, antihierarchy, and countercultural lifestyle. Indeed, the Greens grew out of these movements, not the other way around, as many foreign observers assumed.[14] Within Germany, few people would even attempt to pose the existence of the Greens without acknowledging their having grown out of the extraparliamentary *Bürgerinitiativen* and movements. More commonly, the Greens are conceived as representing these movements:

The Greens were first made possible through the new social movements; with their 40,000 members, they have become no more and no less than an additional, institutional leg for these movements within the parliamentary system of the FRG.... Not the Greens but the new social movements are the forerunners of the new political landscape in the FRG.[15]

From their inception, the Greens were beset with the contradiction of dealing with power as participants while trying to prevent the emergence of leaders, media stars, and a new elite. To mitigate the abuses associated with power, the party demanded strict rotation of elected representatives, formulated precise provisions for the equalization of salaries, and made major decisions subject to direct democracy. For a decade, the "antiparty" held together with its original principles intact, but they were finally jettisoned, leaving the Greens looking like any other established political party. Althouth grassroots democracy was an essential part of the reason for the party's existence for some members, for others, it was a "green hell, as dangerous as the tropical rainforests of the Amazon."[16] Joschka Fischer penned these remarks in 1983, long before the Greens even considered ending internal direct democracy. As prominent leaders consolidated their hold on media outlets and party positions, a silent end to rotation was instituted by 1987.[17] Rotation only ensured the ascendancy of the star system, since the media were free to appoint whomever they pleased as prominent Greens. No countervailing power of elected leaders in a stable organization existed to prevent individuals such as Daniel Cohn-Bendit or Petra Kelly from speaking for the Greens at the national or international level. Rather than eliminating the star system, rotation displaced it, and the contest between these two structures became increasingly vociferous. Two days after the 1990 elections (in which the party failed to maintain any of its seats in the *Bundestag*), party leader Antje Vollmer declared rotation part of an antihuman "mistrusting culture of the Greens."[18] Tired of attacks on herself, Petra Kelly criticized the fetish of the "grassroots sport of hunting" prominent members of the party. Gert Bastian also spoke up, labeling rotation a "dictatorship of incompetence." Finally, in 1991, Ulrich Beck put the finishing touches on the assault on rotation, calling it a "sado-masochistic" Green syndrome that included "publicly carving up leading candidates" and "a preference for rotating incompetence."[19]

The Greens are now the third largest political party in Germany with publicly recognized leaders, one of whom served as vice president of the *Bundestag*. Running for office in national, state, and local elections, they have won thousands of seats at local levels by surpassing the 5 percent needed for representation.[20] As Table 6.1 summarizes, they have held dozens of seats in the *Bundestag* on three different occasions.

Besides winning elections, the Greens have developed a national constituency that has remained faithful through a variety of trying situations and major political transformations. In 1983, they counted twenty-five thousand members; five years later, about forty thousand, a level they have maintained into the 1990s.[21] Their annual revenues were approximately $28 million in 1993 (42.5 million DM).[22]

As they consolidated themselves after their initial electoral successes in the early 1980s, two predominant viewpoints emerged within the party: fundamentalist and realist. From its origin in 1982 in Hesse, this dispute dominated the Greens' existence for years. The fundamentalist wing (or "fundis") demanded that the party serve only as a parliamentary opposition—that they refuse to form coalition governments with other parties in order to maintain their integrity as an antiparty aimed at fundamentally transforming the political and economic structures of the world system. They believed that major social decisions (to rely on nuclear power or to favor absentee landlords and a housing shortage) were made by corporate executives and government bureaucrats, not by elected representatives. Fundis were more interested in putting out a radical message and mobilizing social movements than in getting votes. They felt compelled to act in parliament as one movement arena among many. In effect, fundis wanted to represent protest movements (which they considered to be vehicles of change) in parliament. Petra Kelly was one of those who insisted:

> Within their parliamentary process, the Greens should not enter into the old established structures or take part in the powers-that-be, but should do everything to demolish and control it. Accordingly their role remains one of fundamental opposition that depends upon the success of grassroots movements in the streets.[23]

Kelly called for a nonviolent global general strike to uproot militarism and war[24] and maintained the integrity of her fundamentalism until her murder in 1992. Another fundi, Rudolf Bahro (who helped found the party soon after his release from an East German prison), insisted that the Greens represent voiceless animals and plants and called for the party to embrace all "people of goodwill," especially social dropouts and marginalized youth.

The realists (or "realos") maintained the need to act pragmatically within current economic and political structures. By appealing to middle-class employees, women, and youth, they hoped to gain wide public

TABLE 6.1

GREEN VOTES IN FEDERAL ELECTIONS

Year	Percentage of Vote	Seats in Bundestag
1980	1.5	0
1983	5.6	27
1987	8.3	42
1990	4.8 (West)	0
	6.0 (East)	8
1994	7.3	49

Sources: Markavits and Gorski, p. 290;
New York Times; *Week in Germany*.

support for an ecological restructuring of Germany. The failure of the SPD and other parties to enhance popular participation in government and to integrate the demands of emergent constituencies in new social movements helped motivate the realos' attempt to reform the existing system. They sought to design programs oriented to regional planning and short-term amelioration of specific crises linked to broad structural issues, such as nuclear power and patriarchy. They also wanted to build a national consensus on the need for a new steering mechanism for the political system. Entering the *Bundestag* as a committed but loyal opposition corresponded to a strategy dubbed the "long march through the institutions" in the 1960s by Rudi Dutschke. According to this idea, when possible, a revolutionary movement should introduce its values and ideas within established political forms, thereby reaching millions of people and setting in motion new possibilities for change. The continuing process of reforms unleashed by this strategy is supposed to encourage popular participation and to raise consciousness and expectations. If the existing institutions can be shown to be incapable of creating, in this case, an ecologically viable society, then many people might be convinced of the need for a whole new system with reasonable economic and political policies (or at least persuaded of the need to vote Green).

Besides the fundi-realo schism, more traditionally defined cleavages, along the lines of Left versus Right (neo-Leninist ecologists versus conservative conservationists), also made inner-party discourse refreshingly dynamic, hopelessly argumentative, or boringly trivial, depending on one's perspective. The tension between realos and fundis was a favorite subject of the conservative German press, since they expected the internal bickering to alienate voters. Instead, extensive commentaries on the internal problems of the Greens actually explained the intricacies of the debate within the party to a wide circle of Germans, thereby helping to inject substance into ritualized pronouncements and comings and goings of the established political elite. As fundis and realos pounded each other in seemingly endless and, at times, pointless debates, activists within the party tired of obsessive struggles led by media stars. Women finally upstaged the entire fundi-realo show. Beginning in 1984, a *"Feminat"* of women held all major national positions, and their effect on the party was enormous.

The previous disputes became the backdrop for full-scale clashes, however, as the Greens' historical impact made the party a major player in national power. As many people expected, once the Greens entered parliament, the radical character of the party was constrained. Besides jettisoning visionary demands, the Greens ultimately could not maintain robust ties with radical social movements. As realo cooperation with established politicians estranged the Greens from their activist base, the fundis also cut themselves off from supporters when they insisted on preaching to others rather than participating as equals. An enormous gulf appeared between direct-action movements and what some insisted was their parliamentary expression. In 1983, after autonomists attacked Vice President Bush's limousine with stones in Krefeld, Green spokespersons denounced the Autonomen as "police agents" seeking to undermine popular support for the party. On the other side, Autonomen came to regard Greens as government agents. The identification of inner-movement "enemies" with the government was a telling indication of the wide gulf that opened in this period between progressive forces within the system and radical critics outside it.

For years, the positions taken by the first Green city councilors in Hesse served as a model for Greens around the country. They showed concretely how the Greens could serve as a regional planning mechanism. The fundi-realo debates in Hesse were particularly prolonged and ultimately carried into the federal levels of the party. Like the elections in Berlin in 1981 (see Chapter 3), the Hesse events bring considerable light to bear on the relationship between electoral and extraparliamentary tactics. The battle over the Frankfurt airport expansion (Startbahn West) propelled thousands of people into action and hundreds of Greens into elected positions. In the towns of Büttelborn and Mörfelden-Walldorf, the communities most immediately affected by the new runway, the Greens won 25.2 percent of the vote in local elections in 1981, and in some other districts, ecologists did even better.[24] Buoyed by this success, the statewide Greens won 8 percent of the vote in 1982, enough to enter the Hessian parliament. Their platform had insisted that they could not form a coalition with the SPD, "a party which, when wielding governmental powers, has not shrunk from implementing civil-war like measures, has completed projects such as Startbahn West with brutal police violence against the will of the population, and criminalized citizens' initiatives."[26] For its part, the local SPD refused to work with the Greens. The following year, when the Greens won barely enough votes to remain in parliament, the party's realists argued that a coalition with the SPD was necessary for their future electoral success.

As long as the question of coalition with the SPD concerned the future, the debates between fundis and realos had seemed abstract or personal, but the brutality of power soon changed that. On September 28, 1985, Günter Sare, a participant in a demonstration against one of the neo-fascist parties holding its national convention in a Turkish neighborhood in Frankfurt, was killed when a police water cannon ran him over. The Hessian state budget (which the Greens had approved) included money for this water cannon. To many people in the autonomous movement, the Greens were thus part of the forces that killed Sare. At a mass meeting at Goethe University in Frankfurt, 1960s veterans and former Spontis Daniel Cohn-Bendit and Joschka Fischer defended their realo politics, but enraged activists threw eggs and tomatoes at them. Across Germany, more than sixty demonstrations protested Sare's death.[27]

Riding the wave of resentment against the realos, fundi national spokesperson Jutta Ditfurth, one of three members of the party's federal presidium, went on the offensive. Known for her sharp tongue, Ditfurth was alternately a media darling and their favorite target. As the Hessian Greens moved closer to a coalition with the SPD, Ditfurth and the fundis tried to orient the national party apparatus toward extraparliamentary movements. When fifty thousand people protested in Munich against the Wackersdorf nuclear reprocessing plant on October 10, 1985, the Greens were the only national organization that helped mobilize for the action.

Later in October, the Hessian Greens formally approved the formation of a coalition government with the SPD. Although the realos had not been promised any major concessions (such as an immediate moratorium on Startbahn West or closure of the Biblis nuclear plant), the first "red-green" (SPD-Green) state coalition government was nearly a reality. Calling Joschka Fischer a "Green Machiavelli," *Der Spiegel* reported that 80 percent of the two thousand members present had voted for his proposal. Responding to the Hessian vote, Ditfurth released a biting public statement:

Only eighteen days after the murder of Günter Sare by the police, the Greens in the state parliament in Hesse have decided to go into coalition with the SPD, to join sides with the rulers.... The Greens in parliament haven't even demanded a parliamentary committee of inquiry.... The coalition in Hesse is not realism, it is the pathway towards integration into the ruling system.[28]

In December 1985, when Fischer was sworn in as Hesse's first Green minister of the environment, a chorus of warnings about a "Green nightmare" unified the voices of the president of Hoechst chemicals (the largest industry in the region), executives from the nuclear industry, conservative politicians, and even the president of the chemical workers' union. On the other side, *Taz* jubilantly declared, "The long march through the institutions—one has made it."[29] The disparate character of these responses reflected the uncertainty of the path that the red-green government would take. Seeking to reassure his newfound allies, Fischer humbly promised the established powers that he was willing and able to enter into a constructive dialogue with industry.

Ditfurth and the fundis were caught between the rock of the Autonomen and the hard place of endless meetings with their realo colleagues. They called for antinuclear demonstrations, but they belonged to an organization with Joschka Fischer, whose service as minister of the environment in Hesse made him responsible for the controversial Nukem and Alkem nuclear facilities as well as for the transportation of nuclear wastes on Hesse's highways. To offset the rightward drift of Hessian realos, fundi Greens deliberately scheduled the party's national convention in the vicinity of Wackersdorf. At the Offenbach conference, they orchestrated a fundi coup, winning control of the party's executive by a wide vote (468 to 214) after shuttling hundreds of delegates to a demonstration at Wackersdorf.[30]

When disaster struck the Soviet nuclear power plant in Chernobyl on April 28, 1986, differences within the Greens threatened to tear the party apart. Fundis proclaimed that all "374 nuclear installations on earth are declarations of war against us."[31] Condemning the "nuclear mafia" and "atomic terrorists"—meaning everyone from the SPD to the Pentagon and its Soviet counterpart—the fundis reflected the radicalization of ecological activists after the Chernobyl catastrophe. The next month, demonstrations at Brokdorf (due to go on line) and Wackersdorf were particularly militant, and the media dubbed the "violent" autonomists leading the confrontations "the Greens' steel-ball faction," a reference to the slingshot ammunition used by some Autonomen. One characterization of these demonstrations focused on their militance:

In scenes resembling "civil war," helmeted, leather-clad troops of the anarchist Autonomen armed with sling-shots, Molotov cocktails and flare guns clashed brutally with the police, who employed water cannons, helicopters and CS gas (officially banned for use against civilians).[32]

Those Greens attempting to maintain ties to militant movements paid a heavier than usual price. Press reports (later shown to be false) charged that hundreds of Greens had applauded the injuries suffered by police during the demonstrations. In response, many Greens tried to distance themselves from "violent" protesters (and subsequently called for an entirely different relationship between the party and social movements). At Brokdorf, the Greens and their pacifist allies cooperated with the police search of automobile convoys, leaving those who refused to submit to the searches sitting ducks for police violence.

At the party's federal level, the fundis pressured for a stand for the termination of all nuclear power plants and an end to the Hessian coalition. With 80 percent of Germans reportedly wanting to end the use of nuclear power after Chernobyl, the Greens won a larger electoral victory than ever before (or since) in the national elections of January 1987, with 8.3 percent of the vote (forty-four seats in the Bundestag). Almost immediately, the fundi-realo schism was reinvigorated. Fischer and the Hessian Greens were compelled to pull out of their coalition with the SPD. The fundis, in control of key committees, including those that allocated money, were unable to keep track of hundreds of thousands of marks, leading to a financial scandal. Although they conceded that mistakes had been made, fundi leaders insisted that no one had personally profited from the embezzled party funds. Nonetheless, they lost a vote of confidence during a party convention at the end of 1988, and the entire national executive committee was compelled to resign, paving the way for realo control of the party apparatus. On March 12, 1989, a red-green coalition government was voted into power in Frankfurt.[33]

The fundis' fall from grace was presaged by disturbing events. In November 1987, the bitterness of those marginalized from mainstream parties was a factor in the shooting of eleven policemen (two of whom died) at Startbahn West. The media seized that opportunity to dramatize the split in the Greens. Hard-liners such as Thomas Eberman and Ditfurth refused to condemn the killings, but the party's majority loudly vilified the shootings. In a context in which the state was actively attempting to criminalize militant opponents of the system and a few extremists were seeking a shooting war, the Greens' existence as part of the governing structure complicated their ties to extraparliamentary movements. For Daniel Cohn-Bendit, the antagonisms between him and the Autonomen reached a breaking point. In 1987, Cohn-Bendit was invited to speak at the Free University of Berlin, but he canceled his appearance after leaflets were distributed threatening to disrupt his speech (as had already happened in Karlsruhe with stink bombs). Many Autonomen considered Cohn-Bendit to have "informed" against suspected "terrorists" through his participation in the government's amnesty plans, to have uncritically supported Israel in the pages of his Frankfurt magazine *Pflasterstrand* during the bloody invasion of Lebanon in 1982, and to have refused to abandon the male chauvinism of his magazine. Even in the eyes of sympathetic observers, he was a "cultural relic of the revolt of 1968... integrated into the management of urban conflict."[34] In the mainstream media, Cohn-Bendit was either a favorite son used by liberals to discredit the Autonomen or a scapegoat used by reactionaries to vent anti-Semitic, red-baiting sentiments. The depoliticization obvious in the subsumption of vitally important political issues to Cohn-Bendit's personality was one dimension of the Greens' dilemma. Embodying the generation of 1968, he opposed revolutionary (and even radical) politics. For the Autonomen, Cohn-Bendit proved that the entire New Left had sold out. The Greens were proof of their political cooperation; their nuclear families and the Mother Manifesto (see Chapter 4) indicated their cultural conformity; and their professional jobs and condos were proof enough of their economic integration. As one Autonomen put it:

> A little more than ten years after its founding phase, this party, consisting of a core membership of technocratic ecology managers, has become a political mouthpiece for reactionary conservationists, epicureans, and upwardly mobile petit-bourgeois citizens.[35]

Increasingly distant from insurgent social movements, the Greens' inner life was consumed by the obsessive conflicts between realos and fundis. With their membership calling on the party leadership to stop its "disgusting quarrels," a new pragmatic stratum of professional politicians emerged within the Greens, reflecting the conservatism of the Mother Manifesto. By 1987, all but one of the state (*Länder*) candidate lists in the national elections were headed by women, the first time in German history that a majority of a party's parliamentary representatives had been women.[36] (Only in the city-state of Hamburg was a man awarded the top spot, and that was predicated upon the fact that in the state elections of November 1986, an all-female list had run successfully.) Echoing realo themes, the new pragmatists called on the party to abandon "utopian dreams" and offered a new slogan of "ecological capitalism." According to that notion, because of the existing system's wholesale destruction of the biosphere and the remoteness of any genuine alternative, the Greens needed to put forth proposals for making the market system responsible for the preservation of the environment. Is it any wonder that many ecologists considered the Greens to have betrayed the vision of a qualitatively better society? The parallel with the opportunist history of the Social Democrats at the beginning of the twentieth century is striking.

If nothing else, the Greens provide a bridge to millions of Germans, some of whom subsequently find ways to participate in the movements that originally helped create the Greens. As the third largest party in Germany, the Greens afford visibility and dissemination of ecological, feminist, and progressive ideas that otherwise would simply be ignored by most Germans. Since the Greens have easy access to the media, they have been able to publicize alternative viewpoints on a regular basis. From 1983 to 1987, for example, they introduced 53 bills, made 367 parliamentary proposals, participated in 87 inquiries, and flooded the media with position papers and press releases.[37] Their chief political success was to prod mainstream parties to include many Green issues in their platforms.[38] Soon after the Chernobyl disaster and the renewal of the anti-nuclear movement, the Social Democrats shifted their policy and decided to oppose all nuclear power plants within ten years. Even the sclerotic German bureaucracy has been slowly transformed. In June 1993, the same month in which more than ten thousand people marched through Berlin to mark Christopher Street Day, the Alliance 90 (eastern Greens composed of groups such as New Forum, which had been a leading force in the last days of the East German government) was able to introduce for the first time a proposal to the *Bundestag* that contained the words "gay" and "lesbian" in its title. In March 1994, the *Bundestag* finally removed paragraph 175 of the legal code (which had made all forms of homosexual relations subject to prosecution). For a long time, lesbian and gay leaders had called for such a move, and without the pressure from the Greens inside parliament, it is doubtful that they would have had even this small success. The German Association of Gays also called for the right of gay people to marry, as well as for a status equivalent to heterosexual marriage for unmarried gay couples regarding tax, inheritance, and rental laws.[39] Spokesperson Volker Beck explained, "we will no longer be satisfied with simply being tolerated by society."

Feminism is another of the party's saving graces. Although women constitute only about 35 percent of its members, they are required to hold 50 percent of all party posts, and candidate lists observe a similar quota. Women have veto power within the party and essentially rescued it when it appeared on the verge of self-destruction in 1988. In 1995, the parliamentary fraction of the Greens consisted of twenty-nine women and twenty men. At the same time, however, women have sometimes uncritically accepted the newfound power within the established system.[40]

Concrete gains that can be traced to Green participation in government have been minuscule. On the national level, the first four years of Green representation produced only one successful bill dealing with a ban on the importation of sea turtles. In Hesse, no major concessions were granted: Startbahn West was in full use, and fission power proceeded unabated. Even in the area of women's rights, the red-green coalition produced only miniscule changes.[41] In Frankfurt, plans for a greenbelt were repeatedly shelved, and the red-green government was regarded by many as an exercise in frustration. Although small gains in parks, minority rights, and regulation of Hoechst were made, the Greens became targets of newly emergent citizens' initiatives in the northern part of the city. In Berlin, twenty months of a red-green government produced only a few reforms: major electrical power lines from a nuclear plant were buried in the ground to mitigate the harmful effects of overhead lines; a two-kilometer stretch of the road around Lake Havelchau was closed to traffic; speed limits on highways were lowered (angering many motorists); and new lanes exclusively for buses were designated in the city.

Reforms won must be balanced against the longer-term strengthening of the system accomplished through Green participation in government. Local party branches have some autonomy from the national once, but they are compelled to act in accordance with national party policy. Even more significantly, all officials are obligated to conform to federal government dictate. In Lower Saxony, the state interior minister, herself a Green and a prominent member of Greenpeace, called in police when antinuclear protesters blocked the entrance to the Gorleben nuclear waste site. She had originally forbidden the assembled police to clear the blockade, but when she was specifically ordered by the federal interior minister to end the standoff, she was compelled to relent. Under her administration, arrests were made, and more nuclear waste was buried beneath the earth at Gorleben. As demonstrated by the participation of the AL in the Berlin government at the time of Mainzerstrasse, red-green coalitions have not functioned any differently with respect to social movements.

Since they play the parliamentary game, the Greens have to operate at national and even international levels like any other party. In order to be seriously considered by the electorate, they are compelled to take positions on a wide range of issues and to formulate national or regional policies based on the continuing existence of the established political structures. Unlike the Autonomen, who are free to build (or dissolve) their own groups and create their own scale for political engagement, the Greens must accept the formal aspects of the political status quo.

Self-righteously sermonizing from their nonviolent podium, the Greens mercilessly vilified "violent" Autonomen. For many pacifists, nonviolence is itself revolutionary, and any deviation from it only reproduces the power relations of the established system.[42] Autonomists, for their part, have little respect for the Greens, whom they all too often view as government agents. Their mutual antagonisms are reminiscent of the tragic split in the German Left in the 1930s that provided an opportunity for the Nazis to seize power.

The future of the movement as a whole (Green and autonomous) may well be tied to the continuing tension between parliamentary and extraparliamentary actions. By preventing even a discussion of such a concept, the movement's internal feuds are obstacles to its own future success. If the German movement is unable to accommodate itself to its own internal contradictions, its fate may mirror that of the Italian upsurge of the 1970s, which is little more than a memory today. I am not arguing for formal ties or even informal meetings between people involved in these various forums. Nor am I assuming that the Greens are the representatives of the Autonomen in parliament or that the Autonomen are the militant arm of the Greens. Each of these formations has its own inner logic and reason for existence. I am, however, highly critical of the Greens' arrogance of power and the Autonomen's fetishization of marginality, each of which contributes to the attenuation of the other, not their mutual amplification. If the Greens can stomach working with the SPD and the Autonomen can support hierarchical Marxist-Leninist organizations from Turkey and Kurdistan, why can't they hold their noses and stand next to each other? Why can't the Greens simply adopt a policy of noncompliance with particularly odious federal laws, such as those authorizing the transport of nuclear waste to Gorleben? At a minimum, they should abstain from criminalizing radical activists, who, for their part, should refrain from denying progressive parliamentarians public space for discussion. So long as activists make the assumption that the movement is defined by one set of values or tactics (nonviolent elections versus militant opposition) and that those outside the chosen values are not part of the movement, they fetishize their own positions and ultimately reproduce the very system they oppose.

Defeatism and sectarianism remain formidable internal obstacles to continuing activism. Because they accept the government's version of the closing down of Wackersdorf as related to technical issues, many people refuse to understand it as a movement victory. Among those who do see the movement as the driving force behind victories not only at Wackersdorf but also at Wyhl and five other nuclear facilities,[43] some claim that social movements, not the Greens, are responsible. In my view, it is impossible to separate the combined effects of these two formations.

The Greens' reformism is not their main shortcoming—their inability to act responsibly as part of a larger movement is. Their failure to keep proper financial records is trivial when compared with their other political problems. Rather than act resolutely after the dissolution of East Germany, they refused to participate in the "annexation" of the east. In 1987, they had won 8.3 percent of the national vote in one of their best efforts, but after Germany reunified, they decided to watch from the sidelines. Opposed in principle to the "colonization" of the east, they insisted on running as a separate slate from eastern Greens (Alliance '90) in the national elections of December 1990. As a result, the national Greens did not surpass the 5 percent needed to remain in the *Bundestag*, although Alliance '90 did receive sufficient votes in the first elections after reunification to have parliamentary representatives. If the two parties had run together, they both would have been over the 5 percent mark (although some insist that the Greens would have swallowed up Alliance '90). The West German Greens' "principled" stand cost them their forty-six seats in parliament, a staff of 260, and millions of deutsche marks in income. Speaking at a postelection gathering of their former representatives in the environmentally sound conference room they had built with government money, Petra Kelly angrily denounced the "mullahs of the party factions who have coagulated in dogmatism."

Many prominent fundis had left the party even before the 1990 elections, believing that the Greens had become part of the social repair mechanism of the established system. At a party congress in Frankfurt at the beginning of June 1991, the remaining fundis saw their position erode completely. When delegates voted to give more power to individuals elected as parliamentary representatives (including an end to rotation), more than three hundred fundis decided to leave the Greens and reconstitute themselves as the Ecological Left. The resulting acrimony prompted one of the leaders of Alliance '90 to call the Greens "a pubertarian association." The departure of the Ecological Left removed the last major internal opposition to coalitions with the Social Democrats and left the realos in control. After merging with Alliance '90, the combined list (known as Alliance '90/Greens) won over 7 percent of the vote in the national elections of 1994, enough for forty parliamentary seats. Despite their inability to gain a majority coalition with the SPD, the Greens are stronger than ever at the state level, where they have formed a handful of coalition governments with the Social Democrats. Now that rotation is a memory and the Hessian experiment has become the Greens' model, Fischer has his eye on a national office. In the future, traffic-light coalitions (red for the SPD, yellow for the Free Democrats, and green) are envisioned for every state government and the national government. If the Greens succeed in forming a national coalition with the SPD in the future, Fischer's ambitions may net him control of a federal ministry, propelling him (and a few other Greens) into the national spotlight and endowing them with power—more of a compromise of the party's founding principles than the maintenance of state coalitions has already demanded.

Robert Michels developed his concept of the "iron law of oligarchy" in a study of German social democracy and trade unions, and to many people, the dynamics in the Greens validates his hypothesis that all organizations inevitably produce elites. Awareness of this hierarchical imperative helped motivate many Greens to infuse a critique of hierarchy into their first program and organizational form. Far from their origins of egalitarian rules aimed at preventing the emergence of an oligarchy within their organization, the Greens today appear to be a monolithic party controlled by a few people. Their failure to mitigate the insidious appearance of elites within the party only alienated them further from the social movements from which they emerged and on which they depend for their future vitality.

AUTONOMY AND THE LEFT

As it is commonly understood, democracy means majority rule. Whether a government is considered democratic depends on its ability to sponsor free elections involving more than one political party with access to the media. Elections are the specific mechanism through which conflicting interests are thought to be "democratically" mediated. When suffrage is distributed according to the principle of one person—one vote, representatives are considered "freely" elected. In the modern period, representative democracy supplanted less democratic forms of political decision making (monarchies, dictatorships, and tribal chieftains). Never has the international legitimacy of this type of democracy been greater than it is today. Francis Fukuyama believes that existing democratic states are as perfect as possible, that we have arrived "at the end of history."

An alternative view posits consensual, direct-democratic forms of decision making as having constituted the earliest, the most robust, and by far the longest lasting democratic form of government known to human beings. Exemplified in Athenian democracy and Renaissance *popolo*,[44] a participatory democracy demands more involvement of citizens in their political affairs and affords them more input into decisions affecting them.[45] Communities of hunter-gatherers, in which humans lived for 99 percent of their existence, almost universally resolved issues of group importance in face-to-face meetings where they more often than not made decisions through consensus. This early form of democracy, far from having disappeared, survives in a variety of settings: local town and village councils in rural areas, family meetings, cooperatives, collectives, and (as discussed in this book) various social movements.[46] Political scientist Jane Mansbridge maintains that for most people, face-to-face consensual decisions occur far more often than majority rule.[47] The differences between these two forms of democracy, summarized in Table 6.2, help us understand some of the reasons for the emergence of autonomous movements (as well as their differences with the Greens). In the table, participatory democracy corresponds to what most people refer to as "direct democracy," thought to exist as an institutional form in some New England town meetings. It is also akin to the original form of German decision-making observed by Tacitus nearly two thousand years ago:

> On matters of minor importance only the chiefs debate, on major affairs, the whole community; but, even where the commons have the decision, the case is carefully considered in advance by the chiefs... they do not assemble at once or in obedience to orders, but waste two or three days in their dilatory gathering. When the mass so decide, they take their seats fully armed. Silence is then demanded by the priests, who on that occasion have also power to enforce obedience.... If a proposal displeases them, the people roar out their dissent; if they approve, they clash their spears.[48]

Since Tacitus penned these lines, the world system has destroyed regional autonomy, and various forms of governments (the most recent type being nation-states) have encroached upon indigenous forms of governance. Contemporary aspirations for autonomy attempt to reverse this process by enlarging the scope of direct-democratic forms of decision making. In contrast to groups such as the Greens that struggle within the domain of representative governments ostensibly to reverse their powers over and above people, the Autonomen seek to defend and extend the independence of civil society, to safeguard their neighborhoods and collective relationships from the existing system's ever-thicker web of hierarchy and commodity relationships. Essentially, the world system evolved according to the same process by which the human species emerged from nature—an unconscious struggle to survive and prosper. Never did the species rationally or democratically agree how to structure its social relations. Partial attempts to redesign the structure of society, such as those reconstituting national power in America (1776), France (1789),

TABLE 6.2

FORMS OF DEMOCRACY

	Participatory	Representative
Assumption	Common interests	Conflicting interests
Central egalitarian ideal	Equal respect	Equal protection
Decision rule	Consensus	Majority rule
Level of intimacy	Face-to-face	Secret ballot

Source: Adapted from Mansbridge, *Beyond Adversary Democracy* (Chicago: University of Chicago Press, 1983).

and Russia (1917), produced results that ultimately were subordinated to the structured logic of the global economy.

Although the 1960s paradigm shift from "bigger is better" to "small is beautiful" signaled a transition from "modernist" centralization to "postmodernist" decentralism, the increasing concentration of power and resources in giant nation-states and transnational corporations has yet to be reversed with the notable exception of the Soviet Union (and nearly Canada). As an organizing principle of society, autonomy provides a means of restructuring governments and corporations, of reversing the modernist imperative for uniformity. At its best, autonomy means all power to the people. Communities, institutions, and regions would be governed by their inhabitants, not by managerial prerogatives. To give one example, the now-empty idea of the autonomy of the university would be reinvigorated by student-faculty-staff self-management.

Autonomy is the political form appropriate to postmodern societies (whose contours are discussed in the next chapter). Already autonomy has emerged as a central defining feature of social movements, revealing the phenomenological form of freedom not in speculation but in the concrete universal of history. Autonomous democracy means more freedom not only for those who are judged to be politically correct but for all citizens. No longer should adversary, zero-sum solutions be necessary to social problems. Autonomist solutions to poverty, for example, include creating cooperatives, instituting self-help programs, and providing direct aid to the poor, not disenfranchising the comfortable majority of people in industrialized societies. Nelson Mandela's limited endorsement of a white homeland for those South African whites who insist on one is another example of how autonomy is a new solution to age-old problems. In his day, Black Panther leader Fred Hampton similarly endorsed the idea of "white power for white people." Autonomous communalism, developed from the Black Panther Party's "revolutionary intercommunalism," might obviate the need for centralized bureaucracies and giant nation-states by devolving power directly to people affected by specific decisions. For autonomists, the republican form of government provides too little space for broad participation in decisions affecting everyday life. By subjecting everyone to the same uniform standards, modernist political forms are seen as denying differences rather than enhancing the unique attributes of groups and individuals.

The distance between this conception of freedom and that of the Old Left is great. Both social democracy and Leninism were predicated upon the need for centralizing control, not deconstructing it. In the case studies in this book, I have been careful to point out how parliamentary and "revolutionary" Leninist party politics continually threatened the vitality of popular movements. In the following pages, I discuss the distance between autonomous movements and these Old Left currents, a distance at least as important as that between the Autonomen and the New Left Greens. In contrast to the Old Left, autonomous movements have criticized representative democracy as being too little democracy, not simply because it is a system of democracy for the rich but because it is not a system for direct popular decision making. Soviet Marxism's critique of representative democracy produced a "dictatorship of the proletariat" (originally a concept, anomalously enough, that was supposed to mean an extension of democracy)."[49] A dictatorship of the party, not the rule of the vast majority of workers and peasants, the Soviet Union nonetheless created a social system that negated the twin extremes of great wealth and dire poverty. The Leninist curtailment of liberty for the rich, however, led to the reduction of liberty for all, a drastic step that doomed the Soviet system (and too often gets reproduced within popular movement organizations open to Leninist groups).

For the first half of the twentieth century, freedom meant either liberty in what used to be called the "Free World" or equality in the "socialist" countries. Neither bloc embodied social orders in which fundamental social antagonisms were resolved. Because Soviet Marxists mechanically defined freedom as equality rather than liberty, one result was the uniform design of apartments, each one containing precisely the same number of square meters and, in many cases, the same exact layout. Mammoth concrete jungles built under "socialist" architects differed from their Western counterparts only by their dull uniformity and inferior building materials. In both the East and the West during the Cold War, gigantic projects epitomizing the centralization of power were the rule, not the exception. More significantly, at the same time that the gulags killed millions and "socialist equality" debased egalitarian ideas, capitalist "liberty" enslaved tens of millions of individuals at the periphery of the world system. Making both liberty and equality preconditions for freedom was a defining feature of the New Left.[50]

The lessons of the Soviet Union have not yet been fully distilled, but one thing has always been clear: governments can be overthrown and new ones established, but they remain part of the world system, subject to its economic cycles, military impulses, and political initiatives. The failure of the Soviet Union and Leninist strategy to provide a materially satisfying and more democratic way of life was partly predicated upon its obsession with national power. At least as we have known them, nation-states must maintain sovereign control over their land and people, a necessity that contradicts autonomous notions of self-government, particularly when centralized decision making and a command mentality are enshrined in the canons of government.

In much of Western Europe, elected socialist governments, long part of the political landscape, have failed to alter significantly any of capitalism's essential features. In France, Mitterrand's socialism privatized banks and large corporations, demonstrating anew the tendency of social democracy to aid corporate accumulation of wealth, not society's most needy or insurgent popular movements. As discussed in earlier chapters, German Social Democratic governments and Italian Communists, though often less repressive than their Christian Democratic colleagues, have never hesitated to use force to maintain order when faced with domestic insurgency from autonomists. These were not accidental occurrences, thrust into historical relief by coincidence or particularly bad leaders: the PCI in the 1970s was renowned as one of the most liberal Communist parties in the world, and Hamburg's mayor Dohnanyi had literally written the book on the disruptive effects of youth unemployment.[51]

The clear line that divides both Communists and Social Democrats from the Autonomen means that the latter are often described as anarchists, a label that is not entirely accurate. For the most part, Autonomen do not understand themselves as anarchists, and the movement is often indifferent and sometimes hostile to individuals and groups who call themselves anarchists.[52] "They [anarchists] are scared of us," is how one autonomous activist put it, "because we do the kinds of things they only talk about." To accusations of being anarchists, autonomists sometimes reply that they believe in freedom. Autonomists exemplify self-discipline and self-organization (not imposed from the outside). As radical critics of the Soviet system, some Autonomen did consider themselves anarchists. Anarchism provided a coherent theory explaining the bankruptcy of "real existing socialism." Its insights rang true to many activists beginning to assemble an analysis of their own political experiences as squatters or antinuclear activists. After the demise of the Soviet Union, anarchist theory is consumed eagerly by many in a quest for theoretical clarity and assistance in making strategically viable decisions. Although the anarchist critique of authority may provide an understanding of the problems of Communism as they existed in the countries controlled by the Soviet Union, libertarian Marxism and other currents of Left thought undoubtedly contain important insights as well. To name one, the Marxist ability to analyze the economic forces at work in the existing world system (exemplified in the work of Immanuel Wallerstein and *Monthly Review*) has no parallel in anarchist thought. Judging from the movement's posters and activists' ideas, Rosa Luxemburg (a turn of the century Marxist with an incisive and radical critique of Lenin, as well as a deep appreciation for the autonomy of popular movements) is as highly regarded as any political figure.

In contrast to Communist Party organizations consisting of cells of three to fifteen individuals arranged hierarchically under the rigid authority of a central committee, autonomous movements are structured horizontally or, as discussed earlier, even circularly. One reason for the organizational differences between Leninists and autonomists is that the goals of Leninism are starkly different from those of autonomous movements. Unlike the communist dream of insurrection aimed at capturing and centralizing the political system, many Autonomen believe that as the system destroys itself, whether through ecological degradation or economic stagnation and crisis, the government will become irrelevant to more and more people, and collectives will become the new form of the social organization of civil society. Those autonomists with a less passive understanding of the future of the existing political system see the role of the autonomous movement as being to subvert current conceptions of politics, to critique mercilessly the lack of substance in representative democracy's claims to facilitate popular participation in government.

Just as there is no central organization, no single ideology is vital to the Autonomen, but this does not mean that the movement is atheoretical or antitheoretical. Activists there read—or at least have read—Left classics from Bakunin and Marx to Mao and Marcuse. Although they seem to agree on very little, the Autonomen have a profound critique of authoritarian socialism and refuse to permit Stalin posters and paraphernalia at their annual May Day demonstrations. Many people have had their limbs broken or been seriously injured by Stalinists swinging steel bars to assert their "right" to lead the march with their banners. These injuries are testimony to the vital importance of the movement's critique of Left authoritarianism. The Autonomen distance from what used to be called "real existing socialism" in East Germany and the Soviet Union was vital to the movement's identity. Just as Autonomia in Italy existed in opposition to the Italian Communist Party, the Autonomen's political universe shared little with East Germany. At one point, when a squatted plot of land adjacent to the wall was invaded by West Berlin police, the occupants jumped the wall into the East to escape arrest, but they were promptly expelled by the communist authorities. Although the RAF received aid and sanctuary from East Germany, the autonomous movement was despised and vilified by communists.

Outsiders can easily misconstrue this relationship—all the more so because the movement plays with its radical critique of the conservative Left. Using irony in a fashion reminiscent of their predecessors in the Metropolitan Indians of Italy, some activists in West Berlin habitually dressed in old Communist military attire on May Day and positioned themselves in a balcony overlooking the route of the annual autonomous demonstration from Oranienplatz. As the marchers passed, they held out their arms or saluted, mimicking Soviet generals and party hacks on the review platform in Red Square. Similarly, after the fall of the Berlin Wall, Pinux (a collective bar originally squatted) prominently displayed a glossy photograph of former East German chief of state Erich Honecker, as much of a joke about him in those days as Teutonic humor would allow.

One of the reasons that the movement in West Germany successfully maintained its impetus when the upsurge of 1968 vanished in so many other countries is that Marxist rule in East Germany provided ample daily evidence of the bankruptcy of the Soviet system. For forty years, an everyday political problem for Germans was how to grapple with Soviet control of the eastern part of the country, and radical social movements necessarily differed sharply from its Communist rulers. Many Germans were able to watch nightly news from both sides, daily witnessing the bureaucratic style of Communist control so obviously foreign to concepts of individual liberty. In the early 1960s, key activists in German SDS came from East Germany and were able to infuse an informed critique of Soviet Marxism into that organization.

Leninism was built upon the bifurcation of spontaneous popular action and theoretical consciousness, a split that Lenin believed necessitated the creation of a vanguard party to bring revolutionary consciousness to the working class. The edifice upon which Soviet Communism was built included the defamation of spontaneity. What I have called the "conscious spontaneity" of the autonomous movement reflects the vast difference of opinion regarding popular movements and crowds. Innovations in communications and the immense differences in literacy between the beginning and end of the twentieth century are material conditions that change the character of popular formations. Contemporary cultural-political movements comprising collectives, projects, and individuals who assemble sporadically at conferences and act according to local initiatives might very well represent future forms that even "normal" politics might take.

A century ago, similar initiatives existed. Thousands of people in Paris, Barcelona, and Berlin lived differently, associated as radicals, and even created a counterculture. In Spain in the 1930s, anarchism was an important political belief, yet all these groups were eventually compelled to take up arms, many activists lost their lives, and these movements seldom receive more than an occasional reference. Are autonomous movements doomed to a similar fate? A negative response might be argued on the basis of the fact that contemporary nation-states have diminished powers to use force domestically (although they often do, whether at Kent State, Tiananmen Square, or South Central Los Angeles). The diminished capacity of governments to intervene militarily within their own borders and the declining legitimacy of established forms of politics precondition autonomous politics—or, as I like to call it, the subversion of politics.

In the nineteenth century, both anarchism and Marxism developed from the need to sum up the experiences of vibrant movements and to find avenues for their own future success. Both were responses to the advent of the industrial revolution and its profound transformation of the world. The failure of these movements can, in part, be traced to their theoretical inadequacies, but their shortcomings need to be understood through historical analysis, not simply through the prism of their theory. The history of the 1848 uprisings throughout Europe is unknown to many people who appropriate the theories that these movements developed a century and a half ago. Severed from their historical genesis in the 1848 movements, such theories become empty shells of formal logic, everywhere applicable but nowhere vital. Transformed from an ongoing process to a finished product, such theory is then mechanical and weakens the ability of social movements to find appropriate means of action under contemporary conditions. When ideologies are appropriated as labels, the intellectual process of questioning, probing, and coming to an independent and fresh understanding is short-circuited. Dogmatic recitations of texts and pledges of allegiance to one theorist or another replace careful consideration of immediate issues.

For much of the twentieth century, a standardized rendition of Marxism produced by party hacks provided workers' movements with an already constructed, supposedly universal analysis. In some cases, movements around the world were able to use Marxism as a tool in their revolutionary projects. As time went on, the Comintern's domination of theory and practice undermined the vitality of most popular movements, either by bending them into appendages of Soviet foreign policy or by compelling them mechanically to apply lessons gleaned from the Russian revolution. Beginning with China and Cuba, revolutionaries broke with Soviet Communists and embarked on fresh paths toward revolution. At the end of the 1960s in both Germany and the United States, Maoist and Guevarist sects stifled the popular upsurge and contributed to its internal collapse. Although opposed to the Soviet Union, the second wave of radical Left activism in this century (the New Left) self-destructed in large measure because many within it adopted wholesale stale theories of revolution. Revolutionary movements adopt their slogans and identities from their predecessors, and in a world changing more rapidly than ever before in history, this tendency is part of an internally conditioned defeatism.

IN DEFENSE OF THE DIALECTIC[53]

Collective reinterpretation of revolutionary theory is long overdue, especially after the end of what Paul Sweezy called the first wave of socialist experimentation. History has revealed the tragic miscalculations of Lenin, and verified Marx's belief that world-historical transformation of capitalism must occur from within its core. Antonio Negri's experiences in the 1970s Italian autonomous movement situate him to pose theoretical insights from the point of view of practical action. As the movement against capitalist globalization has gathered momentum, Negri and co-author Michael Hardt seek to theorize the global revolt against neoliberalism.

While their enthusiasm for the revolt of the multitude is refreshingly unusual among academics, their theories have limited usefulness in building liberatory movements. In the following remarks, I hope to make apparent problems that inhibit these theorists' efficacy: their rejection of dialectical thinking, Negri's fetishization of production, and a failure to deal with patriarchal domination.

Although Negri has been enormously self-critical and changed many of his views from the 1970s and 1980s, he retains ideological categories and patterns of thinking that lead him in the same directions he now acknowledges as mistaken. Accordingly, just as his mentor Louis Althusser believed "history has no subject," Negri and Hardt maintain that "empire" has no single hegemonic country. For them, US imperialism is a category of limited or no value, since their understanding of postmodern reality is that the system exists everywhere but in no determinate place. For them, postmodernism differs radically from the modern epoch, and since the modern epoch was dialectical, the postmodern one cannot also be.[54] Their logic is similar to that of Althusser: the philosophical categories of the young Marx are rejected while the economic categories of the "mature Marx" are rigidly accepted. Rather than understanding Marx's later work as an empirical fleshing out of the philosophical categories developed from Hegel's dialectical method, Negri now tells us that dialectical thinking is wrong. Nowhere is Negri's revision of Marx more apparent than in his current rooting of "communist" theory in Machiavelli and Spinoza and in his disavowal of dialectical thought in all its forms.

Agreeing with Francis Fukuyama in a critique of Hegel, Hardt and Negri tell us:

> History has ended precisely and only to the extent that it is conceived in Hegelian terms—as the movement of a dialectic of contradictions, a play of absolute negations and subsumption.[55]

Rejecting a dialectical framework, they mistake essence and appearance. While the contemporary corporate system may appear to have flattened out contradictions like colonialism, class struggle and national exploitation, beneath the surface, these conflicts brew, ultimately pitting the elite against the multitude in what can only be resolved through the overthrow of the current categories of everyday life. In place of patriotism, international solidarity; instead of hierarchy, egalitarianism; rather than individual accumulation of wealth, collective appropriation of the vast social riches bequeathed to the living by generations of labor. Such a dialectical subsumption of the present defies every system of thought that projects the categories of the present onto the future.

Using the "mature" Marx, especially the *Grundrisse*, as a master text, Hardt and Negri mould reality to fit Marx's categories. Marx's own insistence that he was "not a Marxist" was as much a rejection of such a system abstracted from historical specificity, as it was a distancing from Marxists' claims of their infallibility. Marx's last work contains major problems, as he himself acknowledged when he could not solve the problem of expanded reproduction in Volume 2 of *Capital*.[56] Disregarding the problems Marx found in Volume 2, Negri and Hardt seek to reformulate his work in the context of the "postmodern state-form." With typical modesty, they claim "finally to write those two chapters of *Capital* that were never written."[57]

However much they profess to admire Marx and bring his analysis into the postmodern period, they revise his method in much the same way that the Third International did: emphasizing materialism, they jettison the dialectic.

Now that we have claimed the end of the concept of a socialist transition and the notion of a dialectical progression of historical development...we have to reconsider our methodological principles and reevaluate the stock of our theoretical arsenal. Is there, among our weapons, a method for constructing in separation? Is there a nondialectical theory of the constitution of collective subjectivity and social relations?[58]

On the same page, they go on to assert that the tradition of thought from Spinoza to Nietzsche, Foucault and Deleuze

constitutes an alternative to the dialectic and thus provides us with an open terrain for alternative political methodology. Against the negative movement of the dialectic, this tradition presents a positive process of constitution. The methodology of constitution thus shares with the methodology of the liberal philosophical tradition a critique of the dialectical conception of totality...

In the above remarks, one of his central complaints about the dialectic is its conception of totality. Earlier in the same book, however, he asserts:

In fact, in the postindustrial era, in the globalization of the capitalist system, of the factory-society, and in the phase of the triumph of computerized production, the presence of labor at the center of the life world and the extension of social cooperation across society becomes *total*.[59] (my emphasis)

Such examples of anomaly and inconsistency within the same book are not uncommon in Negri's prose. Another level of the vacillating character of his theory can be found in his writings from different periods of time. In the 1970s, he was flush with admiration for Lenin, the diamat notion of base and superstructure, the dialectical method, and the vanguard party—all of which he now rejects.

While Hardt and Negri's collaboration has been incredibly productive in output, it, too, lacks consistency. To give one major example, after September 11, they radically altered their understanding of the centrality of war to the current system. In their bestselling book, *Empire*, they had insisted that, "The history of imperialist, interimperialist and anti-imperialist wars is over. The end of history has ushered in the reign of peace." Four years later, i.e. after the second major US war on Iraq, they tell us (correctly I think) that: "The tradition of tragic drama, from Aeschylus to Shakespeare, has continually emphasized the interminable and proliferating nature of war. Today, however, war tends to extend even further, becoming a *permanent social relation.*"[60]

For decades, I have written about the shortcomings of Lenin, Soviet Marxism, and vanguards—but have done so from what I think of as a dialectical standpoint: from the perspective of the concrete negation of the existing system by millions of people in popular movements that contest power. The strikes of May 1968 in France and May 1970 in the US both consisted of the dialectical transcending of national allegiances through the enacted international solidarity of millions of people. Simultaneously people negated hierarchical authority through the lived experiences of self-management. In Italy in the 1970s and Central Europe in the 1980s, vibrant movements challenged patterns of authority in everyday life, seeking to overturn patriarchy and organizing spontaneously into squatted houses, insurrectionary groups and communes through an "eros effect" of mutually amplified uprisings.

Negri and Hardt's history of these periods contains little or no empirical data, and they ignore such transcendental dynamics. They do not include feminist autonomy in their schema even though it was an early source of inspiration for the broader movements.[61] Now they tell us not only that reality is not dialectical but also that Marx's method was not dialectical. Insisting that Marxism is one stream in the current of revolutionary thinking, a proposition with which I am in full agreement, they postulate an undialectical Marxism (an oxymoron in my view) for the postmodern world.

FROM THE FETISHIZATION OF PRODUCTION TO THE PRODUCTION OF FETISH

Negri developed the term "social factory" to include as "producers" women in the home and students in schools and a vast number of other people. For Negri, the "collective work experience" is more than primary; it is the only real activity of humans. He organizes his own theoretical schema according to his notion of production, and every arena of interaction is understood through that prism: "Production and society have become one and the same thing."[62] Negri's mentor Althusser saw theory as a form of production; Deleuze and Guattari portray the unconscious as the producer of desire;[63] and now Negri tells us that revolution is a production led by "machines of struggle."[64] Metaphors for revolutionary organizations have had interesting formulations: *organs* of dual power, *vehicles* for the propulsion of revolutionary consciousness, a *transmission belt* of revolutionary ideas to the working class, and now Negri's "*machines of struggle,*" or better, his new formulation, "*cyborg*":

The cyborg is now the only model available for theorizing subjectivity. Bodies without organs, humans without qualities, cyborgs: these are the subjective figures today capable of communism.[65]

His choice of words reveals a fetishization of the labor process; more disturbing is his idea that human beings can be emptied of qualities that differentiate us from machines. Negri can only think in terms of this one dimension, so even his political strategy is transformed into a type of production:

> Instead of new political alliances, we could say just as well: new productive cooperation. One always returns to the same point, that of production—production of useful goods, production of communication and of social solidarity, production of aesthetic universes, production of freedom.

His attempt to analyze all reality from within the category of production is part of his systematic reduction of life to work, of the life-world to the system, of eros to production. This is precisely the reduction of human beings that is made by the existing system. It quite escapes him that if revolutionary movements in the future were to adopt his categories, they would be rendered incapable of going beyond the established system. In essence, Negri makes the whole world into a point of production. In a society overwhelmed with the fetishization of commodities, is it surprising that production, the central activity of capitalism, is itself fetishized?

Without a reworking of the psyche and reinvigoration of the spirit, can there even be talk of revolution? On the one side, the system colonizes eros, turning love into sex, and sex into pornography. Labor becomes production, production a job; free time has been turned into leisure, leisure into vacation; desire has been morphed into consumerism, fantasy into mediated spectacle. Autonomous movements respond by rescuing eros from its commodification, expanding its space, moving beyond patriarchal relationships, beyond conceptions of love solely as physical love. The politics of eros infuse everyday life with a content that subverts its would-be colonizers and preserves it as a reservoir of the life-force. The "eros effect" indicates how social movements are an expression of people's loving connectedness with each other. In contrast to Negri's cyborgs, my view of the role of movement participation is that it preserves and expands the domain of the heart—of all that is uniquely human, all that stands opposed to machine culture.

At a time when working people want to escape the engulfment of their lives by the system, Negri's ideas of revolution do little more than assert the omnipresent character of the system of production. His postulation of production as the central category from which to understand life reproduces the very ethos he claims to oppose. Soviet Marxism's reduction of Marxism from a revolutionary philosophy to the science of the Party led to the labor metaphysic and the enshrining of production as the essential defining activity of the proletariat. Labor is just one of several species-constitutive activities (art, revolution and communication being others). If unchallenged, the fetishization of one dimension will lead to a practical inability to sustain a multifaceted movement. Negri and Hardt insist:

> The world is labor. When Marx posed labor as the substance of human history, then he erred perhaps not by going too far, but rather by not going far enough.[66]

Here their substitution of labor for revolution is significant. For Marx, class struggle was the motor force of history. For Negri and Hardt, "class-for-itself" is an irrelevant concept since the dialectic is dead.

THE CENTRALITY OF PATRIARCHY

Negri's fetishization of production reifies Marx's notion of the working class. In Italy in the 1970s, workerism was an obstacle to the autonomous movement's unity and progress. Negri's interpretations of the struggles of 1968 and 1977 portray them solely as workers' movements, ignoring women's struggles and the counterculture as other sources of autonomous politics.[67] Although he has today disavowed his workerist politics of the 1970s, he still understands the vital post-Fordist forces of militant opposition solely as "workers."

In the late 1960s, Italian and German feminists were compelled by the self-righteous workerism of their male "comrades" to assert their autonomy from the Left. Following the lead of African-American activists, US feminists were the first to break with patriarchal dynamics within the movement, and their leading role is recognized in both Italy and Germany. The significance of feminism and, in the US, anti-racist praxis to the subsequent workers' and youth movements is noteworthy and could not possibly be ignored unless one's categories of analysis obstruct one's capacity for seeing. Feminists spoke in the "I" mode, not on behalf of others (the "workers" or the "people"), and their ability to return continually to the reality of their own needs became an essential feature of autonomous movements. Feminism was exemplary, particularly in Italy, where, even before the consolidation of *Autonomia*, women articulated their need for autonomy.[68]

One of the needs of revolutionary theory today is to understand the centrality of patriarchy. By failing to incorporate an analysis of patriarchy that treats its forms of domination as significant alongside capitalist exploitation (and not reduced to the latter), Negri obviates the urgency of women's liberation. Just as capital has various phases (primitive, industrial, post-Fordist) so patriarchy has its own history, which only recently fused with that of capital. Patriarchy has at least two different forms in history: Originally, the man owned his wife and children and was entitled to trade them or sell them. Hegel reminded us that fathers in Rome had the right even to kill their children. In the second form, the wife and children are not legally owned but they reproduce the legal structure of domination within their own character structures.[69]

Workerism is a partial understanding of the universe of freedom. By positing revolution only in terms of categories of production, Negri constricts human beings and liberation within the process of production. His mechanical subsumption of all forms of oppression to the category of work negates the need to abolish patriarchy, racism and the domination of nature alongside capitalism. His politics are thus a suppression of universal liberation.

Negri's fetishization of production is the theoretical equivalent of Soviet suppression of women's issues as dividing the working class or as, at best, a "secondary contradiction." His one-dimensionality magically obliterates issues of sexism within the ranks of the working class. At first glance, his notion of the "social factory" seems well taken: women, students and other constituencies have had their everyday lives penetrated by the commodity form and mechanization. As he recognized in 1990, he was long overdue in understanding them as a central part of the transformative project. But he understands feminism as having demonstrated the centrality of the issue of wages, not of questioning patriarchy. Although patriarchy (and race) need to be understood in their own right, as autonomously existing, not simply as moments of capital, Negri's abstract categories impose a false universality.

He collapses all categories of crisis into a single concept of exploitation, just as he understands all of society through the prism of production. But his facile incorporation of all life to that category is problematic. He subsumes the patriarchal domination of women into the phenomenological form of capital. Patriarchal oppression cannot be made equivalent to class exploitation, no matter how much the concept of the social factory is invoked. What occurs between men and women under the name of patriarchy is not the same as what happens between bosses/owners and workers. Women's liberation from housework will not occur through the path of "wages for housework" but through the abolition of housework as women's domain through the reconstitution of communal households by associations of cooperating equals who share necessary tasks, eroticize them, turn them into play.[70]

NEO-LENINIST RECTITUDE

Exacerbating the above problems is many people's elevation of Negri to an infallible status[71] and Hardt and Negri's own assertion of the absolute truth of their theories. Unable to make more than shallow theoretical responses to dialectical thought (particularly Marcuse and New Left thinking), Negri invokes his own rectitude in place of substantive discussion and debate. When referring to Marcuse, for example, Negri scoffs at "humanism" and calls for the "the exclusion of this insipid blubbering from theory."[72]

Negri's system is NOT one in which a diversity of views is welcomed. Far from it, he continually insists on enunciating positions as though his correctness were a given, and many Negri supporters refuse to consider alternative perspectives. They have little use for a whole range of movement tactics, arrogantly asserting, "Nonviolent actions are thus almost completely useless when deprived of media exposure."[73] My own distance from such ways of thinking is great, since to me, they represent forces of the dogmatic Left that took over popular organizations like SDS in both Germany and the US, leading them to irrelevance and dissolution at the end of the 1960s.

In fairness to Negri, his workerist politics resolutely opposed the reformism of the Italian Communist Party in the 1970s. By 1989, while retaining his critique of reformism, he and Felix Guattari wrote that "It is clear that the discourses on workers' centrality and hegemony are thoroughly defunct and that they cannot serve as a basis for the organization of new political and productive alliances, or even simply as a point of reference."[74] In a self-critical section of a postscript to this same text dated 1989, Negri acknowledged his failure to understand the "participation of the Soviet Union in integrated world capitalism." He employs the concept of *Gesamtkapital* (capital as a whole) that Herbert Marcuse analyzed as subordinating the particular enterprises in all sectors of the economy to corporate globalization.[75] Moving away from his former workerist politics, he also came to consider intellectual work to be at the "center of production." Together with Felix Guattari, he thinks he "ought to have noted more clearly the central importance of the struggles within the schools, throughout the educational system, in the meanders of social mobility, in the places where the labor force is formed; and we ought to have developed a wider analysis of the processes of organization and revolt which were just beginning to surface in those areas."[76]

In reviewing recent history, particularly the struggles of 1989, Negri concludes that it was not mainly the working class or the bureaucracy who revolted, but intellectuals, students, scientists, and workers linked to advanced technology. "Those who rebelled, in brief, were the new kinds of producers. A social producer, manager of his own means of production and capable of supplying both work and intellectual planning, both innovative activity and a cooperative socialization."[77] While he doesn't say so in so many words, he essentially adopts the New Left idea of the "new working class" formulated by Serge Mallet and articulated more fully by Andre Gorz and Herbert Marcuse.

While Negri insists he has gone beyond Leninism, written a "black mark through the Third International," he retains its syntax and grammar. His "politics of subversion" are still a politics that ends up worshiping power, not seeking to dissolve it:

> After centuries of capitalist exploitation, it [the working class] is not prepared to sell itself for a bowl of lentils, or for hare-brained notions that it should free itself within the domination of capital. The enjoyment that the class seeks is the real enjoyment of power, not the gratification of an illusion.[78]

In this formulation of the "real enjoyment of power" we see the real Negri. In the same breath, he dismisses joyful participation in revolutionary struggle as opportunism. No doubt his fascination with power is one reason for his more recent uncritical incorporation of Machiavelli into "communist" theory.

In the twentieth century, the New Left's impetus to self-management and group autonomy represented the consolidation of the historical experience of autonomous social movements. Beginning with the spontaneous creation of soviets in 1905, the council communists and revolutions of 1917, and the Spanish revolution, the industrial working class expressed its autonomy in general strikes and insurrections. Later, the nascent new working class contested control of entire cities (including factories) in 1968 and 1989, and through uprisings as in Gwangju in 1980, peoples' movements autonomously reformulated the meaning of freedom. The capacity of millions of ordinary people to govern themselves with far more intelligence and justice than entrenched elites is evident in all these cases. For example, during the massive strike of May 1970 in the US, the largest single strike in American history to date,[79] an assault was mounted both from within and outside the system that spontaneously generated what a high ranking US government official called capable of constituting a "shadow government."[80] Modeled on SDS, Federal Employees for a Democratic Society, appeared in Washington D.C., not created by any revolutionary control center, but by the movement's conscious spontaneity"[81]

Rather than deal with any substantive histories of these movements, Negri locates his analysis in the categories he imposes. Looking back at 1968, his history becomes a history of workers movements. Indeed, he postulates the initial emergence of the "socialized worker" in 1968.[82] Much like the various M-L groups that sought to appropriate popular New Left organizations like SDS into their parties, Negri seeks to appropriate the history of these popular upsurges into his theoretical schema. While some postmodernists insist on the unique particularity of social action and insist there is no universal, Negri's false universality destroys the particular history of the 1960s. Although workers participated in these struggles, they followed the lead of students and the revolt's epicenter was in the universities, not the factories. While these struggles were not proletarian in appearance, their universality resided in the concrete demands that spontaneously emerged, in the New Left's notion of self-management and international solidarity—the twin aspirations of popular movements of millions of people throughout the world in 1968.

Immediately after the events of May 1968 in France, Marcuse was one of the few theorists who recognized the newness of the subject and was able to connect it with a dialectical theory of history:

> ...the location (or rather contraction) of the opposition in certain middle-class strata and in the ghetto population...is caused by the internal development of the society...the displacement of the negating forces from their traditional base among the underlying population, rather than being a sign of the weakness of the opposition against the integrating power of advanced capitalism, may well be the slow formation of a new base, bringing to the fore the new historical Subject of change, responding to new objective conditions, with qualitatively different needs and aspirations.[83]

STRATEGIC CONCERNS

In 1985 and again in 1990, Negri defined the five tasks awaiting movements of the future:

—the concrete redefinition of the work force
—taking control over and liberating the time of the work day
—a permanent struggle against the repressive functions of the State
—constructing peace
—organizing machines of struggle capable of assuming these tasks.[84]

Where are concerns such as:

—developing interracial bonds capable of withstanding government
manipulation
—creating postpatriarchal human beings with the capacity to live, love
(and work) non-hierarchically
—protecting the environment
—building counterinstitutions and liberating public space
—establishing communes to transform everyday life.

One of the reasons these are insignificant to Negri is because he postulates the revolutionary as a cyborg. He has no notion of changing human beings or of cultural revolution; instead he appropriates "the social" into a schematic productionist model. For Negri, "There exists no consciousness apart from militancy and organization."[85]

The system's assault on autonomous time and space of the life-world intensifies. Negri's fetishization of production renders him incapable of comprehending the significance of youth as non-production strata so vitally important to our future. As young people are drawn into violence and death drugs, Negri calmly remarks:

Let us be clear: violence is the normal state of relations between men; it
is also the key to progress in the forces of production.[86]

How could Negri publish such a statement? In the first place, his use of the term "men" excludes women. Moreover he defames nature. Abundant anthropological evidence of cooperation and group life exists. Here is the crucial point: Bourgeois thought takes the categories of the present and projects them as valid for all time, a feat accomplished above by Negri, since it is primarily capitalist production and struggles for scarcity that pit humans against each other today.

The subversion of politics—the complete uprooting of authoritarianism in our everyday lives—begins by changing our assumptions and includes a restructuring of ideological categories that prefigure our praxis. Reducing humans' capacity for life to categories of production effectively empties freedom of its sensuous content. If freedom is to mean anything, it begins with the subordination of production to human needs, not the subsumption of life in production.

From the vantage point of the nineteenth century, Marx and Engels understood the relationship between freedom and necessity as vitally important. Viewed from the perspective of the twenty-first century, the dialectic of autonomy and freedom becomes salient. In the former case, industrialization and automation had yet to transform the species' infantile dependence on natural cycles. Thus, positivism's insight that human relationships should be modeled on natural science ones had a material basis. A contemporary understanding of freedom incorporates autonomy as a necessary means of dealing responsibly with our species' newfound capacity for technical domination of nature and society. Without recognition of the centrality of autonomy, our destruction of natural ecosystems and social life-worlds is an unreflexive consequence.

TOWARD A RATIONALITY OF THE HEART

In a world where the "sanity" of the monotonous discourse of established politics is as normal as fresh outbreaks of bloody wars in places such as Bosnia, as normal as daily misery for hundreds of millions of people at the periphery of the world system, is it any wonder that the Autonomen appear bizarre, even insane, to those bent on enjoying affluent consumerism amid political stability? Within societies of material wealth but spiritual poverty, those who act according to a new logic, an erotic logic simultaneously passionate and intelligent cannot help but appear as otherworldly. The Greens' integration into the established political system has made them look like any other mainstream party, leaving the Autonomen more marginalized than ever, questioning whether their actions will continue or whether their intervention during the pogrom in Rostock in 1992 was their last gasp.[87]

Inner meanings collapse in a world dominated by consumeristic categories of existence, and attempts to engage in autonomous activities become increasingly difficult. As the capacity for autonomous individuality shrinks, inner nature is colonized, turning eros into an arena for profit. The instrumentalization of eros is a theme taken up by Alberto Melucci:

> A "medicalized" sexuality entrusted to the experts, a body which has become a "scientific" object, an eros reified in the rules of fashion and in the exigencies of industry: advanced capitalism requires the notion of such a body, a body as object, deprived of its libidinal and aggressive charge, of its capacity for eros and delirium.... The body as libido must

be neutralized and deprived of its potential to menace the system. There is no place for play and eros, but only for the regulated pleasure of a sexuality which has become a kind of gymnastic training for orgasm.[88]

So long as apathy defines daily life for the majority, those who choose to live differently have little choice but the alternatives of confronting the system or escaping it through exhilarating otherworldly states. The "otherness" of autonomous movements is most blatantly clear in their acts of "violence," their outlandish dress, and their drug use. Without talking with one another or knowing one another's history, the Metropolitan Indians in Italy, Christiania's communards,[89] and the Black Panther Party[90] all publicly developed identical outlooks on drugs. Embracing "life drugs" (cannabis, mescaline, LSD, and mushrooms), they completely rejected "death drugs" (speed, heroin, cocaine, and their derivatives) and acted to purge their communities of the latter. No doubt this issue will appear trivial to some analysts, but it is significant because it indicates autonomous—and illegal—actions of individuals with regard to themselves and a rejection of government control of inner reality.[91] The preservation and expansion of individual liberty are beginning steps without which no form of autonomy is possible. Without a reworking of the psyche and reinvigoration of the spirit, can there even be talk of social revolution?

On the one side, the system colonizes eros, turning love into sex, and sex into pornography. Autonomous movements respond by recusing eros from its commodification, expanding its space, and moving beyond patriarchal relationships, beyond conceptions of love as physical love. The politics of eros infuses everyday life with a content that subverts its would-be colonizers and preserves it as a reservoir of the life force. In contrast to Negri's cyborgs, another view of the role of movement participation is to preserve and expand the domain of the heart in social relations—of all that is uniquely human, all that stands opposed to machine culture.

Nowhere in the discourse of what passes for political rationality today does such a notion of politics get validated. Individual transformation of inner reality has been a project of aesthetic avant-gardes rather than vanguard political parties. After cubists painted objects as they thought them, not as they saw them, aesthetic rules dating from the Renaissance were shattered, forever altering assumptions about one-point perspective and realistic representation as beautiful. Cubism's transformation of rules inexorably led to more overtly political challenges to aesthetic discourse. Reacting to the brutal application of modern technology to war, Dada broke free of the straitjacket of deadly seriousness that linked art and war. Holding up readymade objects as examples of "artistic" accomplishment, the most notorious of which was Duchamp's urinal, Dada mocked the tight-lipped mentality of science, instead emphasizing chance and spontaneity as the basis for rationally conceived normative standards. When surrealists uncovered the realm of fantasy, dreams, and the unconscious, they explored terrain that contradicted preconceived notions of the "proper" subject matter of art.

Can future social movements learn from these examples? Will they be able to go beyond the boundaries inherited from previous radicals, whose best efforts have only strengthened the engines of government? Socialist realism interpreted the relationship between art and politics to mean reducing art to the level of the mundane, to turning art into an instrument of politics. It may well be that the opposite is now required: engaging aesthetic rationality in the process of political transformation, of turning politics into art, everyday life into an aesthetically governed domain. Already, youthful autonomous movements have embodied principles first introduced by artists. From the appearance of costumed Indians in Italian cities to nude marches in Zurich and Berlin, autonomous movements contain elements of improvisation reminiscent of jazz, of absurd transcendence following from Dada, and of release of pent-up psychic needs modeled on surrealism. These actions speak volumes to the idea that a genuine revolution would be one in which art becomes life. Commenting an the youth movement in Zurich, Max Schmid noted that:

> Despite all these many congruencies in the motivation, expression and forms of appearance, there exists an essential historical difference between the current movement and DADA: The movement of 1916 called itself DADA; the movement of 1980/81 is DADA.[92]

The cumulative effect of dozens of groups transforming regional culture and daily life along the lines of aesthetic avant-gardes could well prepare the majority to take control of their lives.

The common acceptance of the status quo, not its rejection, conditions the rough and tinged appearance of autonomous movements. At best, the Autonomen are the kernels of freely determined social relations, but they are also imprinted with the violence and cultural values of the existing social order. They remain in an infantile stage, smearing excrement in yuppie restaurants, betraying friends for small-minded political reasons, and living in groups replete with purges, expulsions, and recriminations. Insofar as such dynamics parallel the less well-known history of surrealism,[93] the history of aesthetic avant-gardes has already merged with political activism.[94] If the present movement is understood as a small and transitional phase of a larger process in which future autonomous movements can be imagined as involving a majority, the exhilaration concocted through drugs and the otherness constructed by violent and shocking behavior may become unnecessary.

Although often posed as dark and uncontrollable, inner nature may be an ally in such a revolutionary project. The hierarchical imperative of the existing world system is contradicted by our natural tendencies to favor equality and to love freedom. "Man's law of nature is equality," wrote Euripides, a law obvious to anyone who has ever divided candy or cake among children. Today's vast global inequality contradicts this natural propensity, no matter how rationalized its justification (and structures) may be. The unreasonableness of modern rationality originates in its Cartesian categories, specifically its denial of the body. An important dimension of the project of building a society on the basis of equality and autonomy is the formulation of a rationality of the heart.[95] The development of a passionate rationality that is reasonable begins with the liberation of passion from the straitjacket imposed by its vilification, of misogynist notions of reason.[96] As action becomes part of theory (an idea I discuss in the next chapter), social movements become vehicles for the release of psychic needs and the healing of wounds inflicted by the brutality of contemporary society. In the words of one psychoanalyst sympathetic to the autonomous movement in Zurich, participation in movements can be itself liberating:

> Feelings of depression are going to be acted out in individual and collective actions but also verbalized in small and large groups and *worked through*. Sexual and aggressive reactions are going to be less repressed; instinctual blockage and sublimation are possible but not yet very pronounced.... If it is true, that late capitalist industrial society, through the increasing dissolution of family structures, value systems and positive models, destabilizes the narcissistic balance of its subjects, then the youthful subculture and in particular the movements that have emerged from it should be understood as collective self-healing processes. "Only tribes will survive" [a slogan of the movement]. From this perspective, I understand better the Great Refusal, the reactive and compensatory overemphasis on autonomy.[97]

Reintegrating emotions and the body into politics demands a reconsideration of the role of militance. Popular violence can function as an important vehicle for the reintegration of happiness into politics. If, as Ngo Vinh Long maintains,[98] during the costly struggle by the Vietnamese against the United States, joy and romanticism were pervasive among the resistance fighters, should we not hesitate to criticize the Autonomen for their joy in street fighting? Political struggle should and can be joyous.

The release of deeply rooted anger and hostility alongside love and solidarity presents specific problems demanding careful reconsideration of the role of violence. Liberating violence—an entire range of actions not directed at hurting individuals (from active "nonviolent" occupation of public space to militant defense of movement spaces such as the *Hüttendorf*)—reinjects passion and negates the calculating disposition that has made politics deadly serious. The fact that so few police were hurt in the demonstrations described in this book when compared with any one riot in a U.S. city in the 1960s testifies to their antiviolent character.[99] And who can fault those who fight back against sadistic police armed with riot gear beating up helpless demonstrators? Although the immediate benefits go beyond self-defense and protection of friends (i.e., the release of frustrated liberatory impulses), the costs of militance are often paid later, when violence creeps back into everyday life or paranoia interferes with accepting new friends and relaxing with old ones.

Another problem involved with the tactics of resistance is the escalation of militance: from rallies to civil disobedience, civil disobedience to riots, and riots to armed guerrilla actions. The more militant action grabs the headlines and stakes out the macho high ground. Two watersheds exist: from pacifism to militant resistance, and from massive street actions to guerrilla actions. As we have seen in the case studies, guerrilla actions often function to create spectators out of activists and increase the government's repressive tactics. Although some people may celebrate attacks on the rich and powerful, when considered in relation to the building of an activated movement, these tactics are often counterproductive—even when they are linked to ongoing movements.[100] Militant popular resistance, in contrast, can function to build up direct democracy and as a motor force driving larger popular mobilizations. In some cases, a willingness to defend neighborhoods militantly has been successful—as shown by the examples of the Hafenstrasse and Leipzig's Connewitz alternative community.[101] In the history of autonomous movements in the first five chapters, the significance of neighborhoods where the movement has a presence (Christiania and Kreuzberg, for instance) and the usefulness of militance in spreading the revolt and radicalizing it should be clear enough. Although the escalating spiral of repression and resistance often leads to armed resistance, subversive movements can reorder this hierarchy of resistance by keeping clear the goal of increasing popular participation in determining the form and content of public space. Rather than conceiving the goal of autonomy as attacking the heart of the state, the objective of revolutionary movement must be to subvert even the forces of order, to win over the police and the army to the idea that they should act (and be treated) like erotic human beings. At a minimum, movements need to split the forces of order.

In another context, Frantz Fanon similarly discussed violence. Approaching the issue from his psychopolitical vantage point, Fanon understood the function of violence as a necessary procedure in the reconstruction of society:

> Violence alone, violence committed by the people, violence organized and educated by its leaders, makes it possible for the masses to understand social truths and gives the key to them. Without that struggle, without that knowledge of the practice of action, there's nothing but a fancy-dress parade and the blare of trumpets. There's nothing save a minimum of readaptation, a few reforms at the top, a flag waving; and down there at the bottom an undivided mass, still living in the middle ages, endlessly marking time.[102]

As Fanon used to say, violence alone makes it possible for people to understand social truths that otherwise remain hidden and to transcend conditions that restrain us—or rather, that lead to our own self-constraint.

Having made these remarks on the role of violence, I must qualify them. Violence for the sake of violence, whether "chaos days" in Germany or devil's night in Detroit, reproduces the problem of aggression for the sake of itself. Violence for the sake of violence reproduces the oppressor, but violence against neo-Nazis, for example, is a self-liberating act for young Germans. Beginning with the American New Left, the distinction between violence against property and violence against people indicated a rational release of passionate opposition. Despite the seeming irrelevance of such considerations in a context in which the apparent stability of consumer society has brought us to the "end of history," the historical experiences of social movements at the end of the twentieth century (shown once again in measures that sparked the strikes in France at the end of 1995) leave little doubt that modern conceptions of rationality are often unreasonable.

THE THEORY OF AUTONOMY

Never before in the history of humanity has the pace of social change been so rapid. In one year, our species now consumes more of the planet's nonrenewable resources than we did in any five centuries of antiquity, and in that same year, over fourteen million children under the age of five die from easily preventable causes, more than twice the number of Jews killed in the Holocaust.[1] Under such dire conditions, some of the principal undertakings of social theory should be to understand the character of society, to consider the values it should embody, and to discuss alternative directions we might take. The character of everyday life today in advanced capitalist societies militates against such "qualitative thinking." Overwhelmed with the information explosion and the demands of homes, automobiles, and consumer gadgets, many individuals have ceased to think at all, at least in the sense of "negative thinking" that goes beyond the given reality.

Assuring us that we have never had it better, that we have arrived at the "end of history," the system's intellectual representatives seek to stifle "political correctness," as they refer to any form of critical and transcendental thinking. Lumping progressive social criticism with exaggerations about small groups' actions, they seek to portray white males as a beleaguered minority in danger of losing their rights. Championing the cause of these "victims," neo-conservatives have begun abolishing affirmative action and attacking the rights of minorities and women as they take control of Congress, an ominous step on the road toward a renewal of conservative hegemony not achieved since McCarthyism.

Largely denied access to public discourse, critical social theorists can scarcely agree on the character of contemporary society. As Fred Block summarized this confusion:

> This is a strange period in the history of the United States because people lack a shared understanding of the kind of society in which they live. For generations, the United States was understood as an industrial society, but that definition of reality is no longer compelling. Yet no convincing alternative has emerged in its absence.[2]

Block limited his remarks to the United States, but his insight can be applied throughout the world system. What kind of society do we live in: postindustrial, late capitalist, information, service, technetronic, multinational capitalist, consumer, one-dimensional, postmodern, state monopoly capitalist, imperialist, society of the spectacle, or the world system? Even this list is far from complete, and it is continually expanding. Joachim Hirsch adds "post- Fordist," and Alain Touraine prefers "programmed society."

Two problems come immediately to mind. First, anyone approaching social analysis—to say nothing of those who simply wish a bit of intellectual insight—would naturally wonder why so many different descriptions are needed to name contemporary reality. Theory is supposed to aid us, yet the proliferation of terms masks, rather than illuminates, reality's essential features. Second, adopting one or another of the above descriptions is too often a sign of allegiance to the theorist who developed the term (and simultaneously a means of differing with others). When I use the term "postmodern," for example, many people automatically assume that I agree with postmodernists' disbelief in any "grand narrative."[3] Clearly, I disagree with that view, yet I find the term "postmodern" useful. Like Fredric Jameson, I posit a reading of it that understands that

> postmodernism is not the cultural dominant of a wholly new social order (the rumor about which, under the name of "postindustrial society," ran through the media a few years ago), but only the reflex and concomitant of yet another systemic modification of capitalism itself.[4]

To avoid the difficulty of becoming identified with any one particular school of thought, I use several descriptions of society. When discussing the architecture of civil society, I often use postmodernist terminology, since that vocabulary is most appropriate. If I am discussing global economic relationships, I employ world systems theory, and in relation to culture, I employ the terminology of critical theory. The scholastic mind seeking thinly sliced certainty will no doubt react negatively to the simultaneous use of a variety of specialized vocabularies, yet I consider each of these traditions significant resources.

Up to this point, this book has been concerned with actions of social movements, but in this chapter, I consider theories about them and their social context. There are several levels of analysis here. I begin by examining some of the fundamental features of contemporary society. Autonomous movements are collective responses to rapid social transformation, and I seek to uncover the contours of these changes. I believe that on the basis of the analysis of social movements in the first six chapters, a great deal about society can be learned. My analysis of the contradictions that help produce social movements articulates three levels:

1. Within production, automation, coupled with capitalist social relations, dictates increasing unemployment and marginalization for a large fraction (perhaps one-third) of the population of advanced capitalist societies (as well as untold millions at the periphery of the world system).
2. The system's increasing need for arenas of profitable activity spurs colonization of the life-world, destroying autonomous domains previously governed by symbolic reason—particularly in relation to women, youth, and senior citizens—and uniformly subjecting these dimensions of everyday life to instrumentalized rationality that stimulates movements for decolonization of these domains.
3. The system's disregard for "externalities," coupled with the insatiable structural imperative of increasing profitability, leads to the destruction of natural habitat and the unreasonable production of infrastructure such as giant nuclear power plants and megabridges and tunnels that are part of socially unnecessary and environmentally destructive highway systems.

After considering these objective structural imperatives of the existing system, I use the concrete standpoint of autonomous movements to evaluate current theories of social movements, particularly identity politics and new social movement theory. Unlike most analysts, I neither embrace nor reject identity politics but see it as a contradictory formation. Although I find potential universality contained within particular forms of identity politics (such as feminism), I also understand constraints upon such universality and ways that they can create new lacunae. Too often, social theorists develop categories of analysis that they project as universally valid. One of the functions of social movements is to oblige theorists to rethink these categories. In the case of autonomous movements, they pose the need to reconceptualize traditional notions derived from Western philosophy, especially the individualistic conception of autonomy and the relation of theory and practice. I discuss these issues in the course of a detailed textual examination of the feminist theory of Seyla Benhabib. She insists that the often invisible domain of everyday life be analyzed from within the same framework used to delineate standards of political justice. In so doing, however, she fails to consider the problems attached to extending the power of the existing control center. The inadequacy of her understanding of autonomy and her distance from the practical action of autonomous movements are additional constraints on the efficacy and coherence of her theoretical project. As a result, her feminism (like the workerism of Antonio Negri) fails to realize a universal critique of the existing system.

It is my contention that the deep structures of social movements revealed in an empirical analysis of the participatory patterns and aspirations of (tens of) thousands of people (such as I seek to provide in this book) define emergent forms of social relations and new values that future generations will inherit and implement. As such, social movements are not only vital for expanding democracy and liberty; they are also key to understanding society. They are a lens clarifying our vision and helping to remove distorted images we carry from previous epochs. They attune us to new dynamics and inject fresh insight into tired analysis.[5] Very often, social movements transform "objective facts" or illuminate new meaning for them. What surprised every Italian in the 1970s, for example, was how fluidly southerners and northerners came together in the movement, a unity that transcended traditional north-south antagonisms. The dialectical relationship of theory and practice, of human factors and social facts, is vital to understanding social movements. Seldom in the world of theories of social movements, a world with hundreds of researchers (or perhaps a few thousand) employed fulltime, does the idea of changing society get discussed. For most social researchers, social movements are not something they are part of, but merely an object of study. Some of their theories immobilize us, others make us less attuned to dimensions of our lives we know to be significant. Rarely do they help liberate us from unconscious structures shaping our thinking. Social movements bring these hidden structures to consciousness, and when successful, they quickly make long-standing categories of domination (such as slavery, segregation, anti-Semitism) into anachronisms. Even when sporadic episodes define the life of a movement, they can reveal essential issues for people left out of decision-making by the control center.

LATE CAPITALISM'S POSTMODERN FEATURES

Despite the apparent disagreement embedded in the above list of more than a dozen terms used as analytical tools to dissect contemporary society, there is broad agreement that current reality should be demarcated from the epoch of factory-based industrial capitalism. Production itself has been transformed by automation and global communications and transportation. Henry Ford's assembly lines have been superseded by new techniques of production (robotics, quality circles, just-in-time production, CAD/CAM, and computer-integrated manufacturing), a transformation of production that led to the term "post-Fordist" as a description of such societies. Productivity gains have been astounding. To cite just one example, from 1970 to 1977, the output of German computer and office equipment manufacturing rose 48.9 percent while the workforce declined by 27.5 percent.[6]

The dispersal of production, sometimes called the "diffuse factory," means that although the number of production sites has grown, their size has shrunk dramatically. Contemporary craft-specialty factories typically employ one hundred to two hundred workers.[7] In the City of Industry (part of greater Los Angeles), the average number of workers in fabricated metal product plants is 113. In Germany, the automobile industry has undergone a transition from assembly lines to "flexible specialization" involving small component manufacturers and suppliers operating on a "just-in-time" basis. The proportion of car production in plants owned by the major car corporations has fallen from as high as 80 percent in the 1970s to less than half that today.[8]

Increasingly, production of information is central to the post-Fordist economy (in fields such as education, advertising, computer programming, accounting and financial data, sales, and technical knowledge). The preponderant importance of the service sector means that previously marginalized groups become central to the functioning of society and previously integrated groups become dispersed and surpassed. Within the wealthy countries, as Sharon Zukin observed:

> Those places that remain part of a production economy, where men and women produce a physical product for a living, are losers. To the extent they do survive in a service economy, they lack income and prestige, and owe their souls to bankers and politicians. By contrast those places that thrive are connected to real estate development, financial exchanges, and entertainment—the business of moving money and people where consumer pleasures hide the reins of concentrated economic control.[9]

Based on "deregulation" and "flexible accumulation," the new mechanisms of social control involve the increasing fragmentation of production and deconcentration of the working class, the very force that, for more than a century, was expected by conservatives and liberals alike to be the basis of revolutionary change. Spatial deconcentration in the post-Fordist city is reflected in its diffuse character, its destruction of neighborhoods and community ties. Unlike the centrifugal forces driving the industrial city outward from a central business district through concentric zones defined by economic class, the post-Fordist city has multiple nuclei.[10] Dynamics such as the global relocation of production, the transformation of cities through gentrification and migration, the millions of homeless people in urban areas, and increasing automation signal the types of rapid changes that define postmodern capitalism.

The performance principle of factory-based capitalism ("the obligation to work") has been transformed into the post-Fordist struggle for the "right to work." To understand this dimension of post-Fordist reality, one need only realize that in the 1950s, the FRG had virtually eliminated unemployment. Only 271,000 people were counted as jobless in 1960.[11] During the 1960s, the "economic miracle" meant unprecedented affluence and political stability (referred to as *Modell Deutschland*). Unemployment never rose above 2 percent, and the gross domestic product (GDP), which had grown by an average of 8 percent in the 1950s, expanded by an average of 5 percent.[12] In 1970, the unemployment rate was 0.7 percent; in 1974, it was 2.6 percent; in 1975, 4.8 percent. GDP decreased to an average of 1.7 percent from 1970 to 1975, the first sign of the end of the long wave of postwar expansion. In the 1980s, although GDP per capita had surpassed that of the United States, unemployment remained over 10 percent, and it has not decreased to previous levels. In 1994, the German government counted more than four million unemployed, a record number for the post-World War II epoch (and a number that understates the real number of unemployed by as many as 2.5 million people).[13] In 1992, conservative estimates placed the number of unemployed workers in the European Community at eighteen million.[14] Some guessed the number to be double that figure.[15]

The situation only worsens as new technology makes it possible to produce more output with less labor. When German corporations cut back tens of thousands of jobs in the steel industry in the 1990s during a wave of European Community economic restructuring designed to deal with overproduction, steelworkers responded with warning strikes and protests. On February 17, 1993, in one of their most militant actions in decades, thirty thousand steelworkers and miners blocked autobahns in the Ruhr to protest job cuts.[16] The next month, nearly 100,000 workers turned out for a union demonstration in Bonn. In order to avoid massive layoffs, Volkswagen unilaterally reduced the workweek to four days (28.8 hours), and in the steel industry, strikes compelled management to comply with an agreed reduction in the workweek. BMW and Hewlett-Packard shortened their workers' week to thirty-one hours while continuing to pay them for thirty-seven.[17] German workers already enjoy one of the shortest workweeks (an average of 37.5 hours a week) of all industrialized countries. Excluding vacations and holidays, German workers labored a total of 1,667 hours a year in 1992, far below the average in the United States (1,912 hours) or Japan (2,080) and significantly less than in Italy (1,788).[18] Unionized German industrial workers were entitled to forty paid vacation days annually (compared with a U.S. average of twenty-three and a Japanese average of twenty-five).[19]

TABLE 7.1

OCCUPATIONAL STRUCTURE OF WEST GERMANY (IN %)

Occupational Group	1950	1961	1970	1980	1988
Self-employed	29.2	19.5	17.6	12.0	11.1
Civil servants	4.0	7.1	5.5	8.4	8.7
Employees	16.0	22.4	29.5	37.2	42.1
Blue-collar	50.8	51.0	47.4	42.4	38.1

Source: Thomas Scharf, *The German Greens: Challenging the Consensus* (Oxford: Berg Publishers, 1994), p. 45; Datenreport (1989), p. 85.

Although the service sector is growing most rapidly, manufacturing jobs continue to be an especially important component of Germany's economy (the world's leading net exporter). In the 1970s, Germany and Italy had the lowest percentage of employment in the service sector among all industrialized countries,[20] and well into the 1990s, Germany had a higher percentage of workers employed in manufacturing than did other industrialized countries—nearly double that of the United States (31 versus 16 percent) in 1993.[21] As Table 7.1 details, Germany's occupational structure, although becoming more oriented to the service sector, retained a significant sector of blue-collar workers. A higher percentage of German workers than Italians were engaged in manufacturing, yet participation in autonomous movements by factory workers was rare in Germany. Part of the reason is undoubtedly to be found in the "one plant-one union" structure of Germany, and the system of codetermination (*Mitbestimmung*) that gives trade unions in Germany considerably more power than their Italian counterparts.[22] Those workers who were active in Italy (and in the early 1970s in Germany) were semi-skilled factory workers, not their elders with secure skilled jobs and craft unions. They were women who mobilized both on the job and, as the self-reduction movement and the campaigns in both countries to legalize abortion showed, throughout the society.

Within post-Fordist Germany, prosperity for two-thirds of the society exists at the expense of the bottom one-third, a new split called "selective corporatism" by Joachim Hirsch.[23] Trade unions, political parties, employers' organizations, and the government work together to regulate economic integration and political stability for this majority.[24] The interests of the integrated top two-thirds of society are thereby mediated within the established structures, while those marginalized from these benefits are increasingly isolated.[25] New social conditions such as homelessness, the growing sector of part-time low-paying jobs, declining real wages, and the dismantling of the welfare state are all indications of this transition. Post-Fordist conditions of production meant that while European corporations were expanding their international operations, young people faced a shrunken structure of opportunities in their own countries and were unable to find either jobs or places to live. As Elmar Altvater put it: "On the one side, the abundance of capital and its export predominate, and on the other side, there was an industrial reserve army in the millions."[26] The world system's subservience to the profit needs of transnational corporations has produced a shift of factory production to areas of the globe where labor-power can be more cheaply purchased and where taxes and government regulations are minimal.[27]

In post-Fordist societies, young people, women, and minorities increasingly function as economic shock absorbers, smoothing out the system's inability to generate sufficient numbers of jobs. Tens of millions of people are relegated to the periphery of consumer society and denied the right to full-time, decently paying jobs and housing fit for human beings. (Of course, far worse are the living conditions of those confined to the margins of survival in the rural areas of underdeveloped countries.) The entry of young people into the labor force (and housing market) is delayed long past the point at which they are ready to support themselves (and move away from their parents). In 1993, 20 percent of all 16–24 year olds in the European Community were unemployed, nearly double the rate for the population as a whole.[28] Although young people are intelligent and are physically capable of taking responsibility for themselves, the existing system is incapable of providing enough jobs and apartments for them (to say nothing of houses big enough for groups to live in). This contradiction is a continuing source of massive dissatisfaction among European youth. In 1994, the deputy director of the French Institute for International Relations put it in a nutshell: "Seen from Europe, unemployment is the biggest security problem facing the Western world today... if we don't find answers to that problem, our entire system will collapse on itself."[29]

Unemployment is not a unique cause of youth movements. In Britain and France, countries where youth have not been nearly as active as in Germany or Italy in the time frame studied here, estimates of youth unemployment for most of the 1980s were over 20 percent (over 30 percent in 1986 in France), compared with only about 10 percent in Germany.[30] Yet Italy's "two societies" and Germany's "two cultures," phrases used to describe youth milieus in the 1970s, evidently had an economic basis, and different dynamics resulted from the way in which youth were marginalized. Key institutions of post-Fordist society are the vastly expanded universities. Less than a third of young people go to college in Germany, and less than a fourth in Italy (compared with three-fifths in the United States). In Italy, college students in the 1970s were generally compelled to live at home and work fulltime, leaving them little time to attend their already overcrowded classes. In Germany, students generally attended courses regularly, lived away from their parents, and had independent means of support (either from their parents or from the government). This difference meant that although both Italy and Germany had a generation gap, the phrase "two societies" was used to describe the phenomenon in Italy (reflecting the youth culture's greater impoverishment and distance from the possibility of participating in consumerist lifestyles), and the term "two cultures" expressed the same divide in Germany. To enforce discipline, the Italian movement had to be heavily repressed, but in Germany, students and youth remained a subcultural part of consumer society. In both societies, the emergence of autonomous movements coincided with the post–World War II baby-boom bulge in the youth age cohort, a bulge that will become slimmer as time goes on.[31]

To be sure, contradictory forms of youthful reaction to marginalization are possible, depending on the constellation of a variety of social conditions. In the 1990s, a revival of racist and anti-immigrant sentiment, not new forms of international solidarity, took place among some sectors of the youth population in both Italy and Germany. Should we therefore regard youth as a "new kind of lumpenproletariat"[32] whose political orientation depends on cultural values and opportunist leaders? In the formerly fascist societies, the governments simply did not have the long-standing loyalty of the population. Moreover, since remnants of the feudal aristocracy ruled Germany and Italy well into the twentieth century, regional variations in culture were not homogenized as thoroughly as in other countries where the capitalist market had decades to penetrate and transform outlying areas. These regional identities might be part of the sources for autonomous movements.

Even though their economic future seems bleak, youth's values are increasingly informed by postmodern culture. The weakening of the Protestant ethic, the countercultural need for group living, and concerns for international justice, environmental harmony, and democratic participation appear to be ascendant new values. As Klaus von Dohnanyi observed:

> During the 1960s and 1970s, in particular, youth in the Federal Republic, as in most industrial societies, developed a measure of independence, self-assurance, and joy of living that was unknown before. A changing system of values placed love, friendship, and comradeship in the foreground. Work and making a living became secondary. Authority and

achievement were questioned by critical self-awareness and the drive for the quality of life.[33]

If autonomous movements are any indication, youth will remain a continuing source of ethical opposition and enlightened action.[34] As I discuss below, however, such values are contradicted by the structures of consumer society.

COLONIZATION OF EVERYDAY LIFE

Periods of economic decline, like that currently experienced by industrial workers in advanced capitalist societies, are not favorable for generating progressive movements. Italian and German autonomous movements illustrate how, under post-Fordist conditions, the locus and content of social movements assume new forms. Whereas the traditional working class' role in social conflict has been relatively quiescent, and union organizations have been integrated into the functioning of the corporate-state structures, women and youth have emerged as key participants in contemporary movements in these two countries. Explaining the causes of this empirical observation involves two levels of analysis besides their economic and political marginalization: the penetration of the commodity form into previously private domains (referred to as the "colonization of the life-world"[35]) and the systematic destruction of the conditions of life.[36] The accelerating destruction of nature, intensifying degradation of minority rights, attacks on women's autonomy and gay rights, and marginalization of youth have generated opposition movements rooted in dimensions of social relations outside the site of production. Habermas described these movements in new terms:

> In the last ten to twenty years, conflicts have developed in advanced Western societies that, in many respects, deviate from the welfare-state pattern of institutionalized conflict over distribution. These new conflicts no longer arise in areas of material reproduction; they are no longer channeled through parties and organizations; and they can no longer be alleviated by compensations that conform to the system. Rather, the new conflicts arise in areas of cultural reproduction, social integration, and socialization. They are manifested in sub-institutional, extra-parliamentary forms of protest.... In short, the new conflicts are not sparked by problems of distribution, but concern the grammar of the forms of life.[37]

Habermas refers to the new movements as defending the life-world against the system's increasing assaults on the organic foundations of life, as in "the destruction of the countryside, by bad residential planning, industrialization and pollution, health impairments due to the side effects of civilization-destruction... military destruction, nuclear power plants, atomic waste, gene manipulation, storage and central utilization of private data."[38]

As a self-expanding value, capital permeates the private sphere, colonizing everyday life and turning it into an arena of profitable activity. The economy has expanded to include within it many aspects of life previously not part of the system of commodity production. Alberto Melucci explained the new situation:

> In comparison with the industrial phase of capitalism, the production characteristic of advanced societies requires that control reach beyond the productive structure into the areas of consumption, services, and social relations. The mechanisms of accumulation are no longer fed by the simple exploitation of the labour force, but rather by the manipulation of complex organizational systems, by control over information and over the processes and institutions of symbol-formation, and by intervention in interpersonal relations.[39]

The extension of commodity relations into everyday life and the rapid integration of millions of women into the workforce are two sides of the same coin, each of which feeds capital's insatiable needs. Declining real wages compelled women to take jobs, and the new mandate that is essentially a double shift (at home and at work) has effectively given women economic independence and brought them out of the isolation of the family, thereby undermining previous forms of patriarchal control. Increasing opportunities for women lead to financial independence from men, a material basis of feminist autonomy. Simultaneously, old social relations remain in force. Sexism in everyday life, political impotence, male control of medicine and the bodies of women, and patriarchal hierarchies at work all demand a feminist response facilitated by women's increasing economic participation.

The trend today is for increasing government regulation of previously autonomous arenas of life: child-rearing practices, family relations, reproduction, divorce, and individual consumption of everything from food to drugs. What Habermas and Offe call the "refeudalization" of society (i.e., the increasing intervention of governments in private life, a dynamic like that of medieval Europe) dramatically affects young people. Runaways, underage drinking, sexual repression, and all kinds of abuse are indications of the breakdown of the social regulatory mechanisms

TABLE 7.2

COLONIZATION OF EVERYDAY LIFE

	TRADITIONAL SOCIETY	CONSUMER SOCIETY
Food	Grown at home	Grown by agribusiness
	Cooked at home	Cooked by fast-food businesses
	Eaten at home	Eaten in public
Clothing	Made at home	Bought in a store
Shelter	Built by residents	Built by professionals
Health care	Family members	Corporate hospital
Education	Home	Public or private
Employment	Home	Corporations
Child care	Home	Paid day care
Socialization	Parents and family	Television, schools, peers
Seniors	At home	Retirement communities or nursing homes

and, at least for some, the concomitant need for families to be managed by the political system. Yet the more government intervenes in private affairs, the more resistance it encounters from those opposed to its paternity. According to the logic of this cycle, as families break down, autonomous movements will continue to be generated as a means of re-creating some form of group and individual control over the conditions of everyday life.

The systematic assault on the family is undeniable. Increasingly, two adult incomes are needed to meet the household expenses of a typical family. The effects of work on family life are ruinous. Children grow up without parents, and senior citizens are segregated into nursing homes and retirement communities. As segregation by age group is enforced by all major institutions, teenagers are especially impacted, tracked into peer groups by age and denied full adult status (money and independence) even though they are more than intelligent enough to be treated as adults and are physically capable of autonomy. Seniors and children would each benefit from more contact with the other, yet segregation by age proceeds, along with the continuing deterioration of family relations. As Harry Braverman summarized: "the ruined and dispersed U.S. family also forms a major source for the modern working class."[40]

Since the imperative of capital is to grow, pressure on corporations to continually expand profits means that mundane activities revolving around basic needs (food, clothing, and shelter) are severed from group contexts, increasingly mechanized, and made into arenas for financial gain. The life-world in which humans participate as members of families

TABLE 7.3

OPPOSING VALUES

THE SYSTEM	THE COUNTERCULTURE
Individual accumulation of wealth	Shared wealth
Competition	Cooperation
Patriotism	Humanism
Hierarchy	Equality
Patriarchal monogamy	Open relationships
Careers	Personal Growth
Nuclear family or singles	Group houses

further breaks down under the pressures (and allure) of consumer society as human relations are increasingly instrumentalized. As Table 7.2 summarizes, nearly all traditionally private functions of the family have become public and are often part of the system of monetary exchange.

With so many functions of the family having been appropriated by profit-making corporations and state programs, little has been left to the family. There are distinct benefits for some, however, particularly in a society where time spent at work leaves precious few hours free. Ironically, fast food is a partial solution to the issue of wages for housework.[41] Yet the costs to the quality of our lives include increasing atomization and alienation. As family life is degraded or becomes intolerable because of cultural incongruities between parents and children, participation in autonomous movements is one way to create new group ties. As discussed in relation to squatters, communal living expands the potential for individual life choices and creates the possibility of new types of intimate relationships and new models for child rearing. As Table 7.3 summarizes, the oppositional culture of autonomous movements often negates dominant patterns of the established social system.

Although there is abundant anthropological evidence that humans thrive in groups, our lives are increasingly contained in privatized spaces void of communal bonds and collective endeavors. The contradiction between the need for group affiliation and the reality of atomization is one motivation for participation in social movements. Although postmodernism sometimes means a reinvigoration of groups in comparison to the atomization of modernism, the underlying capitalist structure denies the postmodernist impulse its full expression. The need for profit (hence the logic of building single-family homes and condominiums rather than group houses—particularly for youth without money) is a fetter on the human need for self-constructed collectivity. This dimension of the questioning of the premises of industrial civilization grows out of its already having shattered traditional family structures—whether tribal, extended, or nuclear. Simultaneously, it may have created social strata capable of taking advantage of their autonomy from traditional structures of everyday life.

Without any clear sense of their future, however, many people are unable to find themselves in the flux of rapid change and the postmodern transvaluation of values. If there are those who doubt that civil society needs to be defended and protected from its systematic commodification, they need only contemplate the thousands of people who disfigure their bodies to conform to beauty standards dictated by corporate image makers; breast implants, penis extensions, hair transplants, liposuction, and plastic surgery. The heteronomous determination and standardization of individual self-image have never been so extreme as within the mediated culture of the contemporary world system. With a John Wayne model for masculinity, men react in predictably unfortunate ways in a variety of situations, and many women's orientation in the material world is equally skewed by consumerism. Having long ago penetrated preteen age groups, image-makers' influence over school-children often exceeds that of parents and family. Increasingly, social movements are expressions of group identity in a world being changed more rapidly than ever before in history.

NEW SOCIAL MOVEMENTS
AND THE POLITICS OF IDENTITY

The above observations might offer some insight into why women, minorities, and youth are the constituencies of radical social movements in post-Fordist societies. Although it is extremely problematic to treat social movements as simply conditioned by the form and circulation of capital and the structure of social relations, my analysis suggests that the autonomous movements discussed in this book were partially conditioned by impersonal economic forces and political dynamics. Postmodernists generally sever analysis of social movements from such categories, regarding notions of structure as vestigial modernist relics. For postmodernists, "society" is a construct; we live in multiple and decentered contexts. Using the language of postmodernists, simulacra (mediated semblances of life) are more important than history in determining our actions. Once understood from this perspective, social movements are no longer vehicles for the transformation of the social order as a whole (since that is simply a phantom) but are "new social movements"[42] oriented around specific contested sites and questions of identity (such as race, gender, and age).

Locked in debate, the more that postmodernists and Marxists contest each other's assumptions and ideas, the less likely they are to elicit what could be mutually beneficial insights offered by those they define as their intellectual opponents. At their extremes, both become mechanical responses, not dialectical ones, to rapid change. As the adherents of each position become rigid, prospects for clarification of reality dim. Postmodernism is often written off as an academic fad replete with a jargon of discourse inaccessible to all but a select few, and Marxists are dismissed as dinosaurs. Whereas mechanical Marxists fail to appreciate the radical gap between modernity and postmodernity, crippling their capacity to understand the contemporary world, many postmodernists are unable to link their empirical understanding of the decentered autonomy of local contexts to history, leaving them incapable of articulating a transcendental vision for the future.[43]

In the current atmosphere of recrimination and contestation for hegemony, it is difficult to criticize the politics of identity while simultaneously retaining a sense of their radical potential. Many Marxists lament the appearance of identity politics. They see it as shattering the promise of proletarian universalism, but they miss the latent universality present in new social movements. Identity construction can be a form of enacting the freedom to determine one's conditions of existence, to create new categories within which to live. Although the many dimensions of this dynamic are fragmentary, a totality of such quests can eventually become a radically new concrete universal—a reworking of the meaning of human being.

Unlike economic categories imposed by production and social relations, these new categories can be autonomously formulated—or, at a minimum, they are vehicles for the autonomy of groups oppressed by existing structures. The logic of the established system is to enforce particularisms as a means of social control. By bringing control and power to minorities and women, identity politics can be a form of self-defense. As Anthony Appiah expressed it:

> And if one is to be Black in a society that is racist then one has to deal constantly with assaults on one's dignity. In this context, insisting on the right to live a dignified life will not be enough. It will not even be enough to require being treated with equal dignity despite being Black, for that will require a concession that being Black counts naturally or to some degree against one's dignity. And so one will end up asking to be respected *as a Black*.[44]

When Republicans assault affirmative action and abortion rights, they condition responses from minorities and women that reinforce group freedom from encroachment of outside interests.

No matter how much they respond to intrusive outsiders, each form of identity politics contains a latent universality. Gender equality is a universal aim, benefiting all of us. The celebration of racial diversity and the mutual recognition of our humanity are in all our interests. Unlocking sexual repression and ending the compulsory channeling of libido into exclusive heterosexuality benefit all. Cleaning up the environment and disarming the world's nation-states are in the interest of all humanity. At their best, autonomous movements bring these latent connections to consciousness and accentuate the universal content of single-issue identity politics. The function of revolutionary theory is not to persuade feminists and nationalists to give up their particularisms but to aid the development from within these streams of a new concrete universalism, one produced by immanent critiques—not imposed from the outside. As part of the struggle for the reformulation of the concrete universal, members of autonomous movements must be willing to risk being called racist for challenging the exclusivity of black oppression, sexist for challenging women to confront class reality, anti-Semitic for demanding that Jews do not treat themselves as a chosen people.

The present fragmentation of social movements preconditions a universal identity of human beings as a species—not as nations, genders, or races—an end point that can be achieved only by going through, not ignoring or treating as "secondary," categories of oppression imposed on us by a system based on heteronomous control (externally inflicted). The road from the abstract universal of "modernist" thought (the positing of a proletarian or other form of universality which corresponds to that of white males) to the future formulation of a concrete multicultural universal necessarily passes through identity politics. Unlike the proletariat, no one identity is the vast majority of society, nor is one by itself able to stop the functioning of the system and reconstruct it. Therefore, multiple centers of revolutionary thought and action are historical necessities posing the features of a decentered future society in the making. Identity politics begins the process of unlocking the structures of domination, a process that might eventually result in deconstructing ascriptive identities entirely and reformulating ourselves as autonomous human beings essentially free of externally imposed shackles.

Most analysts of new social movements entirely miss this point. One of the distinguishing characteristics of new social movements, at least as the term is commonly used in academic and research circles, is their specialization, their existence as a fragmentary critique of society, as little more than interest-group politics conducted by nontraditional means. Accordingly, the antinuclear power movement, for example, deals exclusively with the issue of nuclear power plants and nuclear waste disposal. Attempts to link that movement with the feminist movement's call for a new technology based not on the domination and destruction of the environment but on a harmonious relationship with nature are thought to mistakenly combine two different movements.[45] The black movement similarly is understood as having little to do with ecology, but in fact, in the 1990s in the United States, it took the lead in green activism.[46]

New social movement theory may be accurate in describing the forms that actions take when observed by outsiders, but it fails to comprehend the sources of protests and the ways in which synchronic movements can form an organic whole.[47] Most significantly, its compartmentalization of new social movements theoretically obliterates in advance the possibility of transforming society as a whole, thereby insidiously maintaining the status quo. Within the vast domain of the literature on "new social movements" in the United States, fragmented pressure groups become real, and the universal reality of revolutionary social movements "untrue." As Margit Mayer described social movement research in the United States:

> Disaggregated and issue-specific movements that refrain from totalizing their demands flourish all over this country, but movements demanding radical societal change have always remained relatively marginal. Such radical or socialist currents were once even more marginalized by their omission in social movement research. Questions pertaining to their development and dynamic hardly appear in recent American social movement research.[48]

In my view, the current fragmentation of social movements is a transitional phenomenon, a response both to the conservative character of these times and to the historic restructuring of global capitalism. The most salient feature of identity politics, the fragmentation of constituency, arose after the popular movement of the 1960s had disintegrated. As the unifying effects of the revolutionary upsurge subsided and the forces set in motion continued along separate paths, the system's logic of compartmentalization and atomization asserted itself within the opposition. The distance between the New Left—the myriad organizations and individuals that converged in 1968 to form what I have called a world historical movement—and identity politics is precisely the difference between the existence of a popular movement challenging the world system and the defeat of that upsurge and dispersal of its many components.

In manifestos such as the Port Huron statement, the early New Left spoke of universal needs such as increasing democracy but framed its discussions abstractly—without any real understanding of racism and sexism. Like Soviet Communists, they were incapable of integrating racism and patriarchy into their analysis of society. When the Student Nonviolent Coordinating Committee (SNCC) expelled white activists in 1965, they sang the first stanza in the contemporary chorus of identity politics. Passing through the phase of black power—the prototypical formulation of identity politics—a new concrete universal was formulated at the Black Panther Party's Revolutionary Peoples' Constitutional Convention.[49]

To Todd Gitlin, identity politics is an unfortunate consequence of this later phase of the New Left. Like other historians whose roots are in the early phase of the movement, he fails to comprehend this history entirely, in part because he dropped out of the movement when it entered its radical phase. For Gitlin and others, identity politics is a term used to establish a hierarchy of importance that prioritizes new social movements over those defined as universalistic. For Gitlin:

> The proliferation of identity politics leads to a turning inward, a grim and hermetic bravado which takes the ideological form of paranoid, jargon-clotted postmodernist groupthink, cult celebrations of victimization, and stylized marginality.[50]

To be sure, identity politics contains its own internal contradictions: within every form it takes are both a universalistic promise and a particularistic chauvinism (Malcolm X contained both within himself). A failure to comprehend the contradictory character of identity politics unites both its advocates and its opponents. Identity politics can keep the movement divided against itself (as Gitlin understands) or point to one structure of domination and overlook another. It can also obscure the existence of a common class enemy—the wealthiest families, top managers, and their corporations and governments. By itself, identity politics is not sufficient to transform qualitatively problematic political-economic structures. Indeed, not only is it insufficient for the formulation of a revolutionary transcendence of the class-structured multinational corporate world system, it often obscures that very system by seeking to treat as identical actors with very different positions within that system.[51]

In an epoch when capital's velocity and mobility are at unprecedented levels, identity politics reflects the fragmentation of the proletariat's universal subjectivity. To the extent that material conditions affect social consciousness, the dispersal of production, the adaptation of capitalist principles to all the major institutions of society, and the commodification of everyday life condition the fragmentation of proletarian subjectivity.[52] Under post-Fordist conditions, capital's global nature makes the seizure of national political power increasingly superfluous (as the fates of Cuba, Vietnam, and Nicaragua indicate). Immanuel Wallerstein has formulated this notion as the transition from the state to civil society as object of transformation. Even within the world of corporations, the demographic reconstruction of the working class calls for a multicultural analysis. The working class does not consist predominantly of white, European males (since production is increasingly global and everywhere involves women and nonwhites). Workers understand cooperation as global and multicultural, not simply "social" in terms of the immediate community. To the extent they become revolutionary, their international commitment will, be to ecology, feminism, racial solidarity, and peace, not to any nation-state. Seen in this context, identity politics provides the basis for a free society worthy of the name. It is a necessary step in the development of a new universality that recognizes race and gender as significant domains of a broader historical framework. It is necessary to deconstruct structures of domination in everyday life.

Making the case for the potential universality of identity politics does not mean that I project its categories as eternally valid. I have already commented on how racial categories are socially constructed by referring to my experiences in Germany. Recognizing the social dimension of categories of identity is a step in their transformation. Time and again, theorists mistake ideas relevant to specific contexts for universal truths, and recent social movement research is no exception. Although movements are increasingly international and even synchronically connected across national borders, analysis of them remains largely within the nationalistic framework of government funding agencies and language communities. In France, where political action is state oriented, Alain Touraine insists that social movements be analyzed by their impact on the state.[53] In the United States, where fragmented activism possessing immense resources abounds, analysis of social movements has been based on the resource mobilization paradigm.[54] In Germany, where the government's response to social movements was to label them as "terrorists," Habermas puts forth the view that societies could resolve their crises if their members addressed one another with respect in an ideal free-speech situation.[55] Habermas' analysis is unmistakably German insofar as he seeks to enhance democratic discourse in a society that for most of the twentieth century has marginalized (if not murdered) its radical critics.[56]

Few theorists attempt to pose methods by which we can universally understand social movements and the historical trends that produce them. In my opinion, one of the few thinkers to do so is Habermas' student

Seyla Benhabib. Benhabib engages feminists, postmodernists, and modern communitarians in a philosophical discourse encompassing themes of Western thought dating to the ancient Greeks. By responding critically to a wide range of contemporary theorists, she hopes to stimulate ongoing debates and exchanges leading to "reasoned argument as a way of life."[57] She believes that such dialogues are themselves both the means and the goal of a freer society, and she therefore adapts Habermas' method of immanent critique of disparate thinkers regarding the very issues they are discussing within their subfields. Benhabib begins with Habermas' work in universal pragmatics and develops it in a feminist direction. She represents one of the most important responses to the changed constellation of civil society after 1968. Her theoretical work is an attempt to ground a notion of autonomy as part of the project of rationally remaking social geography. Essentially, her philosophy represents social democracy as it will appear in the twenty-first century, as a social democracy of everyday life. Like Habermas, Benhabib seeks to make the existing system live up to high ethical standards. In so doing, she propels insurgent impulses into the established forums for justice. At best, her effort leads in the direction of reforming nation-states and empowering international organizations such as the European Community, NATO, the World Court, and the United Nations, not toward the construction of forms of dual power and direct democracy. Will her theory lead toward such desired goals? Or will it only empower vast national and international bureaucracies? No doubt Benhabib's world of reasoned argumentation as the basis for social life should be exalted. But can we demilitarize international relations, clean up the planet, and end poverty (to say nothing of stopping racist attacks) without social movements compelling policy makers to do so? An international general strike would certainly provide a major stimulus to dismantle nation-states' militaries, but that long-discussed idea does not resonate anywhere in her theory.[58]

Since she is one of the most prominent theorists to use the term "autonomy" and feminism as goals, I pause here to consider her theory in detail. In the preceding chapter, I showed how the workerist theory of Antonio Negri fails to comprehend patriarchy and the centrality of autonomy to freedom, therefore limiting the capacity of autonomous movements to realize their own universal potential and maintain their impetus. My goal in discussing Benhabib is similarly to illustrate how her feminist theory limits discussion of collective autonomy and constrains movements to reformist procedures and goals. By exploring her ideas in depth, I also hope to integrate her insights with those gleaned from my understanding of the practical action of autonomous movements.

FROM THE INVISIBILITY OF THE PRIVATE TO ITS RATIONALIZATION: A REASONABLE PROJECT?

For Benhabib, "ordinary moral conversations" have "implicit structures of speech and action" that, if universally practiced, would lead to the resolution of social problems. The main project of her book is to integrate her "interactive universalism" with feminism's insights that patriarchal gender-based power relations permeate virtually all dimensions of our lives. To accomplish that, she deals with both modernist and postmodernist notions of the relation between the personal and political. In a devastating critique of postmodernism, Benhabib concludes that it is incompatible with feminism: "Social criticism without some form of philosophy is not possible, and without social criticism the project of feminist theory which is at once committed to knowledge and to the emancipatory interests of women is inconceivable."[59]

Using her feminism as a background, she simultaneously critiques Hegelian and Kantian notions of justice (pertaining to political affairs) as constituting a domain above that of everyday life. To her, "life in the family no less than life in the modern constitutional state" must be lived according to ethical standards that would emerge from "participatory politics in a democratic polity."[60] Her optimism regarding the unfinished democratic potential of modern political forms is one of her debts to Habermas. Although Benhabib extends his method of immanent critique and derives her model of interactive universalism from Habermas' discourse ethics, she criticizes him for "gender-blind" theories that ignore the "difference in the experience of males versus female subjects in all domains of life," as well as for treating power relations in everyday life (in the intimate sphere) as nonexistent.[61] For her, women's liberation is the crowning force of modernism's impetus toward egalitarianism and discursive will formation.[62] By subjecting the private sphere to public examination and transformation, feminism questions boundaries established by male Western philosophers that treat everyday life as fundamentally separate from issues of justice in the state. As a device to articulate this position, Benhabib distinguishes what she calls the "generalized other" (those with whom we interact at the level of government) from the "concrete other" (those with whom we share our everyday lives and intimacy). She is then able to appropriate much recent feminist theory (such as the work of Carol Gilligan, which insists upon the integration of the voice of the "excluded others" [women and children] into universalist theory).

Here Benhabib's position becomes difficult, because her justification of the opening of the intimate sphere is premised on the primacy of casting out particularly odious patriarchal practices (wife beating, child abuse, and so forth) that were long hidden and unexamined dimensions of patriarchal order. She acknowledges the twin problems thereby generated: loss of privacy, and creation of government bureaucracies overseeing (and disempowering) women. She argues that feminists need to critically appropriate a Habermasian model of public space as a means to avoid the dead ends of "legalistic liberal reformism" such as the program of NOW and a "radical feminism which can scarcely conceal its own political and moral authoritarianism."[63] In Benhabib's mind:

> All struggles against oppression in the modern world begin by redefining what had previously been considered "private."...In this respect, the women's movement, the peace movement, the ecology movement, and the new ethnic identity movements follow a similar logic.[64]

In the dialectic of individual and system, however, Benhabib loses sight of the intermediate social constellations. She is therefore subject to the accusation that she would simply like to construct a more rational version of the existing system—particularly as related to questions of justice. In her zest to radically restructure the patriarchal capitalist system, she underestimates the centralizing impetus of that behemoth. Rather than postulating a model of public space as decentralized and controlled by participants, she would subject all humans to the secular, liberal democratic norms of discourse and interaction.[65] Should polygamists be able to create their own autonomous communities? Should lesbians be allowed to have their own private societies? Benhabib would indicate not, at least not without having to publicly justify doing so—a justification that she insists cannot be made, since some "practices are more just and fair than another."[66] Isn't an underpinning of collective autonomy the capability for groups to self-construct their own norms? As Habermas articulated the meaning of autonomy: "The citizens are autonomous only if the addressees of the law can also see themselves as its authors."[67]

Autonomy as an organizing principle of collective life does not insist upon the invasive evaluation imposed by Benhabib's monocentric notion of public space. As I mentioned already, in the midst of his tenure as chairperson of the Chicago Black Panther Party, Fred Hampton insisted that white power should belong to white people, and Nelson Mandela expressed support for limited autonomy for white homelands for those who insist that that is what they need. A similar respect for diversity exists within European autonomous movements at their best. During the planning for demonstrations at Wackersdorf, for example, the Autonomen used consensus (communicative ethics) to make decisions and encouraged a range of tactics (not simply militant ones) from which individuals could choose, depending on their own consciences and consciousness. Pacifists and others protested nonviolently, while elsewhere, more militant groups acted according to what they deemed most effective. Whereas these movement groups have positions that negate the modernist engine of uniformity, Benhabib's neo-Kantian ethical imperatives create an appearance of central authority lying in her discourse, despite her insistence that she is part of the shift from legislative to interactive ethics. Like Habermas before her, she is trapped in systematic totality despite her genuine intention to free the self from oppressive situatedness in systemic frameworks, including discourse ethics. Benhabib's situated self is not yet free to stand by collectively constructed principles of social organization. The "conscious spontaneity" of the Autonomen provides the universalism of a modernist critique of capital while simultaneously preserving decentered and locally defined milieus discussed by postmodernists. Although the latter, like theorists of identity politics, impose schematic divisions between these various groups, autonomous movements synthesize their memberships into a universally critical movement.

In the final analysis, because Benhabib's reformulation of the philosophical basis for ethical decisions retains a centralized notion of public space, she contributes to the rationalization of the system's control center, not a questioning of the reasonableness of its existence. Like all contemporary advocates of social democracy, she believes in the rationality of her project but fails to deal with the irrational imperatives of the existing structures. As expressions of antisystemic participatory politics, autonomous social movements seek to live without a control center, no matter how rationalized its operation may be.

THE ATOMIZED INDIVIDUAL AND THE CONSTRAINT OF AUTONOMY

In her meticulous appropriation of the categories of Western philosophy, Benhabib uncritically adopts the standpoint of the atomized individual. Since her analysis is undertaken looking through the prism of this one-point perspective, she remains a modernist in the sense of postulating a central point to the world rather than conceptualizing it as a polycentric collective construction. To be sure, the self she understands is not the fixed "Archimedean standpoint, situated beyond historical and cultural contingency."[68] That self, a metaphysical illusion of the Enlightenment, is replaced by a "postmetaphysical" understanding of "finite, embodied and fragile creatures, and not disembodied cogitos or abstract unities of transcendental apperception."[69] In comparison to the appropriation of subjectivity as conceived by Western philosophy, she develops a more "adequate, less deluded and less mystified vision of subjectivity." She reformulates the subject while retaining traditional qualities such as autonomy, self reflexivity, the ability to act on principle, and accountability for the consequences of one's actions.[70]

By understanding the "radical situatedness of the subject," she believes that feminists can reconstruct a universality corresponding to the impetus of feminism to remake the entire social world, not simply to create isolated postpatriarchal pockets within a patriarchal world system. Her analysis is at its best when she challenges postmodern feminists to rethink their assumption that gendered identity can be attributed to "deeds without the doer." By critically examining varieties of feminism that are premised on the dissolution of subjectivity, on the death of the self as creator of a life narrative,[71] Benhabib's own vision of a feminism premised on the integrity and autonomy of both female and male individuals becomes possible to articulate. In the course of intellectually demolishing the nation of deeds without a doer, however, Benhabib continually posits the "I" as the subject, never the "we." Her response to Judith Butler's farewell to the "doer behind the deed" is to reflect on the production of Butler's own book: Benhabib "presupposes that there is a thinking author who has produced this text, who has intentions, purposes and goals in communicating with me; that the task of theoretical reflection begins with the attempt to understand what the author meant."[72] Such an example may neatly illustrate the self's production of a book, but it has very little to do with the social construction of patriarchy, unless we would consider it to be a consciously authored, meticulously crafted system like a book (which it is not!). By failing to move her analysis beyond the level of the individual reflecting self, Benhabib fails to offer an adequate explanation for how social realities are authored and edited—to say nothing of how their grammar and syntax can be transformed.

Retaining Cartesian categories of individual subjectivity, Benhabib ignores the "conscious spontaneity" of autonomous movements, their construction of a "we" seeking to accomplish the theoretical tasks that she only outlines. Like Benhabib, I too search for a "concrete universal," but I find it in some social movements—in certain versions of feminism and ecology, and particularly in autonomous movements at their best. I locate "collective concrete others"[73] in such movements. They have structures, groups, ideas—they are sensuous historical actors. Certain dimensions closely resemble a new concrete universal in the making. This book seeks to situate the self in concrete historical alternatives that have emerged in various contemporary contexts and that aim to create similar goals to those enunciated by Benhabib. My ontology is that thousands of people acting in social movements embody the concrete realization of freedom: outside established norms and institutions, thousands of people consciously act spontaneously in concert.[74] In such moments (which I call moments of the "eros effect"), genuine individuality emerges as human beings situate themselves in collective contexts that negate their individualism. Vibrant democratic movements enhance the autonomy of the individual and simultaneously build groups that break free of the centralizing uniformity of the corporate-state behemoth. As we saw in the case of German feminism, women in Germany came together in the women's centers and transformed their individual lives as they created feminist projects.[75]

Autonomy for Benhabib, like all the concepts she uses, fundamentally pertains to the individual, not to collectivises. Although it is one of the central concepts of her analysis, she never defines it precisely. Extrapolating from her usage, she refers to the personal independence of isolated individuals. At one point, she refers to Nietzsche's Zarathustra as having reached "a state of autonomy beyond community."[76] In so posing autonomy against community, her mechanical appropriation of the concept from Kant is apparent. Although she recognizes the "autonomous" nature of the women's movement in the nineteenth and twentieth centuries, she never acknowledges the existence of Italian Autonomia or the German Autonomen—never uses autonomy as a concept referring to collectivities other than traditionally defined cultural autonomy. By postulating the existence of isolated individuals unconnected to one another as the building blocks of society, she adopts the atomistic categories of analysis that arose along with capital's penetration of the collective forms of social life, categories that subverted the ancients' assumption of a "we" as opposed to the "I" as the basis of knowledge and social organization.

THE AUTONOMY OF THEORY?

Benhabib brilliantly synthesizes currents of contemporary thought, and although she acknowledges the need for action, her shadow world of theory retains notions that predispose her to remain aloof to the realm of action. She recognizes that "our moral and political world is more characterized by struggles unto death among moral opponents than by a conversation among them,"[77] and she points out the necessity of political activity for the generation of new ethics. Her understanding of modern societies includes the idea that they demand enlarged participation in social affairs—what she calls democratization in reference to an "increase and growth of autonomous public spheres."[78] In her repertoire of action, working to "clean up a polluted harbor" or "combating racism and sexism in the media" by writing critically about them in a journal is "no less political" than narrowly defined definitions of political participation such as voting.

For her, qualities of "civic friendship and solidarity" are the bridge between the dual standard currently applied to categories of justice and ethical norms of everyday life. In her view, such a notion of communicative ethics

> anticipates non-violent strategies of conflict resolution as well as encouraging cooperative and associative methods of problem solving. Far from being utopian in the sense of being irrelevant, in a world of complete interdependence among peoples and nations, in which the alternatives are between non-violent collaboration and nuclear annihilation, communicative ethics may supply our minds with just the right dose of fantasy such as to think beyond the old oppositions of utopia or realism, containment or conflict. Then, as today, we still can say, "L'imagination au pouvoir!"[79]

Her discourse ethics are premised upon the possibility of the "utopian community of humankind" using the "gentle force of reason" in conversations in which reciprocal recognition of the participants exists. Her interactive universalism is the "practice of situated criticism for a global community that does not shy away from knocking down the 'parish walls.'" Reconstituting "community" through critical thinking leads her to discuss the communitarian notion of the "reassertion of democratic control over the runaway megastructures of modern capital and technology."[80]

At every point in her analysis when she approaches the resolution of the intellectual problems she raises, however, she flies into the rarefied world of abstraction, in her chapter "Feminism and the Question of Postmodernism," for example, when she approaches the crucial issue of the "death of the subject" (i.e., the self that is to be situated—presumably the central problematic of her book) she remarks:

> To embark upon a meaningful answer to this query from where we stand today involves not yet another decoding of metaphors and tropes about the self, but a serious interchange between philosophy and the social sciences like sociolinguistics, social interactionist psychology, socialization theory, psychoanalysis and cultural history among others.[81]

Her failure at this crucial juncture to theorize the emergence of active subjectivity in the practical movement of history reflects the inadequacies of her theoretical break with the postmodernist idea of the death of history.

If, as has often been remarked, the world for Marx in *Capital* was one big factory, then Benhabib's world is one ongoing conversation. Her belief that conversation in itself constitutes sufficient action is revealed in her statement: "Only if somebody else is able to understand the meaning of our words as well as the whatness of our deeds can the identity of the self be said to be revealed."[82] What if the person in question speaks a language we do not understand but uses violence to force his or her views upon us? Has not that person's self been revealed? The critical question she leaves unanswered is: what happens when the actions of another are physically and psychically destroying people (or other life) and talk is no help?

She insists on a need for universal agreement that dialogue will not be constrained either by those allowed to participate in it or by what they can bring to consideration. For her, "the basic principles of a just order should be morally neutral."[83] She believes that basic liberties are never to be curtailed. That statement is itself a moral judgment in favor of unrestrained individual liberty—including the freedom to incite racist violence against those labeled "other." It is unrealistic insofar as no public project of any magnitude could proceed if it were to necessitate the use of eminent domain to take control of privately owned land. Her formulation of freedom appears to favor greater individual liberty until we ask: whose liberty are we discussing? The oppressed or the oppressor? If liberties are in conflict, whose standpoint do we adopt? As John Rawls pointed out, the liberty of the racist is unreasonable. The racist can be rational (to the extent, for example, that his or her observations have a real basis) but never reasonable. Similarly, the actions of the Autonomen are often irrational (for example, the smearing of excrement in yuppie restaurants) but reasonable (to the extent that one can make a case that the action helps defend the neighborhood from the assault of monied interests).

Benhabib's freedom is formulated in the abstract world of pure mind, not in the sensuous world of living human beings complete with bodies and souls. Real freedom demands continual moral judgment. Not even technology is purely neutral, as Herbert Marcuse convincingly demonstrated.[84] What about the case of people facing brutal treatment at the hands of others? Should Jews have been bound by the constraints of open dialogue while on their way to the concentration camps? Should young Germans stand by and discuss the racial purity of the nation with neo-Nazis actively engaged in attacking foreigners? Those Autonomen who defend foreigners counterpose militant resistance to Benhabib's "gentle force of reason." Her assumption that rationality is preeminent, that our minds exist but not our bodies, fetishizes the discourse of the university classroom, privileging it over other more passionate forms of expression while ignoring the discourse of racist violence affecting the bodies and souls of too many people. As I discussed at the end of the previous chapter, in the course of confronting oppressors—physically, when necessary—individuals are transformed, liberated from the passivity, victimization and acceptance of domination that is a crucial component of oppressor-oppressed relations. Her rationality of the mind is far removed from such a rationality of the heart. In a world without bodies, it does not matter whether there are attacks. Everyone's liberties to speak in that world should certainly be guaranteed. But when we return to the real world, as opposed to seminar rooms, the difference between reasoned arguments and educated indifference reaches a vanishing point.

Despite the unresolved problems in her orientation, Benhabib's insights have much to offer autonomous movements as they try to break out of the managed space of the contemporary world. Who could fault the Autonomen for learning a bit about the "gentle force of reason" in their own internal relations? And Benhabib's analysis would be enriched if she were to integrate autonomous movements into her discourse. By excluding them, she breaks one of her own rules—namely, that nothing should be outside the discourse world she creates. Her synthetic thinking might prefigure the emergence of social movements prepared to take her categories from the rarefied and abstract world in which they were articulated and make them substantive. As I have discussed, however, her reified categories (particularly her notion of autonomy) must first be transformed.

My tripartite critique of the feminism of Seyla Benhabib, the workerism of Antonio Negri, and the critical Germany of Günter Grass and Christa Wolf has clarified how none of these particular analyses reaches the level of species interest realized by autonomous movements at their best. The questions posed by the contradictions of contemporary industrial society are precisely at a species level of discourse—as are the possible solutions articulated in the praxis of subversive social movements. The theorists I chose to critique are some of the most progressive in their fields. No matter how clear-headed or rooted in time-tested philosophical categories, however, any analysis based exclusively on ethnic, gender, or workerist categories cannot attain a species discourse. Instead, the latent potential of these various forms of identity politics remains obscured by their own internal limitations.

DECOLONIZATION AND DEMOCRACY

Since the seventeenth century, political revolutions in Europe posing as carriers of universal interests have constructed nation-states with immense powers and simultaneously produced images of them as ideal forums for resolving conflicting interests. Two hundred years ago, French political history, notably the guillotine (which Hegel regarded as reason incarnate), provided a script from which local variations emanated throughout the world. Backwards Germany could write little or nothing on the pages of the history of democracy, at least not in the actions of its people, but German philosophers distilled the legacy of the French revolution and presented it with a universalism and clarity that—via Marxism—saw theory become a material force. European history in the 1970s and 1980s was in many ways the reverse. In Germany, movements of striking importance emerged, and philosophical developments appear largely to have extended the modernist critique of Kant and Hegel (Habermas' project). Life in France has proceeded apace within a highly centralized state while its philosophers theorize deconstructionism and postmodemist decentered sites of dispersed power.

Under the authority of universal interests, contemporary nation-states have appropriated extraordinary powers over individuals' everyday lives. Like international-style architecture, modern nation-states and transnational corporations were constructed according to a first principle of the bigger the better. In their own day, skyscrapers freed humans from the imperative of building horizontally, but under contemporary conditions, they dominate rather than liberate. Similarly, representative democracy, which once freed humans from aristocratic absolutism, has become incapable of fulfilling its historic promise to expand freedom for all and provide effective means for popular participation. If the term "postmodern" has an uplifting aspect, it is precisely in its potential to re-create a human scale. Whether in architecture or politics, the promise of reinvigorated collective interaction and a better quality of life is increasingly denied by such modern forms as representative democracy and international-style architecture.[85] Although postmodern architecture is a product of capital, it seeks to blend into its surroundings more harmoniously than structures designed by modernists ranging from Louis Sullivan to Corbusier. Much like the kind of democracy envisioned by autonomists, it returns to notions of human scale derived from the Renaissance or ancient Greece.

Despite promises of the good life made in exchange for the penetration of our private lives by new products and services, the existing system increasingly delivers economic insecurity and ecological disaster hand in hand with the production of political apathy. The state confronts us as an alien being. Recent polls show a historically low and rapidly declining faith in government in the United States and in Europe. The immense resources and international mobility of transnational corporations often make nation-states peripheral to critical economic decisions affecting entire regions. As the power of cities and regions to attract major investments has grown, the role of the nation-state in negotiating the terms for capital's impact within its territory has diminished.[86] Like the ability of governments to use force domestically, the unilateral power of nation-states to intervene internationally through force has declined.

Although banks and corporations have downsized in the 1990s (to accommodate their profit needs, not because of any ecological or moral concerns), national militaries and bureaucracies have yet to be similarly reshaped. How long can the public sector scandalously squander a preponderant share of social resources on the military and transfer payments to the wealthy in the form of interest on debt? In this context, three examples from recent history provide entirely different outcomes. The deconstruction of Czechoslovakia was an exemplary action: one nation-state peacefully devolved into two according to the expressed desires of Slovaks. The demise of the Soviet Union, although generally free of violence, is a mixed example of national deconstruction, involving a laudable end to the Cold War and the system that produced Chernobyl, but also an uncertain future. Yugoslavia's fate and the unleashing of ethnic cleansing tragically point to the dangers involved in this new historical process. (Clearly, all forms of autonomy cannot be understood as producing good things.) In Europe, nation-states have declined in power as European economic integration has increased; in the United States, the federal government has appropriated great powers vis-à-vis the states and individuals. One need not be a Republican or sympathize with the militias to understand this elementary fact. Will the United Stares experience its own form of perestroika, its own decentralization of power—perhaps even devolving into autonomously governed bioregional domains?

Making ecologically responsible decisions already calls for rethinking the political power of nation-states and enlarging the democratic control of technology. The entire species (and all life) is today at the mercy of those who make decisions about high technology. Radioactive fallout from Chernobyl was measured in milk in North America less than a month after the catastrophe. Nonetheless, whether a nuclear power plant should be built is an issue that the established system answers through national bureaucracies governed by scientific experts, faceless government employees, and professional politicians who make decisions that will affect life on this planet for seventy generations.[87] No society has democratically determined whether nuclear waste should be produced, even though it will remain carcinogenic and toxic beyond comparison for tens of thousands of years—more time than since the great pyramids of Egypt were built. The average nuclear power plant has a life of less than fifty years, yet for such transitory generation of electricity, we produce toxic repositories, each of which will need to be encased (or somehow dealt with) for thousands of years. Given the insatiable need for energy in contemporary society, this is no trivial problem.

The system's reliance on nuclear energy rather than on solar, wind, and other nonpolluting sources is conditioned by the need to provide big governments and large corporations with massive projects for the expansion of their powers and the realization of profits. Solar and wind energy generation is far more efficient than is popularly understood and provides more jobs than nuclear fission.[88] The development of solar and wind energy would generate increased job opportunities from many small investments (rather than one huge one), and profits would be realized by handyman producers, not big capital—whose essential nature requires massive projects. Nuclear power, in turn, demands militarism of society for the security of the installations. Because nuclear weapons can obliterate a nation in a matter of minutes, militaries must be on constant alert, and immense resources must be devoted to them. A more symbiotic relationship between large corporations and big governments could not be imagined, nor could a better means to block the possibility of substantive autonomy.

Our species' powers have created the potential to destroy the planet at the push of a button, to put holes in the ozone layer, to create and unleash genetically engineered beings, to melt the polar ice caps, or to pollute huge areas (like that around Chernobyl) so badly that they have to be evacuated for hundreds of years. Tragically, at the same historical moment that the human species has been endowed with powers far beyond any possessed in the past, obsolete decision-making processes are increasingly confined to corporate boardrooms and the inner offices of nonelected bureaucrats. Even if elected representatives are part of the formulation of policy, the outcome is often no different. The unreasonableness of the existing system, its undemocratic nature as discussed above in relation to the issue of nuclear power, can be similarly understood in relation to a number of weighty social decisions, such as the choice to use atomic bombs at the end of World War II, to build the interstate highway system in the United States, create suburbs and abandon the inner cities in the 1950s, to fight a Cold War and the Vietnam War, and to maintain astronomical expenditures for national militaries at the end of the Cold War. The future effects of the existing system's unreasonableness, its response to its own crisis tendencies, are already visible in plans to invest more resources in capital-intensive programs and existing industry—notably automobiles. Over the next two decades, the European Community plans to spend over $1 trillion on more than seven thousand miles of new highways, seriously threatening the scant remaining green spaces on the continent, including the last habitat for bears in France.[89] Infrastructural expenditures designed to aid transnational corporations have already been made for massive tunnels in the Pyrenees and the Alps, the Oresund bridge connecting Denmark and Sweden, and the tunnel between France and Britain. Such squandering of resources is not simply a European problem. Canada plans to build a mammoth bridge to Prince Edward Island, and despite the end of the Cold War, the United States spends more on its military than all other nations combined.

Each of these decisions was made in its own time by nonelected persons in conjunction with professional politicians whose differences from their electoral alternatives were seldom greater than those between Coke and Pepsi. Left to direct-democratic forums of local citizens, probably none of these decisions would have been made. With respect to nuclear power, housing policies, abortion rights, and disarmament, autonomous movements have clearly done more to enact what is now recognized as the popular will than did initiatives from within the existing political system. At a minimum, militant protest movements, such as those against segregation, the Vietnam War, and nuclear power, revealed the lack of consensus on specific policies and provided a necessary counterbalance, compelling even the most intransigent politicians to reconsider their positions. In a larger context, the type of subversive social movements portrayed in this book probably constitute more reasonable vehicles for making significant social decisions than corporate profitability, bureaucratic sanction, or votes by the political system's elected representatives. What I call civil Luddism can sometimes enact greater forms of democratic control than voting once every four years or paying dues to a union.

Although greater freedom and prosperity are both necessary and possible, their realization seems remote. Instead of real autonomy in which regions could plan their future as part of humanity's creative powers, we have false autonomy offered us in choices among various consumer products, politicians, and individual careers. In the short run, several factors appear to favor a continuing regeneration of autonomous movements. First, job opportunities and decent housing continue to be denied to a wide cross section of people. The existence of hundreds of thousands of unemployed youth in Europe provides a base from which wave after wave of new activity might emerge. Second, the existing system's top-heavy impetus preconditions its continuing reliance on massive capital projects. Now that construction of nuclear power plants has virtually come to an end, other projects must be found to satisfy the needs of large capital. With any number of boondoggles looming on the horizon, it appears that the existing system will continue to provide more than sufficient reasons for massive opposition to its destructive imperatives. The unreasonable character of large capital is exemplified in Royal Dutch Shell. Yesterday it stubbornly clung to investments in apartheid. More recently, it took international protests to persuade Shell not to discard one of its mammoth oil platforms by sinking it in the Atlantic Ocean. Shell's shadow also was cast over the execution of Nigerian playwright Ken Saro-Wiwa, whose activism exposed the nefarious tip of Shell's African activities.

As suggested by this book's title, the goal of autonomous social movements is the subversion of politics: the decolonization of everyday life and civil society, not the conquest of state power. Based on a politics of the first person and a desire to create direct democracy, these movements oppose the false universality of the control center under whose guise behemoth governments and corporations seek to impose their wills. The subversion of politics would mean more democracy—more than citizens of Athens or Florence ever imagined, more than envisioned and enshrined by the American revolution, and qualitatively more than ever before possible. If Immanuel Wallerstein is once again right (as he was with respect to the existence of one world system encompassing the Soviet Union), "as the present world system crashes down amidst us in the next 50 years, we must have a substantive alternative to offer that is a collective creation."[90] Autonomy might be that collective creation. Under such circumstances, it may not be a choice for more democracy but rather a necessary form for the survival of the species and all life.

NOTES

PREFACE

1   Apparently in Great Britain as well, the media carried the stories of these shootings quite prominently after having ignored the popular movements leading up to them. Two authors of books that mention the Autonomen introduce them in their narratives for the first time only because of the Startbahn shootings. See Sara Parkin, *Green Parties: An International Guide* (London: Heretic Books, 1989), p. 138. In *Televisionaries: The Red Army Faction Story 1963–1993* (Edinburgh, Scotland: AK Press, 1994), Tom Vague refers to the Autonomen as a "new wildcard development" in 1987, despite their having been in existence for nearly a decade.

2   As Green leader Petra Kelly observed: "Extra-parliamentary activity is an important part of the parliamentary system, even if only in sounding the alarm." Although we can appreciate her insight, her statist bias should also be evident. For her, "every new law means a change to the system." *Fighting for Hope* (Boston: South End Press, 1987), p. 3.

3   I use these terms with reservations, since "American" should refer to all people who live in North and South America, and "North American" should include Canadians and Mexicans. The simple fact is that there is no single word that refers to the people of the United States. As my friend Felipe Ehrenberg pointed out to me, U.S. should stand for Untitled State, since "United States" could just as easily refer to the United States of Mexico.

4   The number of deaths attributed to neo-Nazis might have been as many as ninety at the end of 1995. See *Reunited Germany: The New Danger*, a *Searchlight* special issue in association with *AntiFa Infoblatt* (1995).

FROM 1968 TO AUTONOMY

I would like to thank members of the Boston editorial collective of *Capitalism Nature Socialism* for their comments on an earlier draft of part of this chapter.

1   See my book *The Imagination of the New Left: A Global Analysis of 1968* (Boston: South End Press, 1987).

2   The term "postmodern" is loaded with so many meanings that it is difficult to use it without raising questions that properly belong to the category of whether a glass is half full or half empty. In Chapter 7, I discuss postmodern capitalism and its implications for social movements. Two noteworthy discussions of postmodernism are David Harvey's *The Condition of Postmodernity* (Oxford: Basil Blackwell. 1990) and Fredric Jameson's *Postmodernism, or the Cultural Logic of Late Capitalism* (Durham: Duke University Press, 1991).

3   *Newsweek* (Dec. 22, 1986), p. 49.

4   Quoted in Rob Burns and Wilfried van der Will, *Protest and Democracy in West Germany: Extra-Parliamentary Opposition and the Democratic Agenda* (London: St. Martin's Press, 1988), p. 100.

5   Tine Stein and Bernd Ulrich. "Die Kohorte frisst ihr Kind: Die 68er und der Niedergang der Grünen," in Ralf Fücks (Herausgeber), *Sind die Grünen noch zu retten?* (Reinbek bei Hamburg: Rowohlt, 1991), p. 76.

6   *Processo* (January 10, 1994).

7   See Dieter Hoffman-Axthelm, Otto Kallscheuer, Eberhard Knödler-Bunte, and Brigitte Wartmann, *Zwei Kulturen? Tunix, Mescalero und die Folgen* (Berlin: Verlag Ästhetik und Kommunikation, 1978), p. 86. Michael Ryan outlines a similar

conception in his introduction to Antonio Negri's *Marx Beyond Marx: Lessons on the Grundrisse* (Brooklyn: Autonomedia, 1991), p. xxx. To Agnoli's two meanings, Ryan adds a third, "the multilateral productive potential" of the "subject in the communist society."

8   Although there have been few attempts made from within the Autonomen to define autonomy, one exception was made in preparation for the autonomist convention held in Berlin in April 1995. See *Eat It! Reader: Autonomie-Kongress-Reader Teil II* (Berlin, 1995), pp. 6–7.

9   This system assigns a proportional number of seats in parliament (the *Bundestag*) to any party that receives more than 5 percent of the vote.

10   Ingrid Damian-Hesser and Michael Damian, eds., *Handbuch: Bürgerinitiativen in Frankfurt* (Frankfurt: Verlag im Leseladen, 1978).

11   This perspective is best articulated in Holland. See ADILKNO, *Cracking the Movement: Squatting Beyond the Media* ADILKNO (The Foundation for the Advancement of Illegal Knowledge) (Brooklyn: Autonomedia, 1994).

12   Karl E. Meyer, "Germany's Once and Future Capital: A Second Chance for Renascent Berlin," *New York Times* (June 25, 1991).

13   See Serge Schmemann. "Germans' Day of Exultation and Marlene Dietrich Too," *New York Times* (Oct. 4. 1990), p. 16.

14   The eros effect refers to the sudden, intuitive awakening of solidarity and massive opposition to the established system, as occurred in May 1968 in France. See my *Imagination of the New left: A Global Analysis of 1968* for its initial formulation. Also see my paper "The Eros Effect," presented at the American Sociological Association meetings in August 1989. For a debate about it, see my exchange with Staughton Lynd in the *Journal of American History* (June 1990). Much research remains to be done on the spontaneous solidarity and actions generated by popular upsurges. Sidney Tarrow understands a similar global diffusion of movements in *Power in Movement: Social Movements, Collective Action and Politics* (Cambridge: Cambridge University Press, 1994).

ITALIAN AUTONOMIA

1   Frank Brodhead, "Strategy, Compromise and Revolt: Viewing the Italian Workers' Movement," *Radical America* 18, no. 5 (1984), p. 54.

2   Robert Lumley, *States of Emergency: Cultures of Revolt in Italy 1968–1977* (London: Verso, 1991), p. 202.

3   Alessandro Silj, *Never Again Without a Rifle* (New York: Karz Publishers, 1979), p. 102.

4   Lumley, p. 211.

5   Lumley, p. 226.

6   As quoted in Lumley, p. 189.

7   As quoted in Lumley, p. 227.

8   For discussion, see John Downing, *Radical Media: The Political Experience of Alternative Communication* (Boston: South End Press, 1984), pp. 225–6.

9   Robert C. Meade Jr., *Red Brigades: The Story of Italian Terrorism* (New York: St. Martin's Press, 1990), p. xx.

10   Meade, p. 18.

11   Eddy Cherki and Michel Wieviorka, "Autoreduction Movements in Turin," *Semiotext* 3, no. 3 (1980), p. 73.

12   Lumley, p. 300.

13   Lotta Continua, "Take Over the City," *Radical America* (Mar.–Apr. 1973), pp. 93–8.

14   Judith Hellman, *Journeys Among Women* (London: Oxford University Press, 1987), p. 22.

15   Cherki, p. 76.

16   Brodhead, p. 55.

17   The diary of one these struggles illustrates this trend. See *Tagebuch eines Betrieb-skampfes, herausgegeben von Genossen der "Assemblea Autonoma" von Alfa Romeo* (München: Trikont Verlag, 1973).

18   See Carl Boggs, *Social Movements and Political Power: Emerging Forms of Radicalism in the West* (Philadelphia: Temple University Press, 1986), pp. 72–3.

19   *Italy 1977–8: Living With an Earthquake* (London: Red Notes, 1978), p. 110 (here-after referred to as *Earthquake*). This is one of the best single sources of information on the Italian movement of this period, and I have relied heavily on it for parts of this section. Other sources include *Armed Struggle in Italy: A Chronology* (Bratach Dubh Anarchist Pamphlets no. 4, 1979); *Dossier on Torture and Prison Conditions in Italy: 1979–1983* (Boston: Second State, 1983); *Indianer und P38* (München: Trikont, 1978).

20   *Earthquake,* p. 110.

21   Potere Operaio, "Italy, 1973: Workers Struggles in the Capitalist Crisis," *Radical America* (Mar.–Apr. 1973), p. 31.

22   Bifo, "Anatomy of Autonomy," *Semiotext* (1980), p. 151.

23   David Moss, *The Politics of Left-Wing Violence in Italy 1969–1985* (New York: Macmillan, 1989), pp. 90–1.

24   Hellman, p. 78.

25   See Harry Cleaver, *Reading Capital Politically* (Austin, TX: University of Texas Press, 1979).

26   For discussion of this issue, see my book *The Imagination of the New Left: A Global Analysis of 1958* (Boston: South End Press, 1987), chap. 5.

27   Demau's "Manifesto" is contained in an excellent anthology edited by Paula Bono and Sandra Kemp, *Italian Feminist Thought: A Reader* (Oxford: Basil Blackwell, 1991), pp. 34–5. Hereafter referred to as *IFT*.

28   The collectives of Lotta Feminista developed from the groups associated with Female Revolt in the same period when Lotta Continua was formed.

29   See Hellman, pp. 46–7.

30   This was a minimal number. Rivolta Femminile estimated the number of illegal abortions at one to three million per year. The more conservative World Health Organization gave a figure of 800,000 to 3 million, and attributed 20,000 female deaths per year to improperly performed procedures. See J. Hellman, p. 42, and *IFT*, p. 214.

31   Most Italian doctors were hostile to feminism. Even after abortion had been decriminalized, many invoked a conscientious objector clause to abstain from performing them.

32   See *IFT*, pp. 220–1.

33   *IFT*, pp. 216–8.

34   Bifo, pp, 94–5.

35   *IFT*, p. 226.

36   Quotations from *Earthquake*, pp. 85–7.

37   Hellman, pp. 40–1.

38   Lumley, p. 331.

39   Some women were not counted because they worked in nonunionized jobs and were paid under the table. See Susan Bassnett, *Feminist Experiences: The Women's Movement in Four Cultures* (London: Allen and Unwin, 1986), p. 116.

40   See *IFT*, pp. 260–72.

41   Lotta Feminista (1973), as quoted in *IFT*, pp. 261–2.

42   *IFT*, pp. 15, 42.

43   Bianca Beccalli, "Working Class Militancy, Feminism, and Trade Union Politics," *Radical America* 18, no. 5 (1984), p. 42.

44   Beccalli, pp. 43–4.

45   *IFT*, p. 139. The originality and vibrancy of Italian feminist theory are refreshing. They theorized epistemology, not simply politics, and took on Weberian neutral-

ity, the one-point perspective of scientistic thought, the absence of the body from theory, and the notion of dual subjectivity.

46   Joanne Barkan, "The Genesis of Contemporary Italian Feminism," *Radical America* 18, no. 5 (1984), p. 36.
47   Bassnett, pp. 108–10.
48   Deborah Tannen's recent work on male and female conversation patterns reveals a microsociological basis to explain why organizations of women should be so different from male-dominated ones. See her book, *You Just Don't Understand: Women and Men in Conversation* (New York: Morrow, 1990).
49   Carla Lonzi, "Let's Spit on Hegel" (1970), in *IFT*, p. 51.
50   Antonio Negri, *Revolution Retrieved* (London: Red Notes, 1988), p. 236.
51   Silj, pp. xiv–xv.
52   Lumley, p. 80.
53   Lumley, p. 96.
54   Lumley, p. 97.
55   Beccalli, p. 40.
56   Umberto Eco took particular pains to point out that they had not read Bifo. See his article in Dieter Hoffman-Axthelm, et. al., *Zwei Kulturen? Tunix, Mescalero und die Folgen* (Berlin: Verlag Ästhetik and Kommunikation, 1978). The anarchist pamphlet "Workers' Autonomy" (published by Bratach Dubh) illustrates the degree to which any kind of leftist can become isolated from popular movements. What the authors of this pamphlet have done is to construct an ideal type of the world in which they develop the correct line on autonomy. Not only do they fetishize the working class by reducing the broad concept of autonomy (feminist, creative, cultural, and proletarian) to one of its component parts, but their idea of the working class is their own invention. They are unable to relate real-world experiences to their model. Instead, they develop a recipe for autonomy that is nothing but a formal shell of empty logic.
57   *IFT*, p. 276.
58   Hellman. p. 99.
59   *Indianer und P38*, p. 18.
60   Birgit Kraatz, "Der Traum vom Paradies: Über die Stadtindianer und Autonomia in Italien," in Michael Haller (Hg.) *Aussteigen oder rebellieren: Jugendliche gegen Staat und Gesellschaft* (Reinbeck bei Hamburg: Rowohlt, 1981) pp. 39–41.
61   Significantly, media mogul turned prime minister Berlusconi's control of Italy's main television stations dates from this period as well. For an excellent discussion of alternative media, see Downing's *Radical Media*.
62   Bassnett, p. 128.
63   Meade, p. 72.
64   For a detailed view, see Stephen Hellman. *Italian Communism in Transition: The Rise and Fall of the Historic Compromise in Turin, 1975–1980* (London: Oxford University Press, 1986).
65   See *Panorama* (Mar. 20. 1979), pp. 146–56.
66   Bifo, pp. 153–4.
67   *Zwei Kulturen*, p. 63.
68   Quoted in *Earthquake*, p. 56.
69   *Earthquake*, p. 23.
70   A faction of the PCI attempted to take the party away from the conception of attacking "parasites" and "privileged" by instead talking about a "second society." The chief architect of this position was Alberto Asor-Rosa, a theorist associated with the movement of 1968 who subsequently joined the PCI. For Asor-Rosa, "productive labor" remained the "first society," and the "subproletariat" (unemployed, marginally employed, youth, and women) was the "second society" to whom the PCI should reach out.
71   *Indianer und P38*, p. 119.
72   Lotta Continua editorial (Apr. 23, 1977), as quoted in *Earthquake*, p. 73.

73　Roberta Tatafiore, "A Look 'Outside' the Armed Struggle," in *IFT*, p. 310.

74　Bifo, p. 150.

75　Moss, p. 37.

76　Italian Marxists sometimes called them the "subproletariat" to avoid the issue of Marx's disregard for the lumpen because of their reactionary role in France in 1848.

77　Dossier on Torture and Prison Conditions in Italy, 1979–83.

78　Sidney Tarrow, "Constructing Meaning Through Action," in *Frontiers in Social Movement Theory*, ed. Aldon Morris and Carol Mueller (New Haven, CT: Yale University Press, 1992), p. 196.

SOURCES OF AUTONOMOUS POLITICS IN GERMANY

Versions of parts of this chapter appeared in *Monthly Review* (September 1982) as "The Extraparliamentary Left in Europe" and were presented as "Recent Cultural-Political Radicalism in Europe" at the Pacific Sociological Association meetings in April 1982 and "Europe's Autonomous Movement" at the American Political Science Association meetings in September 1989. I wish to acknowledge the special assistance of Ann Acosta, Susanne Peters, and Uwe Haseloff in this chapter.

1　Susanne Peters, *The Germans and the INF Missiles* (Baden-Baden: Nomos, 1990).

2　Mary Kaldor estimated that five million people demonstrated in the capitals of Western Europe in 1981 and 1983. See "Who Killed the Cold War?" *Bulletin of the Atomic Scientists* July/Aug, 1995), p. 58. The numbers of demonstrators at the largest gatherings in the fall of 1981 were approximately 150,000 in Rome, 120,000 in London, 50,000 in Paris, 150,000 in Helsinki, 500,000 in Madrid, 300,000 in Athens, and 350,000 in Amsterdam. See Wilfried von Bredow, "The Peace Movements in France and in the Federal Republic of Germany—A Comparison," paper presented at the annual meeting of the American Sociological Association, September 1982.

3　Andrei Markovits and Philip Gorski. *The German Left: Red, Green and Beyond* (New York: Oxford University Press, 1993), p. 199.

4　For more information on the Easter marches, see Markovits and Gorski, pp. 46–58; Christine Bachmeier, Alexander Ewald, Thomas Fischer, and Sabine Norton, *Mythen knacken: 40 Jahre Westdeutsche Linke* (Darmstadt: Neues Forum, 1989), pp. 85–6, 92 (hereafter *MK*).

5　This observation was first made to me by Gretchen Dutschke-Klotz and was verified by several other participants in SDS.

6　*MK*, p. 118.

7　*MK*, p. 94. When popular movements disintegrate, social democratic and neo-Leninist groups acquire new members. According to Sidney Tarrow, the Italian Communist Party's membership rose from 1.5 million in 1969 to 1.9 million in 1978. See "Political Parties and Italian Movements of the 1960s and 1970s," in *Challenging the Political Order: New Social Movements in Western Democracies*, ed. Russell Dalton and Manfred Kuechler (London; Oxford University Press, 1990), p. 269. The opposite also apparently occurs. At several points in *Feuer und Flamme: Zur Geschichte und Gegenwart der Autonomen* (Berlin: Edition-ID Archiv, 1990), Geronimo (pp. 61–4) discusses how Marxist-Leninist groups loose membership as autonomous movements gain strength.

8　*MK*, p. 106; also see *Die Früchte des Zorns: Texte und Materialien zur Geschicte der Revolutionären Zellen und der Roten Zora* (Berlin: Edition ID-Archiv, 1993), p. 507 (hereafter *FZ*).

9　In a masterful study, *The Politics of the West German Trade Unions: Strategies of Class and Interest Representation in Growth and Crisis* (Cambridge: Cambridge University

Press, 1986). Andrei Markovits analyzed these non-union-sanctioned strikes. "The most common feature of the 1973 strikes were demands to slow down the speed of the assembly line, lower piece-rate quotas, improve the physical condition of the work environment, and introduce more generous rest periods during working hours.... Many of these strikes in the metal-processing industry were either initiated or led by foreign workers and women grouped in the lower wage categories who were disgruntled over the gap between their wage rare and those of their male, German colleagues" (pp. 226–7).

10   *MK*, pp. 111–13.

11   See Ulrike Heider, *Schülerprotest in der Bundesrepublik Deutschland* (Frankfurt am Main: Suhrkamp, 1984), p. 220, for one example of the distance between the Left and the counterculture. The latter's isolation was the central theme of *Autonomie oder Getto? Kontroversen über die Alternativbewegung*, ed. von Wolfgang Kraushaar (Frankfurt Verlag Neue Kritik, 1978).

12   Johannes Schütte, *Revolt und Verweigerung: Zur Politik und Sozialpsychologie der Spontibewegung* (Giessen: Focus Verlag, 1980), pp. 141–2.

13   Geronimo, p. 35.

14   Saral Sarkar, *Green-Alternative Politics in West Germany*, Vol. 1, *The New Social Movement* (New York: United Nations University Press, 1993), p. 36 (hereafter *GAP*).

15   R. Burns and W. van der Will, *Protest and Democracy in West Germany: Extra-Parliamentary Opposition and the Democratic Agenda* (London: St. Martin's Press, 1988), p. 185.

16   Tilman Fichter and Siegward Lönnendonker, *Kleine Geschichte des SDS* (Berlin: Rotbuch Verlag, 1979).

17   The largest student organization of the New Left in the United States was also called the SDS but stood for Students for a Democratic Society. It was less intellectual and more militant than the German SDS. Although both organizations emerged from acrimonious splits from social democratic parent groups, there was no formal link between the two. In the United States, the movement among white students alone was far bigger than the entire German New Left. The ratio of SDS members to total population was one in seven thousand in the United States, compared with one in thirty thousand in West Germany. Despite their smaller numbers, German new leftists were more well developed in the tradition of radical theory, a difference that might explain the consolidation of Green politics in Germany at a time when the movement in the United States was in great disarray.

18   Gerard Braunthal, *Political Loyalty and Public Service in West Germany: The 1972 Decree Against Radicals and Its Consequences* (Amherst, MA: University of Massachusetts Press, 1990).

19   Braunthal, p. 101. Only in the mid-1980s, when members of the Greens sitting in parliament questioned the decree's appropriateness, was it finally disavowed, but by then, new social movements far more radical than anything anyone had expected made the issues associated with the *Berufsverbot* moot.

20   *FZ*, pp. 200, 709.

21   Quoted in Markovits and Gorski, p. 86.

22   See Dieter Hoffmann-Axthelm et al., *Zwei Kulturen? Tunix, Mescalero und die Folgen* (Berlin Verlag Ästhetik und Kommunikation, 1978).

23   The trajectory of the proliferation of autonomous movements is easier to fix than the exact time when the Autonomen was first used as the name for autonomous groups. Geronimo (pp. 83, 151) locates the first visible autonomous groups in the transcendence of single-issue struggles within the Brokdorf antinuclear mobilizations of 1976–77. Documents in the archives of the Hamburger Institut für Sozialforschung demonstrate clearly that the Hamburg Autonomist Plenary met for the first time in December 1979, and that it had been strongly influenced in its choice of a name by the struggle in Zurich. In 1980, a pair of radical leaflets in Amsterdam bore the name Autonomen. In *Marginalisierung und Militanz: Jugendliche*

Bewegungsmilieus im Aufruhr (Frankfurt: Campus Verlag, 1992), Matthias Manrique locates the first meetings of the Autonomenplenum Kreuzberg in Berlin in the late fall of 1981 (p. 168). Although the exact timing of the use of the name "Autonomen" cannot be fixed with certainty, it is clear that similarly minded groups adopted it as a label to show continental affinity with radical politics loyal to no nation-state or political party. The international reproduction of the name is an instance of what I call the eros effect, the intuitive adoption of tactics and analysis by social movement activists.

24　In 1971, a wave of squats and even proposals for a youth center had surfaced in Zurich, but the organizing committee was swamped by cadre groups. "Every party sent its delegates to the committee, who then fought for their resolutions and attempted to recruit shocked inhabitants [of the neighborhood] to their own correct line." Needless to say, the impetus was short-circuited. Hanspeter Kriesi, *Die Zürucher Bewegung* (Frankfurt: Campus Verlag, 1984), pp. 290–3.

25　"Offener Brief an den Stadtrat von Zürich," *Zürich Tages-Anzeiger* (Dec. 13, 1980), p. 34.

26　Kriesi, p. 42.

27　Michael Haller, "Aussteigen oder rebellieren: Über die Doppeldeutigkeit der Jugendrevolte," in Haller (ed.) *Aussteigen oder rebellieren* (Reinbeck bei Hamburg: Rowohlt, 1981), p. 12.

28　Gruppe Olten, *Die Zürcher Unruhe 2* (Zurich: Orte-Verlag, 1981), p. 123.

29　Kriesi, p. 178.

30　See the police chief of Hamburg's report, dated October 30, 1986, "Autonome: Selbstverständnis und Motivation."

31　*Emma Sonderband: Schwestern Lust—Schwestern Frust: 20 Jahre Frauenbewegung* (Nachdruck, 1990; Einleitung, 1991), p. 4.

32　This speech is translated and excerpted in *German Feminism: Readings in Politics and Literature*, ed. Edith Hoshino Altbach, Jeanette Clausen, Dagmar Schultz, and Naomi Stephan (Albany: State University of New York Press, 1984), pp. 307–10.

33　Helke Sander, "Mütter sind politische Personen," *Courage* (Oct. 1978), pp. 38–45. The women's actions in Berlin transformed the groups that undertook them and led to women's councils being established in many other cities. In Münster, a group of sixty to seventy women quickly came together and developed campaigns using irony and defamation of men as key tactics. One of their members produced "The Cultural Revolution of Women," the first radical feminist text of the new wave of German feminism. As women met, they read texts from the U.S. women's movement and adopted them for their own. For the most part, however, the movement was oriented to practice rather than theory.

34　Ann Anders (ed.), *Autonome Frauen: Schlüsseltexte der Neuen Frauenbewegung seit 1968* (Frankfurt: Athenäum, 1988), p. 11.

35　Alice Schwarzer, "Ewig zittere das Weib," in *Emma Sonderband*, p. 137. It should be noted that German law was a hodgepodge of various statutes. After World War II, the United States essentially rewrote Germany's basic laws according to the U.S. Constitution. In January 1949, the *Bundestag* approved an equal rights statute, but it had little enforceability. Another equal rights statute in 1957 modified rigidly patriarchal marriage and family laws.

36　Schwarzer was able to persuade only three groups to join her at first, women from Frauenaktion '70 in Frankfurt, the Socialist Women's Federation in Berlin, and one part of the "Red Women" of Munich. See Altbach et al., p. 103.

37　*Emma Sonderband*, p. 61.

38　*Emma Sonderband*, p. 71.

39　*Emma Sonderband*, p. 75.

40　Kristine von Soden (ed.), *Der grosse Unterschied: Die neue Frauenbewegung und die siebziger Jahre* (Berlin: Elefanten Press, 1988), p. 89.

41　Anders, p. 25.

42   *Emma Sonderband*, p. 76.

43   Out of discussions at the Hornstrasse, a women's university seminar was organized at the Free University of Berlin in 1974. Although there was considerable opposition to its excluding men, the principle of women's autonomy was maintained and explained to a growing cadre of university students. By the fall of 1974, 350 women were involved in the seminar. The group occupied much of its time writing a critique of Herbert Marcuse's essay on feminism. Women's seminars spread to a dozen other cities, and after its Berlin organizers encountered women's studies programs during a trip to the United States, a decision was made to organize a summer university for women in 1976. Over six hundred women arrived for the first summer university, and it became a strategy forum that was particularly important for women whose local towns had few feminists.

44   *Emma Sonderband*, p. 81.

45   *Emma Sonderband*, p. 48.

46   von Soden, p. 145.

47   *Emma Sonderband*, p. 88.

48   *Emma Sonderband*, p. 103.

49   Although these shelters opened autonomously and excluded men, within a few years, state funding insidiously undermined their autonomy, and males were making their way into the shelters as coworkers. By 1983, there were approximately eighty feminist shelters and as many as forty active planning groups for new shelters. Within the feminist shelters, autonomy was the key internal organizational principle: women who came for help found that they could take on as much responsibility for running the shelter as longer-term volunteers and sometimes even paid staff members. Because government monies were often rejected unless strict understandings regarding the autonomy of the centers were reached (including, in many cases, the complete exclusion of men—something most state agencies could not sanction), the feminist shelters were less well funded than they could have been. See Myra Marx Ferree, "Equality and Autonomy: Feminist Politics in the United States and West Germany," in *The Women's Movements of the United States and Western Europe,* ed. Mary Fainsod Katzenstein and Carol McClurg Mueller (Philadelphia: Temple University Press, 1987), pp. 185–8.

50   *Frauenjahrbuch,* 1976.

51   Altbach et. al., p. 107.

52   Anders, p. 23.

53   Marie-Theres Knäpper, *Feminismus, Autonomie, Subjektivät: Tendenzen und Widersprüche in der neuen Frauenbewegung* (Bochum: Germinal Verlag, 1984).

54   *Emma Sonderband*, p. 75.

55   See Ferree's discussion of this important topic.

56   Altbach et. al., p. 48. *Courage* ceased publication in 1984.

57   During a political conflict in Berlin, a butyric acid attack on the automobile of another feminist was made.

58   *The Power of Women and the Subversion of Society.*

59   The discussions around this issue became notoriously acrimonious, dividing women's centers into feuding tendencies that called each other "reactionary." These dynamics led one commentator to remark: "Also the German women's movement was not spared a German sickness: rigid friend/foe and black/white thinking; the widespread incapability to discuss differences while maintaining solidarity and the customary defamation of anyone thinking differently." *Emma Sonderband*, p. 80. I question whether this is a specifically German problem. Suffice it to say that the cultural tendencies of patriarchal interaction emerged within the women's centers. See the end of Chapter 5 for a discussion of the "German problem."

60   It was estimated that women did two-thirds of the socially necessary labor in Germany and men only one-third—meaning that women did twice as much work as men. In 1968, the average woman worker made 1.61 marks an hour less than the average male. In 1973, this gap rose to 2.60 marks an hour. *Emma Sonderband,*

p. 65. In 1939, there were only 700,000 women with jobs outside the home; by 1955, there were more than 4 million, or 36 percent of the workforce. Herta Däubler-Gmelin, *Frauenarbeitslosigkeit oder Reserve zurück an den Herd* (Rcinbek bei Hamburg: Rowohlt, 1977), pp. 32, 45.

61 Altbach et al., p. 247.

62 Hannelore Mabry, "The Feminist Theory of Surplus Value," in Altbach et al., pp. 265–74. Mabry's general point appears well taken, although counter-examples can be found. On September 9, 1978, for example, fifteen thousand trade unionists marched against wage discrimination and female unemployment in Rheinland-Pfalz at an event sponsored by the main union federation.

63 *Emma Sonderband,* p. 95.

64 Eva-Maria Stark, as quoted in *Emma Sonderband*, pp. 115–6.

65 See the discussion in Anders, pp. 34–5.

66 The entire discussion was further complicated when *Courage* published a text discussing the marital problems of a well-known leftist in prison whose wife was suing him for child support and alimony. Because *Courage* painted him as a villain, despite his persecution by the government, many women wrote to the magazine to support him. See Altbach et al., p. 240.

67 Translated in Altbach et al., p. 108.

68 *Emma Sonderband*, p. 118.

69 Vera Slupic. "Love Is Work—but Love Is Also Love," in *Beiträge zur 4. Sommeruniversität*, 1979.

70 Dagmar Schulz, "The German Women's Movements in 1982," in Altbach et al., p. 374.

71 See Werner Hülsberg, *The German Greens: A Social and Political Profile* (London: Verso, 1988), p. 132.

72 A "women's council" was formed that quickly counted a membership of over five million. Along with other groups, it pressured candidates to take progressive stands on women's issues. Governments have begun to make major concessions to feminists in terms of hiring quotas in major universities (where women constitute under 10 percent of tenured faculty) as well as in affirmative action plans for public-sector jobs.

In 1988, Rita Süssmuth's *Frauenlexikon* listed three varieties of feminists: "socialist feminists," who reckoned with class conflict; "cultural feminists," who believed in a superior women's culture; and "ecological feminists," oriented toward a reconciliation of women and nature. At the same time, the more progressive *Feminist Studies* spoke of "political-socialist feminism" and "culturally critical feminism" grounded in either historical or biological otherness of women. Schwarzer took issue with Süssmuth's tripartite categories because they omitted "radical feminists," who had "put everything in question" without being grounded in a conception of "women's nature (or human nature generally)" while raising the issue of power and class.

73 Altbach et al., p. 194.

74 Y. Lenoir, *Technocratie française* (Paris: Pauvert, 1977), p. 95, as quoted in Dorothy Nelkin and Michael Pollak, *The Atom Besieged* (Cambridge, MA: MIT Press, 1982), p. 23.

75 Günter Minnerup, "West Germany Since the War," *New Left Review* 99 (Sep.–Oct. 1976), p. 4. A few months earlier, the same magazine published a report that in Italy, "the long social crisis opened in 1968–9 by the student upsurge and by the most extensive and radical workers' struggles of the post-war period has also ended, at least temporarily." See Paolo Flores d'Arcais and Franco Moretti, "Paradoxes of the Italian Politcal Crisis," *New Left Review* 96 (Mar.–Apr. 1976), p. 35. Social movements often appear unexpectedly and leave analysts of various political persuasions unable to predict their proliferation.

76 Nelkin and Pollak, p. 22.

77 Minnerup, pp. 19, 38.

78   Nelkin and Pollak, p. 39.
79   Anne Dudeck, "Selbstorganisierte Bildungsarbeit im Wandel," in *Neue soziale Bewegungen in der Bundesrepublik Deutschland*, ed. Roland Roth and Dieter Rucht (Bonn: Bundeszentrale für politische Bildung, 1987), p. 224.
80   Enno Brand, *Staatsgewalt: Politische Unterdrückung und innere Sicherheit in der Bundesrepublik* (Berlin: Verlag die Werkstatt, 1988), p. 188 (hereafter SG).
81   Markovits and Gorski, pp. 103–4.
82   *GAP*, pp. 121, 131.
83   *GAP*, p. 165.
84   Nelkin and Pollak, p. 45.
85   *FEZ*, p. 727.
86   See Ulrike Wasmuht, *Friedensbewegungen der 80er Jahre* (Giessen: Focus Verlag, 1987); Markovits and Gorski, p. 111; Brand, p. 234; *FZ*, p. 465.
87   Manrique, p. 65.
88   See Burckhard Kretschmann, Monika Binas, and Broka Hermann, *Startbahn-West: Fotos und Interviews* (Privat Druck); Brand, pp. 213–4; *FZ*, pp. 394–418. Ultimately, courts ruled that the airport was a federal issue and not subject to local referenda.
89   *FZ*, p. 429.
90   Elmar Altvater, Jürgen Hoffman, Willi Semmler, *Vom Wirtschafts wunder zur Wirtschaftskrise* (Berlin: Verlag Olle und Wolter, 1979), p. 100.
91   *Der Tagespiegel* (Berlin), June 8, 1980. The shortage of available houses resulted in standard nonrefundable deposits of around 6,000 DM (then about $3,000) for a small apartment. More than sixty thousand households—largely senior citizens—paid more than a third of their income toward rent. The West Berlin average was 20 percent of income for rent, heating, and electricity. Other major cities were equally bad. In Munich, for example, ten thousand people were registered with the housing office as emergency cases, and even by conservative estimates, an additional twelve thousand Germans were searching for housing there on the "free market."
     Although particularly severe, the housing crisis in West Berlin was also irrational, because the city had been depopulated by an exodus of Berliners after the war. Attracting Germans to work there was so difficult that even in the midst of the recession of 1974–76, a monthly average of ten thousand available jobs existed. For many, the city's geographical and political isolation from the rest of West Germany and its economic dependence on outside help were key reasons for Berlin's lack of appeal. Most West Berliners suffered acutely from "wall fever," and many left the city at least once a month. To help Berliners make life there more attractive, the government subsidized wages (8 percent was automatically added), paid birth bonuses to mothers, gave special allowances to the elderly (30 percent of the slightly more than two million West Berliners were over sixty years old in 1976), provided freely flowing student support money, and subsidized airfares to and from the city.
92   Haller, p. 104.
93   *New York Times*, (May 6, 1981), p. A–17.
94   See the discussion in Kriesi, p. 200. Internationally, much the same could be said of punk. See James Stark, *Punk '77: An Inside Look at the San Francisco Rock n' Roll Scene* (1977).
95   *SG*, p. 207. Quoting government statistics, Margit Mayer counted 54 police evictions, 410 police raids, 4,687 criminal investigations, and 2,287 arrests vis-à-vis the squatters' movement in West Berlin. See "Restructuring and Popular Opposition in West German Cities," in *The Capitalist City*, ed. M. Smith and J. Feagin (Oxford: Basil Blackwell, 1987), p. 353.
96   *Die Tageszeitung* (May 4, 1981), p. 12. Manrique counted 160 by the end of 1981 (p. 159). Kriesi maintained that there were over 500 (p. 170), a figure also given by Manrique (p. 168) for early summer 1981. The police referred to "about 700

known house occupations." See *Verfassungsschutzbericht* (1981), p. 71.

97 See Steven Katz and Margit Mayer, "Gimme Shelter: Self-Help Housing Struggles Within and Against the State in New York City and West Berlin,"*International Journal of Urban and Regional Research 9*, no. 1 (1985), p. 33; also see Manrique, pp. 80, 118.

98 Manrique, p. 133.

99 Nanette Funk, "Take It," in *Semiotexte* vol. IV, no. 2, 1982 (German issue), p. 297.

100 *GAP*, p. 55.

101 By March 1984, only fourteen houses were still illegally occupied, the remainder having been legalized, cleared out by police, or abandoned. *GAP*, p. 54.

102 *Der Spiegel* (Jan. 19, 1981), p. 28.

103 I consistently use conservative estimates, since I do not want to appear to be inflating the scope of events in question. At the anti-Haig demonstration, for example, it was estimated by some that at least eighty thousand demonstrators were involved, probably a more accurate number than the police estimate of fifty thousand. German sources include the *Frankfurter Allgemeine* and *Die Tageszeitung*.

104 Manrique, p. 160.

105 So far, no one has systematically counted the number of Greens elected to office. See Hülsberg, p. 234.

106 For a comprehensive treatment of how the Social Democrats swung around to the Left, see Andrei Markovits, "The German Left: Between a Crisis of Identity and Orthodoxy," *New Political Science* (Spring–Summer 1993).

107 In 1995, *Taz* had a readership of 410,000 and printed just under 60,000 copies daily. Nonetheless, the end of the government's special subsidies for Berlin contributed to a financial crisis. *German Press Review* (Sept. 22, 1995).

108 Petra Kelly, *Um Hoffnung kämpfen: Gewaltfrei in eine grüne Zukunft* (Bornheim-Merten: Lamuv Verlag, 1983), pg. 180–1. Joseph Huber estimated the numbers involved in the national "active movement" at between 6,000 groups / 30,000 activists and 15,000 groups / 135,000 activists in 1980. *Wer soll das alles ändern? Die Alternativen der Alternativbewegung* (Berlin: Rotbuch Verlag, 1980), p. 29. Sarkar quotes numbers of 10,000 alternative self-help and service projects with 80,000 activists, and 4,000 alternative economic enterprises with 24,000 jobs in 1983 (*GAP*, p. 257). In addition, there were as many as 100,000 *Wohngemeinschaften* in the FRG in 1983 (*GAP*, p. 241).

109 Selbsthilfe Netzwerk Berlin, *Ein Jahr Netzwerk* (1979).

110 For an analysis of how *Netzwerk* fit into the overall movement and its context, see Mayer, p. 355.

EUROPEAN AUTONOMIST MOVEMENTS

Versions of parts of this chapter appeared in Z magazine (Sept. and Oct. 1992) as "Europe's Autonomen" and "Mayday in West Berlin" (with Rodolfo Torres) and were presented as "The Autonornen: A New Social Movement?" at Harvard University's Center for European Studies in March 1990. Invaluable sources of information were interviews with 5askia K. and activists in the Hafenstrasse, Frankelufer, Christiania, and the Grootc Keyser.

1 Winfried Kretschmer and Dieter Rucht, "Beispiel Wackersdorf: Die Protestbewegung gegen die Wiederaufarbeitungslage," in *Neue soziale Bewegungen in der Bundesrepublik Deutschland*, ed. Roland Roth and Dieter Rucht, Erste Auflage (Bonn: Bundeszentrale für politische Bildung, 1987), pp. 142–3, 148.

2 Enno Brand, *Staatsgewelt* (Berlin: Verlag Die Werkstatt, 1988), pp. 259–60.

3 Bunte Hilfe Nordbayern, "Repression in der Provinz" (1989), pp. 87–8 (in the archives of the Institute for Social History in Amsterdam).

4   Monika Bauerlein, "Germany's Radical Counterculture: Are They Revolutionary Heroes or an Albatross for Other Activists?" *Utne Reader* (July/Aug. 1989), p. 32.

5   See Rob Burns and Wilfried van der Will, *Protest and Democracy in West Germany: Extra-Parliamentary Opposition and the Democratic Agenda* (London: St. Martin's Press, 1988), pp. 182–3.

6   For an analysis of this action and the mobilization at the international meetings of the World Bank and International Monetary Fund, see Jürgen Gerhards and Dieter Rucht, "Mesomobilization: Organizing and Framing in Two Protest Campaigns in West Germany," *American Journal of Sociology* 98, no. 3 (Nov. 1992), pp. 555–96.

7   Altogether, 475 different events were counted in one study. See Jürgen Gerhards, "Die Mobilisierung gegen die IWF und Weltbanktagung 1988 in Berlin: Gruppen, Veranstaltungen, Diskurse," in *Neue soziale Bewegungen in der Bundesrepublik Deutschland*, ed. Roland Roth and Dieter Rucht, Zweite Auflage (Bonn: Bundeszentrale für politische Bildung, 1991), p. 219.

8   *Der Spiegel*, (Oct. 3, 1988), p. 132.

9   In 1989, the German government counted such centers in more than fifty cities. See *Verfassungsschutzbericht* (1989), p. 62.

10   There were points at which Dutch movements rejected tactics from Germany. In 1988 and 1989, discussions in Amsterdam questioned the idea of wearing black ski masks at militant demonstrations. See Val, "Liebe, Krieg und Alltag," in Geronimo, *Feuer und Flamme 2: Kritiken, Reflexionen und Anmerkungen zur Lage der Autonomen* (Berlin: Edition ID-Archiv, 1992), pp. 34–5. In Denmark, however, the ski masks became part of an autonomous uniform.

11   Brand, pp. 259, 262, 266.

12   *OECD Employment Outlook* (1984, 1985); *Amtliche Nachrichten der Bundesanstalt für Arbeit* (Bonn: 1991).

13   Elmar Altvater, Jürgen Hoffman, and Willi Semmler, *Von Wirtschaftswunder zur Wirtschaftskrise* (Berlin: Verlag Olle und Wolter, 1979), p. 263.

14   See Martin Moerings, "Niederlande: Der subventionierte Protest," in *Angriff auf das Herz des Staates. Zweiter Band* (Frankfurt: Suhrkamp, 1988), pp. 321–2.

15   See ADILKO, *Cracking the Movement: Squatting Beyond the Media* (Brooklyn, NY: Autonomedia, 1994), p. 205.

16   Heiner Luft Kastell, *Christiania: Selbts-organization von Nichtangepassten* (Copenhagen: 1977), and Doris Teller, Heiner Gringmuth, and Ernst-Ullrich Pinkert (eds.), *Christiania: Argumente zur Erhaltung eines befreiten Stadtviertels* (Werdorf: Gisela Lotz Verlag, 1978).

17   Michael Haller, "Schwesterlichkeit: Über die 'Kindermacht' in Kopenhagen," in *Aussteigen oder rebellieren: Jugendliche gegen Staat und Gesellschaft*, ed. Michael Haller (Reinbek bei Hamburg: Rowohlt Spiegel-Bush, 1981).

18   Ria Bjerre, "For Christiania with Love," in Alberto Ruz Buenfil, *Rainbow Nation Without Borders: Toward an Ecotopian Millennium* (Santa Fe, NM: Bear and Co., 1991), p. 89.

19   See Bjerre, pp. 99–100.

20   Michael Haller, "Das Dorf in der Stadt: Über 'Christiania' in Kopenhagen," in Haller, p. 143.

21   For one account of what was involved, see Mark Edwards, *Christiania: A Personal View of Europe's Freetown* (Photographers Gallery of London, 1979).

22   "Danish Police Fire at Anti-Unity Mob," *New York Times* (May 20, 1993).

23   See Andrei Markovits and Philip Gorski, *The German Left: Red, Green and Beyond* (New York: Oxford University Press, 1993), p. 224, for an analysis of the parliamentary dimension of the Hamburg government's weakness as related to a strong showing by the local Greens (GAL) in November 1986 and Dohnanyi's subsequent jockeying to form a coalition with the Free Democrats.

24   See *Die Tageszeitung* (Sep. 3, 1993) for drawings and an interview with the architect, Wolfgang Dirksen.

25 See Michael Hermann, Han-Joachim Lenger, Jan Philipp Reemtsma, and Karl Heinz Roth, *Hofenstrasse: Chronik und Analysen eines Konflikts* (Hamburg: Verlag am Galgenberg, 1987), p. 147. Additional materials for this chapter were found in the archives of the Schwarzmarkt Buchhandlung in Hamburg.

26 For a chronological account that also conveys the guerrillas' contempt for non-armed activists and an unfortunately glib regard far human life, see Tom Vague, *The Red Army Faction Story 1963–1993* (Edinburgh: AK Press, 1994).

27 Vague, p. 55.

28 Richard Clutterbuck, *Terrorism, Drugs and Crime in Europe After 1992* (London: Routledge, 1990), p. 48.

29 Clutterbuck, p. 50.

30 Vague, p. 97.

31 Yonah Alexander and Dennis Pluchinsky, *Europe's Red Terrorists: The Fighting Communist Organizations* (London: Frank Cass, 1992).

32 Alexander and Pluchinsky, p. 228.

33 *Boston Globe* (Mar. 28. 1993).

34 Craig R. Whitney, "'German Guerrillas Assert Leader Was 'Executed'," *New York Times* (July 11, 1993).

35 Jane Kramer, "Letter From Europe," *New Yorker* (Nov. 28, 1988), pp. 67–100.

36 For a comprehensive history and collection of their communiqués, see *Die Früchte des Zorns* (Berlin: Edition ID-Archiv, 1993).

37 Clutterbuck, p. 51.

38 Brand, p. 292.

39 *Die Früchte des Zorns*, pp. 681–2. After her release, Strobl made a documentary film about women's resistance in the Warsaw ghetto and published a book on the politics of population control, *Bevölkerungspolitik: Ideologien, Ziele, Methoden, Widerstand* (Berlin: Edition ID-Archiv, 1991).

40 See *1. Mai 1987–12. Juni 1987* (Berlin: Ermittlungsausschuss, 1988), *1. Mai 1987–1992* (Berlin: Umbruch-Bilder, 1992).

THE AUTONOMEN IN UNIFIED GERMANY

A grant from the Deutscher Akademischer Austauschdienst (DAAD) made it possible for me to travel to Germany in 1993 to research the resurgence of Nazism and the antifascist movement. Additional research was conducted while I was a visiting scholar at Harvard University's Center for European Studies. I would like to thank Susanne Peters, Gretchen Dutschke-Klotz, Victor Wallis, and Billy Nessen for their comments on earlier drafts.

1 Stefan Krätke, "Berlin: A Post-Fordist Metropolis?" in *Cities and Regions in the New Europe: The Global-Local Interplay and Spatial Development Strategies*, ed. Mick Dunford and Grigoris Kafkalas (London: Belhaven Press, 1993), p. 229.

2 See Peter Marcuse, *Missing Marx: A Personal and Political Journal of a Year in East Germany, 1989–1990* (New York: Monthly Review, 1991). Reports of the brutality associated with the resurgence of Nazism left little space in the U.S. media to contemplate the roots of the revival of German fascism—already a phenomenon that history will record as the scourge of the twentieth century. The explanation most commonly preferred for the popularity of right-wing ideas and actions in Germany is the economic dislocation caused by the global downturn and political uncertainty after the reunification of Germany. According to this perspective, high unemployment and rebelliousness against the ideas of the former communist regime were the forces compelling Germans to attack foreigners. Why should Germans be out of work and have nowhere to live when their government provides anyone crossing the border with a monthly stipend and a place to sleep? Although the parameters of this argument are true, it fails to explain why it is in Germany—especially in what used to be West Germany—rather than in Britain

or in France that the intensity of attacks on foreigners is so great.

3 See Claus Leggewie, *Die Republikaner: Ein Phantom nimmt Gestalt an* (Berlin: Rotbuch, 1989); Eike Hennig, *Die Republikaner im Schatten Deutschlands* (Frankfurt: Suhrkamp, 1991); Richard Stöss, *Die extreme Rechte in der Bundesrepublik: Entwicklung, Ursachen, Gegenmassnahmen* (Opladen: Westdeutscher Verlag, 1989); Antifaschistisches Autorenkollektiv, *Drahtzieher im braunen Netz, Der Wiederaufbau der NSDAP* (Berlin: Edition ID-Archiv, 1992).

4 See Ferdinand Protzman, "Music of Hate Raises the Volume in Germany," *New York Times* (Dec. 2, 1992).

5 A similar discrepancy could also be found in the number of neo-murders reported. The government claimed three in 1991 and seventeen in 1992 (*The Week in Germany,* Feb. 12, 1993, p. 1). An autonomous antifascist group's list with names, dates, and places detailed twelve murders in 1991 and twenty-five in 1992.

6 *New York Times* (Nov. 2, 1992). For a deeper analysis of these groups, see Michael Schmidt, *The New Reich: Violent Extremism in Unified Germany and Beyond* (New York: Pantheon Books, 1993). The forty thousand figure did not include approximately twenty-five thousand members of the Republicans. *Der Spiegel* (June 21, 1993), p. 59.

7 "Reunited Germany: The New Danger," *Searchlight Magazine* (Jan. 1995).

8 *Taz* (Feb. 23, 1993).

9 *Dokumentation,* Anti-Rassismus-Büro Bremen, Apr. 1992.

10 *Boston Globe* (Sept. 14, 1994).

11 See Stephen Bronner, "The New Right: Reflections on an International Phenomenon," *New Political Science* 24–25, *Germany's Identity Crisis* (Spring–Summer 1993), pp. 87–98.

12 *The Week in Germany* (Jan. 5, 1990), p. 7.

13 Krätke, p. 222.

14 Figures from the AL reported in the *New York Times* (Nov. 15, 1990, p. 8) were twenty-seven thousand vacant apartments in eastern Berlin.

15 Stephen Kinzer, "Berlin, Named Seat of Power, Now Wonders If It Has Room," *New York Times* (June 24, 1991).

16 Jonathan Kaufman, "Foreigners Feel Brunt of German Strains," *Boston Globe* (Aug. 27. 1992).

17 When the police deal with the neo-Nazis was made public a year later after *Taz's* investigations, the state's interior minister was forced to resign, and prime minister's aspirations to become Helmut Kohl's running mate in 1994 also came to an end. See Bettina Markmeyer and Jan Lerch, "Polizei bestätigt Pakt von Rostock," *Die Tageszeitung* (Feb. 3, 1993). Also see reports on February 12 in both *Taz* and the *Frankfurter Rundschau*.

18 "Destroying Ethnic Identity: The Persecution of Gypsies in Romania," as reported in the *New York Times* (Sept. 23, 1992): "Gypsies in Romania have been the target of increasingly violent attacks since the revolution that toppled Nicolae Ceausescu. Their homes have been burned down and vandalized, they have been beaten by vigilante mobs, and on occasion arrested by police and beaten in police custody, and they have been chased out of one village after another."

19 Times Mirror Center for the People and the Press, 1991 in *New York Times* (Nov. 1, 1992).

20 *New York Times* (Mar. 1, 1992).

21 *Taz* (Feb. 8, 1993).

22 *New York Times* (Jan. 31, 1993).

23 Lea Rosh, "Account of Conditions, Fall 1992," in *The Future of German Democracy,* ed. Robert Livingston and Volkmar Sander (New York: Continuum Books, 1993), pp. 109–10.

24 *Boston Globe* (Mar. 16, 1994).

25 Among many sources of this observation, see Dietrich Staritz, *Sozialismus in einem halben Land* (Berlin: Verlag Klaus Wagenbach, 1976).

26   *New York Times* (Aug. 27, 1993).

27   *New York Times* (Aug. 1, 1993).

28   United States Holocaust Memorial Museum, Washington, D.C.

29   Stephen Kinzer, "A Few Bits of Nazi Past Still Linger," *New York Times* (May 28, 1995).

30   *Der Spiegel* (Aug. 21, 1995), pp. 75–6.

31   An extraordinarily interesting book on Afro-Germans is *Showing Our Colors: Afro-German Women Speak Out*, ed. May Opitz, Katharina Oguntoye, and Dagmar Schultz (Amherst: University of Massachusetts Press, 1992).

32   Descendants of Germans living outside Germany are automatically entitled to citizenship. In both 1989 and 1990, more than 400,000 such persons immigrated to Germany, and from 1991 to 1995, about 200,000 more did so each year. *The Week in Germany* (Sept. 22, 1995). p. 8.

33   Assuming that this thesis is correct, what can be done to ameliorate this problem? In a phrase, the sharpness of a German identity based on bloodline must be blurred. That is one compelling reason that the Bonn government should grant citizenship to millions of foreigners born in Germany (as Ignatz Bubis, leader of Germany's Jewish community, recently proposed) as well as to those who have lived and worked in Germany for decades. At present, even with some reforms in place, these individuals have little chance of becoming citizens and rely on the charity of the government for protection. Guaranteeing Turkish Germans citizenship would not only provide them security but also forever destroy the idea of a biologically based German identity, thereby undermining the pernicious political effects of ethnic pride. Such a measure would clearly communicate the commitment of the national government never again to sanction German chauvinism. Without it, stemming the flow of immigration, as the parliament has done, will only feed the appetite of the Right. France and Britain have already granted citizenship to millions of immigrants, yet the prospect of a similar development in Germany remains highly unlikely. Appreciation for difference and multiculturalism is accelerating as a global imperative, and Germans should get in step with the rest of the world.

34   *New York Times* (Nov. 9, 1992).

35   On May 13, 1994, a hundred neo-Nazis assaulted five African students in Magdeburg, stabbing two and beating all of them badly. The police did not intervene until the Autonomen arrived and began beating up the neo-Nazis.

36   Projectgruppe, *Antifa: Diskussionen und Tips aus der antifaschistischen Praxis* (Berlin: Edition ID-Archiv, 1994).

37   See *Verfassungsschutzbericht* (Bonn: 1989), p. 72.

38   See Klaus Farin and Eberhard Seidel-Pielen, *Krieg in den Städten: Jugendgangs in Deutschland* (Berlin: Rotbuch, 1992).

39   Besides interviews with some of the participants, the source for much of this section is *Dokumentation zur Mainzerstrasse 12–14 November '90: Presse, Flugblätter, Presseerklärungen, Auslandspresse, Soli-Aktionen* (Berlin: Ermittlungsausschuss im Mehringhof, 1990).

40   Excerpted from a letter by Jeremy Warren to Billy Nessen.

41   The ownership of more than 150,000 properties—to say nothing of factories and farmlands—in what used to be East Germany was still unresolved. More than 100,000 people filed applications claiming that they were the rightful owners of private property nationalized by the communists. In the neighborhoods of Berlin where the squats were, 80 percent of the buildings were expected to be reprivatized.

42   Marc Fisher, "Anarchists Face Down Berlin Police," *Washington Post* (Nov. 14. 1990).

43   Ralph Geisenhanslüke, "Kreuzberger Mächte," *Die Zeit* (Mar. 26, 1993), p. 21.

44   *Die Zeit* (Mar. 26, 1993), p. 21.

45   Bernd Nitzschke, "Terror 2000: Schlingensiefs Film, Berliner 'Autonome' und

andere Hassprediger," *Die Zeit* (Mar. 12, 1993).

46 In *Interim* 226 (Feb. 4, 1993).

47 In the United States as well, the mass media (including much of the so-called alternative press) systematically ignore, denigrate, or glorify the Autonomen. In 1989, *Utne Reader* inaccurately blamed the Autonomen for hurting the Greens by influencing them "to advocate legalization of sex of children if the children consented." See Monika Beuerlein, "Germany's Radical Counterculture: Are They Revolutionary Heroes or an Albatross for Other Activists?" *Utne Reader* (July/Aug. 1989), pp. 30–1. *Utne* printed Beuerlein's piece as a response to an article Rodolfo Torres and I had written for *Z* magazine. Although she erred on many factual points, *Utne* refused to print our rejoinder. At the Greens' state program convention in North Rhine-Westphalia, a small group of gays had inserted such a phrase. See Markovits and Gorski, *The German Left: Red, Green and Beyond* (New York: Oxford University press, 1993), p. 210. To characterize the Autonomen on the basis of parliamentary dynamics within the Greens is to seriously misstate the situation. Moreover, Beuerlein characterized Kreuzberg, the Hafenstrasse, Christiania, and other autonomous zones as having an "atmosphere of decay" and being "ramshackle," where bars "not identified by signs play 'progressive' music." For *Utne* to give space to such middle-class sentiments was a projection of that magazine's own values, embedded in its profitable structure and private owner-ship. The commercialization of the counterculture is contested in Germany. In the United States it has proceeded so far that no one seems to comment on it.

48 Barrington Moore Jr., *Social Origins of Dictatorship and Democracy: Lord and Peasant in the Making of the Modern World* (Boston: Beacon Press, 1967).

49 T. H. Tetens, *The New Germany and the Old Nazis* (New York: Random House, 1961); *Brown Book: War and Nazi Criminals in West Germany* (East Berlin: Verlag Zeit im Bild, 1966).

50 Günter Grass, *Two States—One Nation?* (San Diego: Harcourt Brace Jovanovich, 1990).

51 Eugene Weber, film series, *The Western Tradition*—segment on The Enlighten-ment. Another estimate was more than three hundred political entities in 1648. See Gordon A. Craig, *The Germans* (New York: Meridian Books, 1982).

52 In the United States, the term "outside agitator" was used to impugn Martin Luther King Jr. and other civil rights activists who traveled the country to help create insurgent movements. If one were to assert that the term belongs to the special vocabulary of U.S. history, one would be right semantically but substantively wrong. For all intents and purposes, "rootless cosmopolitan" and "outside agitator" are culturally equivalent, and the list of repressive governments that blame popular resistance on outsiders would go on at some length. One need only mention de Gaulle's attempt to blame the uprising of May 1968 on Daniel Cohn-Bendit, a German-born Jew. "Traitor to the fatherland" has its U.S. counterpart, at least in the 1960s context, in being labeled a "communist." No American would use "fatherland" to describe the United States, but there are plenty with a fanatical hatred of those they define as "other."

Like Germany, the United States has its own share of government and media collaboration with violence against those defined as "other." Witness the case of Baruch Goldstein, the émigré from Brooklyn who massacred thirty Palestin-ians at prayer in Hebron. In the two weeks after the slaughter, not once did the *Boston Globe* refer to him as a "terrorist." He was a settler, attacker, or gunman in twenty-five out of the thirty instances he was mentioned, yet the *Globe* used phrases such as "Arab terrorist attacks" to portray Palestinian violence. The *New York Times* ran a feature story on Goldstein's youth, and at the same time, one of the Left's leading personalities, a man who had advocated using nuclear weapons against Iraq, toured the country speaking out against anti-Semitism on the Left. Although this issue is important (in no small way because of the patronizing way the Left deals with Jews), it is simultaneously a sad commentary on the state of the opposition movement in a country that has systematically produced men like Baruch Goldstein ever since the days of Lord Jeffrey Amherst.

53 As quoted in Todd Gitlin, "I Did Not Imagine That I Lived in Truth," *New York Times Book Review* (Apr. 4, 1993), p. 29.
54 *Emma Sonderband: Zwanzig Jahre Frauenbewegung*, (1988), p. 80.
55 See the discussion in Markovits and Gorski, pp. 136–8.
56 Robert Hughes, *Shock of the New* (New York: Knopf, 1991).
57 Geronimo, et. al., *Feuer und Flamme* 2, (Berlin: Edition ID-Archiv, 1992), p. 53.
58 Translations of original documents regarding the controversy about the Holocaust in Germany are contained in *Forever in the Shadow of Hitler?* trans. James Knowlton and Truett Cates (Atlantic Highlands, NJ: Humanities Press, 1993).
59 We in the United States have contemporary racists and neo-Nazis as well, and they are not fawning sycophants who worship German fascists. Indeed, at least one American racist from the Ku Klux Klan traveled to Germany to help organize skinheads in 1991, and according to a German television reporter, he was considered a guru by young Germans. American neo-Nazis regularly provide funds to their German allies, and Americans do much of the printing for the German Right. Between 1988 and 1993, Klanwatch claims that neo-Nazi skinheads, organized in 160 groups in over thirty states in the United States, were responsible for twenty-five murders.
60 *The Week in Germany* (Apr. 16, 1993), p. 7.
61 *Die Zeit* (English edition) (June 24, 1994), p. 7.
62 *Der Spiegel* 15 (1989), pp. 150, 157.

THE (ANTI)POLITICS OF AUTONOMY

Part of this chapter was presented at the Rethinking Marxism Conference at the University of Massachusetts, Amherst, in November 1992 and subsequently appeared as "Alternative Forms of Organization in German Social Movements" in *New Political Science* 24-25 (Spring-Summer 1993). I would like to thank Victor Wallis, Markus Mohr, Susanne Peters, Danny Faber, Roger Gottlieb, Alan Rudy, members of the Boston editorial collective of *Capitalism Nature Socialism*, James Herrod, Gary Zabel, and Yaacov Garb for their criticisms of earlier drafts.

1 From an Autonomen leaflet in Wiesbaden as quoted in *Verfassungsschutzbericht* (Bonn: 1989), p. 63.
2 *Taz* (June 28, 1982), p. 15.
3 Matthias Manrique, *Marginalisierung und Militanz: Jugendliche Bewgungsmilieus im Aufruhr* (Frankfurt: Campus Verlag, 1992), p. 166.
4 Winfried Kretschmer and Dieter Rucht, "Beispiel Wackersdorf: Die Protestbewegung gegen die Wiederaufarbeitungsanlage," in *Neue soziale Bewegungen in der Bundesrepublik Deutschland*, ed. Roland Roth and Dieter Rucht (Bonn: Bundeszentrale fur politische Bildung, 1987), p. 150. This definition was written before the shootings at the Startbahn.
5 *Radikal* 123 (1983), p. 12.
6 Quoted in Geronimo, *Feuer und Flamme: Zur Geschitte und Gegenwart der Autonomen* (Berlin: Edition ID-Archiv, 1990), pp. 103–4.
7 Such theoretical statements often first appear as photocopied essays. If they resonate widely, they are reprinted in the pages of scene magazines, and if enough discussion of them occurs, sometimes the original text and several responses are published as a booklet. For the Heinz Schenk statements and discussion, see Geronirno, *Feuer und Flamme 2: Kritiken, Reflexionen und Anmerkungen zur Lage der Autonomen* (Berlin: Edition ID-Archiv, 1992).
8 One German Autonomen noted that in Padua, Italy, even in 1977, there was not

one bar linked to the autonomous movement, clearly a factor aiding repression of the movement. See Tecumseh 2, "Von kulturellen und sozialen Klassen," in Geronimo, *Feuer und Flamme 2*, p. 29.

9   Usually associated with Leninism, such a view is starkly mirrored in anarchist Murray Bookchin's magnum opus *The Ecology of Freedom* (Palo Alto, CA: Cheshire Books, 1982), p. 366. Bookchin concludes that the role of humans is to provide "'the rationality that abets natural diversity and integrates the workings of nature with an effectiveness, certainty, and directedness that is essentially incomplete in nonhuman nature" (p. xx). Bookchin's language, invoking concepts such as certainty and directness, smacks of scientific bias. Moreover, his assumption that rationality is essentially unnatural posits humans outside our natural origins. A better understanding of rationality is that it develops out of nature. Face-to-face democracy of hunter-gatherers is part of the natural ecosystem that should be preserved and expanded. As I suggest later, intuition and cooperation are values that may lead to liberation far more quickly than scientific rationality. Autonomous democracy is a step in the direction of politics becoming based on face-to-face interaction.

Bookchin has never tired of criticizing the Autonomen, although many younger German activists elevated him to a father figure. In 1980, Bookchin obliged his admirers, making an appearance at the UFA-Gelände in Berlin, where he went on at length about the "anarchist movement in the U.S." being massive and active when he referred to local activists whose ideological affinity had nothing to do with anarchism. In the same fashion, Progressive Labor Party members used to arrive at large demonstrations with their banners, take photographs, and then publish them in their party newspaper with a caption naming all those present as party members. Like these Leninists, anarchists such as Bookchin apparently feel a compulsion to justify their political ideology through a presentation of political reality that is less than accurate. This is another instance in which anarchism and autonomy are exceptionally incompatible. More often than not, autonomists understate their own movement's value, bemoan its setbacks, and fail to comprehend their victories (such as Wackersdorf).

Like autonomous movements, anarchists seek to dissolve the state, but since the early part of the twentieth century, with the notable exception of Republican Spain, anarchism has not developed popular participation. The "other international," founded by anarcho-syndicalists in Berlin in 1922, had a third road strategy that was neither Leninist nor social democratic.

10   See my *Imagination of the New Left: A Global Analysis of 1968* (Boston: South End Press, 1987).

11   Benjamin Zablocki, *The Joyful Community* (New York: Penguin, 1971).

12   Jane Mansbridge, *Beyond Adversary Democracy* (Chicago: University of Chicago Press, 1983), p. 21.

13   For a concise and insightful understanding of the value of Marxism, see Victor Wallis, "Marxism and the U.S. Left: Thoughts for the 1990s," *Monthly Review* (June 1991), pp. 5–14.

14   The earliest book to attempt to transplant the Greens without their social movement creators was Fritjof Capra and Charlene Spretnak, *Green Politics: The Global Promise* (New York: Dutton, 1984). The authors also failed to discuss American racism as a dynamic factor and to include considerations of Rainbow electoral politics here.

15   Lutz Mez, "Von den Bürgerinitiativen zu den Grünen," in Roth and Rucht, p. 276.

16   Joschka Fischer, "Für einen grünen Radikalreformismus," in *Was sollen die Grünen im Parlament?* ed. Wolfgang Kraushaar (Frankfurt: Verlag Neue Kritik, 1983), p. 35.

17   Andrei Markovits and Philip Gorski, *The German Left: Red, Green and Beyond* (New York: Oxford University Press, 1993), p. 217.

18   Antje Vollmer, "Das Privileg der ersten, viele Fehler zu machen," in *Sind die Grünen noch zu retten?* ed. Ralf Fücks (Reinbek bei Hamburg: Rowohlt, 1991), p. 15.

19   Ulrich Beck, "Die Grünen in der Weltrisikogesellschaft," in Fücks, p. 186.

20   In the United States, there was prolonged debate about whether the German Greens were simply the product of the 5 percent rule. Although there is considerable evidence that they are, one is still left with the problem of explaining why in Germany there are also vibrant autonomous, feminist, and other "new" social movements.

21   Werner Hülsberg, *The German Greens: A Social and Political Profile* (London: Verso 1988), pp. 108, 118; *The Week in Germany* (Jan. 20, 1995).

22   *The Week in Germany* (Feb. 24, 1995).

23   Petra Kelly, *Um Hoffnung kämpfen* (Bornheim-Merten: Lamuv Verlag, 1983), p. 31. Unfortunately, this section, like many others, was deleted by her English translator and publisher.

24   Kelly, p. 92, 165.

25   Thomas Scharf, *The German Greens: Challenging the Consensus* (Oxford: Berg Publishers, 1994), pp. 67–8.

26   Quoted in Markovits and Gorski, p. 203.

27   Enno Brand, *Staatsgewalt* (Berlin: Verlag Die Werkstatt, 1988), p. 257.

28   As quoted in Hülsberg, p. 173.

29   A more judicious account of Fischer's politics can be found in Wolfgang Kraushaar, "Realpolitik als Ideologie: Von Ludwig August von Rochau zu Joschka Fischer," *1999* (Mar. 1988), pg. 79–137.

30   Sara Parkin, *Green Parties: An International Guide* (London: Heretic Books, 1989), p. 135.

31   Markovits and Gorski, p. 212. There are 105 nuclear power plants in the United States.

32   Markovits and Gorski, p. 213.

33   For an analysis of this government, see Klaus Ronneberger and Roger Keil, "Riding the Tiger of Modernization: Reform Politics in Frankfurt," *Capitalism Nature Socialism* 14 (June 1993), pp. 19–50.

34   Ronneberger and Keil, p. 33.

35   Geronimo, *Feuer und Flamme 2*, p. 157.

36   Parkin, p. 130.

37   Markovits and Gorski, p. 220.

38   Markovits convincingly argues that nearly all major shifts in SPD policy in the 1980s have occurred in response to pressure mounted by the Greens. See "The German Left: Between a Crisis of Identity and Orthodoxy." *New Political Science* 24–25 (Spring–Summer 1993).

39   In the United States, no state recognizes marriages between couples of the same sex, and the controversy that would engulf the proponent of such a measure in Congress no doubt helps prevent it. Here is a strong indication of one of the advantages of the system of proportional representation.

40   See M. Weg and O. Stein (eds.), *Macht macht Frauen stark: Frauenpolitik für die 90er Jahre* (Hamburg: VSA-Verlag, 1988).

41   See Marita Haibach, "Rot-grüne Frauenpolitik in Hessen," in Weg and Stein, pp. 172–9.

42   Kelly, pp. 33–52.

43   Borken, Biblis-C, Kalkar, Nukem (Hanau), and Hamm's thorium reactor.

44   See Max Weber, *The City* (New York: Free Press, 1958).

45   For one of the most coherent analyses of participatory democracy, see Carol Pateman, *Participation and Democratic Theory* (Cambridge: Cambridge University Press, 1970).

46   Examples in the United States include the Clamshell Alliance, an antinuclear power organization in New England, in which consensus decision making was regularly

used. For discussion of its merits and problems, see Barbara Epstein, *Political Protest and Cultural Revolution: Nonviolent Direct Action in the 1970s and 1980s* (Berkeley: University of California Press, 1991), and Denise Levertov, "With the Seabrook National Guard in Washington, 1978," in *Light Up the Cave* (New York: New Directions, 1981).

47   I am indebted to Mansbridge's excellent book *Beyond Adversary Democracy* for providing insight into these issues. See pp. 10, 32.

48   Tacitus, *On Britain and Germany,* trans. H. Mattingly (New York: Penguin Books, 1965), pp. 109–10.

49   See John Ehrenberg, *The Dictatorship of the Proletariat* (New York: Routledge, 1993).

50   See Chapter 2 of my book *The Imagination of the New Left: A Global Analysis of 1968*. From the Reformation and the English revolution, the synthesis of liberty and equality defined the meaning of freedom. In the twentieth century, however, with notable exceptions such as council communists and Luxemburg, the two concepts became increasingly opposed to each other.

51   Klaus van Dohnanyi, *Education and Youth Employment in the Federal Republic of Germany: A Study Prepared for the Carnegie Council on Policy Studies in Higher Education* (1978).

52   See Geronimo, *Feuer und Flamme,* for a typical example.

53   An earlier draft of this section originally appeared in *Socialism and Democracy* 20:1, March 2006.

54   See Michael Hardt and Antonio Negri, *Empire* (Cambridge, MA: Harvard University Press, 2000) pp. 128, 131, 140, and 209. Discussion of how their concept of empire fails to understand Latin American reality can be found in *Empire and Dissent*, a special issue of *NACLA Report on the Americas* (Vol. 39, No. 2) September/October 2005.

55   *Empire,* p. 189.

56   Rosa Luxemburg noted that by adding the "third person" (those at the periphery of the world system) as well as the continual incorporation of domains of life outside the system of commodity production, Marx's model could be completed.

57   Michael Hardt and Antonio Negri, *Labor of Dionysus: A Critique of the State-Form* (Minneapolis: University of Minnesota Press, 1994), hereafter L of D, p. 20.

58   L of D, p. 286. Further discussion of their rejection of dialectical thinking in this book is readily available. See especially pp. 217, 267-9, and 284-6.

59   L of D, pp. 10-11.

60   *Empire*, p. 189, and *Multitude: War and Democracy in the Age of Empire* (New York: The Penguin Press, 2004) p. 12. (Emphasis in the original.)

61   See my *Subversion of Politics: European Autonomous Movements and the Decolonization of Everyday Life* (Atlantic Highlands: Humanities Press, 1997) new edition forthcoming, AK Press, 2006, Chapter 2.

62   Felix Guattari and Toni Negri, *Communists Like Us* (New York: Semiotext, 1990) hereafter referred to as CLU, pp. 22 and 119.

63   Mark Poster makes this point in his introduction to Jean Baudrillard's *The Mirror of Production* (St. Louis: Telos Press, 1975) p. 3.

64   CLU, pp. 111 and 120.

65   L of D, p. 13. In fairness, they are not alone in their advocating of the cheerful cyborg. See Donna J. Haraway, *Simians, Cyborgs and Women: The Reinvention of Nature* (New York: Routledge, 1991).

66   L of D, p. 11.

67   Michael Ryan's introduction to Negri's *Marx Beyond Marx* completely ignores feminism's influence on Italian Autonomia. He does not even understand the meaning of autonomy to include the autonomous women's movement.

68   "DEMAU (Demystifying Authority) Manifesto," in *Italian Feminist Thought: A Reader* edited by Paola Bono and Sandra Kemp (London: Basil Blackwell, 1991) pp. 34-5.

69 Hegel, *Philosophy of Right* (London: Oxford University Press, 1952) p. 266. Max Horkheimer, *Critical Theory* (New York: Herder and Herder, 1972) pp. 105-106.

70 Andre Gorz, *Farewell to the Working Class* (Boston: South End Press, 1982), p.6.

71 Harvard University press calls *Empire* "a new *Communist Manifesto*." Harry Cleaver places Negri above Marx, asserting that: "If Marx did not mean what Negri says he did, so much the worse for Marx." Following Negri's disdain for Marcuse, Cleaver uses a military analogy to belittle the thinking of the Frankfurt School: "If Patton had read that book of his declared opponent [Rommel] the way Critical Theorists read bourgeois authors, he would still have been sitting in his quarters writing 'critiques' of this point or that when Rommel rolled over him with his army." (See Harry Cleaver, *Reading Capital Politically* (Austin: University of Texas Press, 1979) p. 42.) Cleaver's reliance on the military analogy is a projection of his masculine identity onto the "working class" and perverts the revolutionary project, making it into a simple question of brute force. Precisely such reduction of the working class to brutes is part of the reason why autonomous workers' movements appeared: Normal working-class people refused to tolerate their being treated as foot soldiers by self-appointed Leftist generals.

72 Negri, *Marx Beyond Marx: Lessons on the Grundrisse* (New York: Autonomedia, 1991) p. 154.

73 L of D, p. 291.

74 CLU, pp. 122-3.

75 Herbert Marcuse, *Counterrevolution and Revolt* (Boston: Beacon Press, 1972) p. 9.

76 CLU, pp. 153-4. He is referring to a text he published together with Felix Guattari in 1985. Long before that time, the Autonomen had consolidated themselves throughout central Europe (Holland, Switzerland and Germany). The autonomous women's movement had also created counterinstitutions and campaigns against criminalization of abortion. Negri's silence about these movements is predicated upon his failure to yet internalize an understanding of the importance of non-factory based movements.

77 CLU, p. 172.

78 Negri, *Revolution Retrieved* (London: Red Notes, 1988) p. 138.

79 While not a workers' strike in which wages were at stake, students risked loss of grades, careers, graduation and personal safety. In 16 states, the National Guard was called out to put down protesting students, and besides the four killed at Kent State and two at Jackson State, dozens more were wounded by gunfire from the forces of order.

80 Joseph A. Califano, Jr., *The Student Revolution: A Global Confrontation* (New York: W.W. Norton, 1970) p. 88.

81 To name just one area needing attention in our collective reevaluation of revolutionary thinking after the fall of the Soviet Union: the role of spontaneity should be reopened with a fresh sense of its importance. With their Leninist critique of spontaneity, Soviet Communists continually sought to impose correct ideas on popular movements. Whether in Russia, China or anywhere, their theories were assumed to be universally applicable. Seeking to impose on the "masses" their own particular version of the truth, they mobilized some of the fiercest programs of death of the twentieth century.

82 See Negri, *The Politics of Subversion* (Cambridge, UK: Polity Press, 1989), p. 141 and CLU, p. 68.

83 Herbert Marcuse, *Essay on Liberation* (Boston: Beacon Press, 1969) p. 52.

84 CLU, pp. 146-7.

85 *The Politics of Subversion*, p. 148

86 Negri, *Revolution Retrieved*, p. 131.

87 See *Autonomie-Kongress Reader*, Teil II (1995), p. 10.

88 Alberto Melucci, "The New Social Movements: A Theoretical Approach." *Social Science Information* 19, no. 2 (1980), p. 221.

89   At every entrance to Christiania, signs are posted that read: "Speed, heroin and cocaine are forbidden." At the same time, Christiania is one of the few places in Denmark where hashish is publicly available for sale.

90   See pp. 265–79 of my *Imagination of the New Left* for the complete documents of the Revolutionary Peoples Constitutional Convention. The reference to drugs is on pp. 267–8.

91   In 1994, Germany's high court adopted the "Amsterdam solution," ruling that small quantities of hashish should not be criminally sanctioned. Apparently, these jurists hope that otherworldly states might channel energies away from activism.

92   A lengthy comparison of Dada and the Zurich movement, including the participation of old Dadaists, is contained in *Die Zürcher Unruhe 2: Analysen, Reportagen Berichte* (Zürich: Orte-Verlag, 1981). Schmid's observation can be found on p. 42.

93   Helena Lewis, *The Politics of Surrealism* (New York: Paragon House, 1988).

94   Stewart Home, *The Assault an Culture: Utopian Currents from Lettrism to Class War* (London: Aporia Press, 1988). Although often overlooked, Kommune 1 and Subversiv Aktion were noteworthy formations in the early stages of the German movement.

95   In two insightful articles on a seventeenth century African philosopher, Teodros Kiros shows that Zara Yaqoub developed such a rationality during the same time that Descartes split mind and body. See "The Meditations of Zara Yaqoub" (Boston University African Studies Center, 1994), "Doing African Philosophy: Claude Sumner's Work on Ethiopian Philosophy," *New Political Science* 32 (Summer 1995), and *Zara Yacob: Rationality of the Human Heart* (Red Sea Press, 2005).

96   When the autonomous women's movement refused to work with men, Ingrid Schmidt-Harzbach organized feminist adult education classes in Berlin. She wanted to get "women to speak and perform together with men." In this context, she felt that women's envisioned goals "still corresponded to received sex-specific ideals, to the extent that the logic of men was to be opposed by a 'logic of the heart.'" In so doing, she sought to break with the reasonableness of male discourse from within its reality. See Ingrid Schmidt-Harzbach, "Women's Discussion Groups at Adult Education Institutions in Berlin," in *German Feminism: Readings in Politics and Literature* ed. Edith Altbach et al. (Albany: SUNY Press, 1984), pp. 342–8.

97   Psychoanalyst Emilio Modena in *Zürcher Unruhe 2*, p. 12. Susanne Peters helped with the translation. When movements are vehicles for working through psychic issues, it follows that the repression of such movements results in neurotic symptoms and even psychotic behavior. Yesterday the Black Panthers were all but exterminated. Today the violence of young people in the ghettos is apolitical, out of control.

98   Conversation with Ngo Vinh Long and Billy Nessen, Cambridge, Massachusetts, summer 1995.

99   Hanspeter Kriesi, *Die Zürcher Bewegung: Bilder, Interaktionen, Zusammenhänge*, (Frankfurt/New York: Campus Verlag, 1984), p. 220 points out that in Zurich in 1980, only 120 minor police injuries were reported during more than 250 special details involving 244,000 overtime hours. Only 33 officers missed even a few days work because of injuries. Moreover, in a country where the majority of young men had weapons at home, never did any of the so-called Chaoten use them.

100   In the widely discussed Autonomen "Lupus" paper, a similar point was made regarding the wave of sabotage that destroyed more than 150 power pylons carrying electricity from nuclear reactors in the mid-1980s. Although not against sabotage as a mass action, the authors worried that isolated small-group actions took energy away from developing a militant movement. See "Stand autonomer Bewegung: Langlauf oder Abfahrt im Sturz," photocopied manuscript, p. 8.

101   A description of this countercultural haven in one of eastern Germany's largest cities can be found in Susanne Koelbl, "Sog der Freiheit," *Der Spiegel* 48 (Nov. 27, 1995), pp. 76–82.

102   Frantz Fanon, *The Wretched of the Earth* (New York: Grove Press, 1968), p. 147.

THE THEORY OF AUTONOMY

An earlier version of part of this chapter was presented as "Post-Fordist Social Movements and the Politics of Identity" at York University on March 20, 1995. I would like to thank Barbara Epstein, Eddie Yuen, Teodros Kiros, Victor Wallis, Rudy Torres, and Susanne Peters for their comments on earlier drafts.

1   The United Nations estimates that forty thousand children under the age of five die every day from malnutrition, diarrhea, and diseases with cheap cures. In one year, that amounts to more than twelve million children. If anything, the UN believes that this figure might be too low.

2   Fred Block, *Post-Industrial Possibilities: A Critique of Economic Discourse* (Berkeley: University of California Press, 1990).

3   On the contrary, I think that denying the existence of a grand narrative (or unifying impulse to history) is precisely to assert one, however fragmented it may be.

4   Fredric Jameson, *Postmodernism or, the Cultural Logic of Late Capitalism* (Durham, NC: Duke University Press, 1991). p. xii. David Harvey also integrates his understanding of postmodernism within an analytical framework of capitalism. See *The Condition of Postmodernity: An Enquiry into the Origins of Cultural Change* (Oxford: Basil Blackwell, 1980).

5   Alberto Melucci has a similar view in "Paradoxes of Post-Industrial Democracy: Everyday Life and Social Movements," *Berkeley Journal of Sociology* 38 (1993–94), p. 185.

6   Andre Gorz, *Farewell to the Working Class: An Essay on Post-Industrial Socialism* (Boston: South End Press, 1982), p. 130.

7   Victor Valle and Rodolfo D. Torres, "Latinos in a 'Post-Industrialist' Disorder," *Socialist Review* 23, no. 4 (1994), p. 20.

8   Stefan Krätke. "Berlin: The Rise of a New Metropolis in a Post-Fordist Landscape," in *Cities and Regions in the New Europe: The Global-Local Interplay and Spatial Development Strategies,* ed. Mick Dunford and Grigoris Kafkalas (London: Belhaven Press, 1993), p. 233.

9   Sharon Zukin, *Landscapes of Power: From Detroit to Disney World* (University of California Press, 1991), p. 5.

10   Valle and Torres, p. 7.

11   Klaus von Dohnanyi, *Education and Youth Employment in the Federal Republic of Germany: A Study Prepared for the Carnegie Council on Policy Studies in Higher Education* (1978), p. 31.

12   *Kommission für wirtschaftlichen und sozialen Wandel* (Göttingen, 1977).

13   See *Boston Globe* (Feb. 9, 1994). *Neues Deutschland* (Feb. 6–7, 1993, p. 1) estimated that there were at least six million unemployed when the government's figure was 3.5 million.

14   *New York Times* (Aug. 9, 1993).

15   Jonathan Kaufman gave a figure of twenty-three million. See "Europe: Left Out?" *Boston Globe* (July 18, 1993), p. 56; the *Orlando Sentinel* put the number at more than thirty-six million.

16   See Ferdinand Protzman, "Hard Times in the Ruhr, with No Miracles in Sight," *New York Times* (May 2, 1993), p. F5. All over Germany, workers reacted to the crisis. See the series of articles in *Die Tageszeitung* (Feb. 19, 1993).

17   Jeremy Rifkin, "Technological Gain: A 30-Hour Workweek for All," *Boston Globe* (Nov. 19, 1995), p. 82.

18   *The Week in Germany* (Apr. 2, 1993), p. 5.

19   *New York Times* (Aug. 9, 1993), p. A8.

20   Sergio Bologna, "The Tribe of Moles," *Semiotext(e)* 3 no. 3 (1980), p. 41.

21   *The Economist* (Oct. 1, 1994), p. 38.

22   For an analysis of these dynamics, see *The Political Economy of West Germany: Modell*

Deutschland, ed. Andrei Markovits (New York: Praeger, 1982), pp. 155–8.
23 Joachim Hirsch, *Der Sicherheitsstaat* (Frankfurt: Europäische Verlagsanstalt, 1980).
24 See Margit Mayer, "Restructuring and Popular Opposition in West German Cities," in *The Capitalist City*, ed. M. Smith and J. Feagin (Oxford: Basil Blackwell, 1987), p. 350.
25 This arrangement has recently been revealed again, as Helmut Kohl's response to the fiscal crisis precipitated by the annexation of East Germany was to cut back on welfare and unemployment benefits, student aid, and family allowances.
26 Elmar Altvater, Jürgen Hoffmann, and Willi Semmler, *Vom Wirtschaftswunder zur Wirtschaftskrise: Ökonomie und Politik in der Bundesrepublik* (Berlin: Verlag Olle and Wolter, 1979), p. 274.
27 Wages for manufacturing jobs in Germany are 50 percent higher than in the United States. Counting benefits and corporate taxes, a German factory worker cost $25 an hour in 1992, compared with $16 in the United States (only $5 in South Korea, and less than 3.50 in China, India, and Indonesia).
28 Alan Riding, "In a Time of Shared Hardship, the Young Embrace Europe," *New York Times* (Aug. 12, 1993), pp. Al, 12.
29 As quoted in Paul Sweezy and Harry Magdoff, "Unemployment: Capitalism's Achilles Heel," *Monthly Review* (Dec. 1994), p. 2.
30 *OECD Employment Outlook* (1984, 1985, 1986).
31 Dohnanyi, pp. 27–9, 96–7.
32 Joel Kotkin. "Europe Isn't Working," *Concord Monitor* (Sept. 28, 1991), p. 12.
33 Dohnanyi, p. 13.
34 For an analysis of youth that locates larger reasons for this dynamic, see my chapter on ageism in *Introduction to Critical Sociology*, co-authored with R. George Kirkpatrick (New York: Irvington Publishers, 1987).
35 Since Habermas developed the term from philosophical categories of phenomenology, it has become widely used. See George Kitzer's *MacDonaldization of Society* (Newbury Park, CA: Pine Forge Press, 1993). Habermas' original formulation is in *Theorie des kommunikativen Handelns* (Frankfurt: Suhrkamp, 1981), especially pp. 471 and 577 of volume 2. The English source is *The Theory of Communicative Action*, 2 vols. (Boston: Beacon Press, 1987), pp. 332–73.
36 James O'Connor sees this dynamic as a second level of contradiction. See his articles "Capitalism, Nature, Socialism: A Theoretical Introduction," *CNS* (Fall 1988), pp. 11–38, and "The Second Contradiction of Capitalism: Causes and Consequences," (CNS Conference Papers, 1991).
37 Jürgen Habermas, "New Social Movements," *Telos* 49 (1981), p. 33.
38 Habermas, *Telos* 49 (1981,) p. 35.
39 Alberto Melucci. "The New Social Movements: A Theoretical Approach." *Social Science Information* 19, no. 2 (1980), pp. 217–8.
40 Harry Braverman, "The Making of the U.S. Working Class," *Monthly Review* (Nov. 1994), p. 23.
41 Neither side in the prolonged discussions in Germany, Italy, or the United States seems to have arrived at that conclusion. The two positions tended to be wages for women (which some opposed because it institutionalized women in the household) or equal division of household responsibilities (often unrealistic, and also unfair if one person has overwhelming responsibility for supplying the family with money). I owe Fredric Jameson credit for this observation. see *Postmodernism*, p. 325.
42 A broad range of analysts besides postmodernists employ the term "new social movements" to refer to various types of post-Fordist social movements: feminist, youth, ecology, peace, and gay (and in the United States, black, Latino, Asian American, and Native American). As identity became key to the self-understanding of participants in new social movements, ascriptive criteria for membership defined the various emergent formations. The term "new social movements" is actually a misnomer, since oppositional forces structured along the lines of identity

are not new: women mobilized no later than 1848, and African Americans since the arrival of the first African slaves in America.

The best definition of new social movements I have found is contained in Markovits and Gorski, *The German Left: Red, Green and Beyond* (New York: Oxford University Press, 1993), pp. 10–13. In the first place, they demarcate the difference between old movements, "which concentrated on the expansion of rights," and new ones, which "devote their energy to the expansion of 'autonomy.'" In addition, they delineate eight other characteristics of new social movements, such as eschewing comprehensive theories, valuing the collective good and identity rather than individual interests and class politics, and independence from political parties.

German sociologists Karl-Werner Brand and Roland Roth both characterize new social movements as intermediate levels of communication between isolated citizens and political parties. See Roth and Rucht, *Neue soziale Bewegungen in der Bundesrepublik Deutschland* (Bonn: Bundeszentrale für politische Bildung, 1987), pp. 43, 73.

An early analysis of new social movements was published as a special issue of *Social Research*, vol. 52, no. 4 (Winter 1985). Jean Cohen noted that new social movements emerged from civil society rather than mass institutions and that their unwillingness to make formal calculations effectively placed them outside the resource-mobilization paradigm.

Finally, Enrique Larana, Hank Johnston, and Joseph Gusfield pose eight characteristics of new social movements, including a social base that transcends class structure, pluralism of ideas and values, new dimensions of identity, and autonomy from political parties. See their edited volume *New Social Movements: From Ideology to Identity* (Philadelphia, PA: Temple University Press, 1994).

43   For a critical reading of postmodernism, see *In Defense of History: Marxism and the Postmodern Agenda*, special issue of *Monthly Review* (July/Aug. 1995). Surprisingly, the entire double issue contains only a single paragraph dealing with economic dimensions of contemporary reality, usually *MR*'s specialty.

44   K. Anthony Appiah, "Identity, Authenticity, Survival: Multicultural Societies and Social Reproduction," in *Multiculturalism*, ed. Amy Gutmann (Princeton, NJ: Princeton University Press, 1994), p. 161.

45   One source that demonstrates ecofeminism's breadth is Irene Diamond and Gloria Orenstein's *Reweaving the World: The Emergence of Ecofeminism* (San Francisco, CA: Sierra Club Books, 1990).

46   See Patrick Novotny's discussion of the Gulf Coast Tenants' Organization and the South West Organizing Project in *New Political Science* 32 (Summer 1995).

47   The voluminous literature on the theory of new social movements is itself the subject of articles and books. A good attempt to contextualize theory and practice since the 1960s is the last chapter of Barbara Epstein's *Political Protest and Cultural Revolution: Nonviolent Direct Action in the 1970s and 1980s* (Berkeley: University of California Press, 1991).

48   Margit Mayer, "Social Movement Research in the United States. A European Perspective," *International Journal of Politics, Culture and Society* 4, no. 1 (1991), p. 474.

49   Many activists from the early New Left, particularly those who subsequently became historians, were uninvolved then, and their histories pay little or no attention to the more than ten thousand participants in that gathering in Philadelphia who experienced the energy of commonality amid difference. The documents from the Revolutionary Peoples' Constitutional Convention reveal that identity politics, complete with autonomous female and black groups, can indeed formulate universally transcendent visions. These were small first steps, but the library full of debates about the promise of identity politics would be enriched by consulting this instance of historical praxis. See my *The Imagination of the New Left: A Global Analysis of 1968* (Boston: South End Press, 1987), pp. 203, 265–79.

50   Todd Gitlin, "Fragmentation of the Idea of the Left." in *Social Theory and the Politics of Identity*, ed. Craig Calhoun (Oxford: Basil Blackwell, 1994), p. 166.

51   By constructing the identity "female," for example, to conflate the interests of New York's super-wealthy women and the poorest women of Bombay, enormous differences are obscured, and the world system of stratification unthematized.

In 1991, the United Nations reported that the top one-fifth of the world's population controlled 83 percent of its total wealth and the bottom one-fifth only 1.4 percent. The difference between the world's rich and poor had roughly doubled in thirty years. Alongside 202 billionaires, more than 1 billion people lived in the worst poverty and 400 million were close to starvation. The average per capita income in the South (the Third World) in 1987 was $670, compared with a corresponding figure of $12,000 in the North. See Walter Corson (ed.), *The Global Ecology Handbook* (Boston: Beacon Press, 1990), p. 44.

Identity politics can be a means of glossing over this crucial schism in the world, a means of turning attention to the needs of those at the top in relation to each other, not in relation to the whole. As observed in the case studies of autonomous women's movements, however, Italian and German feminists recognized that emancipation within the corporate world is not the same as liberation from it.

52   Frances Fox Piven's discussion at the American Political Science Association meetings in 1993 was a significant stimulus to this insight.

53   He continually defines social movements in terms of power. For his own discussion of this and other issues, see Alain Touraine, "Commentary on Dieter Rucht's Critique," in *Research on Social Movements*, ed. Dieter Rucht (Frankfurt: Campus Verlag, 1991), pp. 385–91.

Touraine poses a "new central conflict," like the labor movement in the nineteenth century. From detailed studies of the Polish workers' movement, the antinuclear movement, student movements, and regional movements in southern France, he arrives at the conclusion that "we were able to observe...both the growing autonomy of social movements, freeing themselves from the control of political parties and ideologies, and the central role of cultural problems in societies where 'cultural industries' play a rapidly growing role, especially in health, education and mass communication" (p. 388). For him, unlike industrial societies in which workers opposing capitalists was the central conflict, "programmed societies" are sites where social movements centering on knowledge and identity are crucial.

Seeking to construct a critical scientific sociology, Touraine engaged social movement participants in hundreds of hours of discussions, after which his researchers wrote up and presented their views of the "highest" possible meaning of the movement's actions in order to provoke discussion of larger transformative ideas within focused movements. He seeks to infuse social movements with knowledge. But as each of his books makes clear, he is informed by social movements—not necessarily the other way around. Touraine's interventionist sociology is the residue of Leninism in academic theory: the educated outsider bringing knowledge to the committed is nothing but a reformulation of Lenin's notion of the party. In another sense as well, Touraine's conception of social movements is traditional Leninism. For him, diversity and fragmentation go hand in hand and permit the ruling elites to employ tactics of divide and conquer, and universality cannot be present within a diverse array; each stage of social development should have one unifying oppositional social movement. See Ron Eyerman, "Social Movements and Social Theory." *Sociology* 18, no. 1 (1984), pp. 71–82.

54   By focusing on issues such as the availability of resources for movements and the impact of state intervention against and within movements, such analysis moves the study of movements in the direction of natural science. Instrumental factors are assumed to be central, and "actors" are assumed to make utilitarian choices related to participation. In this sense, social movements are considered to be essentially no different from any other form of institutional behavior. Posing atom-

ized individuals as the building block of movements (and society), the issue then becomes whether identities are rationally constructed by abstract individuals or by groups with specific identities in history.

Despite its great differences from Touraine, resource mobilization theory also privileges traditionally structured political initiatives over ones that do not seek inclusion in the existing system. See Mayer, "Social Movement Research in the United States," p. 464. According to the resource mobilization perspective: "Victories generally begin with policy successes and culminate in distributional goals." See Craig Jenkins, *The Politics of Insurgency: The Farm Workers Movement in the 1960s* (New York: Columbia University Press, 1985), p. 21. Their middle-range perspective prohibits their comprehension of the fundamental differences of "postpolitical" movements, and they end up (like the more astute Habermas) advocating traditional forms of political engagement.

55   Habermas fails to see that the entire world cannot live at the standard of living of the integrated middle class, and that the structural imperatives of the system demand intensified poverty alongside wealth. Can societies democratically decide to limit the system's predatory character vis-à-vis private life and the natural environment? Even from within his own set of assumptions, Habermas' search for communicative competence in the rational structures of language and consciousness entirely ignores the intuitive ties between humans, our passions and unconscious impulses. In the work of Marcuse, art and nature constitute dimensions of freedom (that remain unthematized by Habermas).

56   The German idea of justice is predicated upon the *Rechtsstaat*, a government that respects laws and inspires and fulfills moral obligations. In the United States, our liberal tradition emphasizes individual liberty with as little government as possible. As Jameson commented: "the culture of the *Spiessbürger* and the philistine suggests the possibility that in this particular national situation Habermas may well be right, and the older forms of high modernism may still retain something of the subversive power they have lost elsewhere" (p. 59).

57   Seyla Benhabib, *Situating the Self: Gender, Community and Postmodernism in Contemporary Ethics* (New York: Routledge, 1992), p. 38. Unlike Habermas, who believes that consensus will emerge in such an ideal speech community, Benhabib stresses the process of dialogue rather than the certainty of any particular outcome.

58   For discussion of an international general strike, see Petra Kelly, *Um Hoffnung kämpfen: Gewaltfrei in eine grüne Zukunft* (Bornheim-Merten: Lamuv Verlag, 1983), pp. 92, 165.

59   Benhabib, p. 225.

60   Benhabib, p. 11.

61   Benhabib, p. 109.

62   Benhabib, pp. 110–11.

63   Benhabib, p. 113.

64   Benhabib, p. 100.

65   In her discussion of Rawls, she makes clear that "we" are to identify and help the "least advantaged" individuals, not to create a context in which they are empowered to help themselves. For her, a basic problem with Rawls is that he assumes that "we" can somehow identify the least advantaged. She asks: "But who are the 'least advantaged' in our society: the black welfare mother of three? the white Detroit automaker, father of four, who loses his position after 20 years of work? the divorced suburban housewife whose household is liquidated and who has no skills to enter the workforce? etc. I see no satisfactory resolution to this question within the scope of *A Theory of Justice*" (Benhabib, p. 168).

66   Benhabib, pp. 42–3.

67   Jürgen Habermas, "Struggles for Recognition in the Democratic Constitutional State," in *Multiculturalism*, ed. Amy Gutmann (Princeton, NJ: Princeton University Press, 1994), p. 122. In this text, Habermas apparently has a deeper appreciation

of the role of social movements than in his earlier works. He believes that without them, there would be "little likelihood" of the "consistent actualization of the system of rights" (p. 113).

68   Benhabib, p. 4.
69   Benhabib, pp. 4–5.
70   Benhabib, p. 214.
71   Benhabib, p. 215.
72   Benhabib, p. 216.
73   The terms she uses on p. 12 are adapted from Arendt.
74   In *The Imagination of the New Left*, I discuss how millions of people acted in strikes during May 1968 in France and May 1970 in the United States. Their spontaneously generated goals, tactics, and aspirations were remarkably similar and emerged without any central organizations.
75   In dozens of communes in Germany, sexual relations were daily being transformed, yet when Benhabib discusses free love, she reverts to classical Western philosophy for her subject matter and dwells on Caroline Schlegel, when the movement of contemporary history would provide equally significant persons for her purpose. Her focus on the life of one person as the conclusion to her book, while completely ignoring contemporary examples of the transformation of everyday life, demonstrates her inability to theorize the world spirit in history.
76   Benhabib, p. 195.
77   Benhabib, p. 33.
78   Benhabib, pp. 104–5.
79   Benhabib, p. 49.
80   Benhabib, p. 25. Why she uses "reassert" is questionable. When was there democratic control over capital and technology?
81   Benhabib, p. 218.
82   Benhabib, p. 127.
83   Benhabib, p. 76.
84   Herbert Marcuse, "Industrialization and Capitalism in the Work of Max Weber," in *Negations: Essays in Critical Theory* (Boston: Beacon Press, 1969); also see Habermas' essay, "Technology and Science as 'Ideology.'" in *Toward a Rational Society* (Boston: Beacon Press, 1972). Marcuse related to me that Habermas later recanted this view of Marcuse.
85   This point is made by David Harvey in *The Condition of Postmodernity*. It refers to the promise of locally controlled sites—an extension of democracy that is not actualized in contemporary society.
86   Within this context, some analysts see the Greens as providing the system with a new regional planning mechanism.
87   Plutonium 239 takes 250,000 years to decay and is hazardous if only one-one millionth of a gram arrives in lungs or bone tissue (where it tends to concentrate). One estimate placed the amount of radioactive waste produced by nuclear power by the year 2000 at twenty-five thousand tons, twenty-four tons of which would be plutonium 239. See Jerome Price, *The Antinuclear Movement* (Boston: Twayne Publishers, 1982), and Anna Gyorgy and friends, *No Nukes: Everyone's Guide to Nuclear Power* (Boston: South End Press, 1979).
88   A 1994 study of the Bremen-based Progress Institute of Economic Research estimated that a net gain of 120,000 jobs would result from a decision to shift the generation of electrical power in Germany from nuclear plants to water, wind, solar, natural gas, and biomass conversion. See *The Week in Germany* (Dec. 9, 1994), p. 5.
89   Leonard Doyle, "Europe Racing to Build Roads," *London Independent*, reprinted in *Picayne-Times* (Norfolk, VA) (Mar. 12, 1994).
90   Immanuel Wallerstein, "Revolution as Strategy and Tactics of Transformation," paper presented at the Rethinking Marxism Conference, November 1992, University of Massachusetts, Amherst, p. 13.

INDEX

abortion, 28–30, 34, 56, 69–70, 72–73, 75, 79, 132, 155, 241, 249, 271n30, 289n76
AIDS, 2
Agnoli, Johannes, 7, 64, 270n7
Alliance '90/Greens, 170, 208
Alternative Liste (AL), 97–98, 99, 170, 172–73, 206, 282n14
alternative movement, 67, 101–05
Althusser, Louis, 217, 220
Amsterdam, x, xii, xiii, 65, 99, 109, 110, 111–117, 123, 141, 191, 273n2, 275n23
"Amsterdam solution," 120, 290n91
anarchists, 9, 21, 38, 72, 91, 169, 188, 191, 193, 194, 203, 213–214, 272n56, 286n9
anti-Americanism, xix–xx, 69
antifascism, 9, 15, 161, 165–68, 176, 177, 193, 282n5
antinuclear movement, 8, 10, 67, 80–88, 101, 102, 196, 294n53
anti-Semitism, 162, 164, 204, 238, 250, 284–85n52
Ausserparlamentarische Opposition (APO), 61–62, 67, 75, 90
Appiah, Anthony, 249
Autonomen, xiv, 3, 5–6, 100–5, 107–11, 124–28, 166–67, 174–80, 274n23,
autonomy, 6–8, 74–75, 95, 108, 187–89, 210–11, 227–28, 237, 254, 256, 259, 272n56

Bahro, Rudolf, 102, 198
Benhabib, Seyla, 16, 237, 254, 255–262
Berlin, 97–100, 108–109, 140, 149–50, 166, 168–174, 206
Berufsverbot, 3, 10, 64, 74, 274n19
Black Panther Party, vi, xix, 2, 39, 53, 119, 121, 194, 211, 229, 252, 256, 290n97
Block, Fred, 235
Bookchin, Murray, 286n9
Brandt, Willy, 64
Braverman, Harry, 246
Bundestag, xiii, 14, 72, 81, 86, 99, 154, 156, 161, 164, 197, 198, 199, 203, 205, 208, 270n9, 275n35
Bürgerinitiativen, 10, 63, 86, 196
Bush, George Sr., 5, 87, 200
Butler, Judith, 258

capital, 245–48, 252, 267
Chernobyl, xxiii, 83, 156, 202, 203, 205, 265, 265

Christian Democratic Party, 42
Christian Democratic Union, 51, 69, 92, 98, 99, 154, 158, 213
Christiania, 117–120, 121–122, 229, 232, 284n47, 290n89
civil Luddism, 5, 174, 187, 189, 266
Class War, 9, 191
Cleaver, Harry, 289n71
Cohn-Bendit, Daniel, 4, 197, 201, 203–4, 284n52
Cold War, xi, xiii, xiv, 3, 10, 59, 60, 61, 80, 100, 154, 163, 181, 212, 265–66
collectives, 175–76, 191–92, 195, 214, 247
Communist Party of Italy (PCI), 22–23, 24, 28, 30, 31, 33, 34, 41, 42–45, 47, 48–49, 55, 56, 213, 229, 272n70, 273n7
Copenhagen, xxiii, 107, 109, 110, 111, 117–124, 148, 191
counterculture, 63, 193, 247
Cubism, 229
Curcio, Renato, 53
cyborgs, 187, 220–21, 227, 229, 288n65
Czech Republic, viii, 158, 264

Dada, 41, 42, 66, 229–30
decolonization, 16, 237, 267
democracy, 209–12, 263–67
Denmark, xiii, 9, 69, 109, 110, 117–124, 158, 191, 266, 280n10, 290n89
dual power, iv, vii, 11, 55, 107, 110, 120, 125, 175, 178, 220, 254
Dutschke, Rudi, 62, 199

East Germany, 214–215
Eco, Umberto, 2, 272n56
eros effect, v–vi, vii, viii, ix, xi, 15, 220, 221, 259, 270n14, 275n23
Euripides, 231
European Union, 108–11, 124, 240–42, 254, 266

Fanon, Frantz, 180, 233
feminism, 1, 7–8, 10, 67, 132–35, 200, 222–24, 237; Benhabib's, 254–62; German, 67–79; Italian, 27–35; postmodern, 258
Fischer, Joschka, 197, 201–2, 203, 208–9
Fo, Dario, 41
France, 8–9, 59, 81, 88, 158, 213, 233, 242, 253, 263, 266
Frankfurt, 206

Free Democratic Party, 98, 99, 100
Free Republic of Wendland, 84–85, 101,
    142–43
Fukuyama, Francis, 209

genocide, 183
Germany, 88–90, 210; economy, 238–44;
    identity, 153–65, 167, 180–85, 190, 262,
    283n33, 284n52
Gilligan, Carol, 255
Gitlin, Todd, 252
Gorbachev, Mikhail, xii, 60, 174
Gorz, Andre, 225
Grass, Günter, 182, 262
Great Britain, 7, 9, 88, 109, 110, 158, 189
Green Party, xiii, 10–12, 59–60, 79, 88, 97,
    99, 188, 196–209, 228
Greenpeace, 206
Guattari, Felix, 220, 224, 288n76

Habermas, Jürgen, xvi, 244–245, 253, 254,
    255, 256, 263, 295n55, 296n84
Hafenstrasse, 110, 124–128, 151
Hampton, Fred, 211, 256
Hegel, G.W.F., xix, 27, 183, 218, 223, 263
hippies, 35, 42, 43, 44, 45, 91, 122
Hirsch, Joachim, 236, 241
Holocaust, 162, 183, 235
homosexuals, 2, 70, 163, 205, 244
Honecker, Erich, 215

identity politics, 237, 249–53, 257, 294n49,
    294n51
Il Manifesto, 23, 24
International Monetary Fund, v, xi, 12,
    109, 128,
Italy, 17–57, 73, 80, 128, 158, 169, 194, 222,
    240, 241, 242–43

Jackson, George, 53
Jameson, Fredric, 236, 292n41, 295n56

Kant, Immanuel, 259, 263
Kelly, Petra, 4, 197, 198, 208, 269n2
King, Martin Luther, Jr., 86, 284n52
Kohl, Helmut, 99, 154, 158, 160, 163, 165,
    292n25
Kreuzberg, xvi, 89–90, 93, 102, 107–9, 132,
    135–38, 161, 173–77, 284n47

Lama, Luciano, 43–46, 48–49
Le Corbusier, 263
lesbians, 70, 77, 78, 135, 256
Lonzi, Carla, 33, 34–35
Lotta Continua, 23, 30–31, 44, 49–50
Lumley, Robert, 37

Mainzerstrasse, 168–174, 179
Malcolm X, 252
Mandela, Nelson, 211, 256
Mansbridge, Jane, 210, 211
Marcuse, Herbert, 104, 224, 225, 226, 261,
    276n43, 289n71, 295n55
Marxism, 213–17, 218, 220, 222
Marxism-Leninism, 8, 38, 53, 62, 188,
    212–13, 214–15, 225, 273n7
Mayer, Margit, 251
media, 13–15, 101, 197
Melucci, Alberto, 228–229, 245, 290n5
Metropolitan Indians, 26, 38–41, 44–46,
    63, 65
Moro, Aldo, 21, 53–54, 129
Mother Manifesto, 134, 204

NATO, xiv, 56, 59, 61, 86, 88, 97, 100,
    124, 254
Nazis, 61–62, 80, 162–63, 181–85
Negri, Antonio, 15–16, 35, 54, 187,
    217–228, 254, 289n71, 289n76
Neo-Nazis, 152–65, 193
Netherlands, x, 66, 111–17, 280n10
New Left, xiii, 1–4, 105, 159, 194, 204, 213,
    217, 225–26, 251–52; German, 61, 75,
    196, 274n17; Italian, 18, 27; USA, 233
"new social movements," 2, 248, 250,
    292n42
Ngo Vinh Long, 231–232

O'Connor, Jim, 292n36

patriarchy, 222–24, 247
Portugal, xiii, 8, 73
Post-Fordism, 222–24, 236–44, 253
postmodernism, 1–2, 247–49, 258–60,
    263
punk, 88, 90–91

racism, xvi–xix, 160–62, 223, 252
rape, 27, 29–30, 177
RA RA (Anti–Racist Action Group),
    115–116, 120
Rawls, John, 261, 295n65
Reagan, Ronald, xiv, 5, 86, 108, 128
Red Army Faction (RAF), 3, 12, 62, 64,
    94, 128–32, 188, 215
Red Brigades, 18, 53–56, 129, 130, 131
Red Zoras, xi, 72, 132–135
resource mobilization, 253, 293n42,
    295n54
Rock Against Racism, 66

Saro-Wiwa, Ken, 267
Sartre, Jean–Paul, 54–55

Schmidt, Helmut, 60
Schwarzer, Alice, 67, 69, 74, 76, 78, 183, 275n36, 277n72
SDS (German Socialist Student Federation): Germany, 61–62, 63, 67–69, 224, 274n17
SDS (Students for a Democratic Society): USA, 194, 224, 226, 274n17
sexism, 68, 228, 252, 260; within autonomous movement, 177–78
Shell Oil, 115–116, 120, 123, 267
skinheads, xiv, 2, 156–158, 162, 167, 285n59
SNCC (Student Nonviolent Coordination Committee), vi, 252
social movements, 225–26, 230–31, 236–38
Soviet Union, vii, 5, 15, 88, 211, 212–214, 224, 264
Spain, 8, 73, 216
SPD (Socialist Democratic Party [Germany]), 11, 59–62, 81, 83, 100, 199, 201, 287n30
spontaneity, iv, vii, 100–4, 180, 230, 257, 289n81
Spontis, 63, 64–65, 188, 201
squatters, 22. 63, 89–97, 99, 124–28, 151, 154, 168–76, 188, 193; Danish, 118–24; Dutch, 112–15; feminist, 34, 67, 71
Stalin, Joseph, 214
Startbahn West, xiv, 87–88, 108–9, 146–47, 201
students, 36–43
Sullivan, Louis, 263
Switzerland, xiii, 65–66, 81, 110, 120, 191

Tacitus, 210
Tageszeitung, 93, 102, 163, 166, 179, 279n107
Touraine, Alain, 236, 253, 294n53
Tunix, 65
Turkey, xvii, 88, 91, 134–35, 183, 207
Tu Wat, 96, 99, 144

urbanization, 21, 32
USA, xv, 63, 69, 82, 194, 240, 265–66

Vietnamese, 157, 160–62, 231–32
violence, 231–33, 290n97
Von Dohnanyi, Klaus, 125, 126–27, 213, 243–44

Wackersdorf, 11, 88, 107–8, 195, 201, 202–3, 207, 256
Wallerstein, Immanuel, 214, 253, 267

Wolf, Christa, 182, 262
workers, ix, 7–8, 62, 81, 222–26, 241, 252–53; Italy, 18–27
workerism, 7, 15, 26, 54, 222–24, 262, 242–44
World Bank, v, xi, 12, 109,128

youth, 35, 36–43, 110–11, 230, 266

Zukin, Sharon, 239

RECOMMENDED TITLES FROM AK PRESS

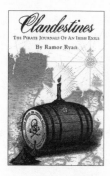

RECOMMENDED TITLES FROM AK PRESS

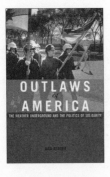

OUTLAWS OF AMERICA
THE WEATHER UNDERGROUND AND THE POLITICS OF SOLIDARITY
Dan Berger

Outlaws of America brings to life America's most famous political renegades, the Weather Underground. Based on detailed and original research, Dan Berger writes a powerful account of the actions and motivations of this group of white people who risked everything to oppose war and racism in the 1960s and 1970s. At the same time, it provides a nuanced and critically engaged study demonstrating the Weather Underground's contemporary significance.

DREAMS OF FREEDOM
A RICARDO FLORES MAGÓN READER
edited by Chaz Bufe and Mitchell Cowen Verter

Along with Emiliano Zapata, Ricardo Flores Magón was one of the most important figures of the Mexican revolution. Through his widely read newspaper, *Regeneración*, which was continuously suppressed, he boldly criticized the injustices of the country's military dictatorship and worked to build the popular movement that eventually overthrew it. This volume collects the most comprehensive English translations of Flores Magón's work. Includes a historical overview, chronology, maps, images, index, and bibliography.

¡YA BASTA!
TEN YEARS OF THE ZAPATISTA UPRISING: THE WRITINGS OF SUBCOMANDANTE MARCOS

The most comprehensive collection of Marcos' writings, *¡Ya Basta!* chronicles the written voice of the Zapatista movement and its struggle to open a space within the neoliberal, globalized landscape for the oppressed people of the world. These nearly 700 pages include the ten-year anniversary communiqués, as well as forewords by Noam Chomsky and Naomi Klein.

"Subcomandante Marcos gives eloquent expression to this movement, revealing both its philosophical foundations and its tactical ingenuity." —Howard Zinn

YOU CAN ORDER THESE AND MANY OTHER TITLES FROM:
WWW.AKPRESS.ORG (OAKLAND)
WWW.AKUK.COM (EDINBURGH)